Undying Passion

Undying Passion

A Book of Anecdotes
About Men, Women, Love,
Sex, and the Literary Life

JOSEPH R. ORGEL

William Morrow and Company, Inc.
New York

Library of Congress Catalog Card Number: 84-61797

ISBN: 0-688-02218-9

Printed in the United States of America

First Edition

1 2 3 4 5 6 7 8 9 10

BOOK DESIGN BY PATRICE FODERO

The author is grateful in acknowledgment to the following publishers, authors, agents, and estates for permission to reprint excerpts from their publications:

Andrew Wylie Agency:
Emily Hahn, *Lorenzo,* (Philadelphia: J. B. Lippincott Company, 1975)
Copyright © 1975 by Emily Hahn
Reprinted by permission of Andrew Wylie Agency, Inc.

Andrews and McMeel, Inc.:
Maisie Ward, *Return to Chesterton* (New York: Sheed and Ward, 1952)
Copyright 1952 by Sheed and Ward, Inc.
Reprinted by permission of Andrews and McMeel, Inc.

Maisie Ward, *Gilbert Keith Chesterton* (New York: Sheed and Ward, 1943)
Copyright 1943 by Sheed and Ward, Inc.
Reprinted by permission of Andrews and McMeel, Inc.

G. K. Chesterton, *The Autobiography of G. K. Chesterton* (New York: Sheed and Ward, 1936)
Copyright 1936 by Frances Chesterton
Reprinted by permission of Andrews and McMeel, Inc.

Atheneum:
Hesketh Pearson, *George Bernard Shaw* (New York: Atheneum, 1963)
Copyright © 1963 by Hesketh Pearson
Reprinted by permission of the publisher

Sergei Tolstoy, *Tolstoy Remembered* (New York: Atheneum, 1962)
Copyright © 1961 by George Weidenfeld and Nicolson, Ltd.
Reprinted by permission of Atheneum, Inc., publisher

David Garnett, *Great Friends* (New York: Atheneum, 1980)
Copyright © 1979 by David Garnett
Reprinted by permission of Atheneum, Inc., publisher

Garson Kanin, *Remembering Mr. Maugham* (New York: Atheneum, 1966)
Copyright © 1966 by T.F.T. Corporation
Reprinted by permission of Atheneum, Inc., publisher

Madeleine Blais:
Interview with Tennessee Williams, *The Miami Herald,* April 1, 1979
Reprinted by permission of Madeleine Blais

To Ella, who inspired and encouraged this project, stood by it throughout, resolved my doubts, and gave without stint of her time, energy, and patience—con amore.

FOREWORD

Sex is no longer a dirty word in literary biography. As a pioneer of sexual emancipation Lytton Strachey put it: "Discretion is not the better part of biography."

Other daring writers sharpened their arrows for the kill. When Hugh Walpole was delivering a panegyric on romantic love, H. G. Wells interrupted him: "Nonsense, Hugh. There's no such thing as romantic love. Every normally constituted young man wants to pop into bed with every normally constituted young woman. And vice versa. And that's all there is to it."

Leo Tolstoy, who probably had more to say about sex and marriage than any other modern novelist, summed up the basic sex drive in seven short words: "The whole story is told in bed."

Too simplistic, countered Bertrand Russell, and added two other elementary forces, money and power, but he kept the human sex drive as the predominant ignition.

Undying Passion is an eclectic compendium of glimpses into the private sex experiences and theories of over a hundred eminent writers. The selections provide fresh insights into such aspects as erotic theories and observations, marital bliss, involvements and entanglements, repressions, brothel diversions, sexual awakenings, inner emotional conflicts, even erotomania. My aim is to satisfy our natural curiosity as well as scholarly concerns about the one overriding human dimension, sexual desire.

My purpose is only partly to amuse, and not all the pieces are intrinsically diverting. Some, like those on Heinrich Heine, Dorothy Parker, Elinor Wylie, and others, betray pathos and arouse compassion. An anecdote is not always droll.

The research for *Undying Passion* led me to examine unpublished correspondence that fortunately had escaped shredding, diaries, personal journals, confessional autobiographies, newspaper files, and off-the-record disclosures discreetly relegated to footnotes and appendices in books long out of print. For the longer pieces I have gone beyond the limitations of an anecdote to a variety of other sources to form composite portraits.

A major difficulty is nailing down gossip and rumor. All the great anecdotalists, like Isaac Disraeli and others, followed the path of the great Samuel Johnson, who defined an anecdote as "secret history." Actually, *anecdote* is often a fancy word for gossip, but a piece of gossip can often be a significant element in a biography. And as G. H. Young points out convincingly, the greatest parts of our inherited literary biographies are little more than what one person said to another about another. After years of research, I have come to agree with Disraeli that an anecdote "frequently reveals a character more happily than an elaborate delineation."

I have tried to have each piece meet several requirements: it must be intrinsically significant; it must be interesting; and, primarily, it should shed light on the writer's character and personality and illuminate his concerns about sex, information crucial to an understanding of his life and writing. Where there are varying versions of an important anecdote, as in the case of Turgenev's account of his first sexual experience, I have preferred the accepted version as being closer to the truth. I have provided a source for every selection in *Undying Passion*.

Regrettably, there are still some unanswered questions. We don't have answers to a number of tantalizing questions: did Franz Kafka sire an illegitimate daughter? How intimate was Henry James's relationship in Rome with the Swedish sculptor Andersen? Did Emily Dickinson have a secret lover? What secret did Edwin Arlington Robinson carry to the grave? And the greatest of all secrets, who was Shakespeare's Dark Lady of the Sonnets? There is no final chapter in a biography.

ACKNOWLEDGMENT

To Nicholas Bakalar, my editor at William Morrow and Company, who believed in this book from the first reading, offered priceless suggestions, and expertly steered it through to publication.

CONTENTS

1

LITERARY FAME INVITES SEX

Fame is the greatest aphrodisiac.

—Henry Kissinger

ANYTHING FOR PROUST

No Marcel Proust buff has been so totally obsessed with the author of *Du Coté de chez Swann* as Mrs. Mina Curtiss. She says that when she touched one of his manuscripts, she felt "an emotion so close to religion as I am likely to experience."

For her edition of *Other People's Letters*[1] she spent two years tracking down every relative and associate of her *cher maître* that she could locate, interviewing him, examining hitherto unpublished letters and memorabilia in the hope that she could dredge up yet another secret or two before the curtain descends forever on the Proustian stage.

She managed to find Céleste Albaret, the wife of Proust's chauffeur, in dreary lodgings in the rue des Canettes in Paris. Every Proustian had long ago given her up for dead. The old woman had been so long in Proust's services as his housekeeper that she even spoke like him.

From here the trail led to Prince Bibesco, now seventy, and probably Marcel's closest and most loyal friend. It was rumored that he had a batch of letters that had not yet been published. The prince took an immediate shine to his American visitor. Gerald Clarke[2] quotes Bibesco as saying, as he dumped an album of letters on her lap, "Now you'll be sweet to me. Now you'll go to bed with me. Look what a lovely bed it is. . . . I thought I was impotent. I have been for months. But you have roused me, you marvelous amazon. Let me kiss your lips."

Clarke says Mina decided to "put quest above scruple," and he quotes her as saying: "After all, I figured, the letters are unique and there are plenty of women who must like this kind of approach or he wouldn't have continued using it."

The widow took no time obliging. Anything to get closer to Proust!

One of the next steps in her research, Curtiss says, was a visit to Harold Nicolson, diplomat, belle-lettrist, and philanderer. One look at her "uniquely-colored eyes" and he was beside himself with lust. During the whole interview he moved about the room and Mina noticed that his fly was alluringly (perhaps inadvertently) wide open. It is anybody's guess what Mina gave to get his letters. For her, obviously no price was too high or too personal.

SPECIAL ACCOMMODATIONS

When Victor Hugo accepted his son's invitation to visit him in Brussels, he agreed with this proviso: "Don't forget that I must have one of the maids to sleep in the room next to mine in the back of the premises. I still have my choking fits at night."

The condition fulfilled, Hugo made the visit. He wrote in his diary: "I have found in the Place des Barricades a new serving wench, Thérèse, who sleeps in the next room to mine. She is plain, Flemish, and fair. I have no idea of her age. Rather I think she must be thirty-three. I asked her whether she was married. Her reply was quite Parisian: 'What a hideous thought!' "

Two days later, he noted: "Five o'clock this morning. Thérèse . . ."

One afternoon, when Hugo's adored fourteen-year-old grandson, Georges, opened the door of the spare room without knocking, he saw the old man *in flagrante delicto* atop the laundress. The boy excused himself and began to bow out when his grandfather called him back. With an arm around the boy's shoulders, Hugo explained, "Look, Georges, mon petit, that's what they call genius."[3]

In his will, Hugo continued to preach the nature of genius to Georges: "Love . . . seek love. . . . Give pleasure and take it in loving as fully as you can."[4]

Part of Hugo's genius was in never forgetting an obligation: he once distributed 500 francs among the drivers of Paris for taking him clandestinely to his mistresses across town. And when Hugo died, the government issued an order granting the prostitutes in Paris 70,000 francs or more so that they could join, unmolested by the gendarmes, the hundreds of thousands of mourners in the streets.

Goncourt recorded in his diary: "It seems that the night before Hugo's funeral, that night of a nation's sorrowful wake, was celebrated by a wholesale copulation, a priapic orgy, with all the prostitutes of Paris, on holiday from their brothels, coupling with all and sundry on the lawns of the Champs-Élysées—Republican marriage which the goodnatured police treated with becoming respect."[5]

Henri Guillemin observed: "Until the very end his virility was demanding and could never be completely satisfying. . . . The diary which he began on January 1st, 1885, records eight sexual performances in four months, the last one being dated April 5, 1885."[6] According to Goncourt, who knew such privacies, Hugo copulated the night before he died.[7]

Olympio would have cherished no other tribute to his genius more highly.

RIBBON OF HONOR

Anatole France was making love to a lady in a grove in the Bois de Boulogne when a gendarme suddenly leaped out of a bush, grabbed him by the lapel, and exclaimed: "I've been watching you for the last quarter of an hour, you old satyr! What's your name?"

Disengaging himself and rising to his full height, France handed him his visiting card and a five-franc note. Looking up, the gendarme caught sight of the ribbon in France's lapel. Tipping his hat, he apologized: "Ah, a member of the Académie Française! Pray forgive me, sir; I couldn't know—all sorts of people come here. Besides, if I venture to interpose, it is on account of the children. The little rascals have eyes, you know, when it comes to seeing what they ought not to see. Apart from that, I don't give a rap. What are woods made for, if not for lovemaking? The unfortunate thing is that your young lady has a red petticoat that can be seen from as far off as if it were a flag. If the lady will excuse the suggestion, black will be much better . . . in that case I should not have come up, but I should then not have had the honor of making the acquaintance of a member of the Académie, sir."[8]

The lady, thrilled, hugged Anatole as they returned to the bushes, and the academician patted his ribbon with affection.

OPEN-END PUNCTUATION

Mistinguette once observed: "A kiss can be a comma, a question mark, or an exclamation point. That's basic spelling that every woman ought to know." It goes even more for punctuation. Nabokov prided himself on being an impeccable proofreader, but a crucial punctuation mark on a piece of paper he once received had him baffled.

After the publication of *Lolita* by the Olympia Press, which relieved Nabokov's financial stress, he was swamped with invitations to lecture, do talk shows, and give interviews. One activity he did not relinquish was his popular professorship at Cornell. Despite the storm his novel had created, surprisingly, the Cornell administration received only one letter of complaint about Professor Nabokov. It came from "Two Concerned Parents" and read:

"Frankly we have forbidden our youngsters to enroll in any courses by Professor Nabokov, and we would be in fear of any young girl who consulted him at a private conference or ran into him after dark on the campus."

Never free from harassment of one kind or another after *Lolita*, Nabokov attempted to keep the commoner species of vultures off by this statement to correspondents:

"I don't fish, cook, dance, endorse books, sign declarations, eat oysters, get drunk, go to analysis, or take part in any demonstration. I'm a mild old gentleman, very kind."[9]

However, this did not protect him much from tons of mail and dozens of intruding nymphets.

Nabokov told Alan Levy about one incident that took place after he had retired from teaching to devote himself to writing and had taken up residence in Switzerland. It was bad enough having to be pestered by mail from Ph.D. candidates seeking help with their theses, but adolescent propositioners tried to crash his suite on the castellated sixth floor of the Palace Hotel in Montreux.

"Not long ago," he told Alan Levy, "there was someone with an American name who kept leaving vague messages for me all over Montreux. I started leaving messages too, that I was unavailable. Then I got one more message—a slip of paper that said 'F——— you'. Well, this was so much more explicit than the others that I asked the desk what kind of person had left this message, and the desk said, 'That wasn't a person, sir; that was two rather wild-looking American girls.' This intrigued me even more, so I looked at the paper again. And there I found something at the end of the message which I hadn't noticed on my first reading: a question mark!"[10]

AFTERNOON SPORT

Cass Canfield has told how old man Scribner used to poke his nose into one editorial cubicle after another to keep tabs on his staff. Of all Scribner's editors, Max Perkins was probably the most prudish, so it can be imagined what Scribner thought when he looked at Perkins's engagement pad one day when the editor was out to lunch and he saw the notation: "Fuck, 3:00 o'clock."

When Perkins returned, Scribner was waiting for him, breathing hard. Casually, he asked his editor what he was planning to do that afternoon.

Glancing at his pad, Perkins replied, "Oh, I'm working on Hemingway's new novel and have been cutting down his use of the word 'fuck' to one per chapter."

Scribner nodded and walked away, considerably relieved.[11]

Some decades later, the four-letter word went public. The two-century hush-up proliferated to the point where a novel had to have at least a sprinkling, if not more, of the obscenity and its close relatives, or forfeit critical notice. Some writers went haywire publicly. Brendan Behan's wife said that *fuckin'* was the only adjective her husband thought existed. *Fuck* paid literary dividends. Three years after Ernest Hemingway died, a letter he had written criticizing William Faulkner for using the word *fuck* sold for $1500, pre-inflation prices.

Apparently not all publishers were keeping pace with the popular trend. Irving Mansfield tells that when his wife Jacqueline Susann's *Valley of the Dolls* was about to be published in England, she received a cable from the publisher there reading: "I WOULD LIKE YOUR CONSENT TO CUT OUT F——K THROUGHOUT BOOK STOP IF YOU CAN AGREE WILL GREATLY INCREASE SUCCESS EMPIRE MARKET STOP."

Jackie did not stop. Within an hour she cabled back: "F——K YOU. LOVE. JACKIE SUSANN." The frightened publisher ignored her instructions.[12]

CLOTHES MAKE THE MAN

When he was still young, before his face was so deeply furrowed, W. H. Auden was followed as far as Venice by a female admirer seeking a liaison. To elude her, he once leaped into a gondola, missed his footing, and got a drenching in the canal.

Another lady, in America, resorted to picketing his house, shouting that she'd had intercourse with Auden and now he was cruelly avoiding her.

The poet, who had met her only once, at the request of her psychiatrist, told Robert Craft, Stravinsky's secretary: "She finally had to be taken to the coop. She was ringing up every minute, banging at the door in the middle of the night, even bribing the manager of the building to be let into my apartment . . ."

Once inside Auden's apartment, he said, she did no more than take measurements of his old suit to buy him a new one.[13]

CORRESPONDENCE WITH WOULD-BE CO-RESPONDENTS

Sinclair Lewis received a letter from a southern girl who offered, first, to be his secretary, and second, to do anything he wanted. "And when I say anything," she wrote, "I mean everything."

Mrs. Lewis (Dorothy Thompson), who took care of such mail, took pleasure in answering that Mr. Lewis had a most competent secretary, and that she herself did everything else. "And when I say everything," she concluded, "I mean everything."[14]

• • •

When crusty Evelyn Waugh, who had said, "I do not believe the expenditure of $2.50 for a book entitles the purchaser to the personal friendship of the author," wrote an article in *Life* expatiating on his disdain for fan letters, he only swelled the volume of nuisance mail. He rarely answered, but one letter from a married woman so aroused his fury that he wrote back to her husband:

"I regret to inform you that your wife has entered into correspondence with a strange man. I return to you her letter, which she impudently wrote me. I trust you will administer to her whatever form of conjugal chastisement is usual in your part of the U.S.A."

He signed the letter "Stuffy Waugh."[15]

• • •

Harold Pinter received many letters from strange women, but the following missive sent to his Kensington home amused him: "I would be much obliged if you would kindly explain to me the meaning of your play 'The Birthday Party.' These are the points which I do not understand: 1. Who are the two men? 2. Where did Stanley come from? 3. Were they all supposed to be normal? You will appreciate that without the answers to these questions I cannot fully understand your play."

Pinter responded: "Dear Madam: I would be obliged if you would kindly explain to me the meaning of your letter. These are the points which I do not understand: 1. Who are you? 2. Where do you come from? 3. Are you supposed to be normal? You will appreciate that without the answers to my questions, I cannot fully understand your letter."[16]

PAPER LOVER

At ninety, G. B. Shaw complained to Stephen Winsten: "Women have been a ghastly nuisance in my life." But Shaw had only himself to blame: he baited a score of female nuisances.

Dozens of women tried to seduce Shaw—one had succeeded in seizing his virginity when he was twenty-nine—but Shaw, who made it a cardinal point in his theories of sex and marriage that woman, not man, is the pursuer, cleverly eluded them all. In his celebrated ardent relationships with Ellen Terry and Mrs. Pat Campbell, he did not forbear from advertising his delight in retaining his status as a paper lover.

To dissuade unwelcome correspondence, GBS would tear off the prepaying postage stamp and send back a printed postcard reply (which was only partly true):

"Mr. Shaw does not open exhibitions or bazaars, take the chair, speak at public dinners, give his name as vice president or patron, make appearances for money on behalf of hospitals or 'good causes' (however deserving), or do any ceremonial public work; and he begs his correspondents to excuse him accordingly."

However, in a moment of weakness during his climacteric, Shaw succumbed. What so many women admirers had been unable to get him to do, one succeeded in doing—and the entanglement lasted for several uneasy years.

Erica Cotterill, a budding playwright in her twenties, asked at first for professional advice and then applied affectionate pressure. Shaw, who had said, "Whenever I get anything in the nature of a love letter I hand it straight to Charlotte," somehow made an exception in Erica's case; probably he enjoyed the role of fatherly patron.

At first he ignored her letters, but his sympathy was stirred after she bombarded him with pleas for professional and personal advice and he sent her long replies, theater tickets, and practical counsel. In time she made declarations of love. When she found that they were failing in their objective, she resorted to radical measures. Shaw later told Hesketh Pearson about it:

> Erica opened with an impassioned plea that we should meet. I warned her that nothing would come of it. But her correspondence became longer and warmer, so I started giving her a little advice. Instead of putting her off, this incited her to more eloquent appeals, and at length I met her, hoping that a rational interview would abate her enthusiasm. It had precisely the opposite effect, and she did a monstrous thing: she took a cottage in this village in order to see me and be near me. I at once explained the whole position to my wife, so as to prepare her for possible incidents and intrusions. Though I had strongly advised Erica to remain invisible, she stupidly called at our house. Charlotte of course was furious and showed by her manner that the girl's behaviour was highly improper. Then, as you know, Charlotte wrote forbidding her to call again. This did not prevent Erica from maintaining a barrage of letters to me, several of which would have led an ignorant reader to believe that we had been sexually intimate.[17]

The severance letter that Charlotte sent Erica was tactful enough, but one can read between the lines her annoyance with GBS for encouraging the girl in the first place:

> I think I had better write to you to explain exactly why I intentionally shewed you that I strongly disapproved of your presence in my house, and that I did not—and do *not*—intend that your visit should be repeated. You might easily think that I was merely annoyed by your coming at an inconsiderate & unusual hour—as indeed I was—or that I disliked you. That was not it at all. I should object to your coming at tea time just as much as I do not particularly dislike you. On the contrary, it is because you are in some ways rather fine and sensitive, so that it is very difficult to be unkind to you, that I am determined to put a stop at once and for ever to any personal intimacy between us.
>
> The matter is a very simple one. You have made a declaration of your feelings to my husband; and you have followed that up by coming to live near us with the avowed object of gratifying those feelings by seeing as much as possible of him. If you were an older and more experienced woman

I should characterize that in terms which would make any further acquaintance between us impossible. As you are young and entirely taken
up with your own feelings, I can only tell you that when a woman makes
such a declaration to a married man, or a man to a married woman, there
is an end of all honourable question of their meeting one another again—
intentionally at least. You do not understand this, perhaps; but you will
later on, when you are married and know what loyalty men and women
owe one another in that very delicate and difficult relation. The present
case is a specially difficult and dangerous one, for my husband is not a
common man; if you become at all intimate with him he would become
a necessity of life to you; and then the inevitable parting would cost you
more suffering than it can now. I could not trust him to keep you at a
distance: he is quite friendly and sympathetic with everybody, from dogs
and cats to dukes and duchesses, and none of them can imagine that his
universal friendliness is not a special regard for them. He has already allowed you to become far more attached to him than he should; and I do
not intend to let you drift any further into an impossible situation.

If I must end by saying that this letter does not admit of any argument
or reply, and that I do not mean it to lead to any correspondence between us, do not conclude that I am writing you in an unfriendly spirit.
It would be no use to discuss the matter now; and later on, when you are
married and as old as I am, it will not be necessary. Meanwhile believe
that my decision is quite inevitable and irrevocable.

Yours sincerely,
Charlotte F. Shaw[18]

Janet Dunbar comments: "The handwriting is Charlotte's, but it is
not her letter. GBS dictated most of it."[19]

It Takes All Kinds

Attractive young women novelists who write about uninhibited sex
are inundated by invitations, and Erica Jong is no exception. After
the publication of her *Fear of Flying*, she was asked by a *Playboy* interviewer whether she had received any propositions from women.
Jong replied:

"I do remember getting a letter from three women who said, 'Dear
Erica, Do you want to be made happy beyond your wildest dreams?
We are dykes and we can make you happy. Please call at such-and-
such a phone number.' "

Erica never called. "But I don't get many overtures like that—I think because my work seems so heterosexual that a lesbian would assume I wasn't interested."

She once got a letter from a man who wrote: "Dear Erica, I would like to tear your poems into little pieces and lick them off your body." It struck her, she said, as destructive, though perhaps he meant well.

"Perhaps the oddest letter I ever received," said Jong, "was from a former nun who wanted me to meet a young man, perhaps have an affair with him. I think she was in love with him but didn't have the nerve to do anything about it herself and was sort of using me as an intermediary.

"Other letters came from men who want to meet me. Sometimes they say things like, 'I have a wonderful 30-acre farm and I'm very wealthy. With a very long cock.' No, they don't say that. . . . They don't use the word cock but sometimes they talk about what good lovers they are."[20]

THE MANY FACES OF LOVE

George Eliot had an extraordinary attraction for women, says her biographer, Gordon S. Haight, although she preferred the homage of men. A social outcast because of her living with Lewes, she invited some men, like Carlyle and Tennyson, to call, and they did so, defying the moral code. When the number of George's readers soared, after *Middlemarch*, she endeavored to keep it high. Becoming the object of admiration from female "groupies," she welcomed (unlike Bernard Shaw) expressions of spiritual kinship from fans and encouraged friendships with them.

In the forefront of her female admirers was Mrs. Elma Stuart, who hailed George Eliot as her "spiritual mother" and lavished gifts on her—an oak table, "a shawl, a letter-case, slippers, gloves, handkerchiefs, a paper-weight, cologne, bonbons." Mrs. Stuart went so far as to plead for an opportunity to kiss the hem of her skirt. They became close friends. When Mrs. Stuart died, she was buried, according to her instructions, next to George Eliot; her gravestone calls her a disciple "whom for 8½ blessed years George Eliot called by the sweet name of 'Daughter.' "

Another fan, Edith Jemima Simcox, twenty years younger than Eliot, was even more insistent on a close relationship and succeeded in becoming practically her alter ego. Edith also called her Mother, sewed undergarments for her, and often made an impromptu or "foolish visit" to Eliot at The Priory. Welcomed warmly, Edith called the novelist "my sweet darling" or "my own beautiful love"; she would kiss her feet, refer to her as her Goddess, and at one time planned to have her ashes scattered over Her grave.

It was an intense and probably lesbian attachment, but George Eliot didn't see it that way and encouraged the attentions. Edith Simcox became a member of the family to all intents and purposes, and Lewes enjoyed her devotion to his Polly. After Lewes died, Edith dropped in every day to solace George Eliot, mourning his death as if he were her own husband and saying, "My loneliness began after he departed."

In her autobiography, Simcox describes one of her meetings with Eliot:

I kissed her again and again and murmured broken words of love. She bade me not to exaggerate. I said I didn't—nor could, and then scolded her for not being satisfied with letting me love her as I did—as in present reality—and proposing instead that I should save my love for some imaginary he. She said—expressly what she has often before implied to my distress—that the love of men and women for each other must always be more and better than any other and bade me not wish to be wiser than 'God who made me'—in pious phrase.

I hung over her caressingly and she bade me not to think too much of her; she knew all her own frailty and if I went on, she would have to confess some of it to me. Then she said—perhaps it would shock me—she had never in all her life cared very much for women—it must seem monstrous to me.

I said I had always known it. She went on to say, what I also knew, that she cared for the womanly ideal, sympathised with women and liked for them to come to her in their troubles, but while feeling near to them in one way, she felt far off in another; the friendship and intimacy of men was more to her.

Then she tried to add what I had already imagined in explanation, that when she was young, girls and women seemed to look on her as somehow 'uncanny' while men were always kind. I kissed her again, and said I didn't mind—if she did not mind having holes kissed in her cheeks. She said I gave her beautiful affection—and then again she called me a silly child, and I asked her if she would never say anything kind to me. I asked her to kiss me. Let a trembling lover tell of the first deliberate touch of the dear one's lips. I returned the kiss to her lips that gave it and started to go—she waved me farewell.[21]

Eliot's marriage to John Cross did not lower the intensity of Edith's love, though she was hurt that she had not been told in advance.

At Eliot's funeral, Edith decked the grave with white flowers and laurel leaves. "I pressed a kiss upon the pall," she wrote, "and trembled violently as I stood motionless else, in the still silence, with nothing to mar the realization of that intense moment's awe." She watched the solemn interment even more tearfully than Cross's son, beloved by Eliot. "Then through the twilight," she wrote, "I cried and moaned aloud."[22]

MARITAL MIGRAINES

When H. G. Wells was asked innocently, "How's Mrs. Wells?" he replied, grinning, "Which one?" By that time he had accumulated three wives, two of whom were living amicably in his house.

Pulitzer Prize winner Norman Mailer did everything on a bigger scale: he had had five wives and was advancing rapturously toward taking on a sixth. They were all living apart, though apparently friendly with one another, and enjoying his fantastic largess, far more expensive than even he, with his best-selling books, could afford. His bewildering financial burdens bound him to his typewriter day in and day out just to provide basics—food, clothes, schools for his kids, several establishments to keep up. He figured that his marital mesh required at least $200,000 a year (by pre-inflation standards) just to support fourteen persons with alimony and child support.

Fortunately, to his considerable relief, Lady Jean (wife number 3) stepped in. Taking advantage of his talents for exhibitionism, she organized, with his hearty connivance, a charity bash to celebrate his fiftieth birthday at the Four Seasons: $30 a head, $50 a couple. Five thousand invitations, printed in purple, went out a month in advance. Norman held out the promise that the celebrants would be the first to hear him launch his sensational "Fifth Estate" plan, a people's FBI and CIA, "the best political idea of my life." The cash inflow would provide a much needed peripheral bonus. After all, "You have to keep the bread coming in," he contended. "I respect Lady

Jean more than any other woman in the world," he said, overlooking his complaint on a former occasion that though she cheerfully gave up millions from her grandfather, Lord Beaverbrook, to marry him, she refused to make his breakfast.[23]

Five hundred and fifty guests showed up, America's literate best— among them Leonard Lyons, Jessica Mitford, Andy Warhol, George Plimpton, Shirley MacLaine, Princess Diana Von Furstenberg, Lily Tomlin, Jose Torres—and attending free were, naturally, mama Fanny Mailer, his second wife, his fifth wife, and four of his seven children.

Mailer, dressed in tux and blue shirt, started the circus off with "a pretty dirty joke," commented critic John Leonard.

The receipts from the bash, however, took Mailer off the hook only temporarily. Fanny Mailer, says Patricia Bosworth,[24] "stood at the top of the Four Seasons staircase. She seemed lost in reverie. "This was the best party for Norman," she confided. "The second best was his bar mitzvah in 1936." As it turned out, the Four Seasons affair netted just $600 for the benefit of the Fifth Estate.

"On certain days," Mailer told a reporter in a calmer moment, "I get real mad." No doubt he had in mind that ill-starred day when he was hauled into court to answer the criminal complaint for having stabbed his second wife, Adele, with a pen knife after a boozing party. Luckily for his career, she survived. Mailer pleaded guilty, but Adele dropped the charge magnanimously, and he was given a suspended sentence and sent for a brief term to Bellevue for observation. Judge Schweitzer told Mailer: "I gamble on human beings, and I intend to gamble on you." Shortly thereafter, Norman and Adele were divorced.

Confronting his mid-fifties, the "nice Jewish boy from Brooklyn," as he boastfully described himself, took time out for private reflection long overdue and found that the time had come to sort out his tangled marital mess. Besides, the IRS had him cornered; the divorce bailiffs were driving him mad. And there were only twenty-four writing hours a day to ease the pressure.

On November 11, 1980—appropriately, Armistice Day—Mailer, 57, married Norris Church, 31, with whom he had been living for seven years. The week before the wedding he went through a marriage ceremony with Carol Stevens, the jazz singer, to honor the years they had lived together and to legitimize their daughter. Exit the biggest headache. Then, a few days later, he married Norris, to make his favorite son, Buffalo, legitimate. Mailer was now the father of eight children, the eldest, a daughter, having been born during his first marriage, to Beatrice Silverman in 1944. *Newsweek* reported that the wedding ceremony with Norris included readings from the groom's book *The Prisoner of Sex*.

2

SEXUAL THEORIES, NOTIONS, AND OBSERVATIONS

The real genius for love lies not in getting into, but getting out of, love.

—George Moore

I am too much interested in other men's wives to think of getting one of my own.

—George Moore

Never fornicate through an ink bottle.

—Dion Boucicault

RATION YOUR SPERM

In their early days in Paris, Ernest Hemingway kept telling Sam Putnam that in his view the three most exciting drives in life were skiing, boxing, and sex. He liked to air his views on sex.

The *machismo* Hemingway, in 1929, gossiped with Allen Tate in Sylvia Beach's bookshop in Paris about Ford Madox Ford's separation from Stella Bowen. Hemingway asked the poet whether he was aware that Ford was impotent at the time. Tate grinned and replied that this didn't concern him, since he was not a woman. It set Hemingway off on a lively exposition of his theory of male sexuality.

The number of orgasms available to a person in a lifetime was allocated at birth, he said. Hence, a young man should space his sexual drive carefully and ration his sperm or he would have nothing left in old age.[1] Hemingway repeatedly quoted Tennyson: "Old age hath yet his honour and his toil."

In his own old age, Hemingway's toil had slowly drained off, though he had his honor; however, in the early days on the Rive Gauche, he put no curbs on his sexuality. According to Scott Donaldson, Hemingway told him that he had once bragged to Thornton Wilder that "he could not be satisfied making love only at night and in the

33

morning; if he could not also have sex in the afternoon, he had to relieve himself privately. On a shipboard crossing in the 1920's he ostentatiously consumed saltpeter to quiet his raging libido."[2]

Hemingway's unappeasable sexuality was the subject of much talk in the cafés, for Kiki, the sex doll of the day, was vocal about her experiences with him. In a letter to Buck Lanham, Hemingway compared intercourse to six-day bicycle racing: the more you do it, the better you get. Lanham observed that the older the novelist grew, the more he boasted of his sexual prowess.[3]

During his most creative period, Hemingway abstained from intercourse in the belief it would block his cerebral juices. After orgasm a writer's head "is cold," he said. He told Charles Scribner, the publisher, that he "always had to ease off making love when he was working hard, because the two things were run by the same motor."[4]

Spare the rod, he enjoined his son. The warning came from a four-times-married father who saw the threatening red light of advancing impotence. What he advised others to do, he was helpless to do himself. He saw no hypocrisy there. Look at Dos Passos, he said, if you want proof: the literary strength of his *Manhattan Transfer* petered out after he married.

The fear of shooting blanks gave Hemingway increasing anxiety, and it has been conjectured that when he killed himself by pulling the trigger of his father's suicide pistol, impotence was the most powerful motive. He had just turned sixty.

Don't Go All the Way

Balzac proposed to his friends at Magny's the theory that sperm was cerebral matter and that every ejaculation wasted one's creative power. Gavarni said that Balzac made a conscious effort to economize on his sperm, but whether his self-control succeeded at all times is another matter.

The Goncourts noted that Balzac "was perfectly happy playing the love game up to the point of ejaculation, but he was unwilling to go further." However, accidents do happen, and in the course of one passionate assignation in a brothel, Balzac tossed his theory aside and pumped all the way. Once, utterly devastated, he burst in on Latouche and wailed, "I lost a book this morning!"[5]

Two Can Sleep Cheaper Than One

During a whirlwind tour at Dijon with Peggy Guggenheim, Samuel Beckett showed signs of wilting under her aggressive lovemaking; he needed some spurts in reserve for literary composition.

Unlike Byron, who pushed aside his bride when she beckoned him into her bed on his hellish *prima nox* with the statement "I always sleep alone," Beckett had a pecuniary reason for his preference. Says Peggy:

"When we went to a hotel he took a double room. This I thought strange, but then all his behavior was most peculiar. We got into separate beds. I soon crept into his, and Oblomov [Peggy's pseudonym for Beckett] jumped out and got into the other bed saying he had been cheated. When I asked him why he had taken a double room, he said it was thirty francs cheaper than two singles."[6]

Off Limits

"Sexuality is one of the most normal parts of life," the poet Anne Sexton told a *Paris Review* interviewer. "True, I get a little uptight when Norman Mailer writes that he screws a woman anally. I like Allen Ginsberg very much and when he writes about the ugly vagina I feel awful. That kind of thing doesn't appeal to me. So I have my limitation, too. Homosexuality is all right with me: Sappho was beautiful. But when someone hates another's body and somehow violates it—that's the kind of thing I mind."[7]

The Literary Bathroom

In Anthony Burgess's opinion, it is an admirable idea for a poet to write while on the toilet, as the author has his poet do in *Enderby*. While Burgess himself does not write on the throne, he told a *Playboy* interviewer: "I've known at least two poets who actually imitated the Enderby method. I know one quite considerable poet who had this little table made for himself just big enough for him to sit on the lavatory seat and work from—which is an admirable idea, because the bathroom was almost *made* for that purpose."[8]

Burgess further told *Playboy* that masturbation in the bathroom was a common release for writers: "I think most artists find that when they're writing something, they become sexually excited. But it would be a waste of time to engage in a full-dress—or undress—sexual act with somebody at that moment. So they often go into the bathroom to masturbate. [Dylan] Thomas did that all the time. Quite a number of artists masturbate when they write. Our sexual energy has been aroused, now we come, now we're able to concentrate on the other aspect of this energy, which is the creative aspect."[9]

ONCE IS NOT ENOUGH

Georges Simenon, author of more than two hundred mysteries, on the mystery of sex: "One knows a woman only after one has slept with her."

At seventy-four, he was still on the search that he had begun in his teens: "I chased after that all my life. Once is not enough," he said.

He added that in the process of trying to find the key to the nature of woman he had slept with ten thousand women in his lifetime.[10]

Put your calculator away—that's a dish of venery every other day in a span of sixty adult years. Simenon, as we know, is a writer of fiction.

• • •

Fenton Bresler[11] takes all this seriously, says reviewer David Price-Jones: "From the moment in 1972 when Simenon ceased writing fiction, the number of women whom he claims to have seduced has been rising inexorably. . . . In his portrait, Simenon can only appear as vain, boastful, destructive, even monstrous. At his sternest, Bresler accuses Simenon of wilful lying, and then believing the lies."[12]

LET IT ALL HANG OUT

Tell all, says Erica Jong.

If a man can go public about his fornications, why can't a woman, she wants to know. And in a *Playboy* interview, she comments on her theory:

> I don't believe one should fuck up one's body with chemicals. I might take a sleeping pill occasionally, if I'm on a tour and can't relax in an unfamiliar hotel room. And I always used to carry penicillin tablets, because I have the greatest clap phobia of anybody in the world. I've always

been tempted when I slept with somebody I didn't know very well. I guess I'm just an alarmist, because when I travel someplace I take V-Cillen K. Lomotil and my diaphragms. . . .

  Playboy: Diaphragms, plural? You have several?

  Jong: A whole collection. I'm planning to send them to the Smithsonian. But—although this may go against the way people see me—I haven't really done all that much sleeping around, just in case a really terrific guy came along—carrying around diaphragms in my briefcase and stuff like that, but the *number* of men I've slept with in my life is very small.

How far is far? Is there nothing private? Why should there be? asks Jong. In the interview she defends her frankness as reflecting the English literary tradition:

  I rarely wear a bra myself . . . I like sexy clothes. . . . We don't have evidence on the possibility of wearing a bra, but Mary Wollstonecraft, the author of *Vindications of Women,* didn't wear any underclothes, though she didn't blab about it. Since lingerie was not *de rigueur* as underwear until the late Victorian era, we can make a safe guess that Jane Austen didn't wear any nor Fanny Burney, nor Anne Hathaway Shakespeare, the closest any woman got to the great Elizabethan poet.

Erica insists that she is no more radical in her candor than Daniel Defoe or Henry Fielding: what is pornographic about them? It is doubtful, however, whether the following conversation could have been matched by either of them. After her *Fear of Flying* came out, Jong was flooded by propositions. "I remember one night before I went to the American Book Convention, I asked Anne Sexton, who was a good friend, 'What do I do when men come up to me on the convention floor and say, "Hey baby, I want a zipless fuck"?' And Anne said, 'Thank them. Thank them and say, "Zip up your fuck until I ask for it." ' "[13]

THE GREEK WORDS FOR IT

André Gide, in his *Journal:*

"Had Socrates and Plato not loved young men, what a pity for Greece, what a pity for the whole world! Xantippe, Socrates' wife, didn't give a fig for the whole world, she kept nagging him, complaining that he didn't satisfy her in bed, was out instead loitering in the groves of Academe fondling his homosexual boys. Aristophanes, who knew the big domed bald philosopher intimately, said that Xantippe must have heard all about her husband's sex habits. Fact is everyone else in Greece knew that Socrates was a pederast."[14]

The highest expression of human existence, Plato says, is philosophy linked with pederasty. He condemned sexual intercourse between a man and a woman as morbid, vile, and loathsome, and advocated avoiding sex except for procreation. No man should marry, if at all, before thirty. Copulation, even during breeding, should be joyless. To those who might protest that abstinence in adults is unnatural and impracticable, Plato points out that Greek athletes always practiced self-denial while in training for the Olympics.

Dr. Thomas Arnold, venerable headmaster of Rugby and father of Matthew Arnold—who probably kissed Plato's *Symposium* every day along with the Bible—took a leaf from Plato and prescribed as a keystone in the Rugby curriculum vigorous physical exercise, to quell the sexual urge.

Plato's disciple Aristotle believed that semen has its source in the brain: hence, sex is in the head. He also believed that women who marry young, since they are strongly lustful, make inconvenient physical demands on their husbands. The ideal time for marriage, Aristotle said, is when both partners are in their prime: women, twenty to forty; men, in the decade or two before fifty. Therefore women should marry at eighteen and men at thirty-seven, so that their sexual powers will decline at the same time.

Men do not marry, Xenophon believed, only to satisfy their sexual desires: the craving for gratification decreases after thirty. He urged that men should not marry before then and thus avoid having too many offspring—a nuisance in old age, he thought.

At My Mother's Breast

Anthropologist-author Ashley Montagu believes that men who are not breast-fed turn into lousy lovers: the male hunger for the nipple persists through life.

"Everyone learns to love sexually at the mother's breast," he says. "One learns tactile response through the skin at the mother's breast during suckling. But today, unfortunately, female breasts are no longer intended for feeding babies. They're intended for Madison Avenue, whose only interest in them is to show a cleavage so deep it could contain the entire collected works of William Shakespeare."[15]

When asked why his analysis applies only to males, Montagu replied, "Because females can compensate later on. Little girls always get a great deal more touching from their parents when they're growing up, so they can more readily recoup the loss. Little boys can't. Therefore, unless a man has been breast-fed he will always be handicapped as a lover."[16]

Montagu is emphatic in assigning superior sexuality to women: "Males flatter themselves about their sexual prowess, but it's nothing compared to a woman's. For instance, there have been laboratory tests where one woman recorded 100 orgasms during one session. Certainly no man can claim that, I dare say."[17]

THE DIVINITY THAT SHAPES OUR ENDS

William Blake said that in one of his visions he was visited by John Milton, then dead more than a century, who "came to ask a favor of me. He said he had committed an error in 'Paradise Lost,' that taught that sexual intercourse arose out of the Fall. Now that cannot be, for no good can spring out of Evil."[18]

Uninhibited physical love inspires creativity, said Blake, and the more lovemaking and the freer, the more paradisiacal. Like Shelley, he believed in free love. So did Blake's wife Catherine ("my dear and too careful and over-gorgeous woman"), except when it touched *her*. She was willing to join him in everything, she believed in his visions, but a husband could go just so far, as he learned. When he was bent on taking a leaf out of the Bible to invite a contemporary Lilith to make a domestic threesome, Catherine balked. She sulked and wept so much because of his proposal to bring in a concubine that he had to abandon the idea, for he could not bear to see tears in a woman.

Blake found that he was especially receptive to messages from paradise while he lay asleep after sexual pleasure. Hearing the divine call, he would spring out of bed and hasten to transcribe the celestial messages on paper ready at his bedside. Then he would return to bed. Catherine believed all this. A. Gilchrist relates, "[She] had to sit up motionless and silent: only to stay near him mentally without moving hand or foot; this for hours, and night after night."

Blake said: "I write when commanded by the spirits, and the moment I have written I see the words fly about the room in all directions. It is then published and the spirits can read. My manuscripts are of no further use. I have been tempted to burn my manuscripts, but my wife won't let me."[19]

Nudity, Blake was certain, transported him to the genesis of the world. He put no fig leaves on his Biblical figures. The penis is a gift from God, he said; why cover it? As T. S. Eliot put it, "Blake was naked and he saw man naked."

The story is told that when a Mr. Butts called at the Blakes' summer home, he found them sitting nude reading *Paradise Lost*. "Come in!" greeted Blake. "It's only Adam and Eve, you know."

Throughout their marriage Blake shared everything with Catherine. "She was no fool," Jack Lindsay writes, "a strong-minded and warm-hearted woman, but she quite lacked the capacity to grasp the real bearing of his ideas. Her sustaining love kept him alive, but every now and then she must have infuriated him by her shallowness, the literal superficiality of her acceptance. He was probably saved by his childlessness. Had there been children, Catherine could not have given him her total absorption."[20]

One opinion of Blake's would probably not please Gloria Steinem: "Let men do their duty and the women will be such wonders; the female lives from the light of the male: see a male's female dependents, you know the man."

THRICE IN A LIFETIME

The French writers who frequented Magny's for the best soufflés in town, shop talk, and gossip about the latest liaisons sooner or later ended discussing their favorite subjects—women, marriage, and sex. The Goncourts, always on hand with enormous cuffs for note-taking, entered it all in their diaries immediately on returning home.

One of the Goncourts had put himself on record as saying, "As for physical love, when I indulge in it I dread its sweet convulsions." He said he'd rather publish a book.

A famous sex symposium is immortalized in a journal entry:

Gautier said that the only woman that really attracted him was the asexual woman, that is to say the woman so young that she banishes all ideas of childbearing and obstetrics; and he added that since he was unable to satisfy this penchant, on account of the police, all other women, whether they were twenty or fifty years old, were the same age to him.

Thereupon Flaubert, with his face flushed and his eyes rolling, proclaimed in his booming voice that beauty was not erotic, that beautiful women were not meant to be bedded, that the only useful purpose they served was inspiring statuary, and that love was born of that mysterious element which was produced by excitement and only very rarely by beauty. . . . he went on to say that he had never really possessed a woman, that he was a virgin, and that he had used all the women he had had as the mattress for another woman, the woman of his dreams. . . .

Flaubert, who was even more than usually verbose this evening and kept throwing out paradoxes, not with the ease of an Indian juggler like Gautier but with the clumsiness of a professional strongman or rather just an egregious provincial, declared that copulation was in no way necessary to the health of the organism and that it was a necessity created by our imagination. Taine pointed out that even so, when he who was no sexual debauchee indulged in sexual intercourse, every two or three weeks, he was relieved of a certain anxiety, a certain obsession, and felt his mind freer for work. Flaubert retorted that he was mistaken, that what a man needed was not a seminal discharge but a nervous discharge; that since Taine went to a brothel for his love-making, he could not possibly experience any relief; and that he needed love, emotion, the thrill of squeezing a hand. Whereupon we pointed out to him that very few of us were in that happy position, seeing that those who did not go to a brothel for satisfaction had an old mistress, a passing fancy, or a legitimate wife, with whom there could be no question of an emotion or a thrill; the result was that three-quarters of the human race never had a nervous discharge, and that a man was lucky if he experienced it three times in a lifetime of copulation.[21]

THE TRAGEDY OF THE BEDROOM

When young Maxim Gorki came to Yasnaya Polyana to pay homage to Leo Tolstoy, the guru to millions all over the world lamented:

"Man survives earthquakes, epidemics, the horrors of disease, and all the agonies of the soul, but for all time his tormenting tragedy is, and will be, the tragedy of the bedroom."[22]

Tolstoy's fulmination against sex intensified with the years. "The chief cause of unhappiness in married life," he wrote, "is that people think that marriage is sex attraction, which takes the form of promises and hopes of happiness—a view supported by public opinion and by literature. But marriage cannot cause happiness. Instead, it is always torture, which man has to pay for satisfying his sex urge."[23]

Unlike Proudhon and Godwin, who kept their doctrines and their private life apart, Tolstoy could not preach one way and live another.

Tolstoy found it harder and harder to act out his unorthodoxy at home. "To get married," he declared, "would not help the service of God and man, though it was done to perpetuate the race. Instead of getting married and producing fresh children, it would be much simpler to save and rear those millions of children who are now perishing around for lack of food."[24]

The outside world knew little of the turmoil behind the scenes at Yasnaya Polyana. His wife helped to keep the lid on their home life. As late as thirty years after their marriage, she was still lying to her brother: "It is as though our honeymoon had just begun, and I think there is only one woman as lucky as I."

It was in 1910 that the world was shocked at learning that at age eighty-two, the revered Tolstoy had fled his home in the middle of the night, a veritable Lear, trudging through the snow drifts to escape his wife's hysterics. He died in a remote railway station. His wife was condemned by all except a few members of the family.

Everyone then came out of the closet. Especially Countess Tolstoy, who affirmed: "How deeply I loved him, and how blunderingly!"

FOOT FETISHISTS

The Victorian novelist James Laver is quoted by Cyril Pearl in *The Girl with the Swansdown Seat* as saying, "One can hardly resist the conclusion that the erotic significance of boots and shoes received partial encouragement from the invention of the crinoline. . . . The crinoline was certainly not a moral garment. . . . The crinoline was in a constant state of agitation, swaying from side to side. . . . Any pressure on one side of the steel hoops was communicated by their elasticity to the other side, and resulted in a sudden upward shooting which gave mid-Victorian men their complex about ankles."[25]

For Havelock Ellis, sexologist and literary critic, the foot constituted a paramount erogenous zone: "Even for the normal lover it is one of the most attractive parts of the body."

Charles Kingsley, the novelist, retained his foot fetish throughout his life. His biographer Susan Chitty recounts one episode in which

Kingsley and his wife, Fanny, went up a mountain on a picnic: "When a slope was too steep, Fanny took off her shoes and stockings and astonished Charles with the beauty of her feet. He found bare feet particularly and peculiarly affecting. He once told Fanny, 'Your letter about bare feet almost convulsed me. I have such *strange* fantasies about bare feet.' Kissing her bare feet made him feel, he said, 'closer to God.' "[26]

* * *

Since Victor Hugo was unusually small as a schoolboy, the headmaster's daughter would place him on her bed and let him watch her put on her stockings. It was then, Hugo recalled, that he experienced his first sexual urge; it also initiated his lifetime obsession with the bare feet of women, especially when he saw them remove their stockings.

Kissing women's feet became Hugo's ploy for making up. His mistress Léonie jealously sent her rival, Juliette (the mainstay of Hugo's harem), a packet of his passionate letters to herself, sealed in wax with the motto of his coat of arms, *Ego Hugo*. Confronted with the evidence of his deceit, Hugo tried a characteristic gesture on Juliette: "What do you want me to say . . . for a long time you were my delight: you are now my consolation. . . . You are an angel and I kiss your feet."

As always, the shower of kisses did its work. This was the way Hugo melted Bernhardt and dozens of other actresses.

INTEMPERATE ZONES

A hotel room

Zelda Fitzgerald said that the moment she stepped into a hotel room and saw a gigantic bed inviting her, she lost all her inhibitions and couldn't wait to jump into it for a session of ecstatic love-making.[27]

The nape of a woman's neck

Goncourt wrote: "Both the round nape and the thin nape, with its indiscreet tuft of curl hair on the glowing flesh, produce an aphrodisiac effect on me. I find myself following the nape of the neck— for the pleasure of looking at—as other men follow a pair of legs."

The swish of a lady's dress

William Hazlitt, the essayist ("Love's Fool"), said that the seductive swish of a woman's dress could make a man desire instant possession.

"Take it off"

Watching his mistress proceed with a languorous, easy-paced strip-tease, peeling off one petticoat after another as she prepared for lovemaking, poet John Donne cried, "O my America! My new-found land!"

• • •

When Fontenelle, the great French writer, approaching the age of a hundred, discovered Madame Helvétius *en déshabille*, he exclaimed, "Would I were seventy!"

(The exclamation has been erroneously attributed to Oliver Wendell Holmes, in a similar situation at ninety.)

A woman's knees

W. C. Rogers tells how James Stephens, early in his career, consulted the self-acclaimed amorist George Moore on how to behave when seated at a dinner party between two strange but apparently accessible ladies.

"You may talk to them about their hair and their eyes and their noses, but don't say anything about their knees," Moore cautioned.

"I will not, Mr. Moore," Stephens said fervently.

"In especial, Stephens, do not touch their knees under any circumstances."

"I will not, Mr. Moore."

"Restraint at a formal dinner party, Stephens, is absolutely necessary."

"I quite understand, sir."

"Moreover, Stephens, women are strangely gifted creatures in some respects: all women have a sense akin to absolute divination about their knees."

"Sir?" Stephens queried.

"When a woman's knee is touched, Stephens, however delicately, that lady knows infallibly whether the gentleman is really caressing her or whether he is only wiping his greasy fingers on her stockings. But formal dinner parties are disgusting entertainments anyhow. Goodbye, Stephens."[27]

SATISFACTION GUARANTEED

H. G. Wells agreed with what Montaigne said: "There is no such thing as an altogether ugly woman—or altogether beautiful." Out of his rich amorous experience, Wells added a corollary: "Never marry a beautiful woman." He believed that plain women provide the ultimate satisfaction.

All that a sex rover requires, Wells assured Alec Waugh, are leisure and convenient premises. H.G. had mighty little leisure, but he always managed to find a convenient couch.

For Wells, freedom in marriage meant the right to be unfaithful. Above all else, he prized his independence. He declared that he "wanted a healthy woman handy"—but she had to leave him time to write.

Intimates marveled at his philandering energy and envied his versatility. It was amazing how he concurrently ran on four or more sex tracks. One domicile was in the country with his legitimate wife, Amy. Another was in Paris, where he did much of his writing. Still another was in London; at his literary-social salon, he was pursued by young women—some ostensibly intellectual and avant-garde—who kept popping in all the time but knew that they had to keep out of sight in the mornings, when he wrote. Things began to stir about one o'clock, after luncheon martinis and some tennis; Wells had it all routinized.

One wonders how he found time to cope with so many liaisons, considering his prolific journalism and literary creativity, constant globe-trotting, personal and business correspondence (he fought over all the fine print), and social obligations. But he felt it was all worthwhile. He kept saying he was having "just as good a time . . . as I can."

His conscience in his sexual adventures was creditable enough. He paid generously for the consequences of his refusal to use contraceptives. After scouring the countryside in search of a home for Rebecca West (who bore him his illegitimate son, novelist Anthony West; she and Wells had a ten-year affair after they met, when he was forty-six and she was nineteen), eventually Wells settled her in a home for pregnant women. At times, when emotional crises threw him into a panic and no storage flat was convenient, Wells brought his women home to Sandgate or wherever his legal domicile was, where his wife,

Amy, was willing to put them up. Beatrice Webb once remarked uneasily that Bertie was set on leading a double life—"on the one hand to be the respectable family man and famous littérateur to the world at large, and on the other hand to be the Goethe-like libertine." Casanova would have been the likelier comparison.

A typical *passade*, as Wells liked to call them, involved his relations with Amber Reeves, an active member of the Fabian Society and the daughter of one of its bigwigs. Norman and Jeanne Mackenzie, in their biography *The Time Traveller*, describe the episode: "Amber Reeves was pregnant and she and Wells had run away to Le Touquet. The elopement (remember he was then married and carrying on with other eager young women) was impulsive and unsatisfactory. Wells was miserable in temporary exile and before long he and Amber returned to England."[28]

Thereupon he sold his Sandgate house, bought a home for Amy and their two sons in Hampstead, and installed Amber in a cottage not far off in Surrey, where Wells visited her often while she was awaiting the birth of their child. Though Wells sweated for months through the negotiations, they didn't interrupt his writing. To some critics, his subsequent novel, *Ann Veronica*, was a thinly disguised account of his personal life. His seduction of Amber Reeves practically split the Fabian Society. He managed, however, to retain his friendship with Shaw and others there—although, naturally, not with Papa Reeves.

Vincent Brome says that when Wells was in his fifties, one of his women exclaimed, "Fancy a man of his age coming to me twice a night!"

Another time, the indefatigable Wells, pausing for breath, declared—half in complaint, half in boast—that his female pursuers at times made him "feel I was wearing glass trousers."

3

PREMIERES

The second night is a success, but the first is a triumph.
—A seducer in *L'Illusioniste*
by Sacha Guitry

PERVERT, SHE SCREAMED

Jim Bishop was fifteen, no longer satisfied with peeking at girls sitting open-legged on upper stairs. He wanted the real thing.

In his memoir, *A Bishop's Confession*, he tells us at seventy-three about his adolescent experience with Tessie.

"Tessie created more hard-ons than Mae Murray, Aileen Pringle, and Nita Naldi did in hours of vamping on the silent screen."[1]

While they were necking in the movie balcony, Jim realized that Tessie was begging for it. But—"What could I do with a grown woman 17 years old? The fellows on the corner said that you spread her legs and put your thing in her thing. But what was her thing like?" The mystery gave him "superb masturbatory fantasies."[2]

Revelation came soon. One night Tessie invited him up to her house to inspect her in her new bathing suit. (Her mother was dead; her father worked nights.) When Jim entered her dark bedroom, Tessie was in her swim suit, lying on her back in a deep sleep.

How was he going to get that tight suit over her hips? It refused to roll down. Luckily, she lifted her leg as she turned over, and he yanked off the suit down to her ankles. Tessie never stirred or opened her eyes. Gently, he parted her thighs. Curiosity over what lay between them made him pause ("I had never seen one"), and he knelt, shivering. Was it high up, deep down, possibly in the middle?

"There was but one way to make certain. I reached into my sagging trouser pockets and pulled out a kitchen match. I struck it on my shoe and, when the flame flared, I held it high up between Tessie's thighs to ascertain the what and the where. For no reason whatever the girl popped straight up in the air screaming. Then she held her hand over her mouth. She stood nude in the dark, whispering: 'Get out, you little son of a bitch! Get out, you goddam pervert!' I ran through the rooms, tugging the trousers up. I made the hall and the stairs two at a time."[3]

Jim was expected home that night ten minutes after ten. When he arrived on the dot, his mother complimented him on his punctuality.

"Good boy," she said, beaming.

In Costume

Playwright Ferenc Molnar's first marriage began with a *prima nox* triumph, but his matrimonial happiness was short-lived. He vowed to be less precipitous and warier in any future entanglement—then he extended his courtship of Sari Fedak, the greatest actress on the Hungarian stage, for seven years before reaching the decision that made her his second wife.

In accordance with Budapest custom, a wedding party of friends called on the bridegroom to escort him to the altar. Molnar was waiting impatiently in his study. His friends were outraged to find him in a casual gray business suit instead of formal garb. When they reproached him, Molnar said, "I only dress for premieres."[4]

Harold Robbins Drops In and Out

This is how sex began for Harold Robbins, according to an exchange in an interview for *Book Digest* conducted by editor Martin L. Gross—but it certainly did not end there, as readers will attest; Robbins's treatment of the subject has made him the most popular and probably the richest contemporary American novelist. He was born in Hell's Kitchen, New York.

MLG: Where did you go to school?

HR: At George Washington High School, until the fifth term. I didn't make it through the year.

MLG: What did you do?

HR: I ran away.

MLG: Why?

HR: I made three girls pregnant.

MLG: What does three girls being pregnant have to do with leaving high school?

HR: The family I was living with got very upset. They thought it was
       bad manners. I ran away and joined the navy.[5]

TAKE THE CASH AND LET THE CREDIT GO

When she was a nineteen-year-old Wellesley junior and already a
promising critic, Nora Ephron told Karl and Anne Taylor Fleming
she lost her virginity in her boyfriend's Harvard dorm:

"It was over quickly, and I don't remember much physical sensation one way or the other. . . . I remember thinking, 'My God, is
this it? Is this what I've been going through all this torment about?'
It was very disappointing. And then, to make matters even more ridiculous, he accused me of not being a virgin at all. I didn't have a
hymen—I don't know anyone who had a remotely athletic adolescence who did—and he assumed that because I didn't, I must be an
old pro. It hardly seemed fair to have finally done it and then not
even get the credit for its being my first time."[6]

IVAN, MAMAN, AND THE CHAMBERMAID

On a January evening in 1872, Turgenev, Daudet, Zola, Flaubert,
and one of the Goncourt brothers were sitting in a café reminiscing,
when they began to match stories of their initiations in sex. Characteristically, Goncourt made sure to record it in his journal the moment he reached home.

"The conversation, this evening," he wrote, "was filthy and de-
praved to begin with." They were fascinated by Turgenev's account:

"I was only a boy, and virginal, with the desire which one has at
fifteen. My mother had a pretty chambermaid with a stupid look, but
you know there are some faces to which stupidity lends nobility. It
was a soft, humid, rainy day, one of those erotic days which Daudet
has just painted. Dusk was beginning to fall. I was strolling in the
garden. Suddenly I see the girl coming straight toward me and she
takes me (I was her master and she—she was just a slave) by the hair
on my nape, saying: 'Come!' What followed was a sensation not unlike the sensations which we all have experienced. But this gentle
seizing of my hair with this single word sometimes comes back to me,
and the bare thought of it makes me happy."[7]

V. S. Pritchett suggests that Ivan's mother, who had all through his adolescence kept tight rein on her son's love affairs, undoubtedly arranged this initiation.[8]

IBSEN CONFRONTS A GHOST

Ibsen's sexual initiation, his earliest "ghost," suddenly reappeared when he was advanced in years. He was long and inextricably married and internationally famous for *A Doll's House* and *An Enemy of the People.*

At eighteen, Ibsen had been working as an apprentice apothecary when he seduced—or was seduced by—his family's twenty-eight-year-old scullery maid. After bearing him a son, she returned home in disgrace. Ibsen paid for Hans Jacob's upkeep until the boy was fourteen and then promptly dismissed him from his mind. He continued to be absorbed, however, by the dramatic theme of the ghosts in our closets.

According to Professor Francis Bull, who, biographer Michael Meyer avers, is usually right in such matters, the bastard son turned up when he was forty-six, a penniless, eccentric, and vagrant alcoholic. He knocked on the door of his father's study in Christiana and begged for financial help. Ibsen glared at him for a minute. Then, after Hans Jacob identified himself, Ibsen slapped down five crowns. When his son scowled, Ibsen reputedly said, "This is what I gave your mother. It should be enough for you!", slammed the door in Hans Jacob's face, and returned to his defense of women's rights.[9]

ALYS IN WONDERLAND

When he took a walk with Alys Pearsall Smith, the twenty-two-year-old Philadelphia Quaker with whom he had fallen in love at first sight, philosopher Bertrand Russell, chanting Shelley's *Epipsychidion* aloud to her, gave her a solemn kiss. It was the second time in his life that he had kissed a woman on the lips. Alys, he said, took away his shyness; he walked a mile and a half to the station in a blizzard, "tired but exultant."

Two people more different in their views of sex were never married. At twenty-seven, internationally recognized as an original thinker, Russell began to realize that he was a man of very strong sexual passions and resolved to gratify them. (Once he discovered sex and had his pyorrhea cleared up, there was no stopping him: in later years, after four marriages and innumerable seductions, he commented that all he was doing was giving women what they really wanted.) On the other hand, although Alys professed to be emancipated and lectured in defense of free love, she was frigid, and a Puritan to whom sexual intercourse was beastly and men were brutes. Copulation, thought Alys, should take place only for the purpose of reproduction.

"Neither she nor I had any previous experience of sexual intercourse when we married," Russell wrote many decades afterward in his *Autobiography*. "We found, as such couples apparently do, a certain amount of difficulty at the start. I have heard that many people say this caused their honeymoon to be a difficult time, but we had no such experience. The difficulties appeared to be merely comic and were soon overcome."[10]

Before he married, Russell said, he was deeply in love but had no conscious desire for any physical relation: "Indeed, I felt that my love had been desecrated when one night I had a sexual dream in which it took a less ethereal form. Gradually, nature took care of this matter."[11]

On a TV talk show, Russell told David Susskind that for his sexual premiere he informed Alys that, like Goethe, he wanted to have light during intercourse; his bride, however, who was surrendering grudgingly, preferred the dark. After some discussion, Alys gave in. "Our first night was spent by candlelight," Russell recorded. Characteristically, he added, "After six months she wasn't any longer a Quaker."[12]

EARLY TO BED

When Casanova was nine years old, his first teacher, the compassionate priest Dr. Gozzi, arranged to have the boy board with his family. Before the year was out, little Giovanni Casanova had his first sexual experience, with his guardian's pretty sister, Bettina, who was an older woman: Bettina was fourteen. It marked the start of a record-breaking career of seduction.

In later years, Casanova described his first sexual act with Bettina as awkward and unconsummated because of his timidity. But, he said, it was a beginning.[13]

In his *Memoirs*, Casanova names at least 116 mistresses who followed Bettina, each with her distinguishing traits. There were hundreds more; undiscriminating, he took them as he found them—young and old, fat and lean, whores and fine ladies, chambermaids and their mistresses. Eating fifty oysters for breakfast may have helped; his main dish, he claimed, was women.[14]

A contemporary writer described Casanova's techniques: "He made love standing, sitting, lying down, in bed, on staircases, in bathing establishments, in the open, with one woman, two women, two sisters at once, with two men and one woman, with fake eunuchs, and with his natural daughter by a former mistress."[15] He even shared a concupiscent nun with an old friend, the notoriously lecherous Cardinal de Bernis.

Casanova's unbridled promiscuity exacted its toll; he had at least eleven attacks of venereal disease. By his own account, in the town of Orsera he spread an epidemic of gonorrhea by infecting at least fifty people. The town physician exclaimed, "For twenty years I have practiced in this town where I lived in poverty, for I had only a few bleedings and cuppings to perform, and scratches and sprains to cure. My earnings were not enough to support me. But ever since last year I can say that my condition has changed. I have made much money and invested it wisely."

"*Io vissuto*," commented Casanova—seducer, gambler, swindler, quack, and celebrated memoirist: "I have lived."[16]

No Children Allowed

"My youthful love, whom I was very attached to and whom a strange indifference on my part allowed to slip from my grasp, seems when I now try to recall her like a character in a book I once read," wrote Bertolt Brecht at thirty-four.

Brecht's first love was Paula Bannholzer, whom he called Bi, short for "Bittersüss" (Bittersweet). She was a luscious seventeen-year-old who lived in Augsburg; Brecht was a lustful, penniless aspiring playwright. He invited her into his garret: "I have given Bittersüss a small ring. She kissed me trembling. We didn't say a word."[17]

Shortly after that, when Bi told him she was pregnant, he fumed and shouted that he was not so much opposed to babies as he was opposed to the status of husband. Marie Luise Fleisser recalls his saying that he had a horror of pregnancies. If he was responsible for getting his lovers pregnant, he railed against the women as if they had done it to spite him.[18]

Bi and Bertolt's son was baptized Frank, in honor of Brecht's favorite playwright, Frank Wedekind. Actually, Brecht was fond of the redheaded child *in absentia.* For the actress Helene Weigel, his mistress and later his wife, it was not difficult to persuade her sister to care for the little Frank until he was sixteen; Brecht paid expenses. Later, Bi took the youth back to Augsburg, where he became a German soldier. He was killed on the Russian front.

Bi later turned up in the widening circle of Brecht's mistresses as a married woman. The two became fast friends for several years and he dedicated *Drums in the Night* to her. Like H. G. Wells, Brecht never dropped a mistress completely, nor did his mistresses dream of disentangling themselves from him. "From time to time," he said, "I shoot at birds who try to get away and gobble them up again."[19]

Brecht reveled in the devotion of women. During an affair with Marianne Zoff, whom he had made pregnant, he asked Bi to marry him. This time it was she who wavered, saying she preferred to wait three years. Brecht said, well, he really was in no mood to marry anyone—he had a stable full of fillies. He wanted "to be able to spit as I wish, to sleep alone, to be unscrupulous."

But Marianne being amenable, he married her, for worse rather than for better, as she later found out. (With wife Helene Weigel, in his final years, Brecht had a very good thing: she was his famous collaborator in their East Berlin theater productions.)

ROUND-ONE KNOCKOUT

In his *Memoirs,* Tennessee Williams describes his first and only consummated sexual experience with a woman. In the Drama Department at the University of Iowa in the fall of 1937, he reports, he was seduced by Sally, a nymphomaniac and alcoholic, in the apartment of one of her friends.

"She had a terrific build, especially her breasts, which were about the most prominent on the campus. . . . we were soon on the sofa, naked, and I couldn't get it up, no way, no way, and all of a sudden I felt nauseated from the liquor consumed and from the nervous strain and embarrassment. I rushed into the bathroom and puked, came out with a towel around me, hangdog with shame over my failed test of virility.

" 'Tom, you've touched the deepest chord in my nature, the maternal chord,' she said."[20]

The next night, when he took her home to her roominghouse, she was wearing red ski pants and a white sweater, which did justice to her extraordinary endowment. She turned out the light in the parlor, motioned Williams to the sofa—and her caresses were "wildly successful." She unzipped the ski pants, but he made love without removing his overcoat. When they were interrupted once or twice by returning roomers, she would zip up her pants and he would button his coat, but no one in that rather raffish house was fooled or cared one way or another.

"The roomers would go upstairs at once and we would at once return to our wild break-through of my virginal status.

"I took to it like a duck to water. She changed positions with me, she got on top of me and rode my cock like a hobbyhorse and then she came and I'd never imagined such a thing, all that hot wet stuff exploding inside her and about my member and her gasping hushed outcries."[21]

He was not yet in love with Sally, but terribly impressed with himself.

"I got home long after midnight. I went straight to the men's room at the ATO house. Another brother was peeing as I peed, and I said, 'I fucked a girl tonight.'

" 'Yeh, yeh, how was it?'

" 'Oh, it was like fucking the Suez Canal,' I said, and grinned and felt a man full grown."[22]

A Noel Coward Opening Night

When a reporter asked Sir Noel, shortly before the death of the songwriter-playwright-actor-director-scenarist-producer with "a talent to amuse," "What are your ideas of heaven?" he replied, "Garbled." And to the question, "Doesn't the eye of heaven mean anything to you?" Coward quipped, "Only when it winks."[23]

Gertrude Lawrence gave thirteen-year-old Noel his first heavenly wink. He had just made his stage debut, to lukewarm applause, as a mushroom in an all-juvenile production; now he was off on a three-week engagement with ten other children and a ballet chaperon in Liverpool and Manchester. He missed his strong, doting mum. But once the train moved out of Euston Station, Gert took over the lonely boy in her own fashion.

At fourteen, Gert was "very mondaine," Noel recalled, "tremendously alive and frequently dabbing her up-turned nose." One night in their digs in Manchester she gave him an orange and told him a few mildly naughty stories. Then, before he could cry mama, she had him alone in her bedroom where in "a labor of love" she gave him "a practical demonstration of the facts of life."[24]

The debut was no smash hit. Once home, Noel was again in charge of his mum, who steered him around the London theatrical offices. For the rest of his life, he was attached to her, as he said gratefully and lovingly, "with an umbilical cord made of piano wire." When Coward was fifty-five, someone observed that "together they behaved like newlyweds." Sir Noel was devoted to many women friends, Gertie Lawrence among them.

JENNY MAKES SHAW'S MIND UP AT TWENTY-NINE

During his first two years in London after coming from Dublin, Bernard Shaw was too busy with polemical journalism, soapboxing on Hyde Park Corner, and heckling speakers in lecture halls to think about sex. Then he met Alice Lockett, a demure Sunday School teacher and hospital nurse as sexually immature as himself. ("I had been perfectly continent," GBS told Frank Harris, "except for the involuntary incontinences of dreamland, which were very frequent.")[25]

After two years of exchanging love letters and writing sophomoric verse, Shaw tired of the fumbling courtship of Alice Lockett and wrote her, "When next we meet let it be as strangers. . . . Lovemaking grows tedious to me. The emotion has evaporated from it. This is your fault. . . ."[26]

He was ripe for someone to take Alice's place. There catapulted into his mother's apartment for singing lessons, and into Shaw's life, the redoubtable sex-hungry widow of forty-two, fifteen years his senior, Jenny Patterson. Well fixed financially, she could pay for their dinners out and had a house across the square convenient for amour. Shaw, living half-starved in a cluttered back room at his mother's, had neither pocket money nor a decent suit to his name.

Unlike Alice, Jenny took possession of Shaw, and appealed to him; she was witty, clever, and shared his passion for music. When his father's death brought Shaw a small legacy, he went out and bought his famous Jaeger suit. It gave him confidence to go out to concerts and dinners with Jenny.

He paid daily calls at her house and found it harder to fend off her attempts to seduce him: "Supper, music, and a declaration of passion. Left at 3:00 A.M. *Virgo intacta* still." (GBS could never be forced to stay out after 3:00 A.M.)

A few nights later: "Forced caresses."

Then, on his twenty-ninth birthday, he celebrated a new experience: "Seduced and raped."[27]

Jenny, whom he found "sexually insatiable," rubbed off most of Shaw's shyness. Her "seduction and rape" he never forgot; six decades later, when Jenny was dead, he described her in his *Sixteen Self-Sketches* and even included a time-worn photograph of her.

Shaw wanted it understood that he was far from being only an observer of London's sex scene. "As soon as I could afford to dress presentably," he told Harris, "I became accustomed to women falling in love with me. I did not pursue women; I was pursued by them."[28] And he was not attracted to virgins; he preferred women, like Jenny, who knew what they were doing.

But for all her wit, Jenny lacked humor and was too overpowering for his taste after a while. She committed the error of barring the door to Shaw one holiday when he was at loose ends and eager for some more night music.

"She put him off one evening," says R. J. Minney, "to see Lord Croft; on New Year's evening he went to her house and found the place in darkness. . . . A week later he went to see her again and the single word 'Revulsion' in his diary records his feelings."

And then on another occasion soon after, Shaw found a rival on Jenny's couch, bent on seduction. "We tried which should outstay the other. Eventually he had to go for a train. . . . To bed late."

Shaw began to go out with other equally attractive women, just as available and far less demanding—May Morris, daughter of the Socialist pamphleteer and poet William Morris; Annie Besant, not yet the activist for India's freedom. Now that Shaw was philandering, Jenny began spying on him; in his absence she read an ardent letter from Annie Besant on his desk and was enraged; in the street, finding him with Annie, she created a highly embarrassing scene. He wrote to Jenny: "Henceforth intercourse must be platonic."

But Shaw could not bring the curtain down so easily. Once at his mother's home, there was "much pathetic kissing and kissing after which she went away comparatively happy," but he repeated his ultimatum, to no avail. Desperately, though she lived just across the square, Jenny moved in with Shaw's mother, who saw it as a step forward to marriage; she had all along expressed the hope that her son would marry an heiress. (So did Shaw.) Now Jenny broke into his room at all hours ("J.P. came, raged, wept, flung a book at my head"); once, with a clamorous Jenny in pursuit, he clutched a sheaf of papers and fled to a stand beneath a park lamp to write.

Jenny left on a tour of the East, and Shaw began to date the divorced actress Florence Farr. He called her "E.E." and persuaded her to play a role in his *Widower's Houses*. On Jenny's return: "Fearful scene about E.E. . . . Did not get home until 3:00 A.M." One night, he came home from the opera to find a terribly wrathful Jenny waiting for him. The denouement occurred one evening when he went to E.E. and Jenny burst in, very late, and made a shocking scene, violent and using atrocious language; Shaw had to restrain her from attacking Florence Farr and was two hours getting her out of the house. He made Jenny apologize to Florence and promise never again to annoy her. He re-created the scene in *The Philanderer*, where Jenny is portrayed as Julia Craven and Florence as Grace Transfield. (Jenny never saw that play.)

Shaw wanted something made clear about his life. He wrote to Frank Harris: "If you have any doubts about my normal virility dismiss them from your mind. I was not impotent; I was not sterile; I was not homosexual; and I was extremely susceptible, though not promiscuously. . . . During the 14 years before my marriage at 43 there was always some lady in the case; and I tried all the experiments and learned all there was to be learned from them. The ladies were unpaid, for I had no spare money. All my pursuers did not want sexual intercourse. Some were happy, and appreciated our understanding that sex was barred."[29]

R. J. Minney observes that Shaw personally attached little importance to sex—"he loved women on this side of adultery" and was able to dismiss the idea that he was sexually inadequate by proclaiming that geniuses were not indifferent to sex.

St. John Ervine said of Shaw: "He was very attractive to women— extraordinarily attractive to women and very intelligent women too. It was a staggering sight . . . the way women cluttered around him like infatuated hens. He wasn't a monk by any manner of means, he was ardent right up to the end."[30]

POETRY LED THE WAY

Frieda Weekley, buxom mother of three and the sex-starved (by her standards) wife of a college professor, did not care that she was not the first woman in D. H. Lawrence's life, just so she had a firm grip on the miner's son.

Long before Lawrence ran off with Frieda, the honor of being his first was claimed by Alice Dax, wife of the local Eastwood pharmacist. She boasted to a friend: "I gave Bert sex. I had to. He was over at our house, struggling with a poem he could not finish, so I took him upstairs and gave him sex. He came downstairs and finished the poem."[31]

Most Lawrence biographers acknowledge Alice Dax's claim to premiere rights; however, Jessie Chambers and Louie Burrows (and probably some others) figured in his early experience of women.

Lawrence's mother strongly objected to her son's marrying Jessie, but was not averse to his wanting to marry Louie, who had attended Teachers Training School with him and who, according to town rumors, was Lawrence's first and only fiancée. He was in fact engaged to her, and they had a close friendship for ten years.

D.H.L. said his mother "hated J. (Jessie) and would have risen from her grave to prevent my marrying her."[32]

Lawrence proposed to Louie but couldn't stick to their protracted engagement of fifteen months. Although Frieda was such a liar that it is hard to credit any of her claims, she pooh-poohed the critics' statement that Louie was the prototype for Ursula Brangwen in *The Rainbow*. "Some of the outer setting in *The Rainbow* was a bit like Louie, but the inside is me," she insisted.

The stumbling block in the Lawrence-Louie courtship was that she was "good, awfully good, churchy," and although he was willing to go to church with her, he couldn't stand her veto against premarital sex. Frieda was a different matter; he eloped to the Continent with her, and as he confided to Edward Garnett, "never knew what love was before." Louie remained on his conscience for a long time, however; considerably later, he broke the news to her, concluding his confession: "The best thing you can do is to hate me."

Apparently, as George H. Ford notes, Louie did not follow Lawrence's advice but carried the torch for him to the grave.

SYBARITE AND SAINT

Henri Troyat described the author of *Anna Karenina* as being "two men—a sybarite and a saint—sewn up inside one skin, each loathing the other."

When Tolstoy was fourteen, he struggled desperately to stay pure. "Could not hold out," he scrawled in his diary. "I motioned to something pink which looked very nice from a distance. I opened the back door. She came in. I can't stand her any more; everything is vile and ugly; I hate her, because she drove me to break my resolution. . . . I bitterly repent of it. I have never felt so strongly as now."[33]

When Aunt Toinette, with whom he was living after he was orphaned at nine, noticed her nephew's long periods of disquiet, she kept nagging him to go out into the village or anywhere on the vast estate to sow his wild oats. "She was always telling me," he says in his *Confessions*, "that there was nothing she wanted so much for me as to have an affair with a married woman. 'There is no better education than an affair with a woman of good breeding.' "[34]

The fourteen-year-old count could ravish with impunity any woman on his estate, but his eyes were on Aunt Toinette's maid, Masha, a country-fresh virgin with orbs "black as wet currants" and seductively swaying hips. He was too timid to do more than follow her into dimly lit corridors, snatch a few kisses, and possess her in his dreams. Then one night he persuaded her to drop her door latch for him. As Troyat describes it, he "clasped in his arms a quaking body huddled inside a coarse linen night shirt."[35]

Post coitus, he cried into his diary, "Is what happened to me wonderful or horrible?" and then dismissed the deflowering with "Bah! It's the way of the world; everybody does it." But then he confessed to being ashamed of the advantage he had taken, called the deflowering brutal, and swore to resist temptation in the future. Like so many other adolescent vows, this one was broken, and his nights were sheer torment.

Aunt Toinette excoriated her maid, Masha, and vindicated her nephew. When Masha could not hide her swelling stomach, Aunt Toinette promptly dismissed her. Later, Tolstoy lamented, "I seduced her, she was sent away, and she perished."

When Tolstoy was past sixty-nine and internationally known for his austere misogyny, he happened to be riding past the field where he had once had sexual relations with another household servant, Dunyasha, not long after his seduction of Masha. And he burst into tears. "I remember the nights I spent there, Dunyasha's beauty and youth . . . her strong womanly body. Where is it? Nothing but bones."[36]

WAITING FOR BECKETT

Act I.

A whore named Lulu picked up restless, gangling young Samuel Beckett as he sprawled on a Dublin park bench, took him home, where she boarded him in the spare room adjoining the one she used professionally and fed his sexual lust, gratis, for several weeks.

One day out of the blue, she told him she was pregnant. "She kept plaguing me with *our* child," Beckett wrote, "exhibiting her belly and breasts and saying it was due at any moment, she could feel it lepping already. If it's lepping, I said, it's not mine." He grinned, picked up his cap and, without another word, slammed the door behind him.

The experience haunted him for decades. He put it in the story *First Love,* which he stored away in manuscript for twenty-eight years, until he surmised that Lulu must be dead. Then he let it be published in French.[37]

Act II.

A hunger to identify with a surrogate father had been a lifelong obsession with Beckett. (He was unable to communicate with his own father throughout his adolescence.) He determined to move compatriot James Joyce into his father's place.

On his arrival in Paris, where he had been appointed *lecteur* at the École Normale Supérieure for a two-year stint, Beckett set out to surrender himself to Joyce, who was twenty-four years his senior. Beckett thought the self-exiled author of *Nocturne* and *Ulysses* was the greatest writer in the world and was resolved to become his acolyte. He persuaded his friend Thomas McGreevy, recognized everywhere as Joyce's alter ego, to introduce him to his idol. The hand that Joyce stretched out to Beckett was tentative and frigid at first; however, after McGreevy recited Beckett's pedigree, academic honors, fame as a cricketer, and zeal to pass on Dublin gossip, which Joyce could utilize for his work in progress, Joyce warmed up perceptibly. In time, Beckett became a daily visitor to the Joyces' home. And he proved decidedly helpful. He brought Joyce books he needed, made abstracts of them, took dictation (Joyce was practically blind), and was so idolatrous that he imitated his expressions and changed to his brand of cigarettes.

Of the dozen people Beckett met at the Joyce apartment that first night, he found the novelist's eighteen-year-old daughter, Lucia, an object of striking interest. A strange girl who made no friends among her father's satellites, she was self-conscious about her pronounced squint and the scar on her chin; she was awkward, shy, extraordinarily affected, and sure that as the daughter of a notoriously eccentric father she would be viewed as an oddity by everyone.

Biographer Deirdre Bair describes Beckett's initial and later reactions:

"Beckett found her a fascinating young woman, albeit one he would rather have studied from a distance than from the delicate, highly involved situation in which he found himself. When Beckett was around, her behavior was nervous, hyperactive and sometimes silly. What she thought was witty, flirtatious chatter was really erratic speech; she leaped from one unconnected thought to another, forcing anyone listening to follow with difficulty as she skidded from one unreality to another. Beckett watched her, fascinated by aspects of the father's mind running rampant in the daughter."[38]

As the months passed, Lucia began to center all her attention openly on Beckett. Her fixation made him uneasy, and he vowed to be wary about encouraging her. When he took her to the theater or dinner parties given by Joyceans Nancy Cunard, Richard Aldington, or Sylvia Beach, he invited others to join them. Observed or no, Lucia made no attempt to hide her feelings. As Bair wrote: "She fascinated Beckett, but more as a case study than a possible love interest."

Beckett realized he was heading for a crisis, but he feared that any upset Lucia suffered on his account was bound to cause a break in his father-son relationship with Joyce. And that was the last thing he wanted. Bair goes on to say: "Lucia was not an attractive woman, and he was flattered that the daughter of Joyce found him interesting, but these feelings were superseded by a genuine feeling of horror that someone he looked upon as a sister found him sexually attractive. Lucia's feeling for him was almost, he confided to a friend, like incest."[39]

Finally, he told her, as tactfully as he could, that he was coming to the Joyce apartment only to be near her father. Lucia blamed her mother for trying to push Beckett into a proposal of marriage and was distressed almost to the point of trauma when she heard Nora tell William Bird, a frequent visitor, "What Lucia needs is a nice young husband." When Lucia conceded to Bird, "The trouble with me is I'm sex-starved," he reassured her, "That's rot. What have you been reading?"[40] The fact is that Lucia, like her mother, had never been able to get through the first pages of *Ulysses.*

Beckett was perceptive enough to understand that if he snubbed Lucia (and he hadn't the heart to do it), he would be offending her father. It had to be both or neither. He decided that the price was too high. The more he studied her condition, the more he was convinced that Lucia was a step from the brink of insanity, and if pushed too far, she would commit suicide.[41]

Mary Colum, on a visit to the Joyces, saw in the first few minutes that Beckett's relationship with Lucia was heading toward disaster, and she suggested to Joyce that he should make a frank approach to the slow-paced Beckett.

Someone must have talked to Paul Léon, Joyce's friend, because Paul soon stepped in and persuaded his brother-in-law, Alex Ponisovsky, who was still smarting from his recent frustrated love affair, to propose to Lucia. It worked. She accepted. Joyce was so overjoyed that he arranged a formal engagement party at a posh restaurant. The result was disaster. Lucia, her heart obviously for Beckett, sat through the party with unfeigned distress and toward the end lapsed into a catatonic fit and had to be taken to Paul Léon's apartment to recuperate.

The event aroused much gossip. Some said that Beckett had proposed, as Bair reports it, "on bended knee and then asked her father for her hand in marriage. Others insisted that Beckett was frightened by Lucia's advances but too passive to resist them and too worried about the loss of access to Joyce to do anything to stop them."

It was Lucia herself who brought about Beckett's "bust-up with Shem." Intent on wrangling a proposal out of him in her own fashion, she invited him to lunch at a restaurant facing the Luxembourg Gardens. For the occasion she was neatly dressed and, for a change, wore makeup. Not wanting to meet her alone, Beckett brought along a friend. The third party upset Lucia immediately. As the meal progressed she became fidgety and tense. Suddenly she sprang up and ran out. Beckett hastened to follow her but she had disappeared.

When she returned home, Joyce knew at a glance that his daughter had been compromised. Nora (Bair writes) "was furious with Beckett, whom she accused of leading Lucia on, ingratiating himself into her affections under false pretenses. Joyce, in tones of icy rage, informed Mr. Beckett that he was no longer welcome in his home or his presence. The break that Beckett had feared became reality."[42]

It was years before Beckett was *persona grata* again at the Joyce apartment.

Act III.

Enter *dea ex machina.* After the calamitous luncheon and break with Joyce, Beckett went off for therapeutic relief. Instead of returning home to his sullen mother, he went to Kassel, Germany, his usual summer retreat. He was sure he would find diversion with his boyhood friend Peggy Sinclair.

According to some authorities, his first meaningful sexual experience occurred during this holiday. News of his serious interest in Peggy reached his mother and drove her to hysterics. (Beckett had left Ireland for good in the first place because of her nagging and threats to throw him out, although his attachment was so strong that he went back home at least once a year.) This time, she smelled unpardonable heresy. Had Samuel forgotten that Peggy was his first cousin? "Holy Mary! It's incest!" she clamored. Even worse: the Sinclair background was Jewish. An aunt had been ostracized for marrying a Jew.

Mama notwithstanding, Beckett came to Kassel intent on cementing his relationship with Peggy. But there was one fly in the ointment: Peggy loved to tease Sam with stories about her other lovers. The siren kept pulling and releasing him; her caprices drove him mad with desire. Finally, as he wrote thirty years later in *Krapp's Last Tape*, he cornered her during a walk. Well, he asked bluntly, would she yield? Gooseberries, she said.

> I said again I thought it was hopeless and no good going on and she agreed, without opening her eyes. (*Pause*) I asked her to look at me and after a few moments—(*Pause*)—after a few moments she did, but the eyes just slits because of the glare. I bent over them to get them in the shadow and they opened. (*Pause. Low*) Let me in. (*Pause*) We drifted in among

the flags and stuck. The way they went down, sighing, before the stem! (*Pause*) I lay down across her with my face in her breasts and my hand on her. We lay there without moving. But under us all moved, and moved us gently, up and down, and from side to side.[43]

This session was Beckett's first initiation in reciprocated sexual passion.

The Green Carnation

Oscar Wilde entered adult life as a heterosexual; his overt homosexuality came after his Magdalen College, Oxford, years.

As a college undergraduate, like other Oxonians he patronized "Old Jess," a popular prostitute there; she gave him his first dose of venereal disease. The mercury treatment decayed his teeth, blackening the prominent front tooth. The syphilis entered the remission stage for several years, only to haunt him later.

Wilde's first love was a seventeen-year-old Dublin beauty, Florence ("Florrie") Balcombe. The Balcombe affair lasted two years, a courtship he called "the sweetest of all the years of my youth." Florrie rejected his proposal of marriage and wed another Dubliner, Bram Stoker, later famous as the author of *Dracula*. Wilde took the rejection hard. Afterward, he wrote her: "I shall always remember you at prayers." Before Florrie's debut in Tennyson's verse play *The Cup*, Wilde sent Ellen Terry, the leading lady, a chaplet of flowers with a note asking her to give them to Florrie without revealing his name: "I should like to think she was wearing something of mine the first night she comes on stage, that anything of mine should touch her. . . . She thinks I never loved her, thinks I forget. My God, how could I?"[44] They never ceased being friends. She went to his theatrical premiere. Who knows what direction his life might have taken had he married Florrie?

Given his eccentric heritage, Oscar could only have developed as a nonconformist. His father was a scholar, an antiquarian, and a celebrated eye surgeon in appointment to the queen. Though married, he ran after Dublin women, siring at least two known illegitimate children. Sir William Wilde's trial, for raping a patient in his office, was a scandal. His reputation never fully recovered, but he did go on to international professional acceptance.[45]

Wilde boasted to Vincent O'Sullivan, the American writer, that he took after his mother. Lady Wilde—the fiery "Speranza" of the Irish nationalist movement—was better known and more talked about than her husband. Gigantic in figure, rather than Junoesque, with a whalelike middle like her famous son's, she was overdressed, turbaned, overpowdered. She was an inflammatory advocate of women's rights and thought not only that she resembled Madame de Staël but that she could claim kinship with Dante. She refused to be bothered over her husband's extramarital involvements. To her son she handed down marked literary tastes.

The Wildes' elder son, Willie, a homosexual alcoholic, died of excessive drinking. Oscar's niece, Dolly Wilde, pretty and wildly impulsive, was a notorious lesbian on the Left Bank in Paris and had a crush on Gertrude Stein. Dolly proudly enjoyed her nickname, Oscaria.

When reports reached Lady Wilde about the eccentric figure that Oscar was cutting in London, she said: "I believe in you and your genius." However, when reports of his homosexual practices reached her, she disowned him, more openly as the scandalous trials proceeded. Bernard Shaw thought she might have had lesbian inclinations herself.

Havelock Ellis believed that Wilde's homosexuality was latent from the start. During the first years of marriage to Constance Lloyd, Wilde enjoyed normal sexual relations with her, boasted how happily uxorious he was, and produced two sons. It is thought that he ceased having sexual relations with his wife when the sign of his earlier venereal diseases reappeared. He feared infecting her.[46]

In his thirties, when his fame as a playwright, essayist, and conversationalist brought him into the limelight, Wilde was bored by the round of social engagements to which he was dragged by Constance, who clearly could not keep pace with him intellectually. He stayed away from home for longer periods of time, once giving the silly excuse, among others, that he was playing golf every afternoon. It was at this period that he framed two of his classic epigrams: "The only charm of marriage is that it makes a life of deception necessary for both parties" and "When a man has loved a woman, he will do anything for her except continue to love her." Actually, Oscar retained affection for Constance, though they were rarely again seen in each other's company.

According to Robert Sherard, one of Wilde's most intimate lifelong friends, Wilde gave evidence of homosexual inclinations at

Magdalen College, Oxford, although there was no homoerotic activity. He was caught up in the swelling tide of the New Hellenism and Pre-Raphaelitism, and joined the avant-garde college milieu dominated by the closet homosexual Walter Pater. Pater collected Greek gem rings. Wilde wore them. Wilde saw much of Ronald Gower, a self-professed "homosexual aesthete." Wilde also became a constant visitor at the London bookshop of Charles Hirsch, a Frenchman specializing in Zola's works and similar books that English booksellers dared not stock. There he found *The Sins of the Cities of the Plain*, about a male homosexual's London adventures. The ultimate conversion was not far off. However, as Montgomery Hyde writes, Wilde's curiosity about homoeroticism was still theoretical, for he retained traces of his native Irish puritanism: "I do not think that people who do these things derive as much pleasure as I do from talking about them."[47]

And Wilde did talk. Brilliantly and far too much for his own security. His buttonhole was never without a green carnation, the public badge of Parisian homosexuals. Dozens of adoring Oxonian boys followed Oscar's sartorial acknowledgment that they were ready to savor unorthodox sexual practices. Aubrey Beardsley, another bold cultist of the new aestheticism, tells how Wilde once bragged (at an after-dinner symposium after the Athenian model) that he'd had five sex sessions in one nocturnal orgy with several telegraph messenger boys: "I kissed each one of them in every part of their bodies; they were all dirty and appealed to me for just that reason." When Wilde's friend Robert Ross warned him of the danger of such public confessions, he waved him off: "The Treasury will always give me twenty-four hours to leave the country as they did in Lord Somerset's case." Pater, who only flirted with homosexuality, was untouched. Wilde, less academic, attracted the notice of the Director of Public Prosecution and ruined his life by boasting that he was indeed practicing what the Greek hedonists preached.

Robert Ross ("Robbie") told Frank Harris that he was "the first boy Oscar ever had." The two met at Oxford when Wilde was lecturing on the new aestheticism and Ross was being tutored for admission to the university. It was love at first sight. Robbie was thirteen years younger than Wilde; clever, and plain-looking, he was a social charmer whose "delightful nature" Sir William Rothenstein described in his *Men and Memories*: "[He] was an admirable story-teller, and a wit; above all he was able to get the best out of those he admired. Oscar Wilde was never better than when at Ross's parties."[48]

At first Wilde took Ross home several times a week; later he had him as his house guest in Tite Street for two months. Ross was Wilde's most loyal disciple through all the three sensational trials, supportive to the very end, when all the fair-weather Oscarites, even Sir Alfred Douglas, had deserted or snubbed him. (The exception was Whistler, who publicly declared that Wilde's scandalous conduct made little difference to him: "Am I to shun a man because he prefers his stout to my champagne? . . . I will confess that the preference to the backside of a Wapping stable boy to the ineffable glories of a beautiful woman's body strikes me as a calamitous error in judgment, a self-deprivation of joy quite staggering to someone like me.")[49] After Wilde left Reading Gaol, Ross helped him with clothes, money, and public support. He later became his literary executor.

Although Emile Zola and George Meredith refused to sign the appeal to Queen Victoria to reduce Wilde's sentence (two years at hard labor), Robert Tyrell, Dublin-born Regius Professor of Greek at Oxford, signed it. Ironically, when Vincent O'Sullivan visited Wilde at Berneval after Reading Gaol, Wilde told him, "The three women I most admired are Queen Victoria, Sarah Bernhardt, and Lily Langtry."[50]

Five years after Wilde's intimacy with Ross began, Alfred Douglas, then a budding poet, seated himself next to Wilde at a much-touted "feast with panthers." After reading Wilde's poems, the young lord prevailed on his friend Lionel Johnson (who was homosexual) to arrange for him to take tea in Tite Street. Bosie—an affectionate contraction for "Boysie"—was then a second-year undergraduate at Magdalen College. Frank Harris wrote that at that first encounter, the most strikingly beautiful boy in England hung upon Wilde's lips "with soul in his eyes."

Thirty years later, Douglas remembered the hypnosis of Oscar's conversation. He told Hyde, "I have never known anyone to come near him. . . . One sat and listened to him enthralled. It all appeared to be wisdom and power and beauty and enchantment."

In a few months Bosie yielded to Wilde's persistent advances. Hyde says, "Douglas found in the older man a most entertaining companion, and it flattered his vanity to be seen in Wilde's company, particularly after the resounding success of Lady Windermere's Fan. Wilde, for his part, was drawn to Douglas's poetic feelings and his gifts as a writer of sonnets . . . and no doubt was also influenced by the fact

. . . that his latest young friend was a lord whose family on both sides occupied a distinguished place in Debrett."[51]

Wilde himself recalled how the two stopped off at the Royal Palace in Kensington: "Bosie has insisted on stopping here for sandwiches. He is like a narcissus—so white and gold . . . Bosie is so tired like a hyacinth on the sofa and I worship him."[52]

Douglas recalled later: "[Wilde] was continually asking me to lunch or dine with him, and sending me letters, notes, and telegrams. He flattered me, gave me presents, and made much of me in every way."

Douglas admitted to Hyde that when he first met Wilde, he was no more innocent than other boys of his age. "From the second time he saw me, when he gave me a copy of *Dorian Gray*, which I took with me to Oxford, he made overtures to me. It was not until I had known him for at least six months and he had twice stayed with me in Oxford, that I gave in to him. I did with him and allowed him to do what was done among boys at Winchester and Oxford."[53]

Constance Wilde slowly perceived the alteration in her husband; she could not be totally blind to it. Ross observed that Wilde "never blamed anyone but himself for his own disaster. He never bore ill will to anybody . . . he did not understand how cruel he was to his wife, but I never expect anyone to believe that."

Wilde's brother, Willie, had the last word. He told Bernard Shaw: "Oscar was not a man of bad character. You could have trusted him with a woman anywhere."[54]

• • •

While Oscar Wilde was going through the three sodomy trials, outraged and stunned homosexuals rushed to Calais to escape from the smut-and-sex hounds. The notoriety of the Wilde name reached even to the canine world: all the dogs named Oscar were hastily renamed. No child was registered with the name of Oscar for sixteen years. During the trials, London truckdrivers and bargemen now cursed each other with a handy obscenity, "You bloody Oscar!"

Years later, Wilde's son, Vyvyan Holland, disclosed to the photographer-memoirist Cecil Beaton: "My mother and I went to Montreux, and when they discovered who we were, we had to leave the hotel. I was seven at the time and it has made a terrible impression on me ever since. I can't bear even to see my name in print: it gives me the horrors. We had to change our name because everywhere we went we were hounded . . . and in my aunt's house I came across a copy of 'The Happy Prince' with the name of the author covered with sticky paper."[55]

"[Holland's wife] disclosed that talk with Vyvyan about his father was a rare occurrence and that for years this had been a forbidden subject in this household. . . . Even the valet found it hard to find further employment when it became known for whom he had worked. It was this being scorned by the world that had killed his father, said V.H."[56]

Vyvyan never saw his father again after the conviction for homosexuality. All he was told by his mother was that he was an unfortunate son of a wicked father whose image he must erase for his own future peace and security, and the less said about it the better. It was only when he reached manhood that he was told the nature of the disgrace.

"Is that all it was?" he asked, dumbfounded. "I thought he was an embezzler."

Some years after the scandal, Oscar Wilde went to his wife's grave in a green cab, holding a bouquet of red roses. He knelt in prayer at the graveside, sobbing uncontrollably and strewing the flowers on the grave. Then he rose and pledged eternal fidelity to the memory of Constance.

"I was deeply affected," he recalled, "with the sense, also, of the uselessness of all regrets. Nothing could be otherwise—and life is a terrible thing."[57]

FEMININE SOUL IN A MASCULINE ENVELOPE

After examining the then available facts of Walt Whitman's life, and in particular the poet's summary avowal "I think to be a woman is greater than to be a man," critic James Huneker labeled the Good Gray Poet a "feminine soul in a masculine envelope." No one has yet changed Huneker's perceptive characterization.

Walt tossed off any number of confessions on the subject. How far can we trust them?

For nearly a century, literary detectives probing Whitman's secret sex life have met with little success. Whitman had pocketed his secrets.

When Whitman, at seventy, read some startling comments by reviewers about his first heterosexual performance and his later homoerotic loves, he hit back, considerably annoyed: " 'Taint true—'taint true . . . I am an old bachelor who never had a love affair."[58] With that, he stopped issuing self-pronouncements—at least for a while.

And yet the stories about his first venture into sex of any kind refuse to go away. There is now no doubt that he was a virgin until he was twenty-nine, with no previous homoerotic stirrings. His first sexual experience was decidedly heterosexual.

The story goes that when Whitman was in New Orleans on a newspaper assignment, he saw an octoroon flower girl passing the saloon when he was standing at the bar. After a few innocent and rather tepid months, she gave him his first experience of sex. Most of the details of this episode are obscure.

Once, responding to Horace Traubel's urging to talk about his prime love affair, Whitman said, "The octoroon was not a whore and yet *was* too: a hard class to comprehend: women with splendid bodies— no bustles, no corsets, no enormities of any sort: large, luminous, rich eyes: face a rich olive: habits indolent, yet not lazy . . ."[59]

Again and again, Whitman dropped hints about his sexual initiation. The conjectures that the octoroon had borne him a child he met with stony silence. But once, when the English writer John Addington Symonds pushed him for an answer, Walt responded with characteristic brag: "My life, young manhood, middle age, times, etc. have been jolly, bodily, and doubtless open to criticism. Though unmarried I have had six children—two are dead—one living grandchild, fine boy, writes to me occasionally." At another time, Walt puffed his productivity up to eleven illegitimates. Was he trying to prove he was a normal male? No one is sure. In his recent biography, Justin Kaplan delivers a dismissal: "This is the first and last we hear of the offspring."

None of the alleged offspring have ever come forward to claim kinship with the foremost poet in American literature. However, Whitman's suspected paternity stirred curiosity long after his death. English biographer Henry Bryan Binns insists that the following lines by Whitman shed light on the New Orleans affair:

> Once I pass'd through a populous
> city imprinting my brain for
> future use with its shows,
> architecture, customs, traditions.

> Yet now of all that city I remember
> only a woman I casually met
> there who detain'd me for love
> of me,
> Day by day and night by night we
> were together—all else has long
> been forgotten by me.[60]

But Justin Kaplan counters: how could Binns accept any versified "confession" as literal truth from a poet who wrote that he grew up in Virginia and Texas and hunted polar bears in Alaska? Whitman changed the story of his life so often that it is hard to give credence to anything he said about it.

There is no doubt, however, about Whitman's longest and most intense relationship. Peter Doyle ("my rebel friend"), twenty-eight years Walt's junior, a Confederate soldier captured during the Civil War, came north to work as a streetcar conductor in Washington. Whitman hailed Peter as ". . . a youth who loves me, and whom I love approaching and seating himself near that he may hold me by the hand . . ."

Doyle proudly related his first encounter with the poet on a streetcar that they often rode together:

"We felt to each other at once. The night was stormy—he had been over to see Burroughs before he came down to take the car—the storm was awful. Walt had his blanket—it was thrown round his shoulders—he seemed like an old sea-captain. He was the only passenger, it was a lonely night, so I thought I would go and talk to him. Something in me made me do it, and something in him drew me that way. He used to say that there was something in me that had the same effect on him. Anyway, I went into the car. We were familiar at once—I put my hand on his knee—we understood. He didn't get out at the end of the trip—in fact he went all the way back with me."

They went to a saloon near the carbarn for a drink. Peter continues:

"Like as not I would go to sleep—lay my head on my hands on the table. Walt would stay there, wait, watch, keep me undisturbed—would take me up when the hour of closing came."[61]

At a later meeting they ate watermelon, and Walt, in gratitude, sent him a bouquet of flowers and a note: "Good night, Pete—good night, my darling son—here is a kiss for you, dear boy—on the paper here—a good long one."[62]

A platonic celebration of sex emerged from their association, as psychologist Paul Lauter writes, a "passionate perturbation, but never, so far as one can tell, in carnality." And Lauter goes on to explain: "Touch was all important to him: bodily contact with him not only satisfied his need to 'feel reality,' but consummated his worship of the male physique. He was throughout his life impelled to hug and kiss his men friends. To Harry Stafford he wrote: 'Dear son, how I wish you could come in now, even if but for an hour & take off your coat, & sit down on my lap.' And Traubel relates a tender moment with Whitman: 'W. said: "Come, kiss me for good night." He was still lying down. I reached over him and we kissed. He took my hand—pressed it fervently. "I am in luck. Are you? I guess God sent us for each other." ' "[63]

In his will, Whitman left Peter Doyle his watch "with my love."

As for women in Walt's life, Doyle observed: "I never knew of a case of Walt's being bothered up by a woman. . . . His disposition was different. Women in that sense never came into his head. Walt was too clean, he hated anything which was not clean."[64]

Walt's brother George told Traubel: "I know well enough that his skirts were clean. I never heard the least about his doings with women."[65]

The fact is that any number of women, one of whom was the widow of William Blake's biographer, Mrs. Anne Gilchrist, proposed marriage to Whitman. Mrs. Gilchrist came all the way from England to avow her love in person. But (as Chard Smith wrote) Whitman succeeded in "cooling her passion into friendship, and formed the habit of visiting her every evening in her house, which became a popular literary salon in Philadelphia."[66] After his second stroke he sent her a ring, which she took to mean betrothal.

Some critics have pointed out that it was Whitman's affair with the octoroon in New Orleans that turned him to writing homoerotic poetry. There is no evidence that the sex celebrations with Peter Doyle ever went beyond kissing, holding hands, embracing, or anything beyond what he catalogued in "I Sing the Body Electric": "the love of the body of man or woman . . . The womb, the teats, nipples, breastmilk, tears, laughter, weeping, love-looks, love-perturbations and rising . . ."

The last word on the subject should be given to the testimony of the naturalist John Burroughs, one of Whitman's closest friends:

"I have known Whitman for nearly thirty years, and a cleaner saner, more wholesome man, in word and deed, I have never known. If my life depended upon it, I could not convict him of one unclean word, or one immoral act."[67]

4

BROTHELIZING

> Verily, I say unto you that the publicans and the harlots go into
> the kingdom of God before you.
>> —Matthew XXI, 31, 75

> She's so bonny and brisk,
> How she'd curvet and frisk,
> If a man were once mounted upon her!
> Let me have but a leap
> Where 'tis wholesome and cheap
> And a fig for your Person of Honour.
>> —George Etheridge, *She Wou'd If She Cou'd*

DREISER REMAINED TO PRAY

"Sex is the business of life," said Theodore Dreiser when it was heresy to say so.

Dreiser went into the sex business while still in his teens. The business flourished until the day he died. At forty he wrote a poem beginning:

The street of whores, O wondrous street it is.[1]

The pursuit was at times overpowering. One woman told Waldo Frank of "a dreadful experience" she had when she happened to be alone in a room with Dreiser and she had all to do to fight her way out—literally. He interpreted a slap as an invitation to bring on the ultimate proposition.[2]

Horace Liveright's private office in New York was often Dreiser's port of call. Bennett Cerf tells that when a pretty aspiring author came to see Horace, the publisher "would have two things in mind—her manuscript and proving to himself what an irresistible man he was." Once, when Cerf entered Liveright's private cubicle without knocking, he caught the publisher *in flagrante* on the casting couch. "This girl," Horace later explained, "is a very promising writer, and the only way I could get her would be to have a little affair with her."[3] Lillian Hellman learned early in her career never to go up the spiral staircase at Boni and Liveright ahead of Horace.

In Greenwich Village, Dreiser picked up dozens of streetwalkers. When the sex itch became unendurable, he masturbated publicly, even in a room with other authors. W. A. Swanberg describes his characteristic way of relieving his genital tension. He would rock rhythmically in his chair, "pleating his handkerchief, then folding it into a cube, finally flinging it out like a flag and starting the folding process all over again."

As an adolescent, Dreiser later recalled, he had an ungovernable compulsion to fantasize "breasts, thighs, underwear . . . hidden physical lines, and my blood ran hot and cold." He fed his sexual desires by devouring *Tom Jones, Moll Flanders*, Balzac, and magazines with pictures of nudes. By the time he was ten, pimply, clumsy, and big-bodied, he had already amassed an extensive collection of sex pamphlets. When he first saw an actress in tights at the opera, he fell, he says, "into the ridiculous and unsatisfactory practice of masturbation."[4]

Not many years later his interest in the social problems stemming from prostitution ran a close second to appeasing his own sex urges. Whether out of guilt or whatever, he followed intercourse invariably with an analysis of the outlawed profession. Had prostitutes not existed, he would have invented them.

As a young reporter in Pittsburgh he went to the whores and, like Zola, lingered long to pump them about their social views. It gave him a mission in life and a literary subject. The inner conflict between his fiery particle and the whole sex syndrome intensified as he grew older. He could never feast enough on pornography, and yet some inherited puritanical streak threw him into shock when he heard a smutty story. He himself never told an off-color story. His buddy H. L. Mencken, an even greater prude and professed womanizer, liked to tease Teddy with a Rabelaisian anecdote to see the reaction. Once when his older brother Paul paraded before Dreiser with only a towel draped about his middle, the twenty-three-year-old Dreiser stamped out of the room in revulsion. Yet Dreiser eagerly went with him to a brothel specializing in "Frenchies." After satisfying his desire, he remained behind for hours with the whore to discuss the deplorable condition society forced upon her.

There were times when he took as many as three whores in a day and yet he could not restrain himself from pawing women and brushing against them in crowded places. He used no guile, no finesse. Sexual promiscuity, he insisted, was an inalienable part of his creative power. He lost one job because he tried to seduce the daughter of the assistant editor.[5]

He was an exceptionally patient listener, ready with his notebook. But there were limits to his patience. Interviewers were themselves put on the witness stand. Rose Feld, assigned by *The New York Times* to interview Dreiser, already a well-known literary figure, said that before she knew it he was propositioning her in his bumbling manner. "He was terribly nervous," she wrote. "Folding his handkerchief interminably, he asked me very personal questions. Was I married? Did I have a fiancé? Was I interested in men? . . . There was an air of tension about him. I could see that if I gave him the slightest encouragement the situation could grow embarrassing."[6]

Female devotees took a chance writing him fan letters. A thirty-eight-year-old reader wrote to tell him that she had read and reread every book of his she could lay hands on. When she accepted his invitation to meet him, hoping to meet the writer she had idealized, he put her up at a hotel and stayed with her eleven days. Of course, Helen Richardson, his current mistress, a few blocks away, knew nothing about this particular encounter, being used to his periodic disappearances.[7]

Years later, he was still rambling about the shady lanes in London on the prowl for prostitutes, then probing them for hours on their views of their sordid existence after he had paid lavishly for services rendered.

Swanberg tells of one harlot who intrigued Dreiser with her beauty and air of absent-mindedness until he saw innumerable needlepricks on her arm: shocked, he railed against the drug habit and demanded to know why she became addicted.

"Oh, great God!" she said wearily at last, "why do you talk? What do you know about life?"

[Dreiser says that his lust vanished on the instant.] "I sensed a kind of misery and hopelessness here, and for once in my life I did a decent thing. I had not much for myself but I took out three dollars . . . and laid it on the nearby mantel.

"That's all right," I said when she looked at me oddly. "I'm glad to give you this. You don't want me tonight, anyhow."[8]

It must testify to some mark of his extraordinary power over women that every one of them he had relations with had a good word to say about him. Some even appeared to share his pride in his amative powers. Helen Richardson, for five years his mistress and later made respectable by his marrying her, was slapped, maltreated, deserted, and abused, and yet she cared for him tenderly.

Something about him made the women stick to him. It couldn't have been his looks. He was anything but handsome. He was lubberly, beetle-eyed, thick-lipped, droopy-jowled. Kirhan Markham stayed five years with him and yet when he went off to his love-in with Helen, she did not reproach him.

After twenty-five years of love-and-run separations, and repossessions, he still refused to give up the skirt chase, though he was obviously getting weary of it all, increasingly hypochondriacal, brain-locked, word dry. One of his last sentences was: "I am the loneliest man in the world."[9]

He kept drinking heavily, brooding and folding handkerchiefs, irrational at times, and suffering memory lapses.

Once Helen missed him a few days too long, and she grew frantic until she received a call from a brothel madam saying that Theodore Dreiser was there, unbearably quarrelsome and paralyzed drunk. Would she come and pick him up? So his "Babu Mio," "My April Girl," and "My December Girl" hurried off, picked him up, and took him home.[10]

Constantly defending his ungovernable tropism to women, Dreiser whined, "Why must women torment me so?" He told a friend, "You walk into a room, see a woman, and something happens. It's chemical. What are you going to do about it?"[11]

A few months before he died, Helen hailed him in a sonnet "To a Poet" and enclosed it in the coffin before they nailed it down. She sent a copy to some of the women Dreiser had been having affairs with, some concurrent with his life with herself, Sylvia Bradshaw, and others.

And she wrote: "It is like a miracle to be loved by such a man. My life has really been a wonderful thing."[12]

Practically the whole Dreiser extramarital sorority would have readily signed that testimonial.

THE PHILANTHROPIST

Recently, when Nobel Prize for Literature winner Gabriel Garcia Marquez was asked which character in his novel *One Hundred Years of Solitude* he identified with, he replied, "The whore. She helped to make the largest number of people happy in the shortest amount of time—and without anybody knowing."[13]

GET THEE TO A BROTHEL

"I know whores," William Faulkner told his Hollywood mistress, Mary Carpenter. "I wrote *Sanctuary* out of what whores in Memphis told me. They were friends, but I don't bed with whores. Not here, not in Oxford, not anywhere."

For writers, a brothel has often provided more than a sexual convenience. When Jean Stein of the *Paris Review* asked Faulkner what he thought was the best environment for a writer, he said:

> Art is not concerned with environment either; it doesn't care where it is. If you mean me, the best job that was ever offered to me was to become a landlord in a brothel. In my opinion it's the perfect milieu for an artist to work in. It gives him perfect economic freedom; he's free of fear and hunger; he has a roof over his head and nothing whatever to do except keep a few simple accounts and to go once every month and pay off the local police. The place is quiet during the morning hours, which is the best time of the day to work. There's enough social life in the evening, if he wishes to participate, to keep him from being bored; it gives him a certain standing in his society; he has nothing to do because the madam keeps the books; all the inmates of the home are females and would defer to him and call him 'sir.' All the bootleggers in the neighborhood would call him 'sir.' And he could call the police by their first names.[14]

Evidently, Robert Benchley agreed with Faulkner's recommendation of a brothel as a nice quiet place to work, for he was a habitué of Polly Adler's famous house in New York, writing his reviews and his humorous essays there, and grateful for her friendship.

ZOLA CAME TO MEASURE

When Émile Zola was researching local color for his novel *Nana*, he dined with La Valtesse, the famous Paris cocotte. He brought to her home a pencil, a notebook, and a tape measure.

George Moore, who idolized Zola, told Barrett Clark: "I don't think he felt at ease there, and evidently he had come for strictly scientific purposes; at any rate he scarcely looked at the woman, but asked to see her bedroom; and what do you think he wanted there? To measure it, and get its exact dimensions! Good God! Art is a coquette, and Zola never knew it!"[15]

THE PHILOSOPHER AND THE PROSTITUTE

"Socrates brought philosophy down from heaven to earth," Erasmus boasted, "but I have brought it even into games, informal conversation, and drinking parties."

When a fellow Dutchman heard this, he challenged the claim, whereupon Erasmus cited the report he got from a studious young man who had visited a whorehouse in Amsterdam. The colloquy between the student and the madam, said Erasmus, fully confirmed his own claim.

> *Young Man:* I took a book along instead of a flask: the New Testament translated by Erasmus.
> *Madam:* Erasmus? He's a heretic, they say.
> *Young Man:* You don't mean Erasmus's reputation has reached this place?
> *Madam:* No name is better known to us.

The evidence was incontrovertible.[16]

Nobody can give chapter and verse to authenticate this colloquy between Erasmus's disciple and the madam, but three centuries of circulation have not killed it. Another rumor was also current in Amsterdam—that the great Erasmus himself had once been "clapped" in a brothel. Again, unverifiable—but if archbishops can, why not an unclerical scholar?

JOYCE CAME TO RECITE

More sophisticated than the Amsterdam whores in Erasmus's day were the harlots of Dublin. James Joyce began to frequent Kips, the night-town brothel, when he was not yet fourteen, but he always came out with a heavy sense of guilt. As a Jesuit seminarian several years later, he visited Kips much like Anatole France's Hippolyte. Instead of re-lieving his sexual desires physically, Gogarty affirmed, Joyce would lecture the madam and her ladies on points of Greek drama and the Gregorian chant. The harlots found him pleasurably strange and no doubt enjoyed the pay.

In honor of Joyce's visits, Gogarty dashed off a limerick:

> There was a young fellow called Joyce
> Who possesseth a sweet tenor voice;
> He goes to the Kips, with a psalm on his lips,
> And biddeth the harlots rejoice.[17]

ANYTHING FOR HENRY

No one tells it so specific as Anaïs Nin in her diary entry for Febru-ary 1932. The account of her visit to a brothel with Henry Miller is so fascinating that it must be quoted verbatim. It shows that only the French madam knows how to run a first-class brothel with all the trimmings. Even Polly Adler could take a lesson or two from Ms. Nin.

> Henry said, "Would you like me to take you to 32 Rue Blondel?"
> "What will I see there?"
> "Whores."
> Henry's whores. I feel curious and friendly towards Henry's whores.
> The taxi drops us in a narrow little street. A red light painted with number 32 shines over the doorway. We push a swinging door. It is like a café full of men and women, but the women are naked. There is heavy smoke, much noise, and women are trying to get our attention even be-fore the *patronne* leads us to a table. Henry smiles. A very vivid, very fat Spanish-looking woman sits with us and she calls a woman we had not noticed, small, feminine, almost timid.

"We must choose," says Henry. "I like these well enough."

Drinks are served. The small woman is sweet and pliant. We discuss nail polish. They both study the pearly nail polish I use and ask the name of it. The women dance together. Some are handsome, but others look withered and tired and listless. So many bodies all at once, big hips, buttocks, and breasts. "The two girls will amuse you," says the *patronne*.

I had expected a man for the demonstration of sixty-six ways of making love. Henry barters over the price. The women smile. The big one has bold features, raven black hair in curls which almost hide her face. The smaller one has a pale face with blonde hair. They are like mother and daughter. They wear high-heeled shoes, black stockings with garters at the thighs, and a loose open kimono. They lead us upstairs. They walk ahead, swinging their hips.

Henry jokes with them. They open the door on a room which looks like a velvet-lined jewel casket. The walls are covered with red velvet. The bed is low, and has a canopy which conceals a mirror on the ceiling of the bed. The lights are rosy and dim. The women are at ease and cheerful. They are washing themselves in the bidet which is in the room. It is all done so casually and with so much indifference that I wonder how one can become interested. The women are joking, between themselves. The big woman ties a rubber penis around her waist. It is of an impossible pink. They lie on the bed after slipping their shoes off, but not the black stockings.

And they begin to take poses.

"*L'amour dans un taxi.*"

"*L'amour à l'Espagnole.*"

"*L'amour* when you do not have the price of a hotel room."

(For this they stand up against the wall.)

"*L'amour* when one of them is sleepy."

The small woman pretended to be asleep. The big woman took the smaller woman from behind, gently and softly.

As they demonstrate they make humorous remarks.

It is all bantering and mockery of love until . . . The small woman had been lying on her back with her legs open. The big woman removed the penis and kissed the small woman's clitoris. She flicked her tongue over it, caressed it, kissed. The small woman's eyes closed and we could see she was enjoying it. She began to moan and tremble with pleasure. She offered to our eyes her quivering body and raised herself a little to meet the voracious mouth of the bigger woman. And then came the climax for her and she let out a cry of joy. Then she lay absolutely still. Breathing fast. A moment later they both stood up, joking, and the mood passed.[18]

Two of a Kind

Edward Dahlberg, author and critic, once said, referring to the nature of fame. "If psychoanalyzed, a writer will have to confess that at bottom he is a whore."

No psychoanalyst was needed to convince one great writer of this truth.

When Anatole France and Bernard Shaw were introduced at a reception in England honoring the great Frenchman, they shook hands.

Stanley Weintraub gives Shaw's version of what followed: "When I was first in company with Anatole France he asked who I was. Answering for myself I said, 'I am, like you, a man of genius.' This was, according to his code, so immodest that it startled him into riposting with, 'Ah well: only a whore (*courtisane*) has the right to call herself a pleasure merchant.'" Whereupon France raised himself on tiptoe and kissed his fellow whore on both cheeks, their beards meshing fraternally.[19]

A Social Call

When e.e. cummings was a freshman at Harvard, he burst into full revolt against all the virtues his clergyman father had preached to him. Papa's worship of chastity became e.e.'s special target. Malcolm Cowley describes one caper cummings's father would have frowned on:

"One night the Boston police were embarrassed to find his father's car, with its clergyman's license plates, parked outside a joint near Scollay Square. Cummings and Dos Passos, both virgins at the time, were not 'upstairs'; they were drinking in the parlor holding a polite conversation with the madam.

> *When you rang at Dick Mid's Place*
> *the madam was a bulb stuck in the door*[20]

* * *

Another compromising trick was played by H. L. Mencken on Tom Mix, the movie idol of innocent boyhood. The story goes that on his only visit to Hollywood, Mencken was bored as hell and longed for some unorthodox fun. Picking up a writer friend, Mencken barged into Tom Mix's house and "borrowed" his hallmark ten-gallon hat and glossy initialed white car, recognized all over Los Angeles. They drove downtown and parked the car in front of a fashionable bawdy house. The two writers, by now thoroughly soused, staggered in. Insisting on keeping Mix's hat on his head, Mencken sat down at the piano, puffed on his smelly, foot-long stogie, and banged out "The Battle Hymn of the Republic."

Fundamentalist Tom Mix never lived down that caper.[21]

SISTERS UNDER THE SKIN

In "Looking Back," Somerset Maugham's sensational series of articles vilifying his wife and daughter, the old writer recalls his first experience with a prostitute. He was then a medical student at St. Thomas's Hospital in London.

"I used to listen to my fellow students' bragging accounts of their sexual exploits, which in my innocence I believed, and I was ashamed to be still a virgin. One Saturday night I went down Piccadilly and picked up a girl who for a pound was prepared to pass the night with me. The result was an attack of gonorrhea and I had very shyly to ask one of the house physicians to tell me what to do about it. Undeterred by this mishap, however, I continued whenever I could afford it, and fortunately without untoward circumstances, thus to satisfy my sexual desires."[22]

Since he was eighty-eight when he wrote that recollection, Maugham may be forgiven for a lapse of memory. Elsewhere he wrote a different account of his first experience of sex, saying that after he left school and long before he became a medical student, he went to study in Heidelberg, where he met John Ellingham Brooks, a homosexual who, he says, "took his virginity."[23]

In "Looking Back," Maugham disclosed that when he was in Mexico City to get background material for a book, feeling restless and bored, he asked Gerald Haxton—sometime lover, secretary and valet, and pimp—to scour the stewpots to bring Willie some boys. One boy, writes Ted Morgan, "was a thin, large-eyed child who said he was fourteen. He undressed in Maugham's hotel bedroom, knelt to say his prayers, and crossed himself before getting into bed."[24]

When Somerset Maugham visited New York in 1926, Carl Van

Vechten took him to a whorehouse in Harlem. Probably Van Vechten thought of it just as an educational tour, but Maugham apparently knew the business more expertly than his guide.[25]

Years later, in the series in *Show,* Maugham revealed for the first time that he had been a homosexual. None of his friends was more astonished than Gerald Kelly: "To think that I have known Willie since 1902 and have only just recognized that disguised as an old Chinese madam, he kept a brothel in Shanghai."[26]

Ho, Hum!

Young Evelyn Waugh could barely suppress his yawns when he went brothelizing. Visiting a whorehouse was *de rigueur* for young writers-to-be and he went along with the mode, but (unlike his pal Randolph Churchill) insisted he was not cut out for it. Waugh tried flagellant orgies in London and a few whorehouses in Paris ("a good place for young Englishmen to get their taste of fornication"), but he noted in his diary that he had to fight "nausea with sexual imaginings," and after a visit to a male brothel in Paris, he "took a taxi home and to bed in chastity." He adds, "I think I do not regret it."[27]

In Abyssinia, where he was usually drunk to the gills, Waugh reports that he tried "three or four *ted* (drink) houses. Brothels. Red cross over doors. Ugly women. Saw exquisitely beautiful girls." Later: "Went into a native brothel with Movietone man and saw a little dance. One of the most boring days of my life."[28]

Not Love at First Sight

When Jorge Luis Borges, the prince of Argentine letters, was a boy, "Georgie" (as his biographer, Emir Rodriguez Monegal, calls him) was taken by his father to a brothel in Geneva to experience life early. However, the whore so terrified the bespectacled, nearsighted boy that the visit ruined his sexual pleasure for life. It was not until he was sixty-seven that Borges dared to marry—he was then practically blind—and the marriage ended in divorce.[29]

Literary Jail

W. H. Auden learned that a woman's prison can harbor literary taste: "I have never been prouder of my profession" (Auden to interviewer Alan Levy) "than when my friend Dorothy Day [the Catholic pacifist and editor of *The Catholic Worker*] told me of something that happened when she did some time in New York's Women's House of Detention. Each prisoner was taken out to be bathed once a week. Dorothy shared a cell with a whore and, when the time came, Dorothy's cellmate was led off toward the shower chanting a line from Auden: 'Thousands have lived without love, not one without water!' "[30]

LITERARY BROTHEL

Noel Coward, reminiscing with David Frost on a TV talk show, told about the time a friend took him on a tour of Honolulu's red-light district. As they passed a brothel, they heard a Coward song played on a recorder coming from a first-floor room.

"How'd you like that?" David asked.

"One of my major triumphs!" Noel exulted.[31]

ALL THE COMFORTS OF A HOUSE

In his basement Eugene O'Neill, who was ailing, kept a player piano that he had taken from a whorehouse. It was covered with pictures of nudes. As a relief from his wife Carlotta's nagging, O'Neill would go down to the basement, drop nickels into the slot, and enjoy some ragtime.

When Bennett Cerf came to visit, O'Neill took him downstairs. The two were listening to a record as Carlotta burst in. "You ought to be ashamed of yourself, bringing Bennett down here!" she shouted. "You're in pain, remember?"[32]

BRUISING CRUISING

Early in his hectic career, Tennessee Williams learned that looking for boys can be dangerous. In 1939, when he began to cruise for young males around Times Square and Tin Pan Alley on West 52nd Street, practically the first pickup warned him away, at least temporarily, from such venture.

In his *Memoirs*, he recalls that Harold Vinal, editor of *Voices*, invited him up to his hotel room to meet a pair of "delightful Georgia boys."

Williams writes: "I had no sooner seen one of these boys, with his great dreamy eyes and willowy figure, than I thought, Baby this one's for you.

"We all started dancing to a band that was playing directly below their room and I no sooner had him in my arms for the ostensible motive of dancing than I began to kiss him and paste my pelvis to him."

This made the other boy jealous. Then the three went walking up and down Times Square. Two sailors followed them upstairs ". . . I was far from enchanted by the brutal sex-bit. When it was completed, the sailors abruptly ripped the telephone cord from the wall. Then they stood me against the wall while they beat up my friend, knocking out a few teeth. Then they stood *him* against the wall with a switch-blade knife while they beat me up."

That ended, Williams observed, his Times Square initiation in cruising.[33]

A TOUCH OF CLASS

Gustave Flaubert once boasted to friends: "When I was young my vanity was such that when I went to a brothel I always picked the ugliest girl and insisted on making love to her in front of them all without taking my cigar out of my mouth. It wasn't any fun for me: I just did it for the gallery."[34]

A steady patron of Paris brothels, Gustave suffered successive doses of clap, but when a friend at Magny's suggested that one can live a full life without going to prostitutes, Flaubert retorted:

"No, you can't! A man has missed something if he has never woken up in an anonymous bed beside a face he'll never see again, and if he has never left a brothel at dawn feeling like jumping off a bridge into the river out of sheer disgust with life. If there's nothing else, there's something about their shameless clothes, the temptation of the unknown, the age-old poetry of venality and corruption."[35]

And he added a personal reminiscence:

"During the first years I was in Paris, I used to sit outside Tortoni's on hot summer evenings, admiring the sunset and watching the streetwalkers pass by. At times like that I used to bubble over with Biblical poetry. I used to think of Isaiah, of 'fornication in high places,' and I walked back along the Rue de la Harpe repeating the verse, 'And her mouth is smoother than oil.' "[36]

Free Loading

In the record of seductions, H. G. Wells outclassed even Dreiser. Wells called them *passades*. When he was a young biology crammer, impecunious, and engaged to marry his cousin Isabel, Wells was also critically ill with terminal tuberculosis. He feared that he might die a virgin. Despite his scientific studies, he had to confess that he was "a very ignorant as well as an impatient lover." He tethered his "sexual and romantic imagination" to his fiancée, but, he writes, he "went furtively and discreetly with a prostitute . . ." The experience was disillusioning: it "deepened my wary apprehension that round about the hidden garden of desire was a jungle of very squalid and stupid laws."[37]

Nevertheless, the one brothelizing incident set Wells in motion; in the early weeks of his marriage, he seduced one of Isabel's friends and made the discovery that "sexual purpose by duplicity" can be fun. He called this "quite the most interesting fact about my early married life." Later, in his *Experiment in Autobiography*, he recorded that "Once or twice at Southsea, or Portsmouth, a prostitute would make an alluring gesture to me, but a shilling a week of pocket-money gives no scope for mercenary love."[38]

As soon as Wells's growing fame opened bedrooms for him, it was promiscuity all the way—for free.

An Absurd Visit

At thirty-two, Franz Kafka drew up a list of comparative decisions:

To remain chaste	To get married
Bachelor	Married man
I remain chaste.	Chaste?[39]

Now and then Kafka permitted himself lapses in chastity. In his diary he records his first sexual experience: "I had never yet been intimate with a woman apart from the time in Zuckmantel. And then again with the Swiss girl in Riva. The first was a woman and I was inexperienced; the second was a child, and I was completely and utterly bewildered."[40]

Years back in Prague, he says, he had often taken casual notice of the Amazonian character of brothels; but in Paris he was taken by "two respectable-looking women upstairs (why two?) who received us; the light switched on in the adjoining room in the darkness or semi-darkness of which were sitting the unengaged girls; the three-quarter circle (we made it a full circle) in which they stood around us, drawn up in postures calculated to reveal them to best advantage; the long stride with which the girl who had been chosen came forward."

Apparently all Kafka got was a look, and all he remembered, he says, was "the one who stood directly in front of me. She had gaps in her teeth, stretched to her full height, her clenched fist held her dress together over her pudenda, and she rapidly opened and shut her large eyes and large mouth. Her blond hair was disheveled. She was thin. Anxious lest I should forget and take off my hat."

Before he knew it, Kafka was outside.

He ends his diary note: "Lonely, long, absurd walk home."[41]

MORE THAN A HALF INTEREST

Coming from a male brothel bubbling with delight, Marcel Proust told his housekeeper, Céleste (wife of Albert, who drove Proust around town in his taxi): "My dear Céleste, what I have witnessed this evening is unimaginable. Le Cuziat told me there was a man who goes there to be whipped, and I saw the whole thing from another room, through a little window in the wall. It is incredible. . . . Imagine—there he is in a room, fastened to a wall with chains and padlocks, while some wretch . . . whips him till the blood spurts out all over everything. And it is only then that the unfortunate creature experiences the heights of pleasure."[42]

Flagellation became such a preoccupation with Proust that he would take time out during his nights to visit birching parlors for observation and note-taking, savoring the experience of flagellation himself. His housekeeper, in her memoirs, quotes his statement that any personal pleasure he derived was secondary; it was all research for his novel. Céleste reserved judgment.

Having a half-interest investment in Le Cuziat's parlor on the rue d'Arcade, Proust enjoyed special privileges—he was never charged a fee and could watch the other clients through the peephole. Proust actually helped set up the place and donated some of his parents' furniture when his own cork-lined apartment was broken up and sold. In turn, he often received information for his books about deviant practices as well as scuttlebutt. Albert became a model for Julien in the novel as a keeper of a brothel.[43]

Obsessed with getting the details right, Proust pumped everyone he met on points of protocol in the massage parlors. Helena Rubinstein, the cosmetician, described Proust to Patrick O'Higgins: "Nebbishy looking. I met him once at Misia [Sert]'s. He smelt of mothballs, wore a fur-lined coat to the ground, asked heaps of questions about make-up. Would a duchess use rouge? Did demimondaines put kohl on their eyes? How should I know? But, then, how could I have known that he was going to be so famous? If so, I might have told him a thing or two. But I was shy . . ."[44]

A House Can Be a Home

Charles Baudelaire denied having intercourse with his mistress Jeanne Duval; he preferred to read poetry to her and to embrace her feet. The syphilis that killed him came from a visit to a brothel, not from her.[45]

All his life Baudelaire was interested in whores and in brothels— interested not as a patron but as a poet. Anatole Broyard points out that Baudelaire "was afraid of women . . . never recovered from his fixation on his mother . . . his letters to her begged not so much for money as for love." Whores were more intelligent than the fine ladies he met in the cafés; he found their company stimulating.

Baudelaire said he went to brothels not as a customer but as a voyeur, to refine his sensations. The whores themselves, to the considerable annoyance of the madam, reported that the poet spent his hour gazing languorously at the merchandise, slobbering over their scented hair and shapely limbs.[46]

Biographer Alex de Jonge writes that a friend once introduced Baudelaire to a striking blonde who was a connoisseur of seduction. She took an immediate shine to Baudelaire and invited him and his friend home. There "the lady grew more and more lascivious and finally began to strip. She had beautiful hair that reached to her feet and a superb body. The friend was tactfully on his way out the door when he heard Baudelaire, tired and worn out, say, 'Get dressed.' "[47]

THE LITTLE TIN SOLDIER

Frightened all his life by sex and too shy to make amatory advances, Hans Christian Andersen tried in many ways to still his sexual urges: "Am unable to sleep," he wrote in his diary; "sensual longings are still strong within me. Fortunate he who is well married."[48]

In Paris, at sixty-two, he summoned enough courage to visit a brothel, not to have sex but to look at the naked girls: "Having dined, I walked up and down in a state of burning desire, then suddenly went into a human shop. One woman was pasted with powder, the next one was very simple, the third one was a complete lady: I spoke to her, paid her 12 francs and left without having sinned in deeds, though mainly in my mind. She asked me to come again, told me I was very innocent for a gentleman. I was relieved and happy when I left that house. Many will call me a coward—I wonder if I was so in this case."[49]

5

I HAVE A LITTLE BOOK

> *Diary. n. A daily record of that part of one's life, which he can relate to himself without blushing.*
> —Ambrose Bierce, *The Devil's Dictionary*

"I Do Not Keep a Diary Myself"

"Lover of the Century," ran the headlines in 1934; "Marathon Lover Exposed."

Who would have dreamed that the forty-six-year-old playwright George S. Kaufman, known to his friends as obsessively fearful of even being touched, had a charge account at Polly Adler's famous whorehouse? Not only the "vicious circle" at the Algonquin but all of Kaufman's fans on and off Broadway were fascinated to learn that the fabulous madam herself regularly sent girls to meet him at a designated lamppost so that he could screen them before taking the choice numbers to the apartment he had rented for assignations. (No money passed hands. Polly sent him a monthly bill.)[1]

The whole story came out when detectives digging for evidence in film star Mary Astor's divorce case found her diary. It "cited, clocked, described with meticulous accuracy and quiet clinches" every Kaufman visit to her. In it, Astor noted "thrilling ecstasy . . . he fits me perfectly . . . many exquisite moments . . . twenty—count them, diary—twenty . . . I don't see how he does it . . . he is perfect."[2]

In Astor's diary, Gene Fowler was said to have been on top of the list as a "skilled lover."

The Astor divorce case threatened to turn into another Fatty Arbuckle bust. When Kaufman failed to appear as a witness in court, a bench warrant was issued.

"It got to be like a Mack Sennett chase," says Larry Adler, a close friend of Kaufman. "He fled his hotel, with the sheriff's deputies chasing after him, to Moss Hart's house. Hart virtuously denied knowledge of Kaufman's very existence while our hero (it was indeed he) cowered in the bushes behind the house. Then on to Irving Thalberg's yacht, to Catalina Island, the deputies now pursuing by plane. Then, most dramatic touch of all, Kaufman disguised himself as a stretcher case, and bandaged to being a double for Claude Rains in 'The Invisible Man,' was put aboard a New York-bound train."[3]

The press finally caught up with the fugitive. "I have one piece of news for The Great American Public," Kaufman told them. "I do not keep a diary myself."

A Russian Don Juan

Alexander Pushkin, smarting under a slight, kept in his private journal a list of the people who had insulted him. He noted them by date and when and how he had repaid them.[4] In the same book he kept a "Don Juan" list of all his love episodes; they were, as one reviewer put it, "hits, runs and errors among all the Dashas, Mashas and Dunyashas of romantic Russia."[5] Careful research by biographer Henri Troyat traced Pushkin's first love affair to the poet's seventh year. Later, like Hugo and Thomas Wolfe, he kept an explicit account of every time he had sexual intercourse, the name, date, duration, intensity, and the amount he paid.

"Les Affaires sont les Affaires" (Business Is Business)

In one of his stories, Arthur Schnitzler tells of a Viennese rake who lost his "little black book" and became bewildered and disoriented in all his appointments because he got mixed up trying to fix the right pet names on the members of his harem.

This could never have happened to Victor Hugo. The insatiable buck kept his little book safe and accessible in a desk drawer at home. Every night before retiring, he would take the book out and, with characteristic Gallic respect for bookkeeping, go over his accounts, including his appointments in the several apartments he rented concurrently for his various mistresses.

Methodically entered in his diary—which would have enriched a blackmailer—were the names of his lovers, all well known in the fashionable salons; their addresses, the exact hours he had set aside for his pleasure; the duration; the number of his orgasms with each mistress; and the amount he paid. To identify his reaction (a detail very important to Olympio), Hugo wrote next to each name *assistance* (not special) or *secours* (the jackpot!).

Hugo never locked the drawer. Adèle, his wife, who regularly examined the memo book, never destroyed it. Her malice did not reach that far. However, her husband's amours eventually drove her into the arms of Hugo's much publicized rival, Sainte-Beuve. So what? Sainte-Beuve was all but impotent. And Adèle didn't much care, for like all traditional French husbands, Victor always came home to *Maman*.

THE STORY OF "A"

You'd expect an amorist like Hugo or the adolescent Tolstoy to keep a record of his women—but John Galsworthy!

Only recently we have learned that Galsworthy, PEN's first president, was human enough to keep a secret diary—and what a diary!—between 1910 and 1918. After his ten-year passionate courtship of Ada, his first cousin's wife, and his success in finally winning her after countless stratagems to avoid scandal, he turned into a lapsed lover. Galsworthy believed in marriage as a sacred trust (except when it was cruel or loveless), but there was one inevitable blot on his escutcheon. He met Margaret Morris, a pretty and rather naïve nineteen-year-old dancer.

Galsworthy fell in love with Margaret, got her to take part in his plays, and brought her home several times to meet the unsuspecting Ada. But he continued to see Margaret secretly, and the attachment heated up to the point where he had to make a critical decision.

Long after Galsworthy's death, Margaret Morris wrote, in *My Galsworthy Story*: "It was horrible weather, and in the taxi back to the theatre John said, 'You look terribly cold,' and he put his arm round me. That was too much—he had never touched me before. I snuggled up against him, and he suddenly said: 'Look at me.' I did not dare, but buried my face in his coat—I can still feel the soft texture of the deep pile of the overcoat he wore; but he insisted, saying, 'I must know, you must look at me.' So I did, and he knew, and of course he kissed me and the world was transformed."[6]

Conscience compelled Galsworthy to break the news to Ada, pleading with her to understand that it in no way replaced his love for her. The defection struck deep in Ada and started her on a long period of illness, which sent them traveling all over the globe. On the beach at Beaulieu, Galsworthy made the decision. He wrote to Margaret: "We must give each other up, and utterly. Ada's life and mine together has been such as to make it a sacred trust . . . And if it's any joy to you to know that I loved you, as it is still joy to me to feel that you could have such a feeling for me—well there it is and will always be, even when we have both got over it. So my poor dear it must be Goodbye—a real lasting Goodbye, and God bless you! Forget, forget and forgive me!"[7]

Galsworthy put his sexual anxieties into his novels, especially *The Dark Flower*, but he buried his deep inner torment in his diary. In this journal (like so many diarists, notably Hugo and Boswell), he resorted to code, referring to Ada with a rounded capital A when he noted the rare occasions when he had sexual relations with his wife. In a diary entry of November 15, 1914, he expresses his despair: "This is what comes of giving yourself to a woman body and soul. A paralyses and has always paralysed me. I have never been able to face the idea of being cut off from her."[8]

Frank Swinnerton tells of a visit he made to Galsworthy at his luxurious estate in the country. The author of *The Man of Property* was then at the height of his career. He had the best of everything— acclaim, prestige, and more wealth than he could use. But Swinnerton got the feeling that his host was not a happy man. It was obvious to him that he was depressed and lonely. "The impression was reinforced," wrote Swinnerton, "when, surveying from his study window a magnificent coloured panorama of the South Downs, I said with dreadful breeziness: 'Beautiful! There's a novel a day in that outlook!' He wistfully answered: 'Not from me, alas!' "[9]

After his death, Ada recovered her health. She destroyed his love letters, keeping two poems to her in a little box with his eyeglass and his Order of Merit.

THE EDITOR IN THE HOUSE

Mrs. Wallace Stevens was a stickler for privacy, her own and her husband's.

The poet was apparently a hostage to his wife. Like Mark Twain's Livy, she not only edited his work, she edited *him*. After Stevens's death, she excised from his private journal many names and episodes (some of which ran to several pages).

Stevens's daughter has said, "While I was growing up, my mother did not read my father's poems, and seemed to dislike the fact that his books were published," and John Updike has commented, "Her 'regard for privacy' apparently led her to resent that a few poems originally written for her birthday were later made public in print."[10]

Fortunately, Stevens did not show his wife everything he wrote. He did not show her the poems he wrote at the office (he was an executive of an insurance company).

Whatever she felt moved to eliminate from his journal, Mrs. Stevens had one consolation: her husband did not go out with other women. She was proud that he was not like the other poet-"degenerates"—William Carlos Williams, Ezra Pound, and Henry Miller.

EDMUND WILSON KEPT LEDGERS

Edmund Wilson took his fornications with extraordinary solemnity.

Joseph Epstein commented on Wilson's outpouring of diary entries: "Without either a lyrical or comic spirit, Wilson explores sex as a great critic might explore terza rima."

Who would have thought that the dean of American letters had so much sexuality in him? It was not until Wilson's diary *The Twenties* and the fuller sequels were published that his closest friend, Dos Passos, became aware of the number and variety of Wilson's sexual activities. By comparison, Frank Harris and Theodore Dreiser were minor-leaguers.

Wilson filled several large volumes of diary notes with the details of his amours; he was apparently afraid to rely on his memory.

How he loved specifics! A characteristic entry in *The Twenties* describes his enjoyment of a prostitute he picked up in New Orleans:

> The first time I saw her she was anxious to get through with it as quickly and with as little sentimentality as possible. Wouldn't take off her clothes, didn't want me to take off mine, didn't want to be kissed in fear of disturbing her rouge . . . simply threw herself on her back across the bed with her feet hanging down at the side and pulled her skirts up over her stomach. After she had told me about her mother trying to get her to go home at Christmas, large tears came into her eyes. I wiped them away with the red quilt and they came again. I wiped them away again, and that was the end of it.—She had a pretty body, but said she was ugly—

whenever I complimented her, she would say, "Yes!" with terrific sar-
casm—some man had told her that she ought to be made over again . . .
Wanted to be married and be somebody!"[11]

Wilson was fascinated by techniques of lovemaking, pillow talk,
the contours of breasts in and out of bras, stationary bottoms, leg
movements, the swirl of dresses, the scent of undergarments. He loved
to hear women talk, relishing the vulgarisms of his "proletarian" pickups. His prolific diary entries don't strike even staid critics as gross or
pornographic. His women, in dress or undress, stretched out seductively on divans or beaches, are a carefully painted gallery of sex subjects: Katze, Marie, Florence, and Margaret stand out; in particular
there is Anna, a fictitious name for a waitress and dancehall girl who
furnished Wilson with the model for the girl in "The Princess with
the Golden Hair" in his *Memoirs of Hecate County.*

Leon Edel, editor of the Wilson diaries, points out that "even before D. H. Lawrence's sexual rhapsodies, Edmund was discovering the
objective language—a mixture of the crude and the delicate—to render erotic experience."

Another characteristic Wilson description is about Marie, said to
be his model for Misa McMein: "She was broad and had olive skin
when she took off her bandeau, disclosed large full breasts of which
the nipples were spread from pregnancy—she was marked all the way
down from navel to the pubes with a long straight dent which gave
her bronze and anatomical look of Dürer's women—her cunt, however, seemed to be small. She would not, the first time, respond very
heartily, but the second, would wet herself and bite my tongue, and
when I had finished, I could feel her vagina throbbing powerfully—
Thrust makes cock up into those obscure and meaty regions. Afterwards, she lay with the covers pulled over her up to the breasts, which
were left bare."[12]

Wilson says that it was Anna who gave him gonorrhea, but apparently he felt she was worth it.

She had loved Sam [her husband] more than me but Sam didn't throw
her the way I did—she used to kiss 'um all over the way I did her.—I
don't believe there was an inch of his body I didn't kiss!—I don't suppose
he minded it. Sam's was longer than mine, but it hurts nice—you know
what I mean?—the doctor had said she was very passionate, wasn't she?
because that opening of her womb was so small—her cousin did'un care

anything about it, but she did it every night her husband liked it, you know—she thought her cunt (I never heard her use the word, she always called it "it") was an awful-lookin' thing—didn't know about her clitoris—washed it but didn't look at it—didn't mind a man's . . . When she came, she'd get a sensation like a thrill that would go through her from her toes, all through her body, you know what I mean? And she'd want to scratch and bite—I don't know where I am or anything—didn't feel the semen, didn't feel herself putting out anything—and (when we're together) I doan wantcha to go, but if you keep on, it makes me nervous— like me, she enjoyed it more the second time than the first . . .

I asked her where she liked best to be kissed—"I like it all!"—never had been kissed by Sam—at first resisted being kissed on neck, breasts, etc. (her coquetry one night, when I tried to take down her chemise: "only one"—Don't you like it?—"In a way!"—) . . . Her soft little face with its white tender skin and its shadows, as she was sitting half upright on the bed, with the bathroom door half open, her eyelids lowered at my compliments—her round and attractive legs from under the short skirt of her pale blue dress, rather snappily draped . . . . which was so smartly short and contrasted so with her white stockings that it made me want to put my hand on her solidly crossed thighs—her bloomers worn by calculation when I first saw her—"I wear them on purpose—when I'd go out with a boy, you know, and he'd try to put his hand up my clothes—when they touch your skin, they go wild."

I didn't like her habit of not washing herself after intercourse ("To hell with that")—Odor associated with Tango Gardens—garlicky breath, which I liked . . . head hanging off edge of couch, "Sweetheart!"—deep husky city voice in amorous bed—"Oh, don't!—Oh yes!"—"What did you say?" straining back with the pillow under her buttocks—my part rendered unsatisfactory and imperfect with condoms, especially so after the first time— only difference for her was that it "didn't slip as easy?"—her shyness, modesty, gentleness—"I don't know what you call them; I call them balls"—sliding her hand under my bathrobe—She'd have to know me a long time before she'd do with me what she used to do with Sam—"Only whores do that, you'll think I'm a pervert' whore!"—I didn't like her pinching me under my shin—Sam hadn't liked it either.

. . . She used to sleep curled up to fit my back and with my cock in her hand—she had always slept that way with Sam. Can't go to sleep unless, etc.—When I had her naked and her little middle elevated by pillow—the little narrow lozenge of her cunt, which had such a slight lining of hair, seeming charming, with her rather slender legs and feet extended and drooping wide.—I used to stroke it and caress it with my tongue—it was so pretty it would make me linger and preoccupy me, so that I almost forgot to do anything else . . . Fucking in the afternoon with her dress on—different from anything else—rank satisfactory smell— peculiar zest, on these hurried occasions, added by shoes and stockings and dress, which would be discouraging and undesirable at a regular ren- dezvous at night . . . The night when she had on a red dress and I was drunk and kissed her, just rubbing my mouth against her wet lips, again and again, till it was almost like some kind of intercourse—a meaty effect like lips below. . . . Perfect feeling of possessing her completely—arms all the way round her slim little figure—tongue in her soft little mouth— legs which I made her put over mine.[13]

In the most recent edition of his diary, *The Forties,* Wilson recalls the first time he made love: "Sunday I kissed her feet with much pleasure, running my lips over her toes. She had just cut and painted her toenails a few days before. Her feet when they are at their clean- est—and they are really always clean, because she takes so many baths—have that faint cheeselike smell that is almost a taste and that I like."[14]

Not even Henry Miller had contributed to the literature of sex such prose descriptions as those of Edmund Wilson, dean of American letters.

6

AND SO TO WED

Happy marriages, like happy nations, have no history.
—Maurice Colbourn

Were man to consult only his reason, who would marry? For myself, I wouldn't marry, for fear of having a son who resembled me.
—Chamfort

When wives come in at the door, wisdom escapes by the window.
—Arthur Schopenhauer
(who died a bachelor, in an insane asylum)

Marriage is the deep peace of the double bed after the hurly-burly of the chaise-longue.
—Mrs. Patrick Campbell

People are always talking about advice you should give brides before their wedding night. . . . Damn it all, what they need more, it seems to me, is advice afterward, on how to be embarrassed.
—Didier, a character in a Colette novel

I was ever of opinion that the honest man who married and brought up a large family did more service than he who continued single and only talked of population.
—Oliver Goldsmith, *The Vicar of Wakefield*

WHAT ARE BUGGERS FOR?

On a lawn in Princeton, New Jersey, in 1939, a *Life* photographer asked Thomas Mann to pose for a family portrait. W. H. Auden took his place beside Erika Mann. Christopher Isherwood also joined the group. The photographer knew that Auden was Mann's son-in-law, but how was Isherwood related, he asked.

"Family pimp," the novelist replied.[1]

The pimping for the Auden-Erika marriage went back to 1934. German-born Erika—actress, journalist, auto racer—was running a cabaret in Amsterdam when she was ordered home by the government. Since she had no passport, she knew her citizenship would be revoked and she would be left stateless if she complied. In any event, as the daughter of the outlawed anti-Nazi novelist, she was risking the gas chamber. But under British law a bride automatically became a citizen, well out of Nazi reach; and so her brother Klaus asked Isherwood, who had known Erika during his boy-chasing days in Berlin, to marry her and give her British citizenship. Isherwood hesitated: it might offend his family and upset his lover, Bubi Heinz. He asked Auden to perform the rescue. Auden wired back, chivalrously: "Delighted."

Years later, Auden said, "On the very day we were married, Goebbels *did* revoke Erika's citizenship. I had never met her before she came to England to marry me. Of course I knew who her pa-*pa* was. And we signed an agreement to make no financial claims on each other."[2]

Immediately after the wedding, Erika returned to Holland as a British subject. Although the marriage was never consummated, the couple remained fast friends. In the years after the war she was introduced to the Hollywood-exile set as Mrs. Auden, but the *Celebrity Register* and *Contemporary Authors* referred to them as "divorced." When Erika died in 1969, Auden was still ignorant of any divorce proceedings, but in filling out his passport a year later, he explained, "I had to say I was a widower." In fact, his obituary noted that he was the husband of the late Erika Mann.

The marriage catapulted Auden into anti-Nazi activism. He felt he had not done enough for the victims of Nazism: "Nothing I wrote saved a single Jew from being gassed."

After rescuing Erika, he urged his bachelor friends to follow his example. "After all," he told E. M. Forster, "what are buggers for?" Forster agreed and induced his friend, the poet John Simpson, to marry Erika's stranded friend, the actress Thérèse Giehse.[3]

For this wedding, Auden came to the registry office as a witness in striped trousers, wearing a boutonnière, an unusual costume for him. He supervised the arrangements and volunteered to answer the clerk's questions to the bride. After the ceremony, he handed around double brandies

"It's on Thomas Mann," he said.[4]

DIRECTED BY THE BRIDEGROOM

Looking back on his marriages, Sacha Guitry commented: "I have always longed to fall into the arms of beautiful women. All I have done is to fall into their hands."[5]

Ironically, on being introduced to the women he later married, Sacha invariably passed a flattering remark about their hands.

Guitry always gave himself the stellar role of lover in most of the 120 plays he wrote and directed, in which the stable ingredients were, as Pierre Schneider observed, "cuckolds, a bedroom, a girl in black panties, and a Poujadist mixture of salacity, greed." It was only natural that he should marry pretty actresses who could no more resist affairs offstage than on.

No one has yet been able to make an accurate tally of Guitry's marriages (the authoritative number is five) and certainly not his adulteries. "Most men," he explained, "have had as many women in their lives. I marry them."

His first bride, twenty-six-year-old actress Charlotte Lysès, considerably older than himself, was lissome, enchanting, coquettish, still country fresh, splendidly exuberant, and irresistible. From his director's chair, Guitry watched enraptured as she minced across the stage. She had electric velvet eyes (though she was terribly myopic), but he couldn't resist a quip, "Behind her glasses she gives the impression that she's looking at you through a keyhole."

For the wedding ceremony he wrote his own scenario. It took place in his bedroom in a villa near Rouen, where he was doing military service. Old faithful farceur Tristan Bernard was best man, a role he played in all Sacha's weddings.

Guitry had Bernard run off to summon the town mayor with the plea that the greatest actor-playwright of his time was on his deathbed and wanted him to officiate at his marriage.

The mayor found the groom in bed, dramatically made up as for a role onstage and groaning pathetically. The great Molière himself couldn't have been expiring more pathetically. Charlotte stood by the bedside holding her groom's hands, sighing and moist-eyed. When the ceremony ended and Guitry had scrawled his signature on a certificate, he leaped out of bed with the agility of a professional gymnast.

At first the mayor grumbled that the deception was an affront to religion and the dignity of his magistracy, but then quickly sized up the situation and joined in the laughter around him. How stupid of him to have expected the most prominent comedian in France to take anything seriously.

Characteristically, Guitry saluted his marriage with a bon mot: "A comedy that ends with a marriage is really the beginning of another comedy—rather of a drama."

That drama came to a close in a divorce court ten years later, with no bitter feeling on either side.[6]

Charlotte herself provided him with her successor in the person of a twenty-year-old musical comedy soubrette, Yvonne Printemps. He did not have to train Yvonne in dramatics; she had made a sensational debut in the Folies Bergères at thirteen and was now a star.

After a few long walks with her and her dog, Guitry persuaded her to accept his marriage proposal.

He planned his second wedding with masterly showmanship. Paris theater royalty came out in full force. Papa Lucien Guitry kept shaking hands around as though he were getting married. To everyone's surprise, even the dean of Paris comedy, Georges Feydeau, appeared, having made an exception to his habit of sleeping all day and getting up at night. But what put the ceremony into the newspaper headlines was not petite Yvonne or her groom but Sarah Bernhardt, still sprightly at seventy despite the amputation of her left leg. She was carried in, to center stage, on an elaborate palanquin. No one would think of upstaging the divine Sarah.[7]

For several years Yvonne starred with her husband in the twenty plays he wrote for her, but then she went on to play a role he did not direct. He knew he was being cuckolded, but fearful of the gossip columnists, he did nothing except grit his teeth after a few verbal skirmishes. When he tried to keep her too close to him, she complained to friends, "It's a gilded cage, but a cage all the same."[8]

However, the time came for face saving when he received a cryptic note from an insidious actress who may have had her eye on a released Sacha: "If you want to know where they go—I'll take you there." Guitry went and trapped the lovers *in flagrante delicto* and, as quickly as he could reach his solicitor, instituted divorce proceedings, to the unfeigned gratification of his informant. The charge— Guitry wanted to be fair—was "reciprocal adultery."

Guitry was great at contriving dénouements. To the end of his life he retained a soft spot for Yvonne. They remained close friends, held hands and embraced in public; he continued to write plays for her and even suggested a flattering epitaph for her tombstone: "Here lies Yvonne Printemps—for the first time cold."

"At last I shall be living on my own," Sacha said when the divorce came through, "and already I'm wondering: with whom?"[9]

He didn't have to look far; his company had any number of receptive soubrettes. Jacqueline Delubac, whom he got to know intimately when he was touring Lyon, made overtures to him, and he succumbed. Jacqueline moved at once into his busy mansion in Paris, helped him rearrange his furniture to her taste, removed the old pictures that might remind him of Yvonne, and prepared methodically to lay the groundwork for the climactic wedding scene. As he had done for his first wives, he wrote her a new comedy in which he was to play the role of the lover.

Guitry set the stage for the announcement of his third plunge into matrimony. He invited some dozen friends to a luncheon at the Ritz. The guests—Yvonne was probably among them—were sure that he had brought them together to celebrate his fiftieth birthday. Jacqueline, more gorgeously dressed than for a luncheon, sat beaming at his side. Laudatory speeches filled the time between courses, and as the dessert dishes were being cleared away, Sacha rose, acknowledged the clatter of applause, and said: "Ladies and Gentlemen, as you know I'm fifty today. Jacqueline is twenty-five. So it was natural today she should become my better half. . . . Before meeting you we made a little detour, via the town hall, and now it's done. You're the first to know it."[10]

For Guitry's fourth wedding, the scene shifts to Switzerland. Jacqueline had long eased herself out of his life when his eye lighted amorously on the actress Geneviève de Séréville. She was at least thirty-eight years younger than himself.

When Yvonne heard he was planning to marry Geneviève, she remarked, "He'll be after Shirley Temple next."

Guitry had a ready answer in lines he himself delivered in a play: "When you're in love at the age of twenty and for the first time, your beloved is the only woman in the world; by the time you've reached your fourth you realize that the world's number of women is limitless."[11]

Geneviève was not so receptive as the first three, and he felt he had to think up a unique style for this courtship. His biographer James Harding provides the details of the master playwright's irresistible suit:

When Geneviève complained, while they were visiting the fashionable spots along the Riviera, "I've got nothing to wear," Guitry went to work immediately to relieve her vexation. Harding writes:

"At half past nine a small pageboy with a small packet knocked at her door. Inside the packet were handkerchiefs of Alençon lace and the opening sentence of a letter: 'Once upon a time . . .' At ten o'clock a slightly taller pageboy handed her a box containing three Hermès scarves and a further instalment of the letter: 'Once upon a time there was . . .' At a quarter past ten came a medium-sized pageboy with a medium-sized box of underwear and the letter: 'Once upon a time there was a gentleman very much in love with . . .' Quarter of an hour later came a large pageboy with a large box of sweaters and coats. 'Once upon a time there was a gentleman very much in love with a girl who . . .' At half past ten the first pageboy returned with a Lanvin parcel, much too big for him, containing a suit, dress and coat: 'Once upon a time there was a gentleman very much in love with a girl who, having nothing . . .' Fifteen minutes afterwards the second pageboy came back with an elegantly wrapped fur coat: 'Once upon a time there was a gentleman very much in love with a girl who, having nothing to wear, was obliged to agree to being dressed entirely by him. But morality won't suffer, because the gentleman is her future husband.' Whereupon Sacha himself appeared on the threshold his arms full of jewelry: 'I forgot all the trinkets that go with it.' "[12]

What woman could say no to such a lover?

Her parents were willing to overlook the difference in their ages. But there remained one major obstacle to marrying Geneviève: their religious differences. Sacha compromised upon a church wedding. But he had to get Church sanction before her parents would give their consent. It was not easy, considering that the Church frowned on divorce. He hastened to see the archbishop of Paris in person. In the first minutes of their interview, the cleric was favorably impressed by his visitor's persuasive charm.

Suddenly His Eminence asked him: "How do you manage to act churchmen so well without having very much to do with them?"

"It's hereditary," he answered. "Though we were all actors on my father's side, my maternal great-uncle was Bishop of Le Mans."

To provide inducement for the archbishop's approval, Sacha told him that he had already bought a country house in his parish. This clinched the case.

Guitry married his fourth wife in a little church in the vicinity. As Harding observed, it was the first time in his theatrical career that Sacha stood with his back to the audience and allowed himself to be upstaged by an actor in parish robes.

Guitry was sixty when he married for (by general agreement) the fifth and last time. Lana Marconi was a stunning twenty-eight-year-old Parisienne. A friend had told him, "She's the most beautiful girl in Paris at the moment!" He invited her to dinner at his home in the avenue Elisée-Reclus. He turned on the charm the instant he saw her. "You have the loveliest hands in the world," he told her. Sacha knew all the tricks, and one more: beside her plate he placed three roses. She knew a trick or two also: she dropped her handkerchief as she was leaving; it was embroidered with the arms of Romanian royalty.

A whirlwind courtship in the Guitry manner began the following day. He loaded her with gifts of fur coats, gowns, jewels, and millions of francs to finance her investments in National Lottery tickets, which she went out to buy by the ton. Her hunch number was 5, a figure based on her numerical order in the succession of Guitry's wives. He loved her for that. He had no difficulty appeasing the Exarch of the Metropolitan Church of Central and Western Europe about their religious differences: "Born and baptized at St. Petersburg in 1885, I wish respectfully to inform you that I belong to the Orthodox Church," he informed him. The signature clinched the point: only a native Russian would carry the name Sacha.

Sacha chose the Russian Orthodox Church in the rue Bizet for a wedding. As they were crossing the threshold of his house, he turned to his bride and said, "I've made a French woman out of you, and you'll make an Orthodox man out of me." Sensing a trace of jealousy still lingering over her predecessors, he reassured her: "The others were my wives, but you, *chérie*, you will be my widow."[13]

And he kept his promise.

APOLLINAIRE PROPOSES

Beckoning Guillaume Apollinaire out of Montmartre was a free vacation where he didn't have to exist on herrings. A hundred francs a month for only two hours each morning was irresistible to one who scrounged for his living copying publicity wrappers at four sous an hour while his poetic genius was bursting for exploitation.

His friend Mme. Nicosia had suggested he might apply for the vacant post of French tutor to the daughter of a rich widow of a German viscount who was returning to the Rhineland. Apollinaire thought he might hammer out a piece on Germany for one of the reviews. When he learned that a pretty English governess of his own age, Anne Playden, would also be there, he became enthusiastic.

Apollinaire knew how to get his way with women. After a few walks in the woods, he and Annie got on famously. He courted her with his gypsy lyrics and his Gallic strategy and dazzled her with his mythomania.

Apollinaire was a man of considerable attainments—an attractive package of charlatan, pornographer, avant-garde poet, poseur, and hellion. He never told a story about himself in the same way twice. In order to hide his bastard birth, he changed his identity a dozen times a week. No one, sometimes not even Apollinaire, knew exactly who he was on a particular day. Even his handwriting changed automatically to suit his altered character, so that his bank required him to supply five or six signatures.

He was, in fact, the illegitimate son of a convent dropout (currently living with a minor Italian nobleman) and of a Polish father he had never seen. On this frail base he embroidered the most fantastic yarns. One story he never changed: he was the bastard son of a cardinal or maybe even of the pope himself. The rest he improvised.

When Apollinaire looked wistfully into Annie's lowered gray eyes and called her his Lorelei, he touched a sensitive feminine nerve. Before she knew it or wanted it, she fell in love.

"He was madly in love," she recalled years later, "and I was a little silly who would not allow herself to fall in love because of her puritan education . . . at certain moments he was violent and impetuous to the point of cruelty, but he could also be very attentive and loving."[14]

She tried hard to resist his importunities. When the advances became too intensely physical, she suffered alternating emotions of ecstasy, fear, guilt, and frustration. A fortuneteller had told them their love was doomed to failure. It worried them, but not for long; it only made Apollinaire press more ardently for the consummation.

The courtship came to a boil. They were standing at the top of Drachenfals, in a spot steeped in romantic legend: here Siegfried allegedly slew a dragon. The scene was right, *le moment* had arrived, and Apollinaire seized his advantage: he asked her to marry him. She hesitated, then in a sudden rush of fear, refused. The old violent glare came into his eyes and she turned away, terrified. Pointing to the steep precipice below, he threatened to push her over if she did not consent to marry him. (Nobody would doubt it was an accident.) She consented, and they descended. When they reached flat ground, she grinned, unlocked his embrace, and ran for cover, shouting her final, irrevocable refusal.[15]

If At First You Don't Succeed

The "troubling" of his life began for William Butler Yeats before he was twenty-three and it held him in thrall until his death at seventy-five. His enchantress was Maud Gonne, the rebellious daughter of a British colonel who was the Irish Joan of Arc, a Sinn Fein plotter and fiery orator. To a compatriot she was "impulsive and fierce"; to Bernard Shaw, she was "outrageously beautiful." Monk Gibbon said of Maud Gonne and Yeats, "It was she who touched his lips with a coal of fire and made him the poet he was."

Yeats misjudged Maud. He believed she reciprocated his love and at the right moment would marry him. But he overlooked a trauma in her past. Scorning his proposal, she said, "I have a horror and terror of physical love."[16] At his near collapse, she softened, kissed him, and suggested "spiritual marriage."

It was not what Yeats had in mind. He retreated for the moment, realizing that he should have gone more slowly with a woman who, before she was twenty, though already an activist marked for execution by the British, had borne two illegitimate children during a long liaison with a French journalist. Maud's Dublin friends were well aware that her "adopted cousin Iseult" was really her daughter.

Maud's rebuff only intensified Yeats's worship of his Irish goddess. He was constantly at her side at political rallies, and they sat up far into the night uttering incantations, weaving mystical legends, and holding hands as they awaited visions. Lyrics of love unreciprocated poured from him; she was, he said, the beam in his eye, the beat of his heart, the spur of his hope for an emancipated Mother Ireland. On the point of summoning up courage for a second proposal—this time, sure of acceptance—he was beside himself with shock and rage:

Maud took off for Paris and, in defiance of everyone whom she respected, married John McBride, hero of the Irish Transvaal Brigade in the Boer War.

Yeats called McBride "a drunken, vainglorious lout." Not long after her elopement, Maud was estranged from her husband. She was widowed when McBride was executed during the Easter Rebellion.

Yeats proposed again, more passionately than ever, and this time unconditionally. And again Maud rejected him. Now, however, it was for political reasons; she refused to marry a man who spent his time writing poems when he should be throwing bombs in the cause of Irish freedom. (She did not go so far as to quote Carlyle's dictum in *Hero Worship*: "The poet who does nothing but sit on a stool and write poetry will never write a poem worth reading.") Once more, on observing his discomfiture, she offered him the consolation of "spiritual marriage."

According to one writer's count, Yeats proposed to Maud at least fifty times over half a century. Either Yeats or Maud must have told, because Dublin gossips like Oliver St. John Gogarty and George Moore made capital fun of the affair.

Iseult later told Richard Ellmann: "My mother was not a woman of much discernment, but she had enough to know better than to marry Yeats, to whom she was not suited."

Iseult also told Ellmann that when she was fifteen, she had such a crush on the handsome poet, now a national figure, that she asked him to marry her. Though flattered, he begged off; he was still nourishing the hope that Iseult's mother would change her mind.[17]

But she didn't. After the next rejection, *faute de mieux* Yeats proposed to Iseult. Apparently, she was expecting it.

At this time Yeats was Ireland's undisputed greatest poet and playwright. The mother hen of literary Dublin, Lady Gregory, worried about her favorite disciple's despondency, urged Yeats to marry one of the many attractive women who boasted of being his mistress.

Characteristically, Yeats consulted a medium, who advised him to marry Iseult at once.

But Iseult asked him, "You wouldn't say you love me, would you?"

He admitted he wasn't sure, but continued to meet her. Finally, at a Lyons Corner restaurant in London, he asked her, "Yes or no?"— and she pressed his hand warmly, kissed him on the cheek, and said, "No." Several years later, when he said to her, in a wave of nostalgia, "If only you and I were married . . ." she cut in, "Why, we wouldn't have stayed together a year."[18]

Still a bachelor on his fifty-second birthday, lonely for female companionship, his poetry seemingly blocked, and realizing that it no longer made sense to preserve his availability for the adamant Maud, Yeats cast an amorous eye on Georgie Hyde-Lees. She was a friend of Ezra Pound and Pound's wife, Olivia Shakespeare. Georgie was witty, cultivated, and friendly. Yeats thought her more beautiful at twenty-six than when he had met her when she was eighteen, and even more beautiful than Maud Gonne or Iseult. In the light of his discovery, the day of their meeting seemed to him "a classical impersonation of Spring, the Virgilian commendation. 'She walks like a goddess' made for him alone." Characteristically, he at once broadcast his intention of marrying Miss Hyde-Lees—news that roused his friends to astonishment and ribaldry. Maud, according to Arthur Symons, "was moved to mirth and spite," and Yeats's father was perturbed to learn that his son was marrying a woman half his age. However, when he was told that the bride was five feet seven inches, the elder Yeats wrote John Quinn: "I think tall women are easier to get on with and live with than little women. They have more sentiment and gentleness, and because they are more conspicuous are more watchful of themselves. The little women are constantly out of sight so that you don't know what they are up to."[19]

Miss Hyde-Lees vowed that she was in love with Yeats, admired his poetry, and fully shared his newest interest—occultism and psychical research. Yeats let it be known that Georgie could be of help in furthering his fame.

She hastened to have the banns posted before he changed his mind; his friends were not sure he would go through with it. When Yeats asked Lady Gregory whether he might bring his fiancée, Georgie, to visit her at Coole, she replied bluntly, "I'd rather you didn't come until you are married."

She married him. Georgie and he took the oath in a secular ceremony in London, with Ezra Pound as best man (Yeats had stood up with Pound when he married Olivia Shakespeare). Maud Gonne turned over her Dublin house to the honeymooners.

From Stone Cottage, Yeats wrote Lady Gregory: "My wife is a perfect wife, kind, wise, and unselfish . . . has made my life serene and full of order."

However, during the first four days of the honeymoon, Georgie detected a shadow of depression in him: he was fidgety, often irritable, and obviously bored. He was then composing "Owen Ahearn and His Dancers," on the theme of being in love and being rejected. One line sparked Georgie's concern: "I ran from my love's side because my heart went bad." Was Willie Yeats still regretting Maud and Iseult?

Georgie decided to resort to automatic writing to discover her husband's errant thoughts. Yeats was obsessed with astral messages, then the rage in Dublin, and had already had proof of the accuracy of divination. When he had received a letter from his mistress in London informing him she was pregnant, he consulted a medium. "Deception," she said, and she was right.[20]

Richard Ellmann describes Georgie's obviously fake experiment: "Her idea was to take a sentence that would allay his anxiety over Iseult and himself, and after the session to own up to what she had done: . . . she encouraged a pencil to write a sentence which I remember as saying, approximately, 'What you have done is right for both the cat and the hare.' She was confident that he would decipher the cat as her watchful and timid self, and the hare as Iseult—a fleet runner. Yeats was at once captured and relieved, and it did not at once occur to him that his wife might have divined his cause of anxiety without preternatural assistance.

"Then a strange thing happened. Her own emotional involvement—her love for this extraordinary husband and her fears for her marriage—must have made for unusual receptivity, as she told me later, for she suddenly felt her hand grasped and driven irresistibly. The pencil began to write sentences she had never intended or thought which seemed to come from another world. As images and ideas took penciled form, Yeats went beyond his marriage. Here was more revelation: he had married into Delphi."[21]

Georgie herself never realized what an extraordinarily gifted medium she was. Amazed by his wife's psychic power, Yeats kept her at the oracular machine three hours and more a day, until it became too much even for her. The revelation inspired him to write "The Second Coming."

Yeats's biographers agree that the marriage was a major factor in his rise to fame; only after settling down with a woman who gave him love, understanding, and complete freedom of movement was he inspired to exploit his great talent to the full. As he told Georgie in "Under Saturn":

For how should I forget the
wisdom that you
brought,
The comfort that you made—[22]

Yet Yeats only appeared to have settled down; he was still restless, thirsting for romance and pursuing liaisons to spark his muse. When his American lawyer, the bachelor John Quinn, found Yeats making passes at Quinn's mistress, Dorothy Coates, when the three were in Paris, Quinn became furious. Yeats denied any sexual interest and he said: "If it had been your wife, yes, but your mistress—never!" The explanation fell flat, and lawyer and client did not speak to each other for years.[23]

Georgie, reasoning that love affairs were necessary to a romantic poet, took a tolerant view of his philandering and his correspondence with female admirers. She knew he loved his family and would always come home to her. It was indeed an extraordinarily happy and productive marriage. He was deeply in love with Georgie. "The marriage bed," Yeats wrote, "is the symbol of the solved antimony." And she assured him, "After your death, people will write of your love affairs, but I shall say nothing, because I will remember how proud you were."[24]

Maud Gonne never lived to see a united Ireland, but she donated a son to her country, the pacifist Sean McBride, who was awarded the 1974 Nobel Peace Prize for his work as chairman of Amnesty International.

When Yeats received the Nobel Prize for literature, Maud refused to send him a note of congratulation. To her, the only poet who merited felicitation was one who had fought for his country's freedom—and perhaps died for it (*"Dulce et decorum est pro patria mori"*).

One Dozen Is Just Right

When young John Donne, the English poet and theologian, was secretary to Sir Thomas Egerton, Keeper of the Great Seal, he fell in love with Lady Egerton's fourteen-year-old niece, Anne Moore.

Four years later, after an intense, clandestine, and sexless wooing, he eloped with Anne and married her without the then mandatory consent of her parents or her uncle. Donne did not have the opportunity to cohabit with her immediately after the ceremony. Sir

Thomas, enraged, dismissed him at once, cut off all his funds, and ordered him hauled off to Fleet Prison. It was there that he wrote impatient, distracted Anne, telling her where he was and ending with the now classic line: "John Donne, Anne Done, Undone."

A year later, parents and uncle relented, and the marriage was legalized.

Anne could not read or understand her husband's poems. The love lyrics he read to her, however, did not fall on deaf ears. Donne loved her dearly. After fifteen years of happy and compatible marriage in which she bore him a dozen children, he resolved that enough was enough and turned celibate. Donne, of course, is famous for his fervent religious poems as well as his beautiful love lyrics to Anne.

DOROTHY PARKER: "JUST A LITTLE JEWISH GIRL TRYING TO BE CUTE"

"I require only three things of a man," said Dorothy Rothschild before going out to play the field. "He must be handsome, ruthless, and stupid."

She should have added: he must be willing to take my wisecracks.

Lovers came and lovers fled, annihilated. Her friend Lillian Hellman said, "She had been loved by several remarkable men, but she only loved the ones who didn't love her, and they were the shabby ones."[25]

When she was twenty-four, "a little woman with a dollish face and basset-round eyes, in whose mouth butter hardly ever melted," she was "the 'verray parfit gentil knight' of the squelch."[26] Dottie was just beginning to savor sophisticated one-liners, epigrams, stories, and verse. About her first husband, Edwin Pond Parker II ("Spook"), she told two contradictory stories: he was her childhood sweetheart; they had met at a summer hotel in Connecticut.

Before the marriage was a year old, Parker shipped off to Europe as an enlistee in World War I. A minister's son, he returned even less sophisticated than when he left and a bottle-a-day drinker. He found Dottie a changed woman, in her element writing clever pieces for *Vogue* and other magazines. She walked him around town with her poodle. When they lunched at the Algonquin with the Round Table wits, he sat mute in a corner, feeling superfluous, and though he never got the point of jokes, he would smile at the stories his wife told at his expense. When it all grew unendurable, he tried to get his wife to leave New York with him, but she refused and he left alone.

Dottie changed the facts of her life as often as she changed her hats. Some thought she was deliberately trying to confuse potential biographers.

Her wisecracks were self-protective; she was sentimental, soft, frightened of life, in flight from herself. Robert Benchley, Lillian Hellman, and Wyatt Cooper saw through her disguises; her husbands and transient lovers did not.

How had she come to marry Parker? "I married him to change my name," she quipped. But her wisest friends knew that they were in love. Dottie would never admit it. To explain his prolonged absence, she told a story nobody believed, that Spook had gone back to Germany, was addicted to morphine, and had to be put in a sanatorium.

She did once say, "Damn it, it was the late twenties, and we *had* to be *smarty*. I *wanted* to be cute. That's the terrible thing. I should have had more sense. A smart cracker they called me."[27]

Donald Ogden Stewart, who knew the couple and sympathized with Spook, said, "Eddie stayed in love with his wife longer than she did with him."

Dottie got at least one famous verse out of the marriage:

> By the time you swear you're his,
> Shivering and sighing,
> And he vows his passion is
> Infinite, undying—
> Lady, make a note of this:
> One of you is lying.[28]

She came out of her first marriage lonely, despondent, and poor. She had several affairs that blew away on a wave of wisecracks. She hitched on to Charles MacArthur (then an Algonquin diner and, before his marriage to Helen Hayes, a womanizer), but he would not field her gibes. When he left her, she remarked, "It serves me right for putting all my eggs in one bastard."

She went back to the canary and the dogs in her apartment and slashed her wrists. Robert Benchley came up and admonished her, "Dottie, if you don't stop this sort of thing you'll make yourself sick."

She tried to get a new grip on life, having an affair with Ring Lardner, but after a few weeks her lethal sallies were too much for him. An interlude with a handsome young Wall Street broker seemed promising, but he too was soon disenchanted and in a blasting finale shouted at her, "You're a lousy lay!" To a sympathetic friend, Dottie commented, "That sounded just like him . . . yes, his body went to his head."[29]

Then the actor Alan Campbell entered her life. She was forty, still attractive, more popular than ever in literary circles, but a lonely and disillusioned romantic living in a cheap hotel. Campbell was twenty-nine and madly in love with her, though friends suggested that he wanted to use her to advance his career as a Hollywood scriptwriter. "He was beautiful," Dottie was to say afterward, "but not very smart."

Lillian Hellman says, "He was also difficult for her and she would talk about him in a funny, half-bitter way not only to me but given enough liquor, to a whole dinner party. But she had great affection for Alan. . . . She wanted to charm, to be loved, to be admired, and such desires brought self-contempt that could only be cured by behind-the-back denunciations of almost comic violence."[30]

Alan was good for her morale and extraordinarily useful. "When they were living together in New York" says her biographer, John Keats, "he had bought the food, done the cooking, done all the interior decoration in their apartment . . . cleaned up after the dogs, washed and dried the dishes, made the beds, told Dorothy to wear her coat on cold days, shaken the cocktails, paid the bills, amused her, adored her, made love to her, got her to cut down on her drinking, otherwise created space and time in her life for her to write, and taken her to parties."[31]

But she found him excruciatingly dull. She needed a sounding-board for her wit, but her putdowns did not amuse him. She circulated funny stories about him, bending the truth so far to get a laugh that even Alan joined in. In low whispers she confided to friends that Alan was a homosexual, but he was admittedly bisexual and did not attempt to deny her gossip.

Intensely jealous of her handsome boy, she openly accused him of imaginary infidelities. Referring to a dry-as-dust woman known to be less giving than most, she taunted. "I know you aren't laying her. If you were, you'd have splinters in your prow."[32]

In his memoir of her, Wyatt Cooper wrote, "No matter what he did she felt victimized. When World War II began, she went about muttering that any man worth his salt would be in there fighting. Then, when he enlisted, she bitterly accused him of deserting her in perilous times." Dottie put it in her own way: "We were married for about five minutes, then he went off to war."[33]

She filed for divorce in Connecticut, where, she said, "You can get it for roller skating." To the Algonquin wits she explained that she had divorced Alan because he was homosexual ("How do you like that for competition?").[34]

While waiting for the divorce to be finalized, she became, her friend Elizabeth Janeway says, "like her friend the lady who spoke eighteen languages and couldn't say 'no' in any of them." She dated playwright Ross Evans, who was twenty-three. John Keats says that some of her friends thought the coupling was "a way of displaying rage at Alan, or was using him in a desperate attempt to prove that she, at fifty-four, still possessed an attractiveness that had nothing to do with her superficial appearance, that she was alluring to young men."[35] Ross now had himself an agent, editor, and woman all rolled into one. Hollywood never looked brighter. Vincent Sheean reports that once, when Dottie and her lover came for a visit, "Ross and Dorothy sat on our great, oversized, red and green tartan sofa. We drank—it was one of our main occupations—and about two or three in the morning they began to make love. I tried to avert my eyes. . . . As they were leaving, she fluttered her lids with becoming modesty and apologized: 'You know, this hasn't happened for about six months. Hope you don't mind. We must have been awfully picturesque.' "[36]

Eventually, Dottie was able to wash Ross right out of her hair. Alone again in her hotel, she took stock of herself and on an impulse called Alan, now doing scripts in Hollywood. Yes, said Alan, he missed her, it was stupid to live apart. They agreed to make another try together. It was three years after their divorce.

Right after the ceremony, Dottie called Lillian Hellman jubilantly. "Lilly," she said, "the room was filled with people who hadn't talked to each other in years, including the bride and bridegroom."[37]

Alan died a few years later, presumably from an overdose of sleeping pills. In *An Unfinished Woman*, Lillian Hellman writes that when his body was taken out to the coroner's automobile, Mrs. Jones, an acquaintance, who had liked Alan, asked Dottie, " 'Tell me, dear, what can I do for you?'

" 'Get me a new husband,' Dottie said.

"There was a silence," says Hellman, "but before those who were left could laugh, Mrs. Jones said, 'I think that is the most callous and disgusting remark I ever heard in my life.'

"Dottie turned to look at her, sighed, and said gently, 'So sorry. Then run down to the corner and get me a ham and cheese on rye and tell them to hold the mayo.' "[38]

G. K. Chesterton Marries a Warden

At her wit's end, G. K. Chesterton's mother had consulted her physician about her son. Although he couldn't read until he was nine, he was now muttering Bible passages and whole chunks of R. L. Stevenson, but he couldn't tie his own shoelaces and drew pictures over walls, towels, blinds, windows. The analyst reported: "Six feet of genius. Cherish him, Mrs. Chesterton, cherish him." The boy's brain was the largest and most sensitive the doctor had ever seen. The prognosis: "A genius or an idiot!"

Gilbert knew he was no idiot, and his mama cherished him as a genius—waited on him hand and foot, let him mark up the napery, encouraged his humor, gave him no pocket money, and silenced everyone when little Sir Oracle opened his mouth. He was probably the most irresponsible and absentminded *Wunderkind* since S. T. Coleridge, but he became the acknowledged greatest essayist of the century, a scintillating dialectician, a prince of paradox, author of the ingenious novel *The Man Who Was Thursday*, and the Father Brown detective stories.

He met his future wife, Frances Blogg, in his early twenties, when he was earning a pound a week as a publisher's reader at Fisher Unwin and doing other literary odds and ends. A secretary for an educational society, Frances had met him in a suburban London debating club. She had humor and common sense; she was fascinated by his originality, good nature, and the sense of wonder with which he approached the commonplace. She agreed when he said that what everyone called his absence of mind was in fact "presence of mind."

Frances's mother had hoped for someone more promising than the gawky, sloppy Chesterton, whom she called on first sight "an aimless, tactless, reckless, unbrushed, strange-hatted, opinionated scarecrow." When informed of Mrs. Blogg's verdict, Chesterton told Frances, "My appearance is singularly exemplary. My boots are placed, after the fastidious London fashion, on the feet; the laces are done up, the watch is going, the hair is brushed, the sleeve-links are inserted, for such is the Kingdom of Heaven."[39]

Mrs. Blogg got a foretaste of her future son-in-law (for Frances had pleaded that if anyone could reshape her suitor's image into a conventional mold, she could) on his first visit. Her apartment had just been redecorated and the drawing room repapered. Gilbert slouched on the sofa, lost in a fog as usual. She asked him how he liked her new wallpaper. The voice shocked him out of fantasy; he leaped up, dug out a piece of chalk from his pocket, went to the wall and, in a lightning flash, drew a portrait of his beloved. Stunned, Mrs. Blogg bit her tongue to keep from exploding.

It took Chesterton a few years to muster courage to propose. He wrote Frances endless poems and love letters (described by his mother as the letters of a poet in love with love), but no subtle prodding from Frances could speed the moment of his coming to the point. Perhaps he came to that stage because all the couples at the debating club were planning to marry. Or perhaps it was the parasol. Frances had forgotten her parasol in the railway waiting room. Later she told Gilbert she had been too tired to go back for it. In the middle of the night, walking home from Kensington to Bedford Park, he had a vision of the parasol. He explains, in his autobiography:

"I happened to see the identical railway station stand up black and bulky against the moonlight, and I committed my first and last crime: which was burglary, and very enjoyable." The station was locked, but he climbed the steep embankment, crawled onto the platform, and recovered Frances's parasol. "As I returned by the same route (still in the battered top hat and considerably deranged frock-coat) I stared up at the sky and found myself filled with all sorts of strange sensations. I felt as if I had just fallen from the moon, with the parasol for a parachute."[40]

Holding the parasol up triumphantly when he met Frances the next day for lunch, he looked into her madonna eyes, clasped her hand, and proposed. She accepted immediately.

The following morning he wrote the news to his closest friend, Mildred Wain: "On rising this morning, I carefully washed my boots in hot water and blacked my face. Then assuming my coat with grateful ease and with the tails in front, I descended to breakfast, where I gaily poured the coffee on the sardines and put my hat on the fire to boil. These activities will give you some idea of my frame of mind.

My family, observing me leave the house by way of the chimney, and take the fender with me under one arm, thought I must have something on my mind. So I had.

"My friend, I am engaged . . ."[41]

To Frances, he wrote an inventory of the items in his equipment "for starting on a journey to fairyland": among them a straw hat, a walking stick ("admirably fitted to break the head of any denizen of Suffolk who denies that you are the noblest of ladies"); a copy of Walt Whitman's poems; "a number of letters from a young lady, containing everything good and generous and loyal and holy and wise that isn't in Walt Whitman's poems"; a pocket-knife; a box of matches ("because fire is beautiful and burns your fingers. Some people think this a waste of matches: the same people who object to the building of cathedrals"); three pounds in gold and silver ("the remains of one of Mr. Unwin's bursts of affection"); a book of children's rhymes, in manuscript; a tennis racket; a soul ("hitherto idle and omnivorous but now happy enough to be ashamed of itself"); and "a heart mislaid somewhere."[42]

Before the wedding, he wrote her: "I shall have no objection to your having an occasional dragon to dinner, or a penitent griffin to sleep in the spare bed . . ."

Frances certainly knew what to expect. She went into the marriage with her eyes open and she had no qualms, sure it would be amusing, at any rate.

They were married at his favorite parish church, in Kensington, and remarkably, he was on time. (A friend had picked him up.) He had once appeared at a debate wearing two ties; this time he wore no tie; a bridesmaid's brother bought one at a local outfitter's minutes before the bride arrived. As he knelt before the altar, his mother, in the front pew, giggled: on the sole of one of his new shoes was a price ticket. What would her boy do with a thirty-four-year-old wife?

On the way to honeymoon in the Norfolk broadlands, he induced his bride suddenly to leave their carriage and join him in a glass of milk at a dairy. Then he took her into a nearby shop to purchase a revolver and cartridges. Always able to provide a logical explanation for seeming lunacy, he said, "I did not buy the pistol to murder myself or my wife; I never was really modern. I bought it because it was the great adventure of my youth, with the general notion of protecting her from the pirates doubtless infesting the Norfolk roads, to which we were bound; where, after all, there are a suspiciously large number of families with Danish names . . . But the ritual consumption of a glass of milk really was a reminiscence of childhood. I stopped at that particular dairy because I had always drunk a glass of milk there when walking with my mother in my infancy. And it seemed to me a fitting ceremonial to unite the two great relations in a man's life."[43]

Why had he chosen the White Horse Inn for the honeymoon? He had, he explained, always "been stirred by a wooden post painted white; and even so by any white horse in the street; it was like meeting a friend in a fairy tale to find myself under the sign of the White Horse at Ipswich on the first day of my honeymoon." The white cow outside the dairy was "a sort of pendant to the figure of the White Horse: the one standing at the beginning of my new journey, and the other at the end."[44]

A few days after the honeymoon, Chesterton commemorated it in a quatrain:

> Between the perfect wedding day
> And that fierce future proud, and furled
> I only stole six days—six days
> Enough for God to make the world.[45]

His first letter from the White Horse Inn went to Annie Firmin, his mother's first candidate for his bride: "I have a wife, a piece of string, a pencil and a knife; what more can any man want on a honeymoon?"

If we are to believe Gilbert's brother Cecil's wife, Ada, the first night was far from successful. How did Ada know? She said she had it from Cecil, who had it from Gilbert. Dudley Barker quotes her account from her book *The Chestertons*. Since the book was published after Cecil, Gilbert, and Frances had died, who was to disprove Ada's remarkable document?

He was fathoms deep in love, and in that first transcendent moment of their honeymoon when far beyond time and space they found themselves utterly, incomparably alone, he must have heard the sun and the moon and the stars singing together. And then the whole world went crash. The woman he worshipped shrank from his touch and screamed when he embraced her. A less sensitive or more experienced man would have regarded the whole affair as distressing but by no means irremediable, but he was haunted by the fear that his brutality and lust had frightened the woman he would have died to protect. He dared not even contemplate a repetition. He went to Cecil, quivering with self-reproach and condemnation. His young brother took a completely rationalistic view of the contretemps, and suggested that some citadels must be taken by storm, while others yield only to a long siege. Anyway he insisted that nothing had happened that couldn't be put right. They could both be happy and have lots of children. But the mischief had been done. Gilbert hated himself for what had happened and Frances couldn't resign herself to the physical realities of marriage. Temperamentally ascetic, physically sick from spinal disease, the experience must have shocked her profoundly. Her tragedy was that desiring children she shrank from sex. The final adjustment between them seems never to have been made, and Gilbert in a vital hour was condemned to a pseudo-monastic life in which he lived with a woman but never enjoyed her. For there was that about the Chestertons which would not let them be unfaithful. . . . Once married, they were dedicated for life.[46]

How much truth is there in Ada's account? One can make what one chooses of the following clue provided by Chesterton himself in an article written three years after the honeymoon:

"For the truth is that however you arrange the rules, or no rules, of the sex relation, however you twist it round or turn it inside out, you cannot make the sex relation anything else but tragic. That is to say, the happiest state for a man, you cannot deprive it of its power to make him the most miserable thing on earth."

Biographer Barker comments that it is evident in her book that Ada did not care for her sister-in-law Frances and that a wedding night that was a fiasco was "frequent in middle-class marriages during the reign of Victoria, when bride and groom alike were not uncommonly, as in the Chesterton marriage, both virgins with only romantic experience of sex. But it is certainly not true that Frances denied her husband sexual intercourse ever after.

"She was, perhaps, not an over-sexed woman. At various times Chesterton set down his views on marriage, and most of them assume a sexual coldness on the part of the wife. During the early years of their marriage, for example, he wrote, 'Man's sexual response to woman is presumed and almost automatic, but woman's can be withdrawn, even permanently withdrawn, for the aura around the virgin is something as man's history . . .' "

Barker supplies what he considers a piece of incontrovertible evidence that Frances did not refuse to have sexual intercourse later:

"Her sexual frigidity may probably have been increased by her frail physique. She suffered, among other illnesses, from arthritis of the spine, an affliction which grew in severity as she grew older." But Frances once said that she hoped to have children, at least seven, and even underwent an operation so that she could conceive. As Barker concludes: "Obviously, no woman would give a thought to such an operation unless she had proved to herself, by several years of copulation, that she and her husband could not breed children without such aid."[47]

If Ada's dislike of Frances emerges in her book, a close friend of all the Chestertons, Maisie Ward, testifies that Frances was more charitable. After Gilbert's funeral, says Ward, "At Top Meadow we gathered to talk. Frances a few of us saw for a little while in her own room. With that other self-forgetfulness that was hers she said to her sister-in-law, 'It was so much worse for you. You had Cecil for such a short time.' "[48]

Whatever Gilbert's and Frances's sexual frustrations were, all the evidence shows that these did not cloud their thirty-five years of marriage. Frances loved Gilbert dearly and pampered him even more than his mother had. She became his valet, time clock, appointment secretary; to preserve her sanity, she eventually stopped trying to reform him. One critic has even said that she fashioned him into a public clown—substituting, for his oversized overcoat and battered top hat, his famous romantic opera cloak and brigand's broad-brimmed slouch hat. She could do nothing about his sloppiness or his spattering his clothes with cigar ashes; she treated all his eccentricities with amused tolerance.

Chesterton called marriage the happiest state for a man. How about a woman? The stories of his absentmindedness and his peculiarities are legion; only a woman who loved him deeply and respected his genius could have endured them. Frances tied his shoelaces for him, helped him in and out of his bath. Dressing him with some semblance of decorum was a problem.

For twenty-four years Chesterton wore a sword in his cowboy belt. One day when Frances was out visiting and he had been left in the charge of Mrs. Mills so he would not get lost if let out alone, a constable near Beaconsfield asked Mrs. Mills: "Is the gentleman all right who's staying with you? He's been going around with a drawn sword."

Maisie Ward repeats a story told by his friend's wife, Ethel Older-shaw: she recalled him "striking matches on the wallpaper and walking in bright sunshine under an open umbrella held over his head. When she asked him the reason for this, he awoke from his musings, looked rather puzzled and said: 'I think Frances put it up.' An hour or so ago it had been raining."

He often had no idea where he was expected to be: once, as it had happened often, he was stranded on a lecture tour. He sent his wife a telegram: "Am in Birmingham. Where ought I to be?"

At home, getting him bathed was a daily trial for her. She had fed him so well that from the one hundred pounds he carried when she first met him, he now tipped the scales at three hundred. "One day," writes Ward, "she had heard him get out of the tub and was hovering around, waiting for her moment, when a tremendous splash assailed her ears. Then came a deep groan and the words 'Dammit, I've been here already.' "

Everyone who knew Chesterton had a story to tell. Gerald Cumberland recalled: "On one occasion I saw him emerge from Shoe Lane, hurry into the middle of Fleet Street, and abruptly come to a standstill in the middle of traffic. He stood there for some time, wrapped in thought, while buses, taxis and lorries eddied about him in a whirlpool and drivers exercised to the full their gentle art of expostulation. Having come to the end of his meditations, he held up his hand, turned round, cleared a passage through the horses and vehicles and returned to Shoe Lane. . . . Nobody else in London could have done it with his air of absolute unconsciousness, of absentmindedness. And not even the most stalwart policeman, vested with full authority, could have dammed up London's stream of traffic more effectively."[49]

He was having a two-hour lunch with E. V. Lucas. At three, they were interrupted by a message from Chesterton's cabdriver: "Would the gentleman please pay him off now as he wanted to eat too."

Like Carlyle, he was completely spoiled. Robert Blatchford recalls that when the two families went on a trip together—in separate cabs because of Chesterton's gargantuan girth—he went out in the driving rain to fetch a taxi while Chesterton sat back cozily reading a book and sent Frances out to get one.

Frances understood. "If he'd gone out in the rain he'd simply get lost," she said.

Once, when he was collecting his things for the usual morning train ride from the country to London, he asked her what time it was due. In a rare rush of impatience, she asked, "Don't you really know the trains to London?"

"My dear," he answered, "I couldn't earn our daily bread if I had to study the time-tables."[50]

It was more than daily bread that he earned. From a 26-shillings-a-week publisher's reader he became one of the richest writers in the world and one of the most prolific. He left an estate of 28,389 pounds, only a small part of which was inherited from his father.

ALL COBB'S WORLDLY GOODS

In a bureau at home were Irwin S. Cobb's two treasures: his mother's obituary and a clipping from a Savannah, Georgia, newspaper about his marriage.

To complete his costume as a bridegroom, Cobb had needed to borrow a pair of gloves from his bride; his granddaughter Elizabeth said that though he was over six feet tall, his hands were tiny.

Cobb wrote about the ceremony: "When we stood up before the minister and I repeated after him, 'with all my worldly goods I thee endow,' I could not help grinning inwardly. All my worldly goods, as nearly as I can recall at the moment, consisted of 2 suits of clothes, a set of Ridpath's *History of the World,* and a collection of birds' eggs. My salary was $18 a week."[51]

A MARRIAGE OF TRUE MINDS

In 1947, following the deaths of Beatrice and Sidney Webb, the British government acceded to the campaign to disinter their remains from Passfield Corner and bury them in Westminster Abbey. As the two similar urns were being lowered into the grave, Beatrice's sister Rosie asked, "Which is Sidney and which is Beatrice?"

No one could say for sure. The Webbs were inseparable in death as they had been in life.

The Webb union almost never happened. Entering her twenties, Beatrice Potter—brought up in an advanced circle of thinkers like Herbert Spencer and the Huxleys—was not averse to getting married, provided it left her independent to use her brains, preferably in social work. Marriage was certainly more interesting than the debutante whirligig or the partnership in the timber business offered by her father. An attractive, vivacious, and knowledgeable suitor presented himself: Joseph Chamberlain. Their dating over several years was not idyllic ("I like him and I do not like him," had been her first judgment). The better she knew his views, the more disenchanted she became. When he told her that he had to have complete authority as a husband, she flared up. She had other plans: "Hitherto the well-to-do have governed the country; it is my aim to make life pleasanter for this great majority." After a particularly severe clash of opinions, Beatrice was discovered sobbing: "I've just refused him," she said.[52]

More determined than ever, Beatrice joined a charitable organization, studied tracts on economics, and before long took up with the Fabians. It was Shaw who arranged for Beatrice to meet the workhorse of the movement. "Sidney Webb knows everything," he said.

They were an odd couple indeed. Beatrice was tall, willowy, from a privileged and moneyed class, and stunning. Sidney was dwarfish, a London shopkeeper's son; he was a clerk in the Colonial Office although already leading the Fabians. "His huge head was covered with black hair," Beatrice's niece, Kitty Muggeridge, has described Sidney. "He had a large nose, and eyes bulging behind thick-lensed pince-nez. He wore a goatee beard. His clothes were not very clean and he dropped his aitches."[53]

Joseph Chamberlain had worn an orchid in his lapel, a monocle in his eye. But Beatrice had wanted more.

"At last," she cried triumphantly after her first hours with Sidney, "I am a Socialist!" Together they determined to turn the capitalist world around. In the process, she would tidy him up a bit and lose some of her snobbery.

After seventeen months, love joined respect. They were to become a collective industry. It took a long time—after intensive shared work, cycling in tandem in country lanes, a little spooning—for Sidney to get up enough steam to write her a proposal. Only a woman like Beatrice could have appreciated it. He wrote her:

> I know perfectly well how little likely I am to be personally attractive to anyone, and I know also how all one's bad habits and tricks of manner are able to be positively repellent. But if we two were alone in an enemy's country, and found ourselves to fight the good fight better together, or if

we were in imminent peril—all those personal details would sink into in-significance before our common aims and mutual sympathy. And that, really, is after all, our position today. Aloneness is not a matter of num-bers or of neighborhood. If you marry me, it will be as a means of greater usefulness, and helpfulness, and our union (like those of the Salvation Army) will be a new consecration of our lives to the service of humanity in the way we think best. That, indeed, is the only thing that enables me to contemplate without shame the fact that I, personally, have so much to gain by it, and you (as the world will say) so much to lose. I do not need to tell you how much I should prefer that you were *not* a person of station and good connections and some wealth; it will not be very pleas-ant to me to have to face the things that will be said about me on this score. Except insofar as they lend themselves to our joint effectiveness your "advantages" are obvious drawbacks to one who is both poor and proud.[54]

Sidney triumphed. "Reason and not love won me," she later ex-plained.[55] When he received her letter accepting him, Sidney sent her his photograph, but she returned it instantly, saying, "Let me have your head only—it is the head only I am marrying."

Months later, she wrote: "Dear Sidney—I will try to love you—but do not be impatient."

The wedding ceremony in St. Pancreas's vestry took ten minutes. Beatrice's sister called it "prosaic and sordid," but a Fabian witness noted: "Beatrice looked remarkably well, being for once tidily dressed." The couple exchanged gold rings inscribed "*pro bono publico*" (for the public good), and Malcolm Muggeridge (husband of Beatrice's niece) reports, "Sidney implanted a kiss on his bride, an experience com-parable, I imagine, with kissing the big toe of a marble saint."[56]

"The only thing I regret," Beatrice said, "is parting with my name. I do resent that . . . Exit Beatrice Potter, Enter Beatrice Webb, or rather Mrs. Webb, Sidney Webb, for I lose, alas, both names."

Directly from St. Pancreas the couple hurried to board a train for Glasgow to participate in the Trades Union Congress and then on to Ireland to inspect the municipal cellars and to gather sociological data. Love would not be permitted to interrupt the advancement of mankind.

Beatrice had frequently liked to boast of her sex appeal, raising a good many Fabian eyebrows. Margaret Cole reports that for years, Shaw said that "Beatrice sampled all the members of the Fabian executive committee in order to decide which one of them she wanted to marry. (There is not a word of truth in this story; its explanation may possibly be that Shaw could never face the fact that Beatrice preferred the ugly and grubby Sidney to his own much more attractive self.)"[57]

Beatrice took her loving in spurts between work. Once, in a rush of emotion, she jumped up from her desk, threw herself upon Sidney's knee, raised his small hand affectionately, and nibbled his fingers.

As for sex, she later wrote, "Physical nature had to some extent dried up at 35 after ten years' stress and strain of purely brain-working and sexless life."

Muggeridge says: "His little legs seldom reached the ground . . . and I wondered how it would have been possible for Mrs. Webb's long, lithe body to sit upon so tiny a lap, as she claimed happened when they broke off their labours after a little while—her term— spooning."[58]

A. L. Rowse wickedly wondered "whether they slept with a fountain-pen between them, as saintly medievals were apt to do with a sword . . . One can almost hear Sidney saying, 'We could not love each other so well, loved we not our work and our duty more.' "[59]

Like a good wife, Beatrice was reconciled, in time, to her husband's ugliness, untidiness, Cockney speech and manners. Sidney perspired easily. Muggeridge says she used to issue bulletins: "as 'Sidney sweats!' or, explaining the impossibility of their sharing a bedroom, 'Sidney snores!'—which he seemed to find totally inoffensive, even, perhaps, endearing."[60]

There was never any question about who was the boss in the Webb partnership. A. L. Rowse says that Douglas Cole told him how Beatrice "dealt with the royal 'We' " on occasions: "She did not take breakfast, merely a cup of tea; so at their hotel (at Labor Party conferences) she gave orders in the form 'We do not take toast with Sidney's breakfast.' "[61]

Bertrand Russell, who spent weekends with the Webbs, said they were "the most completely married" couple he had ever known. Listening to Sidney on a walk, Russell would say, "I know just what Beatrice is saying at this moment."

The Webbs were of course more than a marriage: they were a writing collective, a force for social reform; their work together is still moving and shaking the world. As Laborite Clement Attlee said in his eulogy at their interment in Westminster Abbey (which was attended by 229 Fabians in Parliament and 10 in the Cabinet): "Millions are living fuller and freer lives today because of the work of Sidney and Beatrice Webb."

BERNARD SHAW HOBBLES INTO MATRIMONY

Said Oscar Wilde, "One should always be in love. That is one of the reasons one should never marry." Bernard Shaw, who thought he knew better than his compatriot what women were up to, got to the heart of the matter: "It is a woman's business to get married as soon as possible, and a man's to keep unmarried as long as possible."

Shaw was as good as his word. He never got the marrying business out of his mind or his plays. After his first seduction at twenty-nine, by the widow Jenny Patterson, he never stopped pursuing women. But he deftly eluded the ultimate trap several times. Some of his later affairs were protracted; he emerged battle-scarred from a five-year relationship with the beautiful red-haired and blue-eyed Fabian artist Bertha Newcombe. Beatrice Webb, who had almost succumbed to Shaw's bold way with attractive women, congratulated her: "You are well out of it, Miss Newcombe. If you had married Shaw he would not have remained faithful to you. . . . In his relationship with women he is vulgar—if not worse—it is a vulgarity which includes cruelty and springs from vanity. . . . A good riddance!"[62]

Beatrice, safe now, having fastened on to Sidney Webb, boasted for years about her variety of suitors. Shaw had not been easily put off. Malcolm Muggeridge wrote in his memoir, *The Green Stick:*

"She told me that the first time they were alone together, Shaw 'simply threw himself upon me.' It was something . . . that he did to every woman, and she had so sternly rebuffed him that nothing of the kind ever happened again."[63]

Shaw even flirted with the wives of his friends, Muggeridge was told, and actually became the "Sunday husband" of Kate Salt, an assiduous Fabian. He withdrew graciously, drawing a profit by using Kate as his heroine in *Candida.*

In her diary, as Hesketh Pearson said, Beatrice Webb said of Shaw's philandering: "He imagines he gets to know women by making them in love with him. Just the contrary. His stupid gallantries bar him from the friendship of women who are either too sensible, too puritanical or too much otherwise engaged to care to bandy personal flatteries with him."[64]

Shaw met Miss Charlotte Payne-Townshend at the rectory in Wilt-shire, rented by the Webbs. The guests spent many hours debating socialist theories, bicycling, and going on walking tours (still debat-ing). Charlotte was impressed with the tall, witty dialectician who read aloud his unactable plays to the house party.

The green-eyed, wealthy Miss Payne-Townshend, an Irish aristo-crat, had turned philanthropic missionary for socialism and women's rights after having been cruelly jilted by Axel Munthe—who had not yet written his *Story of San Michele*—allegedly because he thought her not sexy enough.

Eventually, she and Shaw were the only unmarried members of the Fabian circle. One summer's end, Charlotte returned to London with Shaw and became his volunteer secretary on Fabian projects. Prox-imity increased their interest in each other. "She has none of the feminine traits I had expected," he said, but noted she had "all the human qualities I had hoped for." He spent his free time in her flat above the School of Economics at 10 Adelphi Terrace.

Somewhat defensively, Shaw wrote to his paper-lover, Ellen Terry: "I am going to refresh my heart by falling in love. I love falling in love—but, mind, only with her, not with the million; somebody must marry her if she can stand him after me."

His decision came after considerable misgivings. Charlotte had come out of the Axel Munthe fiasco distrusting men and abominating the whole capitalist system of marriage ("unnatural and disastrous, de-grading and vulgar"); Shaw had long ago branded his first experience with physical sex disgusting, if not incestuous. Charlotte's distaste for marriage, however, evaporated when she saw how happy the Webbs were. If marriage worked so well for them, why not for Shaw and herself? Meanwhile, the two never became intimate; Jenny had taught Shaw caution.

Destiny, which Shaw called the Life Force, made the match. In Rome on a world tour with the Webbs, Charlotte received a wire from Shaw. He had fractured an ankle, an operation showed that he had tubercular necrosis, his foot was festering, he was desperately in need of nursing, and unless he was properly cared for, he faced the prospect of dying. As he later said to the Webbs, "Charlotte was the inevitable and predestined agent, appointed by Destiny," to save him. Charlotte caught the first train back to London.

When she entered his small room on the second floor of his moth-er's house at 29 Fitzroy Square, Charlotte was appalled. Hesketh

Pearson has described it: "The mass of matter on the table was cha-
otic: heaps of letters, pages of manuscript, books, envelopes, writing
paper, pens, inkstands, journals, butter, sugar, apples, knives, forks,
spoons . . . a neglected cup of cocoa or a half-finished plate of por-
ridge, a saucepan, and a dozen other things were mixed up indiscrim-
inately." His mother had been ordered to stay out of his room; nor
did she deal with his foot. Shaw defended his indifference to his environment: "I have long resolved myself to dust and dirt and squalor
in external matters; if seven maids with seven mops swept my den
for half a century it would make no impression on it."[65]

Charlotte lost no time on halfway measures; she went out at once
to rent a house in the country near Haslemere, where she was determined to nurse him back to health.

Shaw objected strenuously to this plan: he had to be in London to
write his dramatic criticism and—more importantly—he feared the
scandal from their living together unmarried. He protested: "Go out
and get a marriage license! It is impossible for a woman in your position to have a single man in your house." It was 1898.

Shaw polled his friends. He asked Ellen Terry: "Shall I marry my
Irish millionaire? . . . She believes in freedom, but not in marriage;
only I think I can prevail upon her. . . . What does your living wisdom say to it?"[66] The living wisdom advised him to go ahead at once.
Henry Arthur Jones agreed, but counseled him first to read what Ra-
belais's Panurge had to say about marriage. The verdict of half a dozen
others was unanimous.[67]

Shaw admitted that Miss Payne-Townshend filled his own requirements: a disgust with sex, a horror of convention, a willingness to
stand by him through fair and foul, wit, tolerance of his impudence.
And she possessed a tidy fortune which she was not averse to sharing
with him. His own annual income put him in the poverty class. Finally, he said, he had to marry her to avoid enmeshing "our whole
circle and its interest in a scandal." All objections spent, the rest was
clear sailing.

After wrestling with her own principles and concluding that it was
better late than never to submit to "the final humiliation," Charlotte
helped him into a cab and on the way from Haslemere stopped to
buy the wedding ring, "the symbol of slavery," before going to the
West Strand Registry House.

On the license Shaw described himself as forty-two, a bachelor and
a journalist. He was wearing his customary ragged, leather-patched

jacket; the bride was fashionably dressed. He was standing on one leg, supported by crutches, and grinning. There were two witnesses, one of them his Fabian colleague Graham Wallas.

"The registrar never imagined I could possibly be the bridegroom," Shaw said; "he took me for the inevitable beggar who completes all wedding processions. Wallas, over 6 feet tall, was so obviously the hero of the occasion that the registrar was on the point of marrying him to my betrothed. But Wallas, thinking the formula rather too strong for a mere witness, hesitated at the last moment and left the prize to me."[68]

Shaw could not resist making comic capital of the occasion. He dispatched an anonymous announcement to the *Star*:

> As a lady and gentleman were out driving in Henrietta st., Covent-Garden yesterday, a heavy shower drove them to take shelter in the office of the Superintendent Registrar there, and in the confusion of the moment he married them. The lady was an Irish lady named Miss Payne-Townshend, and the gentleman was George Bernard Shaw.
>
> Startling as was the liberty undertaken by the Henrietta st. official it turned out well. Miss Payne-Townshend is an Irish lady with an income many times the volume of that which "Corno di Bassetto" used to earn, but to that happy man, being a vegetarian, the circumstance is of no moment. The lady is interested in the London School of Economics, and that is the common ground on which the brilliant couple met. Years of married bliss to them.[69]

Charlotte lamented to Webb: "It is a trying thing to be married to a Sprite, but a Sprite with necrosis is the devil."

The master of paradox was not embarrassed by accusations of hypocrisy. He gave any number of versions of how he came to marry.

"She married me because she thought I was a genius. When all that money was left to her (£100,000) she looked round for a useful object. Beatrice Webb intended her to marry Graham Wallas, but I got in first."

Later, he said: "The only difficulty I had to surmount was poverty. It was only when I married wealth that I was able to settle down and write unactable plays like *Back to Methusaleh*."

Years afterward he told Mrs. Laden, his housekeeper, "I never proposed to my wife, you know. It was she who proposed to me and carried me off to marry her."[70]

In time he explained that his love for Charlotte was nonsexual: it was a "moral passion." She was over forty, too dangerous an age for her to have her first child. He would not assume the risk involved.

We now know that Charlotte would never have married him unless he agreed not to consummate the marriage. He had once said, seriously, that prophylaxis is one of the devil's devices. Mrs. Patch, his last secretary, wrote that she could never forget Mrs. Shaw's remark: "Babies! Who could like them? Disgusting little things!"[71] In the dozens of photographs in which Shaw posed with children, he was never seen fondling them. After Charlotte's death, Eleanor O'Connell asked Shaw whether he was sorry they had no children. He said of Charlotte, "She had a feeling against children, but sometimes I have been sorry that I was not more insistent on that point." He paused, then added ruefully: "I don't think I ought to have married. I am not of the marrying sort."[72]

St. John Ervine, who knew Charlotte Shaw well, said, "Charlotte, who was a very remarkable woman, a woman of highly individualized character totally different in every respect from GBS, loathed the whole thought of sex, and she would not marry anybody unless there was an agreement that the marriage should not be consummated, and Charlotte died a virgin. . . . The extraordinary thing about these two very dissimilar people was they were devoted to each other. GBS loved her dearly and she was devoted to him. He once said to me, 'If Charlotte were dying I know an infallible way of bringing her back to life.' And I said, 'What's that, G.B.?' And he replied, 'I should take to my bed and say I was dying. And Charlotte would have come out of the grave to help GBS.' "[73]

Charlotte had revealed her capacity for inner passion to Axel Munthe, before her marriage; later, after her marriage, she wrote with deep feeling to T. E. Lawrence. Reading her letters to Lawrence after her death, Shaw said that only then did he realize that in their forty-odd years of living together he had never really known her.

Shaw was faithful to his wife, though some suggest there is evidence he had intercourse with the raven-haired actress Mrs. Pat Campbell ("you elegant charmer")—she who said that if the vegetarian Shaw were given a beefsteak, no woman in London would be safe.

One phone conversation Charlotte heard between Mrs. Pat and Shaw provoked her; she was miserable for days, then made a scene. It ended with Shaw pledging "only let me have my dreams out." Before Mrs. Campbell retreated, she told Shaw: "It's difficult not to love you—more than I ought to love you." To this Shaw is said to have responded, "Very well, go. The loss of a woman is not the end of the world. You have wounded my vanity: an inconceivable audacity, an unpardonable crime."

In his *Sixteen Self-Sketches*, Shaw wrote a revealing chapter about his marriage, entitled "To Frank Harris on Sex in Biography":

"Not until I was past 40 did I earn enough to marry without seeming to marry for money, nor my wife at the same age without suspicion of being drawn by sex starvation. As man and wife we found a new relation in which sex had no part. It ended the old gallantries, flirtations, and philandering for both of us. Even of these it was the ones that were never consummated that left the longest and kindliest memories. Do not forget that all marriages are different, and that marriage between young people, followed by parentage, must not be lumped in with childless partnerships between middle-aged people who have passed the age at which the bride can safely bear a first child."[74]

Ten minutes past the midnight Charlotte died, Mrs. Laden went to inform Shaw. He gave her a perplexed look as if he were trying to grasp the fact, but he did not go up to his wife's room. Early in the morning, the housekeeper told Robert Minney, she found him on his knees by Charlotte's bed with his hands joined in prayer.[75]

Was Shaw taking no chances? He believed not in an anthropomorphic God, but in the "Life Force," and Charlotte was an atheist who did not pray. Was Mrs. Laden inventing a sympathetic anecdote?

The truth may be that GBS, who bragged he was unsentimental, was letting down his guard because he was alone.

St. John Ervine, his close friend, said: "Shaw was a very emotional man, which was a fact that few people realized, and so ashamed of being emotional and so eager to get rid of the reputation of being emotional, that he pretended to a callousness that wasn't true of him. When GBS was staying once with Lady Gregory and Yeats was there, Yeats told me afterwards that they were talking about death one day, and GBS said that death to him was comic, and greatly shocked both of them. My explanation of it was that that was an attempt to disguise his hate and horror of it."[76]

"Youth" and the Lady

When Samuel L. Clemens went to the Holy Land to write a series of newspaper articles that he later turned into *The Innocents Abroad* by Mark Twain, he became friends with the son of a wealthy, self-made coal operator from Elmira, New York, who had an exquisite photograph of his sister, Olivia Langdon, in his cabin. Sam fell instantly in love with the subject of the miniature and never fell out of love through all the years of their idyllic marriage.

It took a bit of doing for the thirty-five-year-old, breezy writer from the West to win the twenty-five-year-old frail and charming Livy. He took her to Steinway Hall on their first date to hear Dickens read from *David Copperfield;* they held hands; she permitted him to call again. There followed three proposals, which she rejected—her father was not impressed by Sam's cigars and rough speech—but after the third proposal, Livy softened and agreed he might visit her as a "sister." When Sam dropped in on the Langdons, during a whirlwind northeastern lecture tour, and announced, "The calf has returned; may the prodigal have some breakfast?," it became clear to Mr. Langdon that Livy was in love, but before he agreed to their engagement, he asked for character references.

Sam wasn't taking chances with his cronies; he came up with six letters, of which two were from clergymen. Despite his precautions, the references were not altogether complimentary. In his *Autobiography,* Clemens says, the mildest one, from his former Sunday School teacher, expressed "the conviction that I would fill a drunkard's grave." Langdon asked him, "Haven't you a friend in the world?" To which Sam replied, "Apparently not." Already on the suitor's side, Langdon said, "Then I'll be your friend myself. Take the girl. I know you better than they do." [77]

Before the wedding, Sam promised Livy's papa complete reformation. He swore he would give up smoking. (This was the man who had puffed his first stogie at eight and whose mother was still lighting up at sixty-seven.) No more bawdy jokes, no more profanity, no more hard liquor. And before they came to the altar, Sam sent Livy more than two hundred love letters. "I believe in you," said Livy, "even as I believe in the Savior." Sam was not too sure he'd trust her Savior.

After the ceremony in the Langdon parlor, the bridal pair set out for Niagara Falls in a private railway car offered by the president of the Pennsylvania Northern Central as a gesture to the Langdons. Their wedding present from the now jubilant Mr. Langdon was a completely furnished elegant home.

Clemens's reformation never came about; all the old habits crept back; Livy slowly gave up attempts to civilize the husband she called Youth. But he did try; less than a year after their honeymoon, he is reported to have remarked, half seriously, "I would deprive myself of sugar in my coffee if she wished, or quit wearing socks if she thought them immoral." But he stopped at giving up cigars. To please Livy, he went to church and pretended to listen intently to the preacher. For years he would not swear in her presence, but Livy was sympathetic; she came to accept his cussing, tantrums, occasional slugs of whiskey, foot-long cigars. It took a heap of loving to stand forty cigars a day!

Livy had not married an angel—Sam squandered her fortune on one of his pet get-rich-quick projects—but by all standards the marriage was idyllic. In his eyes, "his own dear sweetheart" was perfection; he wrote her an ardent love letter on every wedding anniversary. Their daughter Clara said her parents behaved like lovebirds, constantly kissing and caressing. Sam would take Livy's hand surreptitiously. "Then, while squeezing it with sentimental devotion, he would look around to see if any of the children were noticing. If his glance met our eyes," said Clara, "he gave a tiny toss of his head and a half-embarrassed little laugh."[78]

Clemens conceded, "After my marriage, Livy edited everything I wrote. And what is more—she not only edited my works—she edited me!" There was not a trace of regret in his admission. He always listened patiently to her criticism. Once, when she insisted that he excise *stench* and *offal* from his manuscript, he did object—"You are steadily weakening the English language, Livy"—but he drew a line through the offending words. We do not know to what extent Livy was responsible for there being no evidence of sex or lechery in his later works.

After years of being an invalid, Livy died, and Sam's spirit was crushed. Pangs of conscience set in; he regretted that he had caused her mental suffering, particularly by his public flailing against orthodox religion. He had converted her to a mild brand of atheism. "I am full of remorse for things done and said in these thirty-four years of married life that hurt my Livy's heart," he said.[79]

Relieved that her suffering was over, he gave way to expressions of bleak pessimism and increased heterodoxy. He damned the whole human race. His life had hurt him in three of his children—his one small son had died and Sam had blamed himself for supposed neglect; one daughter had become an epileptic; another, his cherished Susy, had died of meningitis. He had one ray of light left—Clara, who married the pianist Osip Gabrilowitsch.

A year after Livy's death, Sam wrote his sister-in-law: "The wedding is never otherwise than a tragic event, and all present should be clothed in black, and upon the wedding bell should be written 'A day is coming when one of these hearts shall break.' "[80]

From the day after Livy was buried, Samuel L. Clemens wore only white. It is the color of mourning in many lands.

OH, THE BLARNEY!

In his autobiography, *Home Before Night: Memories of an Irish Time and Place*, Hugh Leonard, Ireland's distinguished playwright—*Da, A Life, Stephen D*—tells how he met his wife.

As a sharp young writer who enjoyed using his wit on an audience, he lectured to a group one evening and managed, in one way or another, to insult everyone there. Evidently he had missed someone, however. A pretty Belgian girl, Paule Jacquet, presented herself before him after the lecture and demanded to know why he had neglected to insult *her*.

Leonard (whose real name is John Keyes Byrne) married Paule in 1955. Today they live in Dalkey, County Dublin, and have a daughter, Danielle.

In his interviews, Leonard is not above pulling a reporter's leg when discussing his wife. He refers to her as "my present wife"—he has never had another—because, he explains, it keeps her on her toes. When a reporter in New York, where the couple was visiting for the opening of one of Leonard's plays, asked him where his wife was, he replied, quite cheerfully, that she was out spending his unearned royalties.

ONE FRENCHMAN COULD BE WRONG

Jules Verne (*Around the World in Eighty Days*) complained, "All the delightful ladies whom I honor with my attentions invariably become

engaged within a fortnight. It is really a bizarre attribute of mine."
For a Frenchman, that is quite a confession.

But he had himself to fault for his madcap antics and risqué *bons
mots*. He was once head over heels in love with a girl who had "eyes
of velvet darkness," but when he heard her say that her whalebone
corset was hurting her ribs, he volunteered to help her: "Ah, why
may I not go fishing for whales on that coast?" That spelled *fini* to
the romance.

Verne did eventually marry. On his honeymoon, he took his bride
to the Louvre. Pointing to the statue of the Venus de Milo, he said,
"This is the only woman you need ever be jealous of."

H. L. Mencken Joins the Booboisie

When someone told H. L. Mencken that marriage is a wonderful institution, he bit his stogie and drawled, "Yes, but who would want
to live in an institution?"

A hundred jibes on wedlock are attributed to him. Charles Angoff, his assistant on *The American Mercury*, kept a notebook handy
in his desk; he recorded that the boss once told him that wedlock is
"far and away the most sanitary and least harmful of all the impossible forms of the man-woman relationship, though I would sooner
jump off the Brooklyn Bridge than be married."[81]

In print, Mencken railed against women, calling them leeches, sluts,
whores, and vultures, but he enjoyed buying his friends' wives and
sweethearts princely gifts, flattering them, and acting the chivalrous
Confederate planter in their presence. At the *Mercury* office, he kept
on preaching misogynist gospel to bachelor Angoff: "Only a jackass
ever talks over his affairs with a woman, whether she be his sweetheart, wife, or sister, or mother."[82]

He was disgusted when a friend lyricized his fiancée ("She has him
by the short hairs, all right"). He assured Angoff: "No jezebel will
ever snare me into one of those 'obsequies' " [his term for weddings].
. . . "When you begin to push fifty, you really don't need to get
yourself wet in the central heating so often as before. Sometimes a
whole week goes by now and sexually I'm a Prohibitionist. I'd rather
drink than diddle now."[83]

The Sage of Baltimore, editor of *The Smart Set* and *The American
Mercury*, had for years built up his public image as a heathen, an

abominator of the Church ("that racket"), a beer swiller, a debunker
and smasher of idols in the American marketplace. Yet like any other
southern gentleman, he would gallantly kiss a lady's hand when introduced and would melt over love poems. One could not tell a dirty
joke in his presence. One of those who knew him well said, "Within
that bibulous exterior there lurked a heart of gold."

At the age of forty-nine, without warning, the perennial bachelor
took the plunge. His young disciples were outraged; his friends rubbed
their eyes in disbelief. After a serious seven-year courtship, he was
ready for the altar. He packed a dozen cigars in his wallet, slipped
away silently, and married Sara Haardt of Alabama, an English in-
structor at Goucher who wrote short stories for women's magazines.
They had met at one of his college lectures; she had fallen for his
style.

Despite Mencken's efforts to keep his heresy under wraps, the
newspapers gave the wedding announcement first-page coverage, and
the publicity went on for days. George Jean Nathan, Mencken's alter
ego in *Nathan and God, Inc.*, skulked down Shubert Alley to avoid
reporters. Hank had gone too far; it was a breach of contract, god-
dammit! He sent Mencken a blistering note. Mencken beamed and
advised Nathan to go and do likewise: "It is a grand experience to be
able to look a hotel detective in the eye."

The headlines had fun: "WEDLOCK SCOFFLAW TO MARRY"; and "ET
TU, H.L."; "MENCKEN, ARCH CYNIC, CAPITULATES TO CUPID."

To avoid publicity, Mencken had given reporters the wrong date,
but it didn't work; they smoked him out of his lair. One reporter
pressed Sara Haardt for a comment on Mencken's reference to the
institution of marriage. She said, "Mr. Mencken's present views on
marriage will have to come from him. I agree with him on everything he has ever written about matrimony. You must remember,
though, that he was writing in the abstract." What about his saying
"Marrying is like enlisting in a war or being sentenced to a form of
penal servitude that makes the average American husband into a
slave"? Sara replied with extraordinary cool, "I think Mr. Mencken's
views are well put, and he's absolutely right. They don't apply to every
marriage, however."[84]

Mencken had picked his own rector to officiate at the ceremony,
a one-time contributor to *The American Mercury*. He told his publisher, Philip Goodman, "The nuptial high mass will be very quiet.

. . . We shall follow the rite of the Church of England—after all, a very high-toned ecclesiastical organization, say what you will. I have rejected all evangelical bids."[85]

Step one in the reformation: he had been reared as a Lutheran; obviously Sara was pleasing her family. As Mencken wrote Goodman years after Sara's death: "She was herself a complete agnostic, and much more anti-clerical than I am, but I had to call in a High Church Episcopal rector for her funeral, to avoid scandalizing her Alabama relatives beyond endurance just as I had to call in another to marry us. In the latter case, there was the further consideration that civil marriage is unknown in Maryland. One must either submit to a pastor or go outside of the state."[86]

When *The New York Times* used a Mencken title as a headline for its story of the wedding ("MENCKEN FINDS WISDOM/RECANTS JIBES/AT TENDER PASSION")—recalling his book *In Defense of Wisdom*—Mencken was compelled to concede, "I formerly was not as wise as I am now." He added, in character, "Being married with all your friends about you is as private and discriminating as eating in the window of a restaurant."

Sara brought a Victorian wedding certificate by Currier and Ives to the ceremony. For once Mencken was dressed to the nines. Bride and groom smiled a bit uneasily as they were showered with rice (he had once blasted the custom as "a barbaric relic of primitive tribal rites").

Their honeymoon was in Canada because Sara wanted to see the historic sites. It was the first of many concessions. On the honeymoon he wrote many *apologiae pro vita sua*, but Sara was in the heart of the matter; he sent an urgent plea to Dorothy Hergesheimer: "If you write to her say nothing about my heavy drinking or about the trouble with that girl in Red Lion, Pa. in 1917. I still maintain that I was innocent of any unlawful or immoral purpose."[87]

He answered Clarence Darrow's congratulatory note: "All I ask is your prayers. Get on your knees and let the Holy Spirit feel the full force-power of your eloquence."[88]

From Canada he complained to another friend: "Jesus, what a swell hotel! *Two Gideon Bibles*—and one towel."

Back home he found an apartment near his favorite *Bierstube*, Schellhase's, famous for the best Pilsner in town. But he was a changed man: "In marriage, as they say, there must be give and take." He assured everyone he'd never felt better in his life: "Sara is the grandest of gals, and will help me in my chosen art. As for me, I have promised to behave with relative decency. I am to be allowed five sessions at Schellhase's a week, not counting the anniversaries of the great German victories. More details anon. I count on your advice. But don't tell me I am too young."[89]

To Blanche Knopf he wrote: "Enemies have told the bride that I am a beer drinker. I am having a hard time putting down the slander."[90]

Though Sara obviously brought about some changes, she was compassionate and let him keep his cast-iron plug hat, black outside and white inside, beside the fireplace, to be used as an ashtray. "I spit in it," he confessed. "But only once! The ensuing uproar dissuaded me therefrom."

To a disciple outraged by Mencken's wedding ceremony, he said, "I have no objection to honeymoons, nor to church weddings, nor to wearing a plug hat. In all matters of manners, I am, and always have been, a strict conformist. My dissents are from ideas, not from decorums, and I do not favor wearing old clothes, or living in eccentric houses, or making odd noises."[91]

Unblushingly, he admitted to Blanche Knopf, "I am henpecked, but am getting used to it. It begins to seem that I'll make a perfect husband."[92]

Angoff, who adored the Menckens, wrote: "Apparently, Sara knew how to manage her benedict—she let him talk as he wanted to and about everything he wanted to, and she never took issue with him on major subjects—major, that is, to him. . . . When he railed against 'the bloody English' and 'the stinking frogs' and 'the dirty wops,' she merely smiled . . . she lived up to his notion of the ideal wife: 'A woman who smiles at her husband's prejudices, ignores his ignorance, tolerates his peccadilloes, and is ready to embrace him, even immediately after Mass, as soon as the shade is down, and even before she has a chance to disrobe completely!' "[93]

W. A. Swanberg, drawing on Sara Mayfield's The Constant Nymph, summed up Sara Mencken's refining influence on her husband by saying that in time he began to swear by such bourgeois virtues as honor, courtesy, good taste, payment of one's debts, and orderly living. He came to disapprove of his old friends Ernest Boyd and Scott Fitzgerald because they drank too much and owed money; of Sinclair Lewis, because he made drunken scenes and short-changed Paul de Kruif in the Arrowsmith collaboration; of Theodore Dreiser, because he was deficient not only in taste but also in courtesy and common sense; and of Thomas Wolfe, because he lived chaotically and treated Aline Bernstein as no gentleman would.[94]

"While her death five years after their marriage was expected (she had been seriously ill), it was a shock to Mencken," Angoff writes. "Not once did he complain about her illness—how it cut into his time, how it complicated his life, how expensive it was—even though she spent about half their married life in the hospital or under the care of physicians."[95]

Once, in a taxi, Angoff found him strangely silent; Mencken explained that Sara had been very sick:

"I got worried in the middle of the night early this week. She was in terrible pain. I got a couple of quacks down to look at her, and they had her taken to the hospital right away. Her pleurisy was acting up, and there was a pile of complications—they had to tap the pleural cavity. She was filled up like a balloon. What a courageous girl, Angoff. I've never known the likes of her. Not one goddam peep. . . . What a life, what a life! These quacks don't know. They're all witch doctors, shamans. . . ."

"Well," said Angoff, "if there is anything I can do . . ."

"Nothing, not a goddam thing, Angoff. God himself can't do a thing. He never even heard of pleurisy. The son of a bitch knows a great deal about pleurisy, but He isn't talking. That's the real trouble, of course, with Sara. I wanted to stick around the hospital, but she told me to attend to my business. What courage, what consideration!"[96]

In the early morning of the day Sara died, Mencken dropped into Hamilton Owens's office, drawn and lachrymose, and told him, "When I married Sara, the doctors said she could not live more than three years. Actually, she lived five, so that I had two more years of happiness than I had any right to expect."[97]

For a year after her death, he floundered, finally pulling himself together by working hard on *The American Language*.

The change to a compassionate and warmhearted Mencken is seen in the epitaph he composed for himself:

"If, after I depart this vale, you ever remember me and have some thought to please my ghost, forgive some sinner and wink your eye at some homely girl."

THE RIVALS

Nothing was sacred to Sinclair Lewis, not even his own wedding. None of his friends ever praised his good taste, but Hal thought he was funny, and—to a point—he was. But his sense of humor was odd and could be insulting. An example was the time he was guest of honor at a Yale alumni dinner. Warmed up by bourbon, he struggled to his feet to respond to the round of laudatory speeches, bowed solemnly, then grinned broadly and snarled: "When I was in college, you fellows didn't give a damn about me, and I'm here to say that now, I don't give a damn about you." And he slid into his chair. His audience was grimly silent.[98]

In view of how he behaved about the wedding ceremony, it is worth noting that it was he who wanted his marriage to Dorothy Thompson to be ultra conventional, nothing like his first, to Grace Hegger at the Ethical Culture Lecture Room. (Even the bride said *that* one fell flat: "no bridal veil, no church aisle, no ritual, no lovely tulle-swathed attendant to the bride.")

Miss Thompson, then on a newspaper assignment, wrote back to Lewis that she too was all for a formal ceremony: "I will marry you so gladly with the old marriage service: for better or for worse in sickness and in health, and forsaking all others—until death do us part. Hal!—Hal!"

Hal wrote her ecstatically from Naples: "I kiss your eyebrows, and temples and heart."[99]

He wanted the works, and he had everything his own way. After a civil service in fashionable St. Martin's Registry, London, they had a Church of England ceremony in the Savoy Chapel. Then he arranged an elaborate luncheon to which he invited the cream of British literary society, including Rebecca West, Hugh Walpole, and Mrs. Bertrand Russell. Champagne corks popped and Hal sat back grinning as the toasts hailed him as the greatest American novelist and Dorothy as the most prestigious and fearless journalist in the world.

When it was Lewis's turn to respond, he couldn't resist buffoonery. He rose, surveyed the luminaries with his bulging, bloodshot eyes, stretched his tight wing collar, took a sheet of paper from his vest pocket, put on his gold-rimmed glasses, and pretended to read. Everyone sat back prepared for a literary gem.

Lewis let them have what he considered humor. Punctuating it with occasional fake coughs, he launched into a long mock speech on the jute industry over the whole British Empire, statistics and all, in the style of a corporation mogul addressing a convention of jute dealers. He returned to his seat with a pleased expression that seemed to say, I have heard your damn toasts. Now what do you think of my clever speech?

No one applauded; no one laughed. There were a few uneasy coughs. Dorothy had shifted in her chair as Lewis spoke; her tugs at his coat failed to stop him. Later she said she had been on the verge of throwing up.

Their summer honeymoon in a caravan with a trailer attached was a fiasco from the start. Each brought along a typewriter and reams of paper. Lewis was revising *Dodsworth*; Dorothy had a dozen articles to wire. Naturally, most of their time was spent writing.

A stormy quarrel marred their first stop at Durham. "Tonight," Dorothy wrote in her diary, "because I disagreed with him in an argument he got up and left me sitting alone in a public restaurant."

Pecking away at two typewriters apparently was not Dorothy's idea of a honeymoon, though she was as responsible as Hal. "I can't bear it," she wrote. "I *won't* bear it. I had rather go and work in someone's kitchen than lead this sort of life, chased, pursued, harassed by fear's fear."[100]

In his heavy boozing and drunken rages, Lewis was not the model benedict. Biographer Mark Schorer writes: "Once when they were hiking, each shouldering a pack, they approached the inn of a secluded village. Lewis proposed that his wife carry both packs and follow him meekly into the inn. The innkeeper responded with predictable astonishment and contempt: 'Is it customary, sir, for men in America to allow their wives to carry the luggage?' Lewis replied, 'Certainly. That's why we marry.' "[101]

Dorothy gave a less facetious reason for marrying him. She said she married him because she loved him. "Why else should I have married him, considering my position when we met, except because of that pull of genius and my faith in his almost agonized protestations, at times, that he *needed* me."[102]

Lewis could not cope with a rival in his own household. He wanted catering, and this Dorothy couldn't give him; she had far too many journalistic commitments. She was away too often on lecture tours (once to as many as forty cities). But he wrote her letters professing ardent love. When they were together, they quarreled like hostile competitors. Headlines about her bothered him. He once shouted, "Goddamnit, if I hear anything more about 'conditions' and 'situations,' I'll kill myself!" When a mob of reporters came to interview them, he sulked jealously because they centered attention on Dorothy. When he suggested that Dorothy join him on a trip to Florida, she replied that she had to stay in Europe for lecture dates. "He then got angry," she said, "sneered at me—'You with your important little lectures—You with your brilliant people. . . . *You* want to talk about foreign politics which *I* am too ignorant to understand.' When he talks so my heart freezes up. And then in a minute he is very sweet again. Oh, my God, I really don't know whether I love or hate him—but tonight I was *bored* with him. . . . He is like a vampire—he absorbs all my vitality, all my energy, all my beauty—I get incredibly dull. If ever I begin to talk well he interrupts the conversation. He is not above calling me down in front of people because the dinner is bad. . . . He orders me to send flowers to Noel Coward who is ill in the hospital, but not once since our marriage has he ever sent flowers to me, nor did he do so when I was sick. . . . He insults people in the home which is mine as well as his—the house where I am hostess. He invites strangers to dinner and goes away and leaves them. All social finesse, all delicacy & gaiety of intercourse, all." She concluded: "It's either give up work or give up Hal. My work! I cannot live & work in a world where I cannot plan from one day to the next."

Lewis retorted that her work ruined their marriage and robbed him of his creative powers. Finally, she told him, "I must save myself. I really tried hard not to love you: I confess it. I have been too hurt in my life, Hal, before, to dare even to think of being hurt in the same way again."[103]

Eventually, they separated. He began to satirize her publicly. He took up with a young actress, Marcella Powers, whom he introduced as his niece.

From her apartment, Dorothy wrote him: "There is a bedroom for you, very quiet and comfortable, should you care to live there." Repeatedly, she wrote: "Darling—come home soon—I count the days."[104]

Hal never came back.

Lewis asked for a divorce: "We have not lived together for four and a half years," he wrote her, "and there is no chance that we shall ever live together again. I know that it is impossible for me, and I imagine that it is impossible for you, to compose any sort of normal and decent life so long as we are held together in this bondage." He suggested the grounds: "desertion, mental cruelty, or what you please, with speed, ease, and little or no publicity."[105]

She responded: "I do not like a divorce and I am not going to get one. . . . I have never been able to repudiate our marriage, even to myself. Now you ask me to do it publicly. Such a step would be an unbearable self-violation. . . . I still live every day in the crazy illusion that the door will open and you will come back—as though from Bermuda."[106]

He retorted: "You say that your highest desire was that 'our marriage should be productive—creative.' Well, to my powers of creation, it has been disastrous. That is why I want it broken, before it is too tragically late. Do you relish the notion of keeping me lonely and disfranchised, year on year until I die? I'm sure you don't . . . Dorothy! Be generous!"[107]

Marcella Powers waited patiently in the wings.

Dorothy saw that it was hopeless to persevere. "I shall continue to give you your way. . . . If you wish to divorce me, I shall not contest the suit. I shall keep still. . . . I will not go into court and make a case out against you. I would fight through all the courts and through all eternity for the exclusive custody of Michael. That is my only condition."[108]

Four months later Lewis agreed to give her custody of Michael. The divorce followed.

The marriage was one more proof of the time-honored argument that no two literary "egoarchs" can live together or work in harmony under the same roof.

"You Want a Mother, Jemmie, not a Wife"

In his review of J. M. Barrie's *Peter Pan*, Max Beerbohm put his finger on the playwright's obsession: "To remain, like Mr. Kipling, a boy, is not at all uncommon. But I do not know anyone who remains, like Mr. Barrie, a child." Barrie took this as a compliment: "Nothing that happens after we are twelve matters much." And like Peter Pan, he romanticized: "I want always to be a little boy and have fun."

Fourteen years after the little boy from Kirriemuir married, he learned he could not have it both ways.

It came as a shock. On the day before his play *What Every Woman*

Knows closed, he was at his desk in his country place, Black Lake, Farnham, preparing the evidence he was to give jointly with Bernard Shaw and G. K. Chesterton to the Censorship Committee in London. Hunt, the gardener, interrupted apologetically, looking profoundly disturbed. He told the Guv'nor he could no longer hold back. He and his wife knew that Mrs. Barrie was carrying on with the novelist Gilbert Cannan.

Arthur H. Calder-Marshall reports the substance of the affair: "Cannan played the romantic ass, while Barrie flirted with the Duchess of Sutherland and others in London. Gilbert could have solaced Mary in the seclusion of Black Lake Cottage, Farnham, if only he had tiptoed down the corridor to her bedroom. Instead, to preserve her reputation, he got a ladder and climbed through the window, leaving the gardener to find the evidence of adultery as he started to work in the morning. Mary had put the finishing touch by quarreling with the gardener about horticulture."[109]

The evidence was too clear-cut for Barrie to dismiss, and he took the train at once for his London home in Leinster Corner to confront his wife, hoping she would deny the adultery.

But when Mary found Jemmie tremulous and white in their apartment, she readily admitted her adultery, relieved that her concealments were at last at an end. She made no excuses. With as much theatrical calm as she could muster, she admitted she was deeply in love with Mr. Cannan and was determined to marry him. She wanted a divorce.

Barrie couldn't believe such a thing was happening to him. He begged her to reconsider, but she would not be budged. She chose at this time not to cite the basic cause—his impotence—but her concluding barb hit Barrie below the belt: "You want a mother, Jemmie, not a wife."

Barrie's mother fixation had been disturbing Mary for years, but she had never alluded to it. She felt certain it would disappear in time. But it didn't. The distrust of sex that Margaret Ogilvy had implanted in her third son, one of ten, was too deeply rooted. Mama had lectured him that sex was "regrettable," the sooner it was dismissed from one's mind the better, and Barrie accepted her teaching. It embarrassed him to hear his schoolmates giggle over women's underclothes on washing lines. Even more disturbing were his sex nightmares. "Greatest horror—dream I am married—wake up shrieking."[110]

The maternal obsessiveness persisted to her last day. "You are a precious God-given son to me," she wrote him when he was making a thousand pounds a year, "the light of my eyes." Given the choice between satisfying Mary Ansell Barrie or his mother, Barrie opted for the widow of Thrums.

A ladder brought the fourteen-year marriage to an open break. Cannan, who towered over the diminutive Barrie, was a blond and good-looking romantic novelist. When the facts of the marital relationship were disclosed by Mary, who was vibrant, flirtatious, and ambitious, friends who had for months suspected her affair with Cannan were sure the marriage would not last.

Biographer Janet Dunbar offers this revealing information:

"When her friends asked her why she had not left Barrie earlier, she had replied that after the shock of the honeymoon, she had hoped that her husband would take medical advice and that something could be done. But Barrie had always refused to discuss the matter, let alone do anything about it. In the end she had withdrawn into herself, and except for keeping up appearances before others, they had lived as strangers."[111]

Barrie's proposal of marriage had promised Mary much. He had hesitated for months before broaching it. He had met her when she was acting in his first play, *Walker, London.* In the prosperous playwright she perceived a handle to an impressive theatrical career. He took her to expensive after-theater suppers *à deux.* He was bewitched by all the qualities he liked in an actress: "beautiful, quite charming, a genius for preference, and able to flirt." To Barrie, an incurable flirt, flirtation was a satisfying substitute for the casting couch.

Mary readily accepted him. Then he made conditions: the engagement had to be kept secret; he himself had to break the news to his mother. The puritanical widow Ogilvy had an unspeakable moral horror of actresses.

When news of the impending divorce leaked out, mutual friends began to take sides. Mary said she was indeed sorry to have to hurt Barrie, she loved him dearly, but she had an independent life to lead, and she wanted children. She confided to H. G. Wells: "He seems to have developed the most ardent passion for me now that he has lost me; that frightens me. I must go back to what I was, but to fight that, in the circumstances, is more than I can promise to do. Poor thing, he is distracted and I am dreadfully sorry; he says he knows I would be happier with G.C. and that we ought to marry, one moment, and the next clamours for me."[112]

After several fruitless conferences, at Barrie's insistence the scene shifted to the chambers of their friend Sir George Lewis, a solicitor known for his skill in patching up marital disruptions. Sir George pleaded with Mary to return to her husband if only to head off a public scandal. He pointed out the disparity in the lovers' ages: Cannan was twenty, Mary was forty. But she replied that if she went back to Barrie, adultery would happen again.

Barrie pleaded with her, practically on his knees, and on the brink of tears, but she refused. As the offended party, he then generously offered to forgive her, going so far as to pledge that he would never again mention the affair if she cut Cannan out of her life. Impossible, she retorted. Denis MacKail said: "It was though, if she couldn't escape now, then she could never escape. She had been robbed of her happiness, and now she had found it. She didn't want anything except freedom to marry her lover, and no argument or appeal of any description could make her budge an inch."[113]

After hours of caustic exchanges, Barrie, shaken by self-pity and obvious humiliation, saw he was driven into a corner by a stubborn woman whom he now perceived he had never really known, and he begged her to accept, *faute de mieux*, a Bill of Separation on her own terms. Mary insisted on a divorce, and at once. In an outburst of generosity, Barrie told her she could keep all the cars, their chauffeur, their Black Lake cottage (actually, the house was in her name)—everything. His offer of an allowance she rejected as an insult.

Today a popular writer's divorce would hardly be earth-shaking and might in fact boost the sale of his books, but in the priggish early twentieth century, while extramarital liaisons were tolerated when discreet, divorce would ruin a writer's career.

The court proceedings in the undefended case of *Barrie* v. *Barrie & Cannan* took minutes. Barrie muttered his testimony. The gardener's wife gave her evidence. A *decree nisi*, with costs, was granted. The newspaper accounts were muted, thanks to a letter sent to friends in the press by Mary's partisans—Henry James, Gosse, Pinero, Wells, and Beerbohm.

Barrie retreated from the battlefield a crushed man, his pride hurt, irrevocably, and on the brink of mental and spiritual collapse. He felt he had failed as a husband and a man. What cut him to the quick was that so many of his close friends—Wells, the Lawrences, Bertrand Russell, among others—had abetted Mary in her adulterous deception; so few blamed her, so many others blamed him, and so few dared to side with him.

He couldn't face Leinster Corners, and moved to 3 Adelphi Terrace, across the street from Shaw. As the movers were taking the old tables away, he asked, his voice breaking, "Where is my mother's table?"

Barrie did not remarry, but entered into an intimate relationship with the widowed Sylvia Davies and her five children. He became a doting father to "my boys," played children's games with them, and indulged them extravagantly. He appointed himself their guardian when their father died and paid all family expenses. He was a boy again. In effect he was doing what Mary had told him in the solicitor's office he was best fitted for. Probably not lost on him was the irony implicit in his renewed preoccupation. He had written in *What Every Woman Knows* what would echo in his memory for years: "What we all know is that Eve was not made from a rib taken from Adam, but from his funny bone."

A perpetual mooning look betrayed his lingering despondency. Some say he was never seen laughing, and if he put out a "wee" smile it was as if Mary was inside him blocking his elfin lightness. He became a popular after-dinner speaker, but his wit was only surface froth. Inside, the vital spring had jammed.

Duchesses and wealthy widows pursued him. He proposed to Thomas Hardy's widow in a flirtatious moment, but when she accepted, he ran for cover to "my boys" in Sylvia Davies's home.

Two years after the divorce became final, Mary became Mrs. Cannan, but she was no more happy; in fact, she was less happy than she had been with Barrie. Cannan tried to keep up the romantic role with younger women. Her Galahad had turned into a crashing bore, and he couldn't give her the babies she desperately wanted. Gilbert's juices slowly trickled to a stop. How sexually satisfying he had been during his courtship of Mary is anyone's guess, but he was powerless to make Mary pregnant. He did succeed, apparently, with her maid. According to his niece, Diana Farr, "Gilbert fled in a state of mental confusion from his angry wife and the pregnant maid but also from life."[114]

Cannan became obnoxiously paranoid and schizophrenic, a rabid anti-Semite, showing greater love for animals than for people. After hanging on for thirty years, he died in an insane asylum.

Middleton Murry, the gossipy husband of Katherine Mansfield, said after Cannan's death: "What we were given to understand by Gilbert and Mary was that Barrie was guilty of unmentionable sex behaviour toward Mary. . . . And I am pretty certain that Gilbert had no sexual relation with Mary at any time. The divorce must have been a put-up job, Gilly having put himself into the role of Perseus-Galahad rescuing Andromeda, had to live up to it."[115]

Diana Farr says that according to one rumor, "while in bed with Mary, Barrie made sex with himself." But Farr is quick to discount Murry's catty statement, pointing out that he was miffed with Mary for having rejected his own sexual advances.[116]

When Barrie read several years after the divorce that Mrs. Cannan was playing a role in a theater in Broadway, a village in Worcestershire, he ordered everyone in his household to avoid that town. One day, driving back from a funeral, he neglected to repeat his injunction to his chauffeur. As the car was crossing the main street in Broadway, it swerved to avoid running down an elderly woman in its path. She was thrown to the curb in shock and narrowly escaped being killed.

After dinner that evening, Barrie's secretary, Cynthia Asquith, tells us, Barrie "white and trembling told me *who* the elderly woman was. It was Mary Cannan. What Barrie had refused to do in a trying moment in his solicitor's office he had now missed doing by an inch."[117]

Despite Barrie's reticence on the subject of his wife, he really never forgot her. If he bore grudges, he apparently kept them to himself. When he heard through friends that she was in dire financial straits, he offered assistance through an intermediary. Reluctantly, Mary accepted a regular allowance and she went to France to live. When she was informed that Barrie was dying, she came and stood by his bed silently for a few moments.

The son of a handloom weaver in Kirriemuir (romanticized in his book *Thrums*), who had come to London with £10 in his pocket and "a penny bottle of ink," bequeathed to "my dear Mary Cannan with my affectionate regards" £1,000 and a life annuity of £600. He left an estate of £173,000. He willed his secretary and close friend Cynthia Asquith £30,000.

"AM I NOT YOUR SISTER, YOUR FIANCÉE?"

André Gide was early slated for neurosis. Shortly before her death, his mother, the wife of the stern Protestant Professor Paul Gide, told him that she hoped he would marry his first cousin, Madeleine Rondeaux, with whom he had been thrown together for years and who respected him deeply. His aunt—the second repressive mother figure in his life—felt that the only thing that would relieve his emotional stresses was marriage to Madeleine. To Mme. Gide and André's aunt it was obvious that Madeleine loved him tenderly, but in her own odd, chaste fashion.

"The only thing left for me to cling to," he said, "was my love for my cousin; the will to marry her was all I still had to guide my life.[118]

He did not see Madeleine as a wife to be loved but as a surrogate mother, the embodiment of virtue. The attitude by its very nature inhibited carnal love. And the more he deliberated, the more his inner conflict grew.

Seventeen days after his mother died, Gide became engaged to Madeleine Rondeaux, under an agreement which is no longer extant. She wrote him: "Dear André, am I not your friend, your sister, your fiancée? *Sister* might perhaps seem ridiculous to others—to me it also corresponds very well to what I am, to what I feel."[119] His fiancée was apparently steering clear of any notion he might have of consummating the marriage, and she warned him, "I'm not afraid of death, but I'm afraid of marriage!" And he wrote back: "Ah, what queer people we are!"[120]

The engagement period was most harrowing for both of them. The secret of his homosexuality that he had withheld from Madeleine kept gnawing at his conscience. He was inwardly tortured by his doubt about his fitness for marriage, and he kept wondering whether an open homosexuality would not in fact be easier and more tolerable for him than marriage. Did Madeleine realize his dilemma? He was not sure. When she read the early pages of his *Le Voyage d'Urien,* she found them too incredibly shameful and revolting to continue reading the rest of the novel.

To help him resolve his critical problem he consulted a nerve specialist. Gide wanted to learn whether in the doctor's opinion he could function adequately as a husband, and whether he should have sexual relations with his wife and at the same time indulge in homosexual practices. In good conscience he asked himself if he would be fair to Madeleine.

The specialist assured him that he could marry and have children. Didn't Oscar Wilde have two children? Gide confessed to having a horror of orthodox copulation. But even more pressuring was still another basic fear: wasn't there a danger in marrying a first cousin?

The doctor told him that he was biologically virile and he should have no problem. The fact is that he had already had heterosexual relations, even if they had proved distasteful. The specialist sent him away with a firm handshake: "Get married without hesitation," he said. "You will quickly discover that all the rest exists only in your imagination."

Four months after Mme. Gide died, André and Madeleine were married in a little country church, a ceremony that he later recalled in L'Immoraliste: "I had the impression that everyone was moved and therefore I myself was moved. After leaving the church, you joined us at the bride's house for a short meal, at which there was no laughter and no shouting; then the carriage we had ordered took us away, according to the custom that associates in our minds the idea of a wedding with the vision of a departure."[121]

The newlyweds did not consummate the marriage. Neither thought this extraordinary, since it was mutually understood to be a brother-sister relationship. Gide's unpublished journal has an entry dated three months after the ceremony which furnishes a major clue: "How often, with Madeleine in the next room, have I mistaken her for my mother?" His very soul revolted at the perceived incest if they had sex. Madeleine was too pure to be defiled; he would be betraying his own purest instinct if he touched her. "What I fear she could never understand was that the spiritual force of my love is what inhibited any carnal desire."[122]

The honeymoon was seven months long, but for Gide it was a lifetime of torturing self-analysis. They drove to Switzerland and on to northern Africa, his third trip to the desert. He spent countless honeymoon hours writing Les Nourritures terrestres. A fortnight after the wedding he wrote to a friend in a rare moment of emotional release, "Now I am beginning an indefatigable rest beside the calmest of wives."

The wifely calm was only surface deception. Gide knew in his heart they were acting out their relationship in a silent struggle. There was not a word of complaint from Madeleine, but her conflict took its toll in continual migraine headaches, which troubled Gide, particularly when he saw her eating without appetite and sleeping without rest. He was annoyed with himself for making her suffer, and he felt he was taking it out brutally on Madeleine for letting him do it.

Gide was then writing a commissioned piece, his cynical tale "Manalque," which contained allusions to his homosexuality. He finished it while honeymooning in Switzerland and read parts of it to his wife before sending it to the publishers. In it he was candidly reacting to his mother's puritanical morality and his need to fulfill himself. It is a strange *cri de coeur*, a kind of artistic compensation for the humiliation he was being made to suffer and to make another suffer for his impotence. It was one more conflict in the series of battles waged between his angel, his soul, and his demon's demands on his flesh. It was a relentless search for honesty in facing up to his inner confusions, "Was it not virtue itself I loved?" [123]

Two decades later, Madeleine said that for a long time she knew nothing of her husband's homosexuality. She had some idea of what homosexuals were and what they did, and she had in the course of time read enough to recognize the signs in her husband's conduct. Gide himself said after she died that she must have known almost from the start but preferred to plead innocent of the knowledge, probably for the sake of the family name.

On reading the newspaper account of the Oscar Wilde trials and the sentence of two years in prison at hard labor, Madeleine told Gide: "Did you read the sentence given the two English defendants? Inclosed is a newspaper clipping on the subject. If the details are accurate, the penalty of hard labor would be worthy of being added, as an extra chapter, to those of the sinister *House of the Dead*—or also Dante should have thought of it. It's frightful, isn't it?"

In the early period of the marriage, despite her agreement not to force herself on him, she tried, with the sudden daring of a bride, to draw him to physical love, but when her advances met no response, she blamed herself: "I am not attractive enough. . . . It's all my fault," she thought. She turned to endearing empathy: "I have had the best of your soul, the tenderness of your childhood and youth, and I know that, living or dead, I would have the soul of your old age."

In *Et nunc manet in te*, Gide reveals a flash of his attitude toward his wife in her old age: "I never loved Madeleine more than when she was old, bent, suffering from varicose sores on her legs which she allowed me to dress, almost crippled, and giving in at least to my attentions with sweet and tender gratitude." [124]

During the honeymoon, when their carriage drove into an Italian town, it was surrounded by shouting, gleeful *ragazzi*. Madeleine saw that André suddenly came to life. His sensuality, until then submerged in boredom, leaped to his eyes and lit up his features. With her he had been irritable, but the Italian urchins aroused his whole body; his senses went mad, his nerves tingled, he panted as though in some demonic possession. He literally glowed with lust; he was a different André.

In Florence, he was beside himself when he saw Donatello's statue of the nude boy David; he was aroused by the "oriental grace," the "fold in the belly directly under the ribs, and hollowed out by his breathing . . . that extraordinary flatness of the loins directly above the sacrum." [125] On visits to the museums, he lingered only before the nude figures. In Rome, while his wife went sightseeing by herself or stayed at the hotel nursing her headaches for hours, he remained behind, intensely curious, watching the young male models who were offering themselves to him. Some he took to his small rented apartment in the Piazza Barberini, giving Madeleine the pretext that he was motivated primarily by his interest in photographing them in the nude. He even showed her some of the prints. "I did not feel that I was being unfaithful in seeking from someone other than her a satisfaction in the flesh I was unable to ask of her. Besides, I was not reasoning. I was acting irresponsibly. I was inhabited by a monster." [126]

Madeleine swallowed his deception, but in time he even abandoned the pretext. In Tunis he haunted the cafés looking for shapely boy musicians. It was in their previous visit to Florence that she got the first inkling that André was homosexual, but so great was her respect for the genius of the man she loved deeply that she never made open reference of it. Once she did blurt out, when her irritation was too strong to suppress, "You look like either a criminal or a madman." But the issue was never pursued further.

At the time of Gide's marriage it never occurred to him that he was desecrating his marriage vow or depriving his wife of marital privileges she was entitled to. It was only after she died that he fully expressed his realization that his wife had craved physical love and children. As he looked back on their unconsummated union, he wrote, in *Et nunc manet in te*, "It was not until much later that I began to understand how cruelly I had wounded and devastated the woman for whom I was ready to give my life." [127]

Gide once confessed to Paul Claudel: "I have never felt any desire for a woman," but he added, "I beg you to consider only this: that I love my wife more than life itself."

FAREWELL, MY LOVELY

Raymond Chandler was lunching with several other writers in a Hollywood studio cafeteria when an old man approached his table, extended his hand, and told him how much he admired his books. Chandler, more embarrassed than the stranger, replied icily: "I never shake hands."

Flustered, the man hesitated, then shambled away. Turning to the writer beside him, Chandler inquired loudly, "Who's that old bastard? Imagine coming here and making a nuisance of himself!"

Chandleresque cruelty? That was what the public would say. Actually, Chandler had an allergy that made contact excruciatingly painful. As a cover, he blasted handshaking as "an overdone habit."[128]

"I am exactly like the characters in my books," he said, but he knew otherwise. His arch literary rival and close friend Ross Macdonald had Chandler's measure: "Essentially, I think, Chandler was a romantic, and so's his private eye Philip Marlowe."[129]

The author of *The Big Sleep* and *Farewell, My Lovely* posed as a two-fisted, tough-talking rough guy, a rabid woman hater—but privately, he was a softie, sentimental, supersensitive, and shy. What he could never hope to be he put into his novels. Marlowe was Chandler idealized.

Momism governed him from the age of seven, when his mother took him from his native Chicago to London after she divorced his father. He never forgot—she would never let him forget—the sacrifices she had made for him. When the time came for marrying, he was faced with the choice of leaving Mom or taking his prospective bride home. Mom won.

Returning to Los Angeles after World War I, in which he served in the Canadian army, he renewed his earlier close friendship with Julian and Cissy Pascal. He preferred being with this down-to-earth couple to gallivanting with the fast-living actresses at the Hollywood studios where he worked on script writing assignments.

Cissy and he became lovers.

She took a possessive interest in the thirty-year-old Chandler. Vivacious and charming, she was a sympathetic listener to his literary ambitions, and maternally warm. She did not look her forty-eight years. Her photographs, says biographer Frank MacShane, "show her as an exceptionally beautiful woman with a delicate profile, soft hair and a romantic look about her."

After months of tolerating the undisguised, growing closeness of his wife and Chandler, Julian Pascal thought the three should reach an understanding. He was fond of Chandler, perhaps too much so, but there are limits to friendship, he thought. Cissy was blunt. According to MacShane, she told her husband that she loved him but that she loved Ray more. "What, then, were they to do? They agonized over it for some time in an open and civilized way, and in the end it was agreed that Cissy should file for a California divorce. . . . They were too conventional to think of a quick divorce in Reno and were resigned to a year-long moratorium before the divorce was made final." [130]

When Hollywood learned that Raymond Chandler, kingpin of the whodunits, was going to marry the frilly old blonde he had been introducing as his fiancée, they could not believe it. He could have had any one of a number of stunning actresses: how had he come to pick this woman? Bemused columnists asked how Cissy had done it.

Mrs. Chandler openly disapproved of the marriage, stressing the great difference in their ages. Her son vacillated. He adored his mother too deeply to cross her. "I knew my mother had affairs," Chandler wrote; "she was very beautiful, and the only thing I felt to be wrong was that she refused to marry again for fear a stepfather would not treat me kindly, since my father was a swine." [131]

Cissy understood Chandler's dual loyalty and was delighted that now Raymond's mother finally accepted the possibility of his marrying once she learned that her son was already living with Cissy, and particularly in an apartment in Hermosa Beach not far from the house he had arranged for her to live in.

Chandler waited four years, until his mother died, before he married Cissy. He saw in his beloved qualities that made her an acceptable surrogate for his mother. Cissy comforted him when he was depressed, just as his mother had done. In marrying her, friends said, Chandler "married his mother." As MacShane described his new mother, ". . . had strawberry blonde hair and a marvelous figure and complexion. She was lively and original and liked to be naked when she did housework. She was an excellent cook. . . . By this time Chandler had wandered a lot and was tired from the war.

Here was a woman with sexual maturity who also had brains to be an intellectual companion as well. She seemed just right to Chandler."[132]

It was two weeks after his mother's death that Ray and Cissy were married. The registrar blinked when she gave her age as forty-three—she was in her fifties. The groom was thirty-five.

His mother's prophecy came true. A few years after the marriage, the age disparity began to show. When Cissy was entering her sixties, Chandler had not yet entered his forties. MacShane writes: "Cissy tried to disguise her age by dying her hair blonde and dressing as stylishly as she could. Sometimes she overdid it, wearing young women's clothes that did not suit her. In her manner, she would be skittish and unpredictable, sometimes vague and distant. Undoubtedly she was suffering from the realization that she was no longer convincingly young; accordingly, she exaggerated her femininity. Her bedroom was full of pink ruffles and Hollywood-style French furniture. It was exotic and stagily erotic."[133]

In Chandler's eyes his wife was springtime. He admired her efficiency and her absorption in his professional career. She scrutinized his royalty statements, advised him on contracts, kept in touch with publishers at the same time that she ran the household with the sole view of making her husband comfortable. What man could hope for more? It was a happy, satisfying marriage.

After twenty-eight years of marriage, when he went out with much younger collaborators and their wives, an ungovernable itch suddenly made him feel that he was missing something in life. Chandler was no saint. Pressures began to build up. For relief, he resumed his heavy drinking. Besides writing, which was not paying enough, he worked as an executive in an oil company. There he made a play for the girl in his office. When his employers discovered that he had taken a love nest for weekends, they fired him, and the penitent returned to mama. After this episode, Cissy came first in his life. He now refused to go to dinners with his publishers and his writer friends; she was ailing and he wanted always to be with her. Some friends felt she was only pretending in order to win his sympathy.

Cissy's death (she was in her eighties) hit him hard. He sorely missed the one person who had believed in him. He went on a long binge of weeping and drinking, "a useless and probably foolish gesture," he once conceded, "because my lost love is so utterly lost and I have no belief in any after-life. . . . All us tough guys are hopeless sentimentalists."

"The sentimentalism alternated with fits of depression and self-pity," MacShane writes. "He withdrew more and more, staying in Cissy's room and hardly leaving it."[134]

He tried suicide, miffed it, and was rescued in time. To friends, he pleaded: "For thirty years, ten months, and four days, she was the light of my life, my whole ambition. Anything else I did was just the fire to warm her hands at."[135]

He went to England to seek forgetfulness. It didn't help. He told reviewer Leonard Russell, who had come to cheer him up: "She was everything you say and more. She was the best of my heart for thirty years. She was the music heard faintly at the edge of sound. It was my great and useless regret that I never wrote anything really worth her attention, no book that I could dedicate to her. I planned it, I thought of it, but I never wrote it."[136]

His whole life thereafter turned to one continuous, effusive nostalgia, a large part of it touching his boyhood in England, where he had been naturalized.

"I do not come to England as a visiting author, God forbid, but as a man who loved England when his heart was young, and has never loved in the same way since, and never shall."

But he was inordinately proud of being lionized. "In England I am an author. In the U.S.A. I am just a mystery writer."[137]

He would pace his room restlessly at the Hotel Connaught, where all he found, he said, was "ghosts. Memories that keep me awake. I get up and dress, wander round the old haunts. Trying to recall our wonderful time together. Remembering. Life has lost something."[138]

His anglophilia extended even to his brand of cigarettes, Craven A. "I smoked a pipe from morning to night when my wife was alive, and I loved it. I used to drink a great deal of tea, and my wife loved that, just as she loved to see me smoking a pipe."[139]

It was a recurrent lament: "All that is really wrong with me is that I have no home, and no one to care for me in a home, if I had one."

He let one of his characters speak for him: "I was one of those, one of the perhaps two per cent, who are blessed with a marriage that is forever a courtship. I never proposed marriage formally to anyone. My wife and I just seemed to melt into each other's hearts without the need for words."[140]

The time came when he tried to satisfy his long-repressed sexual drive by courting Stephen Spender's wife, Natasha, with the poet's hearty approval. He went holidaying with her to Italy. But he could not recapture the old feeling.

Cissy claimed him to the very end. Shortly before his death, he proposed marriage to his agent, Helga Green, but he died before the wedding.

Mrs. Green became his heir and executrix.

WE HARDLY KNEW YOU, TOM ELIOT!

T. S. Eliot's private life was a tantalizing mystery while he lived, and the mystery, with some new biographical facts cropping up, deepened after he died. If anything, he had only himself to blame for published distortions of some crucial facts in his life and for the continuing shafts of derogation at his character, probably undeserved. He brushed aside without comment any gossip touching him. And to ensure permanent silence, he included this blunt veto in his will: "I do not wish my executors to facilitate or countenance the writing of any biography of me." For years after he died, his second wife and executrix, Valerie Eliot, constantly alert to detractors, has sedulously obeyed her husband's caveat.

Only recently and in the face of a swelling public demand to know more about T. S. Eliot personally did she permit, so we have been told, an authorized biography. It has not yet been published. It will most likely slide over many of the facts about his private life one is most curious about. Such is the nature of an authorized life. Until it is published, and certainly afterward, we will still be left with a host of speculations clamoring for resolution. T. S. Eliot is too great a poet and playwright to be left alone.

The campaign has already begun. In his recent biography, T. S. Matthews attempted to open up the hoard of secrets by raising and answering in part such questions as: "Who *was* T. S. Eliot? Why did he want to keep his private life secret? Was he a phony saint? Was he a homosexual? Why was Eliot's first marriage so unhappy? Did Bertrand Russell seduce Vivienne Eliot? Why did Eliot abandon his first wife? Because she was mad? *Was* she mad? Should he have abandoned her, in any case? How deep did Eliot's affections go?"[141]

Answering one question he raised, Was he a homosexual?, Matthews affirms that Eliot was not a homosexual, despite biographer

Robert Sencourt's claim that he was. Matthews says he can understand why one would think so, since Eliot did manifest a lifelong, deep horror of women, and the poet's mother and sister were "terrified of sex and disgusted by it, and ashamed of their female bodies."

Eliot was twenty-seven at the time of his marriage to Vivienne Haigh-Wood. The ceremony took place secretly in a registry office. None of their few witnesses have come forward to be identified. His parents did not attend. Secrecy was characteristic of all of Eliot's private actions.

According to biographer Robert Sencourt, a friend of the Eliots for twenty years, the marriage got off to a good start but gradually deteriorated because of Vivienne's chronic drug taking, continued illnesses, and breakdowns. It lasted seventeen years. Sencourt suggests that the reason Eliot was reluctant to disclose all the facts of this marriage was that during that time, in 1921, he had a nervous breakdown for which he was treated at a psychoanalytic clinic in Lausanne for three months. "The Waste Land" was written during this period. We now know as a fact that his breakdown was brought on by overwork as well as by the instability of his first marriage.[142]

Characteristically, when he planned to bring his marriage to an end, Eliot told no one, not even longtime associates in his publisher's office. He moved out of London quite suddenly and went to lecture at Harvard, leaving Vivienne, who was ailing, expecting him to return as he had promised. Settled in Cambridge, he wrote her the news, which shocked her, that he would not see her again except in the presence of a solicitor. He had chosen a London lawyer to serve her with separation papers. When Eliot later heard that she had died in a mental hospital, he said that he felt he had committed murder.[143]

Ten years after Vivienne's death, Eliot, sixty-nine, married his second wife, his secretary, Valerie Fletcher, thirty, at the crack of dawn in a locked London church. Not a single friend had been informed. Later he telephoned the news to John Haywood, the crippled British bibliophile with whom he had shared a flat for nine years, severing all contact with him.

Eliot's obsession with privacy invoked considerable snide remarks about him as a person. Since he had few intimate friends, guesses about the real T. S. Eliot proliferated, attracting uncomplimentary characterizations. Henry Miller called him a "lean-faced Calvinist"; his friend and mentor Ezra Pound referred to him as "the Rev. Eliot" and "Parson Eliot." And Cyril Connolly quoted Logan Pearsall Smith as saying that Eliot married Vivienne because he had been to bed with her, and this would account for the furtive nature of the marriage ceremony and for his subsequent recoiling from his conjugal privileges.[144]

Several writers, who were friends of the Eliots, have expressed sympathy for Vivienne, probably more than took Eliot's side. William Plomer commented on the first time he met Vivienne and Eliot together in someone's house: "I couldn't help noticing her and her neurotic behavior and what seemed a morbid fear of being slighted, and when I came to sign the visitors' book after her I was disturbed, graphologically, by her tremulous signature, 'Vivienne Haigh Eliot.' "[145]

There must be a considerable amount of truth in all the speculations about Eliot's personal life and his two marriages. Unfortunately, conjecture will have to do for the present, until the Eliot archives are opened at Princeton in 2019. Until then, T. S. Eliot's secrets are safe.

ROBERT FROST HAD PROMISES TO KEEP

Robert Frost and his wife, the former Elinor White, had two weddings: the first, private; the second, public. He met her when they were students in Lawrence High School, Massachusetts. He was seventeen and she was two years older. He was jealous of her poetic ability and of her school marks. They became covaledictorians.

Frost courted her by reading poetry to her, in particular Shelley's *Epipsychidion.* Both let everyone know they were free thinkers and rebels against rituals and marriage as an institution, but this did not prevent him from proposing. Elinor vacillated. He threw tantrums. Was she playing hard to get? After a tearful session, they agreed to defer the union until he could support her. He went off to Dartmouth, she to Lawrence University at Canton, many miles away. When he was twenty, he produced a volume of poetry, *Twilight,* containing four love poems. Only two were printed, one for himself and one for Elinor.

Secretly, they conducted their own marriage ceremony. They exchanged plain gold bands to seal their troth until he could support her. They became schoolteachers.

When both felt the time was ripe financially for marriage, they set the date for the ceremony for the vacation period. Frost insisted on a public wedding. Elinor wanted none of it. She was now more iconoclastic than ever. She took her Shelley seriously. When Elinor told him of her firm objection to any formal ceremony, she handed him the wedding band; in a rush of anger he threw the ring into the stove fire and, threatening suicide, ran off.

"I broke her to my will," Frost said years later. Elinor's parents remained inflexible. So adamant were they in their objection to Frost that they would not countenance the wedding in their home. Instead, the ceremony took place in the converted schoolroom the Swedenborgians were using as a meeting place.

The Whites were conspicuous by their absence.

One witness, a Swedenborgian friend, then ten, recalled later: "I gazed at Robert, and couldn't understand how our happy-go-lucky playmate could change into this solemn young man who replied to the pastor in such serious tones. Congratulations, handshaking, kissing—bewildering! First wedding ever I attended, and I didn't like it too well."[146]

Frost's biographer Lawrance Thompson wrote: "As for the bridegroom, standing with the bride before the pastor and making his replies in such serious tones, there were some things he himself did not like too well about this wedding. He would never forget, and would never quite forgive the fact that while he had been courting Elinor White—and even after he thought he had completely won her and had privately married her—she had hurt him so deeply and terribly by making him think she loved and wanted to marry someone else. It seemed to him that she had indeed driven him to the verge of suicide on two occasions, and that the injury which he had suffered as a result of those wounds was one from which he could never completely recover."[147]

At some point in the ceremony Frost promised himself Elinor would pay for his first major trauma.

Deep down he felt Elinor was marrying him out of pity for his distress, and that he married her out of hurt pride. A determined lifelong vendetta poisoned his relationship with Elinor and their daughter.

Elinor never forgot or forgave. She too had a promise to keep. When she lay dying, she refused him even access to her room.

It Was Good Casting

When Eileen Reynolds Carey, an Irish actress, was touring the United States, she consulted a fortuneteller in New York. In her memoirs, she says she was told to return to England at once "to meet there a man with piercing eyes and heavy boots, a man who would be world famous and whom I would marry." Eileen was holding a copy of her favorite play, *Juno and the Paycock,* then auditioning in London. She packed her bag at once and sailed for England to try to get a part in the production.

In the seat next to her in the theater where the auditions were being held (Eileen writes) sprawled the playwright Sean O'Casey. Sure enough, he had strangely piercing eyes. Within minutes they were chatting as though they'd known each other for years. He said later that the moment he saw her he knew he had met his predestined wife.[148]

They were married the following year.

O'Casey, in his autobiography (the volume *Rose and Crown*), describes his first view of Eileen slightly differently: he says it was when she was picked to replace the actress playing Nora Clitheroe in his play *The Plough and the Stars.* Speaking of himself in the third person: "He had rarely seen a lovelier face or figure anywhere in this world, and didn't expect to find anything better in the delectable world to come."[149]

O'Casey was forty-seven, Eileen was twenty-two, but the disparity in their ages didn't matter. As she said, she always fell for older men. He was a "lapsed" Protestant and she was then a practicing Catholic. They were married in a Catholic church. Their three children—Breon, Niall, and Shivaun—were baptized, though apparently not raised, as Catholics.

For the church ceremony, O'Casey discarded his cloth cap, nailed boots, and turtleneck in favor of a well-pressed suit, probably borrowed or rented, a dashing fedora, patent leathers, and a colorful handkerchief in his pocket.

Eileen brought more possessions to their first home than the impoverished Sean; he had but a few things, mostly books, which wouldn't even furnish one decent room for his own use. She brought some lovely things from her flat, in mahogany; linen and cutlery; a beautiful Bechstein piano. So Sean, in the end (as he says in *Rose* and Crown), "found himself in intimate touch with a few of the elegant things of life." He didn't know what they would have done had not Eileen brought as her dowry the furniture of her four-room flat: "With all my worldly goods I thee endow; an easy endowment, indeed, for all he had were two pictures, a chair, a desk kept together by the mercy of God, a cheap divan, a crowd of books, a spoon, knife and fork, a kettle, teapot, and a few articles of delftware."[150]

Living with her dream man was not unadulterated bliss. O'Casey was eccentric, moody, and so seclusive that he even slept in a room of his own. But he was tender with Eileen and he adored her. Gradually, she took over. Despite their financial insecurity, she somehow managed to get all the bills paid, saw that he could write undisturbed, acted as his agent, and solaced him in their personal tragedies. (Their son Niall died of leukemia when he was twenty.) She gave up a promising acting career to devote herself to him; she championed him in his continual battles with the critics, the Abbey Theatre managers, and the religious establishment.

In his autobiography, O'Casey wrote: "Eileen had faults; a lot less than he had himself, for these were many; but faults were trivial things in a nature worthy of all men to be accepted."[151]

And Eileen said, in her memoirs, "From the first afternoon I met him, until his death 38 years later, I don't suppose I ever lost him."[152]

O'Casey, however, almost lost Eileen. During the early bleak years of their marriage, she had a prolonged affair with a former lover, a London producer, and became pregnant. However, she decided to have an abortion and to remain with the man whom she never ceased to laud as the greatest playwright Ireland had ever known.[153]

HONEYMOONING AND ALL THAT JAZZ

When their twenty-two-month courtship culminated in their wedding at St. Patrick's Cathedral in New York, Scott Fitzgerald scooped up his bride to whirl her through a decade of boozing and frolics, until Zelda suffered her first mental breakdown.

Scott bragged that Zelda started the flapper movement in America. He christened it the Jazz Age, boldly declaring himself the spokesman of the "lost generation." Scott and Zelda were set on making it "the greatest, gaudiest spree" in history. He said that he was in love with a whirlwind and must spin a net big enough to catch it.

Mrs. Sayre had rejected Scott as a suitor for her daughter because he wasn't rich, to put it baldly. Later, Scott was to say, "Zelda was cagey about throwing in with me before I was a money-maker." Zelda said afterward, when they were shooting the works in Paris, "You can't have too much money. I believe in money and lots of it. I have to believe in it—because after all there's nothing else to believe in. Nothing."

When Fitzgerald's first novel, *This Side of Paradise*, went into its huge second printing, the suitor had proved to Mrs. Sayre that he was worthy of the belle of Montgomery, Alabama. But she wouldn't let him off without injecting a religious note. The Sayres were Episcopalians; Scott was Catholic.

"As you know," she said, "Zelda has several admirers, but you seem to be the only one to make anything like a permanent impression. . . . Your church is all right with me. . . . It will take more than the Pope to make Zelda good. You will have to call on God Almighty direct." [154]

Scott saw no need to petition God when he had Zelda. "Don't you think I was made for you?" she asked him. "I feel like you had me ordered—and I was delivered to you—to be worn—I want you to wear me like a watch-charm or a button-hole boquet [sic]—to the world." [155]

Pockets bursting with twenty-dollar bills, the honeymooners ran about New York yelling "Whoopee," broke into one booze party after another, created traffic jams, got thrown out of George White's Scandals, and rode off to the Plaza, one squatting atop the taxi and the other doing handstands on the hood. In front of the Plaza, they stripped and went splashing in the fountain. They broke up a May Day parade by tooting and holding their sign: WE ARE THE REDS FROM PARNASSUS.

Their base operations was the Hotel Biltmore. Andrew Turnbull says, Scott did "headstands in the Biltmore lobby, because he hadn't been in the news that week, and, as Oscar Wilde said, the only thing worse than being talked about is being forgotten. . . . After several weeks of honeymooning at the Biltmore, the Fitzgeralds were asked to leave, the continuing hilarity of their presence being considered prejudicial to good order." [156]

Of course, Scott felt they had to go to Princeton to show off. With grandstand swagger he introduced Zelda as his mistress, invited brawls on Nassau Street, and shattered reunion parties. He boasted to a friend, "Zelda and five men in Harvey Firestone's car and not one of us drew a sober breath." When a crowd gathered to watch him strumming a lyre, crowned in a halo of leaves and wearing a pair of wings, he toasted the president of Princeton with a bottle of hooch: "Here's to John Grier Hibben. He ought to be selling ribbons."

They scampered over to the portico of Scott's favorite professor, Christian Gauss, greeted him effusively as he opened the door, and wrapped his dome in a laurel wreath as Scott orated: "We are going to give literature the greatest boost it has ever known." Professor Gauss responded coolly, "Who knows, you may give it a fatal shove."[157]

Then the pair boarded the *Aquitania* to continue their honeymoon in Europe. They were kicked out of Paris bistros, disrupted traffic on the Champs Élysées, and started drunken fights along the boulevards.

Reflecting on her life abroad, Zelda said, "In a small way I was an original." Scott added: "Liquor on my mouth is sweet to her. I cherish her most extravagant hallucinations."

The Jazz Age kids were obviously showing signs of physical and mental strain. Michael Arlen wrote: "Scott Fitzgerald came by one evening, hours late for dinner, striped blazer, white flannels, full of booze from one of Gerald Murphy's parties, embarrassed, garrulous, then silent, leaned his head down on the table top (hair halfway in the soup), 'This is how I want to live . . . this is how I want to live,' he said. And fell asleep."[158]

By this time the Fitzgeralds' "festival conception of life," as Hemingway called it, was drawing to an apocalyptic finale.

Scott's friends had advised him strongly against marrying Zelda, but he had a ready answer for the prophets of doom: Scott told one friend "No personality as strong as Zelda's could go without criticism. . . . I've always known that, any girl who gets stewed in public, who frankly enjoys and tells shocking stories, who smokes constantly and makes the remark that she has 'kissed thousands of men and intends to kiss thousands more,' cannot be considered beyond reproach even if above it. . . . I fell in love with her courage, her sincerity, and her flaming self-respect and its these things I'd believe in even if the whole world indulged in wild suspicions that she wasn't all she should be. . . . I love her and that's the beginning and end of everything. You're still a catholic but Zelda's is the only God I have left now."[159]

SEX IN THE HEAD

Had the miner's son married his village sweetheart instead of eloping with a highstrung Wagnerian blonde, the mother of three, English literature might have taken a totally different direction.

The D. H. Lawrence-Frieda Weekley love story began years earlier in her native Bavarian *schloss*. Baron Friedrich von Richthofen gathered his three impressionable adolescent daughters together and cautioned them: "I don't care whom you marry, so long as it isn't an Englishman, a Jew, or a gambler."

Nusch's first husband was a notorious gambler; Else married a Jew— Edgar Jaffe, a Freudian who became finance minister for Bavaria and later a propagandist for Zionism—and Frieda, in haste, married Ernest Weekley, a noted English philologist, who took her right off to England so he could assume his post as professor of modern languages at Nottingham University. The baron had to be restrained from putting a bullet through his head.[160]

In the end, the baron was proved prophetic; all the marriages were stormy, scandalous, and catastrophic.

Frieda's marriage was a disaster from the start. Weekley, a virginal thirty-three, humorless and solemn, was dreadfully dull. She was nineteen, had already had some sex flings, was full of the new Freudianism, and burned for romance.

Emily Hahn describes their *prima nox* at a provincial hotel:

Several times, under various guises of fiction, she [Frieda] recounted the lamentable story of her wedding night when Ernest, shy in matters of sex, left her alone in the bedroom to prepare for bed while he went downstairs, as he awkwardly explained, for a drink. Frieda was undressing when she noticed a huge, old-fashioned wardrobe at the side of the room. On a sudden impulse she climbed to the top of it and sat there half-dressed, legs dangling, stifling her giggles in anticipation of Ernest's reaction at finding her gone. She would wait a bit to enjoy the joke and then say "Boo!" But when he did appear and stared blankly around at emptiness, he looked so crestfallen that her heart misgave her and she called to him. He looked even more frightened when he saw where she was. Of course she climbed down quickly, but he still seemed shocked. And their first experience of love-making was a miserable disappointment, because Ernest seemed to know just as little about that as he did about jokes. After he fell asleep she stood for a long time at the window and contemplated jumping out. But no, reflected the baroness, only housemaids jump out of windows. She went meekly back to bed, hating Ernest.

In time she got over hating him. She even got used to living in Nottingham, though, like Ernest, it was not terribly amusing. For one thing, she hadn't enough to do. Other Nottingham women liked to follow a rigid routine in housework—Monday washday, Tuesday ironing day, and the rest of the week for cleaning room by room. Meals were fixed, too: the joint appeared on Sunday to reappear cold as a mince on Tuesday, and so on. Not that Frieda did any of these chores herself; the Weekleys had a cook and another woman to clean and launder. Madam was expected to supervise, that was all, and it is only fair to say that the arrangement suited her well enough.[161]

Soon enough, a bored Frieda knew she had stumbled into a provincial trap. Once, in between pregnancies, she thought of leaving her husband, but decided to stay for the sake of the children.

Then the blue-eyed, red-haired D. H. Lawrence crossed her threshold. Weekley had invited Lawrence, his former night-class student, home for lunch—"a genius," he told Frieda, who was coming to discuss a lectureship opening at a German university. Professor Weekley made the mistake of being a half-hour late, just enough time for his wife and their guest to talk uninterrupted. It was love at first sight.

Lawrence was ready for a critical leap. He was still smarting from a failed love affair. He had been depressed for months after his mother's death. His health had broken down, he had chucked his teaching job, and he was determined to begin a new life as a writer. It had taken him fruitless years to escape the mother-incubus. His mother, says John Middleton Murry, had been "determined, consciously or unconsciously, that no woman save herself could have her son's love; and he obeyed." The inner struggle is described in Lawrence's masterpiece, *Sons and Lovers*. Frieda helped revise the novel in more ways than one.

The visits spread over six weeks. Lawrence came to life in Frieda's presence; for him there was no husband in the house. He was drawn to her greenish-tawny eyes, her maternal touch; she found him an irresistible enchanter. ("Once you looked into his eyes," says the

Lawrences' friend David Garnett, "you were completely charmed, they were so beautiful and alive, dancing with gaiety. His smile lit up all his face as he looked at you.")[162]

Giddy from the first visit, Lawrence wrote her: "You are the most wonderful woman in all England." She sent back at once a coy demurrer: "You don't know many women in England, how do you know?"

The second visit was longer; they sat closer and held hands. "You are quite unaware of your husband," he told her, "you take no notice of him." She pretended to dislike the directness with which he declared his love. Later, Frieda said, "I certainly did have what he called 'sex in the head,'; a theory of loving men. My real self was frightened and shrank from contact like a wild thing. . . . Suddenly I knew I loved him. He had touched a new tenderness in me. After that, things happened quickly."

She asked him to come one Sunday evening, knowing that her husband would be away.

"Stay the night with me," she pleaded.

"No," he replied, wincing. "I will not stay in your husband's house while he is away, but you must tell him the truth and we will go away together, because I love you."

"I was frightened," she recalls. "I knew how terrible such a thing would be for my husband, he had always trusted me. But a force stronger than myself made me deal him the blow. I left the next day. I left my son with his father, my two little girls I took to their grandparents in London. I said good-bye to them on Hampstead Heath, blind and blank with pain, dimly feeling I should never again live with them as I had done. . . . He seemed to have lifted me body and soul out of all my past life. This young man of twenty-six had taken all my fate, all my destiny, into his hands. And we had known each other barely for six weeks. There had been nothing else for me to do but submit."[163]

The confrontation with Weekley that Lawrence had insisted on was cyclonic. Trying to make it easier for her husband, Frieda admitted that she had been unfaithful with others, giving names and dates. Even then he was unwilling to let her go, tearfully forgiving her. In the end she said she would go to Metz for her father's fiftieth anniversary celebration of his enlistment in the army, and would think things over. But when she left for Bavaria, she was as inflexible as ever.

That night she dreamed that Lawrence and her father had a fight and Lawrence defeated the baron. Early the next morning, the lovers embraced in Charing Cross station and entrained for Metz. Lawrence carried in his pocket all the money he had in the world—eleven pounds. They consummated their union in a Metz Hotel. "I never knew what love was before," Frieda wrote.[164]

Anxious about his wife's extended absence, Weekley bombarded her with pleas to return. As usual, as David Garnett, friend of the Lawrences, shows, he struck the wrong note in writing her: "How could she so demean herself as to elope with a miner's son? With a man who was not a gentleman? What would his friends in Nottingham be saying when they learned that she had so betrayed her birth and upbringing?"[165]

Frieda laughed throatily, then handed Lawrence the letter. . . . He read it aloud, then thrust it aside with contempt. " 'To think,' " she said, " 'that I was married for twelve years—yes, for twelve years—to a man who cares only what his neighbours will think! And do you know why I married him? I had been reading Tennyson, and I thought Ernest was Lancelot! Our marriage started badly. I went to the bedroom first and climbed up by the door, and when Ernest came in, I threw myself naked into his arms. He was horrified and told me to put on my nightdress at once. Can you imagine such a man? And he wants me to go back and live with him for fear of what his neighbours in Nottingham will say when they find out I have run away with a miner's son!' "[166]

The letters grew harsher; Weekley refused to let her visit the children or to see them away from their home. When she learned that the children had been told "Your mother has left you," she shot back, "I want to tell them I left your *father*, not *you*." Cut to the quick by Frieda's misery, Lawrence consoled her: "Don't be sad. I'll make a new heaven and earth for them, don't cry, you see if I don't."[167]

Lawrence wrote to Weekley: "I love your wife and she loves me. . . . Mrs. Weekley is afraid of being stunted and not allowed to grow, so she must live her own life. . . . Mrs. Weekley must live largely and abundantly: it is her nature. To me it means the future. I feel my effort to live was all for her. Cannot we all forgive something?"

Weekley replied promptly to Frieda: "I bear him no ill-will and hope you will be happy with him. But have some pity on me. . . .

Let me know at once that you agree to a divorce. . . . You have loved me once—help me know—but quickly."

Weekley used Lawrence's letter two years later when he filed for divorce.

Lawrence's and Frieda's honeymoon was rough. Walking all the way to Italy, they subsisted on black bread, fresh eggs, and berries. And love. Once (Lawrence said), huddled on a bed of warm pine needles, "Frieda smiled at me and suggested we make love. It was the natural thing to do." And Frieda recalled that he said, "Take all you want of me, everything, I am yours." And she added, "I took and gave equally, without thought. When I asked him: 'What do I give you, that you didn't get from others?' he answered: 'You make me sure of myself, whole.' And he would say: 'You are so young, so young!' When I remonstrated: 'But I am older than you.'—'Ah, it isn't years, it's something else. You don't understand.' "[168]

Frieda cried all through the honeymoon, saying she missed her children. Lawrence wrote to his friend Garnett: "She lies on the floor in misery—and then is fearfully angry with me because I won't say 'Stay for my sake.' I say 'decide what you want most, to live with me and share my rotten character, or go back to security, and your children—decide for *yourself*—choose for *yourself*.' And then she almost hates me, because I won't say 'I love you—stay with me whatever happens. . . .' I do love her. If she left me, I do not think I should be alive six months hence. And she won't leave me, I think. God, how I love her—and the agony of it."[169]

Yet quarrels that persisted through their marriage began in their first days together. The quarrels grew fierce when Lawrence started to show signs of impotence and Frieda was openly seeking sex with their friends. During a violent encounter one night, their cabin was reduced to shambles. When Frieda was later asked how she could love her husband and break a plate on his head during one of their wrestling matches, she explained: "What does it amount to that he hit out at me in a rage, when I exasperated him, or mostly when life around him drove him to the end of his patience? I didn't care very much. I hit back and waited until the storm in him subsided. Then there was peace. . . . Battles must be."[170]

Lawrence had heard all this before. His mother had warned him that his life would be "battle, battle, battle," and he agreed that his future life program would make him "retire to the desert and fight."

Lawrence did not have to retire to the desert and fight. There was always Frieda!

Douglas Goldring wrote: "Voluble, full bosomed, Prussian Frieda was built to weather storms. Like a sound ship, broad in the beam, slow but seaworthy, she could stand any amount of buffeting."[171]

David Garnett concurs: "No woman who hadn't got a constitution of triple brass could have lived with Lawrence for long."

JAMES JOYCE JOLLIFICATES

When James Joyce, self-styled "egoarch," introduced his fiancée, Nora Barnacle, the baker's twenty-two-year-old daughter working as a chambermaid in Finn's Hotel, Dublin, to his father, the elder Joyce remarked: "With a name like that she'll cling to him." The two had met on June 16, 1904, which is now universally recognized as Bloomsday, the day of Leopold Bloom's twenty-four-hour odyssey through Dublin (*Ulysses*).

Joyce promised Nora "my sin, my folly, my weakness and my sadness." These he gave her and much more. Stuart Gilbert says the two were inseparable: "during all the years I knew him, Joyce never spent a night or even a full day away from his wife." Even when Nora was in the hospital for a hysterectomy, he took a bed in her room. However, Nora is quoted as having said, "I wish I had never met anyone of the name of James Joyce." She told Sylvia Beach of Shakespeare and Company that she would have preferred to marry a ragpicker, but had to admit he is "unique, there's nothing like him."[172]

The two had eloped to the Continent (but not to marry), to the considerable derision and gossip of Dubliners. Oliver St. John Gogarty said that Joyce did not want to be forgotten back home and kept up a ceaseless, lively correspondence with Dublin friends. Almost a year after Joyce's "honeymoon," Gogarty met Vincent Cosgrove, who, he says, "with eyes dancing and his quizzical mouth smiling, asked, 'Did you hear the latest about the 'artist'?

" 'No.'

" 'He sent a telegram to his father to announce the birth of his son with 'Mother and bastard both doing well.' "[173]

Twenty-seven years later, two illegitimate children having been born in the interval, Joyce felt he should marry Nora in order to secure legal status for his family and ensure their rights to his property, already a booming industry, and to provide for "the patron saint in his eyes," Lucia, his retarded daughter, who was his main worry.

During the six months that the Joyces spent in England, they appeared before the clerk at the Kensington Registry Office to solemnize their marriage. They chose July 4, Joyce's father's birthday, as their wedding day, as a sop to the elder Joyce, who had never gotten over their elopement and their sinful unmarried status. For some strange reason, Joyce told the clerk he had already been married to Nora under a different name. The official insisted he could not marry them a second time unless they submitted to a divorce action. But Joyce's solicitor convinced the clerk that the statutes permitted such a marriage, and the ceremony proceeded. Joyce gave his age as forty-nine and Nora's as forty-seven.

WE'RE IN THE MONEY

Cables from London kept coming fast and furious, increasingly insistent, telling Winifred Ellerman ("Bryher") that the end to her long holiday had come. For the first time in her life she had been enjoying independence, and in America besides, writing stories and poems and sharing the company of other writers. "It was time to go back to England," she conceded to friends, "but my family insisted that I go back to live with them again. I was desperately afraid of hurting their feelings."

Winifred indeed faced a crisis and it didn't make her happy. She was the daughter of Sir John Ellerman, the shipping magnate and "the heaviest taxpayer in England." Under his will, she would come into a fortune if and when she married.

The only solution then—marriage!

Her American friends William Carlos Williams and Hilda Doolittle (H.D.) put their heads together, and after considerable shuffling of names produced a likely candidate: Robert McAlmon, the penniless poet and short story writer from Minnesota. He was short but incredibly handsome, pugnacious, charming. The turquoise earring he wore attracted talk. They had met him a year before at a *Broom* gathering and had been impressed by him. He was now in New York posing in the nude for mixed classes at Cooper Union. At the moment he was planning to ship aboard a freighter to China, but they knew he had been desperate to go to Paris to meet Joyce and would chuck his plans if a better proposition came along.

They put in a call to him: hold everything until Bryher came to see him. In her memoir, *The Heart to Artemis*, she describes the encounter: "I put the problem before him, and suggested that if we married, I would give him part of my allowance, he would join me for occasional visits to my parents, but otherwise we would lead strictly separate lives . . . arranged marriages were perfectly familiar to me. It never occurred to me that there was anything irregular in my suggestion."[174]

McAlmon leaped at the idea—anything to get free passage to Paris! It was only days later, when he was getting the license, that he learned her family name and realized he was marrying one of the richest women in the world.

Bryher liked what she saw: he was a sparkler, an Adonis, and ebullient. McAlmon was impressed by her turquoise earrings, which matched his own.

In New York she took him to a tailor to be outfitted.

H.D., Marianne Moore, and William Carlos Williams were witnesses at the wedding ceremony. The marriage was to be kept secret; she would introduce the groom to her parents when it was too late for opposition. In all innocence, Sir John reserved a bridal suite for them on the *Celtic*.

In Paris, McAlmon appeared at le Dôme, his pockets bulging with hundred-franc notes. Soon he was launched on a career of spreading money around where he thought it would do the most good. The drinks for the circle at le Dôme were always on him. But behind his back they sneered at him. He founded *Contacts* and published Williams, Stein, and Hemingway. He took Hemingway to his first bullfight.

Malcolm Cowley got to know him well and said, McAlmon "regarded himself as an unacknowledged genius . . . Hemingway had never liked him and took to insulting him in public. McAlmon, a homosexual, revenged himself by spreading baseless tales about Hemingway's relations with Fitzgerald; it was one of the feuds that kept tongues busy at the Dôme."[175]

McAlmon came up to Joyce's apartment daily: he promised him fifteen hundred dollars a month to tide him over until *Ulysses* was published. He induced his mother-in-law to subsidize the American composer George Antheil for two years.

When Bryher and McAlmon were divorced, Sir John added to the agreed-on annuity fourteen hundred pounds McAlmon had been given to sweeten the divorce settlement.

In his first three years in Paris, McAlmon published thirty American and British books by William Carlos Williams, H.D., Ezra Pound, Gertrude Stein (*The Making of America*)—books that would otherwise never have seen print.

Morley Callaghan insists that they all had McAlmon wrong on the marriage to Bryher: "I had always believed his story that he hadn't been aware it was to be a marriage in name only; he had insisted he was willing to be interested in women. And with the money, what did he do? Spend it all on himself? No, he became a publisher, he spent the money on the other people he believed in."[176]

A WONDERFUL COMBINATION

Sir Max Beerbohm—essayist, critic, caricaturist—was much amused to hear that his friend Bertrand Russell was marrying for the fourth time at the age of eighty. But when it was Max's turn to take the plunge again, he was considerably older than Russell.

At eighty-three, Beerbohm was a widower. The first Lady Beerbohm, the former actress Florence Kahn, had lived happily for many years in the "Villino" in Rapallo, Italy. The "Incomparable Max" was so rich in admirers that his *Festschrift* at eighty was a treasury of tributes from the most distinguished littérateurs and artists in England.

Sir Max was visited in Rapallo by the American playwright S. N. Behrman, whose book *Portrait of Max* offers rich evidence that even shortly before his death, Beerbohm was still very elegant in his "color of primrose suit," and his talk was as delicious as ever. To have dinner with Max, Edith Wharton wrote, "was like suddenly growing wings." But he was very frail now. His rheumatic asthma and other illnesses were getting to him. Since the death of his beloved Florence, he had been looked after in the "Villino" by Elisabeth Jungmann, his devoted friend, secretary-companion, and nurse.

Behrman writes: "I gradually discovered Miss Jungmann's story. She had been for many years the secretary of the German playwright Gerhart Hauptmann. . . . 'Hauptmann loved Rapallo,' Miss Jungmann said. 'Rothenstein, on a visit here, introduced Max to Hauptmann. That is how I met Max.' "[177]

But then the war came and it all ended. Miss Jungmann got a job with the British Foreign Office. Max's wife, Florence, was ill for a very long time. Miss Jungmann continued her story to Behrman: "Everybody said, 'What will become of Max when Florence dies?' I made up my mind. I dropped everything. I came to the Villino. . . . I said to Max, 'Max, if anything happens, you have only to call me and, wherever I am, whatever I'm doing, I'll come the moment I hear from you, the *moment*.' "[178]

Miss Jungmann never left Max from the day that Florence died.

When Max's health suffered a turn for the worse, he was taken to the clinic in town, where doctors hinted he had not much more time to live. Max became alarmed. What would happen to Elisabeth after his death? Something had to be done to make sure she would inherit his money, and done quickly before he might not be able to hold a pen to sign the necessary transfer papers. Earlier that year he had drawn up a will giving her all his property, but according to Italian law, the beneficiary had to be a relative. He had been thinking for months about proposing marriage but refrained lest it appear to the world that she was marrying an octogenarian for his money.

Elisabeth herself had long been thinking how wonderful it would be to marry the dearest person in her life, but scruples prevented her from suggesting it.

One day Max looked serenely up at her from his bed in the clinic and asked, "What do you think of the idea of getting married?"

She paused, then said, "I adore you more than anything else. I think it would be a good idea."

"I am so delighted you think it *is* a good idea," he answered.

Max put in a call at once to the British consul to arrange for a civil ceremony in his hospital room. He pleaded for secrecy; he did not want Elisabeth to face all the photographers and journalists who would be hurrying down to Rapallo to interview her.

The mayor of the town performed the ceremony. As David Cecil writes, Elisabeth was "dressed in her best but looking lost, Max in bed and unusually pale."

Beerbohm's sense of humor did not desert him. The bride was taller than himself. He said, "I am glad that I can never call you my sweet *little* wife."

When the ceremony ended, he turned to Elisabeth, smiled weakly, kissed her, and said, "I think Elisabeth Beerbohm is a wonderful combination."[179]

A few months later, the last words he spoke before he went into a coma were addressed to her and to his doctor: "Thank you for everything."

Elisabeth, the second Lady Beerbohm, survived her "darling Max" by less than three years.

WHAT'S THE RUSH?

Leo Tolstoy stalled for time before getting to the altar. On the wedding day he called on his betrothed—a horrible breach of protocol—and asked her whether she was absolutely sure she loved him. She still had time to take back her promise. Sensing he was looking for an excuse, she burst into tears. Her mother rushed in crying, "You've chosen a fine time to come and worry her to death!"

Customarily, the best man was to come and inform her at home that the groom was on the way to the church. Mother and daughter waited impatiently for one and one-half hours for the best man to call. Instead of the best man, Tolstoy's servant came explaining that in packing his master's things, already forwarded to Sonya's home, Tolstoy had forgotten to leave out a clean shirt. It was Sunday; the shops were closed. Sonya's ma was busy unpacking his trunks looking for a clean shirt.

After the ceremony, while the couple appeared impatient to leave, the entire bride's family were sobbing. The bride was weeping profusely.

Tolstoy kept looking at his watch. It was raining. In the carriage, Sonya sat in the corner still sobbing. She was terrified of the bearded groom who, at thirty-four, was twice her age. He told her she couldn't love him much if going on a honeymoon with him was making her so miserable. She did not reply. The couple had been given the tzar's chambers at the hotel on the way to Yasnaya Polyana, but Tolstoy was impatient. He stopped the coach and raped his bride.

When the coach stopped at Yasnaya Polyana, his aunt rushed out with the traditional tablespoonful of salt on a tray. The couple bent low, crossed themselves, kissed the proffered icon, and embraced her.

At dawn Tolstoy scribbled a diary entry: "Incredible happiness. . . . It is impossible that all this will end except with life."

For thirteen days Sonya found herself still blushing over Tolstoy's recorded premarital raking and she entered a consoling note in her own journal: "I think to myself, 'Well, I'm not the first woman.' "

The rush was over, and years later she confessed to her daughter that she had felt so humiliated that on awakening the morning after the consummation, she could not face the figure huddled beside her and buried her face in the pillow and cried.[180]

Pregnancy set in at once. It took all of Tolstoy's moral strength to try abstaining from the "swinish crime" while she was in that condition. As usual, he was morose and contrite after each crime. According to his son's account, Sonya was pregnant for 117 months and bore 13 children.

Marriage exacted a heavy price. From creating novels, Tolstoy turned to social philosophy and wrote voluminously against the entrapment of sex in marriage. To curb his private temptation, he transferred his bed to a separate room. It brought no relief.

For Sonya, the bedroom turned nightmarish. At last, carrying their fifth child, she took a bold stand and pleaded enough is enough. But Tolstoy turned a deaf ear to her pleas and continued to creep into her bed. Henri Troyat describes one bedroom scene at the time Tolstoy was thundering against sex in marriage:

"Later, lying beside her in bed after the light was out, desire awoke in him again. A certain warmth, something in the odor of her skin and hair made him dizzy. He wanted to hurl himself upon her as he used to do, drown his sorrows in the pleasures of his senses. She refused him. It was hardly a month since the baby was born. It was too soon, she told him. He was hurt by the tone in which she rebuffed him—cold, 'wilfully mean.' She was simply provoking him, of course. He could not sleep all night. He wanted to run away again. He got up and packed his knapsack, woke up his wife, and, trembling with desire, disgust and resentment, poured out everything he had on his mind. 'I told her she was no longer a wife to me. A helpmeet for her husband? She ceased to be a help to me long ago, she is a hindrance. . . . The companion of my nights? She provoked me, she makes it into a game. It was very unpleasant, and I felt how weak and pointless it was. I was wrong not to go.' "

A momentary pang of conscience distressed him: "What if another baby came? How ashamed I should be, especially before the children! They will compare the date [of conception] with that of the publication [of the Kreutzer Sonata]."[181]

Almost to the year when he died he was still invading her dark bed. Their last child, Ivan, was delivered when Tolstoy was sixty and Sonya was forty-four, and all this time, between writing *War and Peace* and *Anna Karenina,* he wrote pamphlet after pamphlet declaring that it was wrong even for married people to have sex. If men could not restrain themselves, there was still the alternative. "I believe the prostitute is necessary for the maintenance of the family."[182]

The children had eyes and ears and they read in amazement much of their father's thunderous advocacy of chastity. They began to see other disturbing evidence of Tolstoyian hypocrisies. "He had talked about the criminality of wealth and the evil of money," said his son Ilya, "yet he himself lived in a fine manor house, slept on expensive mattresses, and ate tasty, satisfying food."

As for his poor mother, she deserved better: "a wonderful woman, an ideal mother, and that she would have been an ideal wife for an ordinary man, but not for a giant like my father."[183]

Her husband's hypocrisy slowly invaded Sonya's mind. Troyat phrases her growing discontent: "After twenty-five years of preaching to all Russia that woman's most noble calling was marriage and childbirth, how could this man publicly [now] deny his ideal? How could he tell others to be chaste, when at sixty, he had got her with child for the thirteenth time?"[184]

Other sexual involvements cropped up in Yasnaya Polyana. At fifty, after having gone through the endless series of pregnancies, Sonya realizing she had become frigid, said, "I so long for spiritual intimacy with Lev, not just this disgusting bodily intimacy. . . . the physical side of love played a great part with *him,* for *me* on the contrary that is nothing." For a diversion she developed a therapeutic crush on the young homosexual composer Taneyev, who was living on the estate. She did not hide it. When in a blistering fit of jealousy she accused Tolstoy of having relations with his chief female disciple, he reminded her that she should be the last to talk.

Konstantin Bazarov reveals the heated-up climate: "It seemed to poor Tolstoy that every female in his home had been bitten by the devil, and he wrote, 'They are scampering about in every direction like cats on a hot tin roof.' "

When his daughter Masha succumbed to the spreading virus and despite her father's opposition married Prince Obolenski, Tolstoy wrote: "I feel all the compassion for her I would feel for a pure-bred race-horse put to work hauling water."

Tolstoy's son Sergei recalled the time he was present with some of his father's celebrated visitors when he asked Turgenev: "Tell us which was the happiest moment in your life!" The novelist was quick to respond: "Of course, the happiest moment of life is concerned with a woman's love. It is when you gaze into her eyes, into the eyes of the woman you love, and you realize that she loves you."

Eyes veered to the master. Tolstoy sat mute, letting his memory roam over his long life with Sonya and some others, including the serf whose bastard son he had sired. Then he said, with marked emotion, "This has happened to me once in my life—perhaps twice."

He gave no names, but Sergei was not so sure his father had Sonya in mind.[185]

• • •

John Ruskin, the foremost English art critic in the nineteenth century, was a thirty-four-year-old naïf when he married Effie, eighteen. He had by then published his greatest opus *Modern Painters*, the result of countless visits to all the important museums on the continent and faithful sketches of their nude statuary.

On his wedding night, however, he proved he had still a long way to go to match even a plowman's knowledge of the female form.

James McNeill Whistler was the worst person to make any statement on Ruskin, but his capsule description of what happened on Ruskin's marriage night is authentic:

"On their wedding night he [Ruskin] made an alarming discovery: pubic hair. He explained to his bride, after he got his breath back, that he had never seen a female body before (he was over thirty, mark you) and hers was not what he had been led to expect. He had formed his expectations of a woman's body, he said, from his observations of Greek and Roman statuary, Aphrodites and Venuses, and they hadn't this curious disfigurement. It was clear, therefore, that this pubic hair must represent a deformity peculiar to his bride. The sight so staggered and repelled Ruskin that he spent the next six years in a solitary bedroom."[186]

The whole event was ominous from the start. Ruskin's parents refused to attend the wedding because it was to be held in the room at Bowerswell where his grandfather had committed suicide, the very room in which Effie was later born.

Robinson Jeffers commented on the Ruskin old couple poetically:

> If God had been good enough
>   to give you a poet
> Then listen to him. But for God's

sake let him alone until
he is dead; no prizes
no ceremony,
They kill the man.[187]

The *prima nox* experience altered John Ruskin's life. He feared to touch his bride and told her she had to wait until she reached twenty-five before he would consummate the marriage. Intercourse at eighteen would desecrate her; he wanted to preserve her beauty.

The bridegroom spent the rest of his honeymoon correcting page proofs, examining rocks, collecting minerals, and watching twilights. In one of his first daily letters home, he reported: "I seem born to conceive what I cannot execute."

The marriage was annulled six years after what Effie characterized as a "hideous" first night, she having been declared *virgina intacta.*

Effie married Ruskin's best friend, the painter Millais. She gave birth to eight children in quick succession.

The elderly Ruskins drew a measure of compensation from their son's uncoupling: "We shall at least have John all to ourselves."

MY YIDDISHE MAMA

Though plagued by a heavy cold, Lytton Strachey, on an impulse even he couldn't explain, rushed across London and knocked on Virginia Stephen's door at 29 Fitzroy Square, London, to propose marriage. It was February 17, 1909. "I proposed," he later wrote his brother, "and was accepted. It was an awkward moment . . . especially as I realized, the very moment it was happening, that the whole thing was repulsive to me."

Virginia, with little show of emotion, accepted him.

Then, in a calmer moment, he had second thoughts and admitted to himself that he was really, says Virginia's nephew Quentin Bell, "alarmed by her sex and her virginity; he was terrified by the notion that she might kiss him," and was even more horrified by perceiving that "his imagined 'paradise of married peace' was an impossibility; it would not do at all. He was horrified by the situation in which he had placed himself, all the more so because he believed that she loved him."

Virginia told him she did not love him. "Nor did she," Bell thinks. "She might accept his personality, but not, when it came to the push, his person. She had always been, as she was later to admit, a sex coward and her only experience of male carnality had been terrifying and disgusting." Bell was referring to her stepbrother's sexual advances to Virginia when she was not yet a teenager. And Bell adds, "Lytton's homosexuality might even have been a source of reassurance; as a husband he would not be sexually exigent and a union with him, almost fraternal in character, might perhaps grow by degrees into something real, solid and deeply affectionate."[188]

Strachey was relieved. Virginia was disappointed and saddened. He sent off a letter to Leonard Woolf in Ceylon to suggest he marry Virginia, and Woolf replied: "Do you think Virginia would have me? Wire to me if she accepts. I'll take the next boat home."

It was probably not so simplistic as all this sounds. Woolf returned to England, relieved to get out of his seven-year stretch of diplomatic service. Back home, he joined the Bloomsbury cultist friends around Strachey in "The Apostles," a group that had a restricted membership. His Cambridge friend Thoby brought him and introduced him to his sister.

Virginia then was twenty-seven. The sun was setting. When Leonard met her, she had had at least one mental breakdown.

After a whirlwind courtship, Leonard proposed to her. He had no money or job. She had an annual income by legacy of four hundred pounds. "It took me 48 hours to come to a decision," he says in his autobiography *Beginning Again*, "and on Wednesday I wired to Virginia asking whether I could see her the next day. Next day I went up to London and asked her to marry me. She said she did not know and must have time—indefinite time—to see more of me before she would make up her mind."[189]

"He interests me immensely," she wrote to a close friend. "L. thinks my writing the best of me . . . wants me to say that if I ceased to write when married, I shall be divorced."

She felt she had to get prior approval from her lesbian friend Violet Dickinson.

My Violet,
I've got a confession to make. I'm going to marry Leonard Woolf. He's a penniless Jew. I'm more happy than anyone ever said was possible—but I *insist* upon your liking him too. May we both come on Tuesday? Would you rather I come alone? . . . You have always been such a splendid and delightful creature, whom I've loved ever since I was a mere chit, and that I couldn't bear it if you disapproved of my husband. We've been talking

a great deal about you. I tell him you're 6 ft 8, and that you love
me . . ."[190]

Eventually Violet did get to like Leonard.

Strachey was the first to get the news of her decision, the "gentle
disengagement," in a postcard message:

> Ha! Ha!
> Virginia Stephen
> Leonard Woolf

The religious barrier did not ruffle Leonard, if it ever entered his
mind. He had by this time become a confirmed atheist and decidedly
opposed to following the contemporary rush to conversion. One cannot, however, fail subliminally to cut the umbilical cord and take a
step to bridge the difference between a Lord Sackville direct descendant and a Maimonides heir.

"Both my parents were respectably religious," Woolf noted many
years later. "They believed in God. My mother went to synagogue
on Saturday mornings fairly often, my father on major feasts and fes-
tivals." He conceded to take religious instruction and bar mitzvah
and a year later informed them he was an unbeliever and would no
longer go to synagogue.

"When I solemnly announced to my mother that I no longer believed in Jehovah, she wept, but her tears were not very convincing,
I think, either to me or to her. She was genuinely distressed, but not
very acutely. That I should repudiate the deity and refused to go to
synagogue caused a family sensation, but only a mild one which lasted
a very short time."[191]

What Mrs. Woolf said when her prize son informed her of his decision to marry out of his faith we shall never know. Fortunately,
Mrs. Woolf was practical and sensible enough not to provoke a mother-
in-law nuisance and, inwardly reluctant but outwardly gracious, she
accepted Virginia.

Protocol required that Virginia and Leonard make the rounds of
their respected *mishpochas*. Meeting her future Jewish mother-in-law
constituted a daunting experience for Virginia. Her nephew tells us
that Mrs. Woolf was "a matriarchal figure living with her large family
in Colinette Road, Putney; seemed very alien to Virginia. No place
could have been less like home than her future mother-in-law's house.

And how did the Woolfs regard her? Did they perceive that she thought their furniture hideous? Did she seem to be a haughty goy, thinking herself too good for the family of their brilliant son? I am afraid they probably did."[192]

Virginia was thinking of that first visit to the Woolfs when she described a similar situation in her novel *Night and Day*. She felt she disgraced herself at the "get-acquaintance" tea at Putney.

"A sandwich, Miss Stephens—or may I call you Virginia?"

"What? Ham sandwiches for tea?"

"Not *ham*: potted meat. We don't eat ham or bacon or shellfish in this house."

"Not shellfish? Why not shellfish?"

"Because it says in the Scriptures that they are unclean creatures and our Mr. Josephs at the Synagogue. & . . ."

"It was queer."[193]

What a way to break down the religious barriers! That barrier never came down. Virginia was probably too biased to bend altogether. She once wrote to Leonard's sister, an Orthodox Jew, "I do not like the Jewish voice; I do not like the Jewish laugh."

Leonard could not have picked a more clear-cut symbol of his complete break with Jewish traditions than to have chosen to be married on a Saturday or to have agreed to stand before an altar as unsanctified in his mother's eyes for the marriage ceremony as the St. Pancreas Registry Office. To Virginia, who was on the verge of another nervous breakdown, a civil ceremony like this seemed an exemplary way to get legally married. The rite was simple and soon over with.

Because it was the Sabbath, Leonard's widowed mother did not attend. Most likely she was listening to Rabbi Josephs' sermon at temple. Besides, she would have felt out of place in the registry, even if she had been urged to come. But she wasn't invited, nor were any other of the prolific Woolf family.

Witnesses to the ceremony have given various versions of what took place. According to Bell, "the Registrar found it trying, partly because he was, or so it seemed to Virginia, half blind, partly because a violent thunderstorm was raging and partly because, when it came to witnessing the marriage, he got muddled by names which to him seemed unfamiliar: Virginia and, still worse, Vanessa."[194]

The groom's own version reveals more of the spirit hovering over the occasion. In those days St. Pancreas Registry Office was in a room that looked down into a cemetery. "In the ceremony before a Registrar," he writes, "one makes no promise 'to love and to cherish, till death do us part, according to God's holy ordinance,' but in the St. Pancreas Office, facing the window and looking through it at the tombs behind the Registrar's head, one was, I suppose, appropriately reminded of the words 'till death do us part.' Apart from the tombstones, our wedding ceremony was provided with an element of comic relief (quite unintended) characteristic of the Stephens. In the middle of the proceedings, Vanessa interrupted the Registrar, saying: 'Excuse me interrupting; I have just remembered: we registered my son—he is two years old—in the name of Clement, and we now want to change his name to Quentin—can you tell me what I have to do?' There was a moment of astonished silence in the room as we all looked round sympathetically and saw the serious, slightly puzzled look on Vanessa's face. There was a pause while the Registrar stared at her with his mouth open. Then he said severely: 'One thing at a time, please, Madam.' "[195]

Surprisingly, Virginia did not provoke a mother-in-law problem. Phyllis Grosskurth, reviewing her letters, said that John Lehmann, who took charge of the Hogarth Press, told her that "Virginia often made antisemitic remarks in Leonard's presence" and he refused to induce her to remove some offensive passages about Jews from her novel *The Years*.[196] Inwardly, she was contemptuous to the Woolf clan, Leonard's mother in particular. In a note in her diary, she wrote "Work and love and Jews in Putney take it out of me." She fretted at the sacrifice of the one day in her writing or reading proofs when Mrs. Woolf and her son Herbert made their annual visit for lunch at Monks House. "She has, I think, the qualities of a person who has never altogether grown up, in spite of 9 children & all her cares. She gossips & enjoys herself & bursts into tears because she feels she ought to burst into tears; . . ."

Yet when Mrs. Woolf died, Virginia was truly saddened.[197]

From a sexual point of view, the honeymoon was unpropitious. Virginia was frigid. Apparently, she did lose her virginity and expected to have children she ardently desired. Clearly, the honeymoon was disappointing to both Leonard and Virginia. She reveals her mood in the letter she wrote during the honeymoon to Ka Cox:

"Why do you think people make such a fuss about marriage & copulation? Why do some of our friends change upon losing chastity?

Possibly my great age makes it less of a catastrophe; but certainly I find the climax immensely exaggerated. Except for a sustained good humor (Leonard shan't see this) due to the fact that every twinge of anger is at once visited upon my husband, I might still be Miss S."[198]

Quentin Bell makes a telling observation: "Vanessa, Leonard, and I think, Virginia herself were inclined to blame George Duckworth [Virginia's stepbrother]. George certainly left Virginia with a deep aversion to lust; but perhaps he did no more than inflame a deeper wound and confirm Virginia in her disposition to shrink from the crudities of sex, a disposition which resulted from some profound and perhaps congenital inhibition. I think that the erotic element in her personality was faint and tenuous."[199]

When she accepted Leonard's proposal, Virginia wrote him, "I want everything,—love, children, adventure, intimacy, work." Children were on their minds when they returned from the honeymoon. Fearful of any strain pregnancy might have upon her, he induced her to visit the doctor at the nursing home where she had been a mental patient. Another doctor whom they consulted said unreservedly that it would be dangerous for her to bear children. They accepted the verdict. For years she could not hide her envy of her sister's maternity.

Virginia was fifty-eight when she wrote a note to her husband saying she intended to drown herself: "Dearest, I want to tell you that you have given me complete happiness. No one could have done more than you have done. . . . But I know that I shall never get over this: and I am wasting your life."[200]

MY YIDDISHE MOTHER-IN-LAW

Of a radically different stripe was Jessica Mitford's Jewish mother-in-law, Aranka, mother of Jessica's husband, Bob Treuhaft. She was headstrong, aggressive, and blunt. She would not let go of Bob, who in turn was firmly attached to her, especially after she became a widow. Fortunately for her marriage to her Bronx-born husband, Jessica applied her sense of humor to Aranka's ceaseless charges that she was responsible for his becoming actively involved with the leftist movement and joining marches against the capitalist system of which she was proud to claim herself a loyal supporter.

Jessica had joined the Communist Party, attended cell meetings, peddled *The People's World,* went to Mississippi in behalf of the Willie McGee cause, took the Fifth defiantly before the McCarthy hearings, and was constantly in collision with the authorities.

Virginia Woolf, encouraged by Leonard, simply ignored his mother, having found her silly and boring but with at least the redeeming trait that she kept out of her Lenny's personal life. Aranka felt that her Bob's future was hers for direction and kept poking into his domestic trivia.

The diversity of two mothers-in-law couldn't have been more pronounced. The whole family from whom Jessica had made a much publicized breakaway moved in a different world from that of the Treuhafts. Her father, Lord Redesdale, was an eccentric, a rabid anti-Semite whose lineage went all the way back to the Saxons. Jessica could use the prefix *Hon.* Her mother felt privileged dining with the Führer. Her sister Unity was a notorious Hitlerphile and always carried a pistol in her handbag. "It's for practicing to kill Jews," she told everyone. Another sister, Diana, was wife of the fanatical Jew-baiter Sir Oswald Moseley, founder of the British Union of Fascists.

Jessica's Jewish mother-in-law Aranka came to America from Hungary and had, by dint of hard work, artistic talent, and gutsiness, lifted herself out of a New York millinery sweatshop into owning a fashionable hat shop on Park Avenue. The crown of her success was Bob. She never let him forget how he had glorified her by being the first Jew to be accepted at Harvard "within living memory." Maternal pride could go no higher.

Then along came this unholy alliance with a minx who threatened to demolish everything Aranka worked for, wanted, and stood for. What if this was no ordinary girl her Bob married? Worse: she was, *horribile dictu,* a Communist!

Jessica was bent on a policy of appeasement. "I had looked forward to meeting Aranka," she says in *A Fine Old Conflict,* "to being clasped to the warm and loving bosom of a Jewish family, as I inferred from Jewish literature would be my good fortune."

But Bob, she writes, "was far from sanguine about this prospect—a *shiksa* of radical persuasion with a two-year-old child [from her previous marriage to no lower celebrity than Sir Edward Romilly, cousin to Winston Churchill!] he suggested, was arguably not the ideal bride for the apple of Aranka's eyes."[201]

When Aranka came out to California, her son felt he had to use masterly tact to control the confrontation between his mother and his wife.

The introductory meeting took place at their boardinghouse on a note of impending disaster. But Jessica was resolved on making peace, on any terms. "After this inauspicious beginning," she says, "things did not improve. I tried to be a good daughter-in-law, to fall in with Aranka's ideas about the proper care and treatment of Bob, yet I seldom succeeded in pleasing. She confided that Bob, 'like his father, may he rest in peace,' suffered from a lack of ambition, that he was not sufficiently motivated to rise in the world, to get ahead to earn more money. My role as a wife should be to instill these aspirations by being more demanding. I should insist on having a fur coat, a better car, costly objects that would compel him to set his monetary goals ever higher."[202]

The relationship turned out better than either belligerent or son had expected, and a disarmed Jessica turned it into *théâtre comique.* She enjoyed parodying, without a trace of offending, Aranka's idiom on the subject of success as Bob's mother viewed it. Jessica writes that when he set out the next morning to take the Haight Street trolley, she leaned out of her window and yelled, "Get to work, you lazy good-for-nothing bum! How do you think you'll ever amount to anything? I want a new coat! I want a car! Off with you!" Aranka, who was within hearing all this, Jessica says, was not amused.

"I can't seem to do right," she told Bob. "Really, there's *no* pleasing your mother."[203]

During her short stay in California, Aranka often dropped in to explore the territory. When she heard Bob was in Phoenix on a union case, she turned to Jessica: "So where is he? Always for the union he's doing things. Isn't it about time he did something for himself?" She faulted them for the way they brought up the children in the house. When she found Bob preparing a formula bottle for their boarder's child, she commented *sotto voce:* "I sent my son to Harvard he should baby-sit for a longshoreman's children?"[204]

Jessica couldn't resist injecting an occasional teasing note in letters to her mother-in-law, who had returned to her shop in New York: "Thank you *so* much for the perfectly heavenly coats from Best's, the children look *too* lovely in them, just the thing to wear on the picket line Saturday." And in another stab: "Bob and I have been subpoenaed by the House Committee on Un-American Activities on account of being subversives, so could you be an angel and send me a smart hat from your shop to wear at the hearing?" And this, the sticking point: "Bob's left the Gladstone's firm because they were making too much money."[205]

"I must have appeared to her as the wrecker of all her dreams," Jessica admits, likely suppressing a guffaw. "Once, when I was showing her some photographs of Chatsworth [her sister's estate] . . . she turned on me in exasperation: 'So why couldn't *you* marry a duke like your sister?' 'But, Aranka, then I should never have met you,' I said laughing. Which, I surmised was the unspoken wish behind her outburst."[206]

Eventually they became friends, but the baiting continued, says Jessica, though by now regarded appreciatively by Aranka, "gradually she became reconciled to me. She even dimly began to see the joke of herself through my eyes. Once in New York, Bob had gone to fetch some delicatessen for a party we were having in her apartment. Opening up the package of cold cuts, she exclaimed, 'This he sold you for three dollars a pound? You should take it back and throw it at his head!' Thereafter, whenever we bought food I would say, 'Aranka, shall we nip back to the store and throw it at his head?' And far from minding, she would let out an appreciative giggle."[207]

Jessica had run away from home, and her father excluded her from his will. Her mother, called Muv affectionately, however, kept writing to her but carefully avoided politics. She sent presents to Jessica's children.

Suddenly, replying to Dinky, one of Jessica's children, who had written, "Dear Granny Muv, Thank you for the lovely book. I wish you would come to see us in Oakland one day," the climate changed.

Next week, to Jessica's consternation, a telegram came back: "Have accepted Dinky's invitation. Arriving San Francisco in a fortnight."

It was like a bombshell. Jessica had not seen her mother in nine years. In 1937 she had tea with the Führer, which had outraged the Treuhafts. "I was at once immensely excited at the thought, pleased and touched that she would make the long expensive journey, and deeply apprehensive that the visit would be a disastrous failure. How would she get on with Bob? And the children?"

When she came off the plane Dinky met her: "Granny Muv, when are you going to scold Decca [Jessica's family pet name] for running away?"

But Granny came to Oakland for a reconciliation and had resolved to say nothing hostile.[208]

Before Lady Redesdale came to America, she expressed a desire to meet Bob's mother in New York. "Though dubious as to the wisdom of bringing two such wildly disparate characters together," Jessica says, "I was nonetheless intrigued by the situation-comedy possibilities their meeting might offer. . . . [and] arranged for Muv to spend a day with Aranka during the stopover in New York on her return journey. If this worked out well, I said to Bob, I would make our fortune by opening a West Coast-East Coast Mother-in-law Coordinating Bureau, charging steep fees for arranging transcontinental encounters between unlikely in-laws.

"The meeting was a huge success. We got rave reviews from both participants. Aranka wrote in her idiosyncratic spelling, 'Your mother is a wonderfull person, a real laddy, so gratfull for everything, I loved her.' And Muv: 'Mme Aranka was *too* kind, she gave me the most beautiful hat it will be my summer joy.' "[209]

The armistice between the families—except Lord Redesdale, Diana Moseley and Unity Mitford—resulted in peace agreements, with only an occasional flare-up, not too seriously disruptive. Jessica's sister Nancy met Aranka in Paris at a fashion show and wrote to Jessica: "Aranka. Well, I absolutely love her, she is a *dear*. Also she's the only person who gives me news of you, so I eat her up whenever she comes. She simply thinks the world of you, she says you're so wonderful that I thought *you must have altered considerably.*"[210]

Some Whores Make the Best Wives

"If you're married to a whore," observed Arthur Koestler, with a jaundiced eye on his old whore Russia, "it doesn't make any difference that you know she's a whore, that she sleeps around. You tell yourself every time: 'At least not with that one.' "

There is plenty of evidence that some whores make the best wives.

At the end of World War I, W. H. Davies, poet and author of *The Autobiography of a Super-Tramp*, was middle-aged, ailing, and impecunious. He decided that he was tired of bumming around the globe and set out to find a wife who would be lover, nurse, and housekeeper. This combination, he was convinced, could be found in a streetwalker.

The first likely candidate he picked up one night turned out to be a sergeant-major's spouse—dishonest, alcoholic, and an experienced whore. The affair petered out.

Davies's second find was the gentle Louise, a French girl very eager to please. However, the lovable Louise left him for another man.[211]

Desperately, he continued to roam the streets, but it wasn't easy for him to find an honest lover, tired or bored by "the life," who wanted to exchange it for the duties of caring for a sick man. One night his luck turned. He saw an attractive young woman step off the bus at Marble Arch. Because of the lateness of the hour, he knew she must be out on business. She had beauty and youth—would she want him? After an hour of earnest conversation, she asked him to take her home with him, and in his modest little house the next morning, she agreed to move in with him. But she had to have a week to make arrangements.

During the week, he feared she had returned to her former profession, but when she came back, she seemed eager to take him on.

Complications set in. In a few days he began to hemorrhage. (Had he contracted venereal disease from a streetwalker he had pitied, who had once tried to strangle herself with a silk stocking?) Then Helen herself hemorrhaged—but hers turned out to be a miscarriage. She was carrying another man's child.

Arthur Calder-Marshall pictures the household: "Each lies helpless on a different floor in the house. When she is taken to hospital, the poet is looked after by a harridan who makes life hell."

Meanwhile, Davies made up his mind to clinch matters. Marriage was the only way. He had never felt such love before. He proposed and she readily accepted. She was not marrying him for his money; she had probably never read his poems or his magnum opus; clearly, she had fallen in love with him.

At fifty-one, a battered man, but famous and with royalties mounting, Davies was beginning to show signs of wear. He was in and out of hospitals with crippling rheumatism and trouble with his leg. But he still had a lot of living in him and he didn't want to lose Helen. He had many solicitous literary friends and, at long last, a social life.

When Davies asked his closest friend, Conrad Aiken, to be a witness at the marriage ceremony, Aiken agreed, but wondered how the union could last; the groom looked old enough to be the bride's grandfather. Aiken recalls that before the wedding, Davies "was scarcely able to speak for fright, though he laughed heartily at the old joke about the bridegroom who carried a ring in every pocket in case of a lapse of memory."[212]

"The old poet had incorrectly remembered his bride's name," Aiken wrote to Robert Linscott, "and the registrar was disturbed; books were consulted; in which by-laws were engraved in old granite; the old poet trembled and licked his dry lips; the bride giggled and looked at [me] with humid eyes. After all, thus spoke the old registrar, the name Matilda is not *wholly* unlike the name Elizabeth; let them be married."[213]

The first months of marriage proved the most idyllic of the poet's life. Davies wrote:

> With this small house, this garden large,
> This little gold, this lovely mate,
> With health in body, peace at heart—
> Show me a man more great.[214]

* * *

H. G. Wells once said: "The trouble with Gissing was that he thought there was a difference between a woman and a lady, but we all know there is no difference at all." George Gissing ruined his life by a refusal to make love to any woman he could regard as a social equal.

Depressed and lonely, wandering about the streets of his native Manchester, Gissing, just eighteen, picked up a prostitute, Nell Harrison, no older than himself; bent on reforming her, he shacked up with her in his lodgings in a slum in order to get her off the streets. He was then a brilliant student of Owens College, now the University of Manchester. He was desperately poor. He pawned his father's gold watch to buy Nell a sewing machine. He was torn by the conflict between buying books and meeting his bodily needs. He tried resolving his problem by stealing money from overcoat pockets in the lockers of his fellow students. When the thefts were discovered, he was expelled and imprisoned, and then, so he could have a fresh start, his parents shipped him off to America. There for a year, he nearly starved to death.[215]

Returning to England, he married Nell and wrote frantically on the themes of all his novels: social injustice and the ghastly conditions of the poor. In time Nell became bored by respectable matrimony and living on bread, drippings, and thin lentil soup, and left her husband for more alluring and profitable streetwalking. After months of searching for her, he received a summons to a mortuary in Lambeth to identify her corpse. She had died from alcoholism, tuberculosis, and venereal disease.

Frank Swinnerton tells us that Gissing was "unable to imagine himself in a sexual relationship with any of the few educated women he knew."

Two years after Nell's death, to relieve his overpowering loneliness, he picked up the first girl he encountered in Regent Park on a Sunday afternoon, a servant girl, Edith Underwood, the wholly uneducated daughter of a tombstone cutter. He proposed to her on the spot, and married her. She bore him two children. He had kept the marriage secret from his well-born friends. His first wife had infected him with syphilis, and he in turn infected the second. She eventually had to be locked up in an asylum and was still there when he died in 1903.[216]

. . .

When Stephen Crane left Lafayette College, he vowed that if he ever met a girl with golden hair he'd propose marriage to her on the spot. This is just what he did when he visited Miss Cora Taylor's Hotel de Dream in Jacksonville, Florida.

There was something about the seamy side of life that held an allure for Crane. As a reporter in his early twenties, he deliberately picked the New York Tenderloin district for his beat. His experience with flophouses and sex crimes paid off in his novel *Maggie: Girl of the Streets.*

Along with other correspondents and adventurers, Crane was forced to linger in Jacksonville for two weeks before taking ship to Havana to cover the Cuban rebellion for the *New York Journal.* He mingled with bums in the town's honkytonk joints, played poker there with sharpies around the clock, until one evening his eye caught the blazing sign HOTEL DE DREAM. He decided to give the place a try. It called itself a "Class A" nightclub but was actually a fashionable whorehouse. That visit proved to be the watershed of his short life.

The proprietor, Miss Cora Taylor, found the twenty-four-year-old Stephen appealing in his cowboy leggings and open plaid shirt. A gun at the ready in his holster signified adventure. Cora looked a cut above the madams he had known in the Bowery fleshpots. She was pretty, winning, vivacious, and fragrant. And she had golden hair!

She took a seat beside him and began to talk as if they had known each other for years. When he told her he was a writer and gave his name, she moved closer and they fell to talking, not shop, but literature. She told him she had been fascinated by his *Maggie* and *The Red Badge of Courage*, loved writers, and had herself writing ambitions. Before the first hour was up he was smitten.

Cora felt that she had met her father confessor. She held nothing back. She admitted to being thirty-one, six years older than he; she added that she had had a few crushes, but they got her nowhere. Taylor was not her real name: she had taken it for business reasons.

Crane gushed out a proposal of marriage. She hesitated, told him with lowered eyes she couldn't marry because she was still legally married to Captain Donald William Stewart, who had walked out on her after six months, but adamantly the bum refused to give her a divorce.

Crane waved the flaw aside. What will Miss Grundy say? He didn't care. As for Cora, she had long been accustomed to abusive gossip. She had a will of iron.

Those hours in her private office were probably the shortest courtship in literary history. After much pressuring, Cora agreed to become his common-law wife. She pledged to lock her fate in with Crane's. She took no time about cementing the new link. She pulled up her stakes in Jacksonville and told him she would go with him to the ends of the earth. She welcomed the opportunity to be the first woman war correspondent, and they left together for Cuba on the first available ship.

Fearing he might never return alive, he made out his will giving one third of his estate to his brother William, whom he designated as his executor, and the rest equally to his two other brothers.

From Cuba they sailed to cover the Greco-Turkish war and then on to England.

Joseph Conrad went down to London to meet Crane. He had already sent him a copy of *Almayer's Folly* and inscribed it: "To Stephen Crane with the greatest regard and most sincere admiration." He suggested that he settle in Brede Place on the Sussex border. The place was swarming with celebrated authors. Literary England took him in with open arms. It expressed great respect for him as a war correspondent and the author of two great novels. Conrad exulted over Crane's short story "The Open Boat."

He was already a well-known writer. He was feted at a Fabian Society dinner, where dozens of England's great writers shook his hand warmly. Galsworthy praised his *Red Badge of Courage.*

The decision to expatriate permanently appeared as the only next right step to take. "There seems so many of them in America who want to kick, bury and forget me purely out of unkindness and envy— my unworthiness, you choose," he said. Stories had reached his ear that gossips had been having a field day saying he was an untouchable, a drug addict and foul-swearing alcoholic.

More than anything, he had the gut feeling that here in England no one would think of throwing dirt at Cora or of hounding them for their unsanctified relationship.

Crane notified his brother that he was settling permanently in England with Cora and intended to marry her there. Obviously, he didn't. Henceforth he introduced her as Mrs. Stephen Crane.

It was taken for granted everywhere he went that Cora was his wife. People were too polite to ask questions. How could they? H. G. Wells, who became one of his first friends and admirers, lived for years with his common-law wife Amy (he called her Jane), and was at the same time a self-professed shameless womanizer. Ford Madox Ford was an unprincipled sexual freewheeler. Henry James, although a prude, who openly expressed great regard for Crane's novels, would not have ventured to visit him had he known. As Howard Moss points out in his review of *Group Portrait:* "If James had known the facts about Cora, it's doubtful he would have allowed himself to be photographed at a garden fete." Meredith snubbed her. No great shake there! But A. E. W. Mason, James Barrie, and others accepted her warmly. Conrad became Crane's neighbor and close friend.

Somehow Cora did not attract most of the writers who came to Crane's home, Brede Manor. Richard Harding Davis, an old correspondent and crony, remarked after his first visit to Brede: "She is a commonplace dull woman old enough to be his mother with dyed yellow hair." R. W. Stallman is quick with a rebuttal: "Her sunny hair was not artificial and she wasn't dull and commonplace. She was plump and dowdy."[217]

Another visitor remarked, "She looked like a dance-hall girl in the morning." But being with the hero Crane made up for his wife's lack of class.

Jessie Conrad loved Cora.

Obviously, the Cranes were in love. Stephen's eyes showed his enjoyment at seeing her run their home as if to the manor born.

It was that way from their first hour together. A telegraph operator who saw them together after Crane survived as a hero in the *Commodore* disaster noted how she rushed out to embrace Crane. "They sat in a corner of the waiting room with their arms around one another, kissing and hugging like love birds, until time for the afternoon train."[218]

Years later, over half a century after Crane died, one of his spongers at Brede could still recall: "I have never known two people more deeply in love with one another than were Stephen and Cora. Their sweetness and confidence each for the other were touching and charming."[219]

For all the stimulating ambience provided by a group of encouraging neighbors, Crane could not have picked a worse place for a tubercular person to live in. The venerable pile was drafty, damp, broken down, uncomfortable. Bats flew about the ceilings. The place lacked plumbing, gas, toilets—visitors had to use the shrubbery outside. Heating came only from open fireplaces.

Even if he had rented more modern, luxurious, and smaller living quarters Crane would have faced the same problems given his personality and eccentricities. In effect, he was trying to make the place his dream hotel. And he ran it like a hotel. He spent thousands of pounds, which he didn't have, trying to restore it, with the result that he had to work feverishly to meet its basic maintenance.

To be sure, he had only himself to blame if the manor got beyond control. He wanted to act the baron of a manor; in fact, he often heard himself referred to as Baron Brede. And it delighted him. He lived in splendor far beyond his means. Visitors were always dropping in for free lunch and champagne. Others were asked to come and stay as long as they wished. The weekend crush rivaled the traffic around Sandgate, where H. G. Wells lived. Like Crane, Wells could hardly afford the expenses and like Crane was driven to write beyond his strength to pay the bills. Conrad called Crane "poor Stevie" and "dear old chap," but he loved the free meals and the brilliant author talk. When the American ambassador congratulated the expatriate celebrity on his success, Crane replied, "I wish success paid me a salary, sir."

Needless to say, Crane was not cut out to be a baron, or Cora a baroness. He was plagued by creditors, overdrawn accounts, grocers, butchers, and other tradesmen who barged in to press for payment. He put them off with promises of "sure and quick money." And he had perforce to resort to all manner of stratagems. In a letter asking his literary agent James B. Pinker for a one-hundred-pound advance, he asked him to word his telegram vaguely since the letter carrier was also his unpaid grocer. When Wells urged him to write fewer stories and relax and play tennis as he did of an afternoon, Crane threw up his hands and said, "I got to do them!"

Henry James tried to contribute a bit of comfort, Ford Madox Ford said: "Once he telegraphed to Wanamaker's for a whole collection of New England delicacies from pumpkin pie to apple butter and sausage meat and clams and soft shell crabs and minced meat and . . . everything thinkable, so that the poor lad should know once more and finally those fierce joys."[220]

London bohemians came to Brede in droves—Conrad called them Indians—popular writers passing by, and his more friendly celebrated neighbors came and admired the man who brought something special and exotic to the countryside, a breath of the wildness of America.

And Crane lapped up the praise hungrily. Ford gushed: "Crane was the most beautiful spirit I have ever known. He was small, frail, energetic. . . . He wore breeches, riding leggings, spurs, a cowboy's shirt and there was always a gun near him. . . . In that ancient edifice he would swat flies with precision and satisfaction with the bead side of his gun."[221]

Another literary idolator, Edwin Pugh, was more lovingly graphic: "To say that he was rather tall, inclined to stoop a little, very fair, with a slight moustache and resplendent hair of pale brown, seems trivial. To say that he was beautiful and brave and careless, might be misleading. . . . He talked with a lazy American accent, and he flopped and lunged about a good deal. His hands were miracles of strength and cleverness."[222]

However, to say that Crane loved the invaders, however disruptive and expensive, is only half true. There were times when he felt depressed and overwhelmed, and he was privately caustic over strangers—"lice," he called them—who signed up at his hotel. "How does it come to pass," he asked Sanford Bennett, "that anybody in England thinks that he can come and stay with me before I've asked him and patronize my wife's housekeeping?"[223] But then he corrected himself and sent out half a dozen invitations to "friends" to come and stay as long as they wished.

Crane realized they were sponging but he enjoyed the deference, the conviviality, the flow of champagne, bracing talk. Pinker was always good for a touch, but the canny agent made sure he got signed notes in return.

There was bound to be a breakup, and the end of the three-year concert came one Christmas night at the end of a glorious house party with Wells and Conrad and others when Crane suffered a massive cerebral hemorrhage. He had to be taken to a sanatorium in Germany, where he died.

Cora probably had an inkling that Stephen had TB. No one who heard the racking coughs and saw him struggle with night sweats could not have known he was in a crisis. Stephen sedulously kept the seriousness of his condition from her and seldom complained. He once warned a friend: "Please have the kindness to keep your mouth shut about my health in front of Mrs. Crane hereafter. She can do nothing for me and I am too old to be nursed. It's all up with me but I will not have her scared. For some funny womanish reason she likes me. Mind this."[224]

Wells knew. "He did his utmost to conceal his symptoms and get on with dying," he said.

Before he left for Germany, Crane wrote a will leaving Cora all his personal effects—until she should marry—and the income from his royalties.

Conrad went down to Dover to see him off and later wrote that "one glance at that wasted face was enough to tell me that it was the most forlorn of all hopes. The last words he breathed out to me were: 'I am tired. Give my love to your wife and child.' " Conrad was the first to welcome him to England; he was the last friend to see him leave.[225]

After Crane's death at twenty-nine, Cora had to face a situation for which she was ill equipped. She was stranded on foreign shores, sat in her chair dazed and irresolute.

The estate was in a mess. Penniless, she tried to recoup some money by pursuing a semblance of the literary career she so ardently had wished for, but no publisher would take her stories.

Friends fled like rats from a scuttled ship—all except Jessie Conrad. There were no more teas, no more champagne parties, no more weekenders, except a last hurrah Cora arranged on Christmas Eve. With Stephen no longer around as a drawing card, his admirers dropped her cold. James was genuinely depressed for days but, except for one act, took an unceremonious leave. Knowing that the estate was on the brink of bankruptcy and seeing creditors in siege about the manor, he sent her a fifty-pound check as a "sort of convenience" for "whatever service it may best render my stricken friend. It meagerly represents my tender benediction to him." Then his smiles stopped forever.

H. G. Wells didn't deign to answer her pleas for money. In fact, he did not come to the funeral, giving the excuse that he couldn't stand funerals because they affected "me so darkly." Amy Wells sent her a New Year's card but no money. Henry James did not visit the mortuary. The Conrads came, says Stallman, "looked through the glass lid of the coffin for a last sight of Stephen and left cards."

To Cora's plea for assistance, Conrad pleaded: "What can I do? I am already in debt to my two publishers," and he asked her, "Won't Stephen's relatives come forward?"[226]

Playwright Arthur Pinero wrote her a note of sympathy, adding, "I never for one moment imagined you desired charity." When she asked Crane's publisher, Heinemann, who had never liked her, for all the contracts in his possession, he wrote back: "As you are aware, I advanced money to Mr. Crane on the security of the contracts and Ms which I hold, and I scarcely think I can give up all the contracts and papers until my account is settled."

When she threw that final Christmas Eve party before returning to America, Henry James, who had been a regular caller while Conrad was alive, begged off the invitation to her farewell party, saying he was "fast down" at Lamb House, and later peered through the curtained window when she passed but refused to invite her in.

Back in Jacksonville, after hauling luggage full of creditors' bills, Cora clung to her legal claim to her relationship with Stephen.

A battle royal over the estate followed. Her brother-in-law Judge Crane told her that as she was not Stephen's legal wife, she had no title to any money accruing from the Stephen Crane royalties. In the long drawn out probate proceedings, Stallman writes, the court named her merely as one of the next of kin. "Judge Crane had known his brother had never married Cora, and he did not let her know that he knew it, and thus he misled her as she had deceived him. She finally recognized that he had duped her, and declared her defeat to

Pinker on July 9, 1905: 'Judge Crane has not acted as a gentleman should.' "[227]

She took the casket to America and arranged a dignified service. A sprinkling of people attended, mostly out of curiosity.

Wallace Stevens attended as a reporter for the *New York Tribune* and wrote that he found the service "absolutely commonplace, bare, silly."

Cora had no alternative but to return to her original style of life. She became a madam again in Jacksonville, operating a whorehouse with the significantly new name the Court.

7

LAY FRIENDS

Get married, but never to a man who is at home all day.
—G. B. Shaw

Few men have made a wife of a mistress who have not repented it.
—Montaigne

It is easier to be a lover than a husband for the simple reason that it is more difficult to be witty every day than to say pretty things from time to time.
—Balzac

Male artists have more of a female component to their nature than the average male. I think that's why I've always stayed away from homosexuality.
—Norman Mailer

THE POET AND THE SHOP GIRL

There were only two things Heinrich Heine took seriously: money and God. With his personal Jehovah he waged a lifelong debate. With his mistress (later his wife), Mathilde, he played the baiting game for twenty years, cracking jokes (albeit *con amore*) at her expense and finding it hard to explain even to himself why he was obsessed with the simpleminded girl: "I seem fated to love the lowest and most foolish."

Mathilde's real name was Crescentia Eugénie Mirat. She entered Heine's life when he was thirty-seven, an expatriate in Paris with a price on his head, a political maverick, an ex-Jew. Though a "German Byron" by the age of twenty-four, he was restless, bored by other exiles like Karl Marx, and despondent. He lived on doles begrudged him by his banker in Hamburg, Uncle Salomon, who feared being blackmailed by his sharp-tongued, unpredictable nephew. Every day the few gray hairs on Heine's head reminded him he had little time left to reap fame and fortune.

Crescentia bewitched him at first sight. She promised a more permanent cure for his *mal de coeur* than the grisettes around the cafés.

Nineteen, the illegitimate daughter of a nobleman, she sold boots in her aunt's boutique. Charming, dimpled, and pretty, she pouted alluringly, a fresh country vision as she stood in the doorway of the bootery and smiled seductively at the young men who passed by.

Heine knew a good thing when he saw one. She liked him, too. He returned at the same time each day, brought her flowers and a pair of thrushes in a cage, and invited her to dances. As they strolled down the rue de Rivoli arm in arm, he noted with fear and pleasure how the young boulevardiers eyed him enviously. He called her his Helen of Troy, the *blume* (flower) he had sung about years before, "so bold, so schön, und rein." At long last he had found someone different from his bluestocking cousins, who flirted with him but snubbed him in the end because he wasn't rich, or the others, who loved only his bittersweet lyrics. This shopgirl captivated him because she loved him for himself: he was delighted that she had never read his *lieder* (songs). Hadn't Nietzsche and Kleist gone to pieces for lack of such a *naturelle*?

Because, he said in jest, her mouthful of names stuck in his German throat, he changed her name to Mathilde. (He was an expert at changing names; he had changed his own from Chaim, given him at his circumcision, to Harry, assimilated to Johann by his mother, who hated her Jewishness, to Heinrich at one of his first conversions, and now to Henri.) Mathilde called him *Einé*.

Even after living with him for five years, she didn't know he was a poet; she told her friends: "They say my Einé is a great poet. Is it not funny I should know nothing about it?" And he told one of his friends that he now had two sweethearts, a French mistress and a German muse, "but the two were not on speaking terms." His attempt to get the two to speak to each other was a dismal failure; the only German she could grasp was "My wife" and "Please sit down." He sent her to school so she could at least read her grocery bills, but it was a waste of ten thousand francs.

But what if she had never heard of Goethe or Shakespeare? He repeatedly complimented himself on his good fortune: would an intellectual have made him so happy? This unspoiled natural soul never plagued him with embarrassing questions; all she cared for was a fetching dress, a good restaurant meal, and the arms of her Einé. Highbrow talk he could get at the café.

A *hausfrau* Mathilde never became; the house was never cleaned, the beds seldom made. But her beautiful voice charmed him.

Afraid he'd lose her, afraid of being cuckolded, he would tease her about infidelities; she smiled and shrugged off the charge and made no scene. It was rumored that she was probably unfaithful when he was away on trips to Hamburg.

When famous writers—Sand, Béranger, Gérard de Nerval—found his address in the Paris directory and climbed four flights to see him, Heine kept Mathilde in her room. What would this cute thing know about their talk? In the early years of their living together, Heine found her ignorance so refreshing he liked to show it off. A caller reported: "We were in his more intimate little ménage on the Rue Cadet, and he was joking with his lady. . . . He told her that Christ had once been Archbishop of Paris—and she believed it!"[1]

He chuckled appreciatively when she went wild shopping for dresses and lingerie; when his brother called her a spendthrift, he replied, "It is better to have an extravagant angel than a stingy devil." To his mother, he wrote that he was blessed with "the sweetest little spendthrift. She has a weak head but a very good heart. . . . We live in the greatest harmony, in the most beautiful and expensive peacefulness. . . . We live harmoniously—that is, I yield in everything."[2]

Perhaps someday it will be understood why so many poets of love, with the exception of Byron and Burns, have had less sexual proficiency or even hunger than the average farmer. Heine was admittedly undersexed. His sexual gratification came from the *sehnsucht*, the romantic melancholy, of his lyrics. It was not until he was nearing forty that he sought the permanent sexual relationship provided by a mistress. Mathilde he found most satisfactory in bed: "forthright sexually irresponsible." She was slatternly, temperamental; they squabbled (over trifles only), but what couple in love did not?

When she made scenes, she bore no grudges and he let her have her way. His close friend Alexandre Weill sized up the domestic relationship: "Mathilde was in no way a bad character . . . but she liked to make scenes. In a rage she was capable of striking herself with her fists. But two minutes later, her wrath ended in tears and sobs. Heine sometimes had to treat her like a badly brought up girl, sometimes like a little pet animal one brings to reason with a slap; but he loved her all the more for that."[3]

She cajoled him into going on shopping sprees, taking her to restaurants, buying her a collection of parrots and cats. Her tantrums sometimes drove him wild; once when she bit on a glass with hysterical force he had to pick the pieces from her bleeding mouth. If he denied her a piece of lingerie, she would throw herself screaming on the floor. Of course he gave in—but he said, "There is something to be said for Platonism too!"

In *That Man Heine*, Lewis Browne said that Heine's problem was Mathilde's lack of sympathy with his work: "She could not even understand what he was doing, let alone inspire him. Mentally and spiritually these two lived in utterly different worlds; they spoke two different languages. And what made it worse, the grisette resented this even more than the poet. It angered her that most of her husband's acquaintances paid almost no attention to her, and she did her utmost to make it uncomfortable or even impossible to call on him at his home."[4]

After six years of living together, a crisis brought their illicit relationship to a head. Heine insulted a friend's wife—ironically, he attacked Börne for living with a woman out of wedlock—and was challenged to a duel. He asked himself what would happen to Mathilde if he should die. Since she didn't bear the Heine name, Uncle Salomon would surely cut off the 4800-franc allowance. As a common-law wife, she would not be entitled to a French pension. The only solution was marriage.

"The music at a wedding procession," Heine once said, "always reminds me of the music which leads soldiers into battle." He now had no alternative but to go into that battle.

A week before the time set for the duel, Heine went through a civil marriage with Mathilde at the Hotel de Ville. That was a sufficient safeguard to legalize their union should he die. Mathilde then pleaded for the traditional dual ceremony, civil and religious. She did not know that her Einé was Jewish. But to please her, he went through a solemn consecration at the St. Sulpice Church, quipping that all he was doing was adding one more farce to the long list of jokes in his checkered life.

Théophile Gautier was best man. Heine and Mathilde were an odd couple; at the time of their marriage, she was well over two hundred pounds, and he was barely half her weight. For the wedding breakfast, Heine invited only couples he knew were living together without benefit of clergy.

At forty-four he was a married man, and Mathilde was an honest woman. He broke the news to his sister: "On the 31st of August I married Mathilde Crescentia Mirat, with whom I had previously quarreled daily for more than six years. Yet she has a noble and pure heart, and is as good as an angel." To a friend who asked him how to explain this farce to the musician Rossini, Heine said, "Tell him that my happiness was decided with a pistol at my throat!" To please the priest, he pledged in writing that any children born would be reared in Mathilde's faith.[5]

Heine still visited his aged mother in Hamburg, whose favorite child he was, and every absence provoked a crisis. He was afraid to leave Mathilde alone for fear she would stray, and to keep her spirits up, he wrote her a long, touching letter each day. (There was always a girl in her aunt's bootery who would read it to her.) "You are the only joy in my life," said one letter. "Do not make me miserable. . . . Sit quietly in your nest, my little dove; do not show yourself in public, lest any of my friends should discover that you are in Paris without me." In the back of Heine's mind was the witticism circulating in the cafés: "Any Frenchwoman can be seduced in five minutes."

For the last decade of his life Heine struggled with his God, who he felt was testing him with afflictions greater than Job's; and like Job, he ended by praising his Maker for His wisdom.

The nature of Heine's basic disease is undetermined but the symptoms are recorded: cerebro-spinal syphilis (probably dating from his brothelizing youth); consumption of the spinal marrow; paresis; partial paralysis of his face, tongue, one good eye, writing hand. To read, he had to hold his good eye open. He confided to his sister that he was now impotent. Breathing was difficult and he lost his sense of taste. Heavy doses of morphine gave no relief. Mathilde had to lift him in and out of his chair onto his mattresses—"my mattress grave . . . a tomb without quiet, a death without the privilege of the dead."

Toward the end he wrote in severe pain, though not in self-pity: "I am no longer a divine biped; I am no longer the 'freest German since Goethe,' as I was called in the better days; I am no longer the Great Heathen, No. 2 . . . I am no longer a joyous Hellene, sound in body, smiling down gaily on the melancholy Nazarene. I am now only a poor sick Jew."[6]

For all her good intentions, Mathilde could not cope. She badgered him endlessly. She was outspoken in her jealousy of Camille, a lion hunter who came daily to take Heine's dictation (for he still scribbled with his limp hand). His teeming brain, the one organ mercifully left to him, drove him on to write his *Last Poems* and his masterpiece, a collection of narrative and lyric poems.

It took Mathilde an unconscionably long time to grasp the full implications of Heine's illness. She still shopped extravagantly, and he defended her: "She complains that she is no longer as pretty as she used to be, and that she must therefore dress to be more beautiful." She seemed to care more for her pets than for her invalid. To his complaint that the mewing of her cats made the pain in his ears and head unbearable, she asked him to consider the plight of her sick parrot, Cocotte. Eventually he had someone secretly poison the screeching Cocotte. To his visitor Meissner, Heine said he was not able to close his eyes all night when the cat fell from the mantelpiece and scratched an eye. "My good Mathilde remained up and applied cold poultices to the cat all night long. She never remains awake for me."

When Mathilde could take it no longer, she would leave, saying she couldn't bear the odor of sickness. The physician's remark that Heine required better nursing she took as a personal affront; she stopped the doctor on the landing and hit him full force in the eye.

At long last, even Mathilde realized Heine was dying. As he tossed on his cot, in his final "agony and revolt," she grew hysterical: "No, Einé, you couldn't do that to me, you couldn't die! . . . Have pity on me! . . . This morning I lost my parent; and if you die too, I should be too wretched!"

Through it all, Heine's mordant wit did not desert him. To calm her, he joked about his infirmities.

He now had the frame of a child. During a rare pause in his agony she carried him to a chair on the balcony and gave him her opera glass. He whispered to a caller: "You can't imagine how I felt. After all those years I was able once again to look out on the world—even though with only half an eye! . . . I took my wife's opera glass and looked with unbelievable delight at a little baker's boy who was offering his cakes to two ladies in crinoline, and a little dog standing against a tree. But I had to close the glass; I did not want to see any more—for I envied the dog!"[7]

Mathilde discouraged his visitors and brought in her own friends to relieve her boredom, who annoyed Heine. When Berlioz came to see him, the poet jested, "What! Someone is actually visiting me! Ah, but Berlioz was always original."

Heine called himself lucky. With Camille's help he wrote his mother that he was getting along well. "With doctors I will have no more to do. I observe that all the people who died here this winter had medical attention."[8]

When his friend, the director of the Comédie-Française, climbed the hundred steps to wish him well, Heine told him: "Do you know why you still find me here alive? Juliette [i.e. Mathilde] holds me here with all her might. She loves me so much, and when I am about to die she cries so wildly, that I wake up again to drink her tears."[9] And all this time he was writing his most lyrical verses, his most popular volume, *Romancero*. He complained that his lips were so paralyzed that he could not even hiss at one of Scribe's plays.

Heine told Weill, "When, after leaving the church, I made my will, I bequeathed everything to my wife. But I stipulated one condition: that she marry immediately after my death. You see, I have thus made sure that there shall be at least one man on earth who will regret my passing!"[10]

In three later wills he turned serious, enjoining Mathilde to have him buried not in overpopulated Père la Chaise but in Montmartre, in a simple service, with no priest, rabbi, or minister and no German words on his stone. "Everything German acts on me like an emetic. The German language tortures my ears." He wanted no Kaddish, no mass.

Mathilde followed his wishes to the letter. Two hundred people came to the grave in the rain. There were no relatives, and among celebrated Frenchmen, only Théophile Gautier and Alexandre Dumas fils.

Mathilde did not come. Some people jested that she had run off with her *maquereau*, her pimp. She returned to the apartment after the funeral.

Mathilde arranged to have a simple tombstone with the sole inscription *Henri Heine*.

At the unveiling, Heine's niece cried out in fury: "Not so much as a *Requiescat in Pace!*"

Mathilde died twenty-eight years after Heine.

NOT TONIGHT, MARGUERITE

When Arnold Bennett first met Marguerite Soulié in his Paris apartment, where she recited poetry for invited writers and artists, he exclaimed, "What a woman!"

Marguerite was then a *vendeuse* in a fashion house in the rue de la Paix and doing odd bits on the stage. Bennett had already produced *Anna of the Five Towns.* "I gave up the hope of a dramatic career to become the wife of the man I love," she wrote. She was first his mistress. He regularly commuted from England to visit her.

They both fell in love on the rebound. She had just come out of an unhappy love affair with a young lawyer, and Julian Green's sister had broken off her engagement to Bennett. Marguerite Soulié was thirty-three, a sophisticated Parisienne; he was forty, a bachelor already set in his ways.

"Bennett set about marrying as he sets about house-hunting," said H. G. Wells. "To him it was as objective a business as any other."

After they had lived together for several years, Bennett suddenly stammered, "Do you know what my friends are telling me? They are saying I ought to marry you!" Marguerite had long been expecting the declaration, but she responded coyly, "Oh, don't dazzle me with such a prospect if you are not serious."

He reassured her he was most serious. She badly wanted A. B., as she called him. He needed considerable fixing, but the alteration could come in good time, she was sure. In later years she knew how mistaken her early assessment of him had been, cynically noting in her journal: "I leave it to the biographers of the future to decide whether when he asked me to become his wife, Arnold Bennett was suffering from a broken heart or an overdose of stuffed cabbage."[11]

In time Marguerite realized she was the last person Arnold Bennett should have married. He had been too firmly indoctrinated by his Five Towns bourgeois background to bend before a wife; he turned out more complex than she had dreamed. He was proud of his accomplishments, practical ("I am a low-brow"), prudent, reserved, rigid, and, in her view, sexually repressed. On the other hand, she was emotional, demonstrative, willful, amorous, with Gallic regard for the amenities of the boudoir.

Petty disagreements arose the moment they left the altar and Bennett insisted on the upper hand even in domestic minutiae. He let her know in no uncertain terms that he could live only in a well regulated *ménage.* "I am a writer first," he told her; "the rest comes afterward." She had all she could do to swallow his terms.

Raymond Mortimer sums up Bennett's view of what he expected in a wife: "an elegant wife at ease in good society, whom he could display proudly to his friends, who would run his house perfectly, never interfere with his work or his social engagements, always agree that he was right about everything, and also prove an alluring, skilful bedfellow, whenever he had not too much work to do the following day."[12]

Marguerite had been bred in a different soil and a warmer climate. In *Arnold Bennett in Love,* by George Beardmore (Bennett's nephew) and Jean Beardmore, is an account of what Marguerite thought Bennett had in mind when he married her:

"He did not marry me just because he happened to want a wife (he had many women admirers); he did not marry me out of spite just because another woman had chucked him; he did not marry me just because I nursed him through an attack of indigestion. He married me with his eyes open and of his own free choice. He was no bashful lover, no victim of mooncalf love. He was an experienced bachelor of forty. He married me because I suited him."[13]

Bennett had to get it all down on paper. His Five Towns prescription was framed in the Bennett Plan—which his wife jotted down in her journal—sacred as the tablets of Moses:

Department A—Determined to keep the writing machine well oiled and his creative juices flowing freely, Bennett alone was to decide when he and Marguerite were to have sex. Evenings of love making were to be by his appointment only, two evenings a week at most, and never on a night before the morning he was working.

Department B—His great principle is that a husband should never give way to his wife whether she be right or wrong. . . . I have to accept his view on the running of the house. Here are the most important of the unwritten laws:

(1) The garden is Arnold's department; it is forbidden to interfere with it in any way.

(2) Wife and servants are another department, but he will give them any order he likes.

(3) The home is his and he will furnish it how he pleases. Once he says a piece of furniture goes in a certain place, it stays there. . . .

(4) He has time only for writing. As for me, his wife, I must be happy, smile, and always be on time. I must look after myself. Also see that the meals are good and the house is well attended to. . . .

(5) When the time comes, if ever, when he must talk to me about his money affairs, he will do so. Meanwhile if I ever ask him about questions of finance he will reply that it is a very complicated business which it

would take days to explain. My duty is to see that he is not disturbed when he is trying to sleep as he is a very bad sleeper.[14]

Even before they were married, Bennett made one item clear to which Marguerite reluctantly consented, despite any reservation she may have had: he would sleep alone, and he alone would decide their sex arrangements. On their sex night he would sleep in the master bed, she in the small bed in the next room.

Other incidents reveal the "master nagger." Once, when she shut some folding doors in the Comarques house in the country and had the piano in the living room moved a few inches, he left a four-page reprimand on her dressing table.

"You are mistress in the house, but I am master. I am the one who earns and pays out, and who directs the overall finances and it will be always me."[15]

The separation was already marked. Though he loved their Comarques estate, he rented quarters in the Royal Yacht Club, no women admitted. "I have to see my publishers early in the morning," he explained.

Later, he conceded two nights a week for sex; when she wanted more, he wrote: "Last week I spent three evenings out of four with you, but that can't always happen."[16]

Quarrels, sometimes violent, were inevitable. An emotional scene made him stammer very badly. Even while they were living together he left memos for her to avoid the stammer. Once, he wrote her crossly: "You asked me to dine with you tonight. But you did not ask yourself what I should do after dinner. Was I to go back and work, or was I to go to bed?"[17]

After hearing that Galsworthy liked to have his wife play the piano softly in the adjoining room when he was writing, Bennett asked Marguerite to sew in the corner of his room while he worked. But the sound of the needle against her thimble distracted him and he banished her.

Seeing matters moving toward a major break, Marguerite tried to head it off in various ways, but eventually she moved into a flat of her own on Oxford Street. He readily yielded to this arrangement. By now they had three residences, but he could afford them. All he demanded was to be left undisturbed to pursue his writing. When she complained about his sleeping at the Royal Yacht Club for increasingly longer periods, he retorted: "I took a room here permanently because . . . it is cheap. I didn't take it for pleasure but for business." [18]

Marguerite grew impatient over his sexual neglect. She wrote him a sharp note that she would leave him if she had the money. He suspected she was spending too much time with a younger man who was taking her to dances, concerts, and theaters. But Bennett insisted he was not jealous; he replied that he would not hold her back: "Husbands who keep their wives solely by the hold they have over them in material things are idiots and worse. I consider that it is the duty of a husband to facilitate the departure of a wife who seriously wants to leave him. *If the other day you were serious*, I will guarantee you a maintenance—not of 500 frs. but of 1000 frs. a month. . . . I write without ill will and without bitterness and simply as a duty." [19]

Marguerite was certain that after a separation of a few weeks he would return to her.

Raymond Mortimer observed: "Though she never ceased to love him, it was she who suggested a separation. . . . The marriage had lasted so long, I believe, because he depended on her sexually, having a distaste for casual affairs." [20]

Her harping on his absences from home once led him to write her impatiently:

"I imagine that if you understood a bit better what the work of a creative artist is like you would not have told me that it is my duty— and that I knew it—to sleep away from here [i.e., at Marguerite's flat] on Wednesday and Thursday. The process of writing is so delicate, so easily thrown off balance, that I have given up trying to explain it to you. But I can tell you that . . . to wake up in a strange bed in strange surroundings and to be forced to leave then and adopt new surroundings before beginning to write, is very frustrating, and might well spoil a whole morning's work." [21]

Many reasons have been given for their eventual permanent separation, but Marguerite's says it all:

"One day I shall perhaps learn to organize my life and my feelings as though I didn't have a man for a husband but a creative artist husband."

Feeling that his marriage was beyond repair, Bennett formed a liaison with Dorothy Cheston, a "dazzling actress . . . a synthetic highbrow," as Frank Swinnerton described her, twenty years younger than Bennett. It was the first time, he said, he was truly in love. Marguerite refused to give him a divorce. Dorothy Cheston became his common-law wife for the last eight years of his life, and the mother of their daughter. The legal complications over the divorce stretched out for years. Dorothy changed her name by deed poll to Dorothy Cheston Bennett.

Bennett tried desperately to marry Dorothy, but his divorce had not become final. He himself probably caused the impasse, because he refused to face cross-examination in court, fearing he would stammer under stress. Besides, unwillingness to have sexual relations was not then regarded as a valid reason for divorce. There was also endless dickering over the financial settlement; Bennett had deep respect for his money.

Frank Swinnerton, Bennett's closest friend, who enjoyed the confidence of both Bennetts, waited until Marguerite and Dorothy were both dead to write A Last Word. Since Bennett's wives trusted and loved Swinnerton, his testimony may be accepted. He was then ninety-three, still had a strong memory, and had nothing to gain by distorting facts.

Swinnerton did not have a high opinion of the second Mrs. Bennett. He wrote that he thought she used Bennett primarily to advance her own theatrical career. Their first years together were moderately happy, but eventually Bennett tired of indulging her, found her unbearably domineering, insensitive, egotistic, coarse, and boring.

Dorothy was considerably distressed that Bennett's best friend for thirty years, H. G. Wells, who lived in the same building three floors above them, had not once visited during Bennett's final illness, and she suggested that Swinnerton ask Wells to come down. Swinnerton found Wells reading Bennett's obituary in The Evening News, tears rolling down his cheeks. To Swinnerton's message, he shrieked: "No! I won't! She's a bitch; and she killed Arnold!"[22]

When Bennett died, Swinnerton testifies, "She did not weep. She was quite composed. Her chief thought, apart from resentment at neglect, seemed to be that without Bennett's income she would be in a financial difficulty; but she had hopes that the doctor would not present a bill and that Beaverbrook, as a rich man, would provide for her."[23]

Dorothy had no need to be anxious about finances. Bennett left an estate of £36,600, in addition to securities valued at £7,900, copyrights at £4,225, and manuscripts at £7,500. Two thirds of the estate had already been committed to Marguerite, but Margaret Drabble points out that he secured Dorothy's future "by making over to her the royalties and copyrights in eleven of his plays . . . in forty-seven volumes of manuscripts, and the rights in his unpublished journals."

Before Swinnerton left Dorothy, at Bennett's death, she asked him to go with her into the room where her husband's body lay. "As we gazed, however," Swinnerton writes, "Dorothy caught sight of the translucent brandy-coloured ring which he always wore on the little finger of his left hand. To my horror, she moved quickly across the room, wrenched the ring from his finger, and said, 'I'm sure he'd wish me to have this.'

"There was no suggestion that the ring was to be a treasured keepsake. She was appropriating something she fancied."[24]

To the Last Toothpick

Theodore Dreiser learned, to his consternation, that fame can sometimes be more of a handicap than anonymity, that a celebrity cannot hope to flout contemporary sexual morality in public without getting scathed.

As the big shot on *The Masses* and fresh out of Moscow, where he was enchanted with the idea of a workers' paradise, Dreiser volunteered to head a committee of writers going down to Harlan County, Kentucky, to fight for unionizing the striking coal miners and to publicize their brutal treatment by company hirelings.

His famous name is what undid him.

Proletarian novelist John Dos Passos, Lester Cohen, and Samuel Ornitz went along. Senators Norris and LaFollette declined Dreiser's invitation to join as being impolitic. Felix Frankfurter bowed out gracefully.

Neither could Sherwood Anderson be persuaded. "I was indignant enough about the treatment the miners had been receiving," he said, "but I preferred to express my indignation on paper. Frankly, I was afraid to go. I think it quite possible that when it came to facing death from a bullet, I might be able to stand up to it all right. But to be beaten. The thought appalled me."[25]

Helen Richardson, Dreiser's typist and mistress, with whom he had been sharing his apartment at the Ansonia for five years—he was not yet divorced from his wife—begged to go along. But Dreiser refused to take her. She pleaded with him not to go.

The presence of a famous writer in Harlan made local headline news. The governor acceded to Dreiser's request to call out the National Guard to protect him. He was too important to be lynched.

Hernon Evans of the *Pineville Sun* interviewed Dreiser to get a big spread for his paper. Ostensibly, he wanted facts to blacken Dreiser's character:

"You are a very famous novelist, and have written several books. Would you kindly tell me what your royalties amount to?"

"I do not mind. $200,000 approximately. Probably more. . . ."

"Do you contribute anything to charity?"

"No, I do not."

"That is all."

Then Dreiser added, "I am a writer, and I am mostly interested in the theory of equity. . . . I am conducting this investigation at my own expense, as I do most of my investigations. . . ."

"What I was trying to say," Evans cut in, "was that me, with my $60 per week, give more to charity, and believe more in the standard of equity than you do with your $35,000 per year."[26]

This kind of publicity was not what the delegation was after.

When Dreiser entered his hotel at about midnight, he was escorted by a comely young woman he had brought from New York and who went everywhere with him. He had introduced her as Marie Pergain (allegedly a fictitious name). His comrades rebuked him for messing up their crusade. Why bring this chick in? Dreiser shrugged them off. That was his personal concern.

"We all thought it was a foolish thing," Lester Cohen recalled. "We almost knew there would be trouble."

The trouble turned out more damaging to the cause and Dreiser's own name than even the novelist had ever dreamed. Word soon got around that the woman with Dreiser was not his wife. Kentucky was not going to let Yankee free-lovers get away with this. The alerted sheriff's men put the pair under constant surveillance, hoping to trap them in some illicit act and get evidence to prosecute. They watched the hotel from across the street.

John Dos Passos gave this account of the trick the sheriff pulled off: "When she went into his room late one night they stacked a row of toothpicks against the door. Finding them undisturbed in the morning they arrested him at breakfast for infringing some local ordinance against fornication. I did not see the trial but I was told that in court Dreiser confounded everybody by declaring that he was an old man and impotent. Nothing immoral could have happened."[27]

After Dreiser took the train for New York, his native ground, the news hit the wires that the county grand jury had indicted the author and his girl friend on a charge of fornication.

Back in the Ansonia suite in New York, resorting to his usual bumbling, Dreiser issued a press release deploring the Harlan conditions and used the occasion to preface his attack with a statement which sounds like a Restoration comedy rake's defense. "At this writing," he said he was "completely and finally impotent," and added, "In fact, today, you may lock me in the most luxurious boudoir with the most attractive woman in the world, and be convinced that we are discussing nothing more than books or art or some aesthetic problem of one kind or another."[28]

Friends called Dreiser's public apologia one of his clumsy jokes: he was about as impotent as Casanova.

One of Dreiser's buffs, W. A. Swanberg says, who was worried about Dreiser's professed impotence, sent him advice: "That is easy to cure. I cured myself of it when I was past sixty, by the proper food and exercise."

Max Eastman exulted: "It's both funny and sublime—an event in the cultural history of man." Dreiser appreciated this.

The phones at *The Masses* rang without stop. In the hullabaloo the unfortunate striking miners were overlooked, but the publicity over the toothpicks was alive for days and attracted more attention than the conditions Dreiser had come to Harlan County to redress. Dreiser kept issuing press releases about Harlan County conditions as well as his impotence.

His rooms at the Ansonia swarmed with callers. Claude Bowers, historian and later American ambassador, found the novelist boiling mad over the Harlan notoriety. When he called on him, Bowers says, "the telephone was constantly ringing . . . he paced the room like a caged lion, bitterly describing the treatment of the miners, and indulging in profanity that amazed me, since ordinarily he never swore. On the table was a pitcher of wine, and time and again he stopped to fill a glass and drain it with a swallow."

"I told them I was impotent," Dreiser exploded. "They can't prove I'm not."[29]

Dreiser's friends and enemies cracked lots of jokes at his expense. No one dared kid him to his face. Horace Liveright once tried that with disastrous consequences, but William C. Lengel, an old friend, braved it and telegraphed a dash of comfort: "I am with you to the last toothpick."

A week later the whole delegation, including Ms. Pergain, were indicted for syndicalism, but Dreiser and his attractive companion escaped extradition since Kentucky law regarded adultery as only a misdemeanor.

MAXIM GORKI COULDN'T SLIP BY

Theodore Dreiser had better luck on his European tour. Wherever he went with his mistress, he was hailed as the number one American novelist. The public dinners in his honor were lavish and were attended by England's literary luminaries. The adulatory toasts flowed as freely as the champagne. Dreiser pulled no boners. He encountered no snubs.

Even the magazine writers, who were noted for smoking out scandal, were exceptionally deferential; the Americans asked no embarrassing questions, and without blinking accepted the lady constantly at Dreiser's side for what she was presumed to be, his wife or his mistress. No one seemed to mind. She was beautiful, charming, and intelligent.

Alexei Peshkov's American tour met a different reaction. Flaunting his famous sobriquet, Maxim Gorki (Russian for *Maxim the bitter*), the author of *The Lower Depths* landed in Hoboken with his "wife" and adopted son. He had come fresh from the bloody barracks of the 1905 Moscow uprising. He had chosen New York as a natural starting point to agitate against an American loan to czarist Russia and to raise funds for the Bolshevik section of the Social Democrat Party, which was desperately in need of relief.

Faced with the collapse of his mission, the Russian ambassador tried pulling strings to have the popular playwright barred from America on the legal grounds that he was an avowed anarchist, but civil libertarians succeeded in getting the immigration authorities to admit him. Fortunately, they had an activist partisan in the White House, Theodore Roosevelt.

Gorki's universal fame made him a natural canvasser. He was the New Russia, and he looked it. He stepped off the ship wearing a blue peasant blouse, Ukranian cotton trousers stuffed into Tartan leather boots. Thousands of partisans turned out to give him a rousing welcome at the pier. The very next day he was feted at a fund-raising banquet sponsored by Mark Twain—resplendent in tuxedo and white tie—Jane Addams, who had come all the way from Chicago, and William Dean Howells, novelist and dean of American letters.

Addressing the guest of honor, Twain said, "If we can build a Russian republic to give its persecuted people the same freedom which we enjoy, let us by all means go on and do it." The New York *World* cartoonist had Twain appear as a "Yankee in Czar Nicholas' Court" tumbling the Romanov tyrant from his throne by a nudge from Gorki's feather pen. Newspapers were vying for the celebrity's exclusive interviews. A reincarnated Kossuth had come to town! The city went wild.

Until . . .

The miffed Russian ambassador pulled the decisive switch. He called in a reporter from the *World* and produced indisputable evidence that this nut Peshkov was traveling under false colors. He had abandoned his legal wife and their two children, and the woman he had been introducing as his wife was in fact his common-law wife, American for mistress; in short, she was a prostitute.

Strangely enough, no one had recognized the woman with Gorki as Maria Andreyeva, the talented actress of the Moscow Art Theater. Gorki couldn't understand the fuss. As far as he was concerned, the link with Andreyeva was moral even in Russia, though not according to American puritan standards. After all, he had been amicably separated for several years from his legal wife and was still corresponding affectionately with her. Since Russian law did not permit divorce for anarchists, Gorki went on to live in common law with Maria, an active revolutionary, the woman he loved. His status was accepted as natural even by such purists as Anton Chekhov and Leo Tolstoy.

The reporter the ambassador called in exploited the scoop to the full. When he pressed Gorki to say whether the lady hanging on his arm was indeed his wife or his mistress, the revolutionist shrugged his shoulders and said nothing, but the gesture clearly indicated what his answer would be.

The next day the most popular New York newspaper appeared with a banner headline across page one: "GORKY BRINGS ACTRESS HERE AS MADAME GORKY." Hearst, not with clean hands himself, whipped up the clamor and doubled circulation on his papers. Moral turpitude! The radical *Forward* reserved judgment. The *Sun* blasted him: "the purity of our inns is threatened." Only *The Independent* took Gorki's side. Brander Matthews said that adultery "did not mean putting sand in sugar." But the defenders were all impotent in the face of the condemnations that swept the metropolis.[30]

As if Gorki's introduction of Andreyeva as his wife had not been enough of a faux pas, Gorki publicly read the congratulatory telegram he had sent to miners who were then on strike. He made it a point at every rally to inject a plug for the strikers. It offended even his staunchest sponsors, who decried it as gratuitous meddling by a foreigner in a native issue.

Reporters jammed the lobby at Twain's hotel at 21 Fifth Avenue while the two chief sponsors were upstairs debating on how to deal with the crisis. Any decision they would make had to be ugly. Plans had already been broadcast that Twain was going to chair a dinner in Gorki's honor. Howells was to be the keynoter.

The conferees upstairs were apparently sweating it out. The "unhappy look" on Howells's face when he emerged to face the reporters confirmed it. Twain followed Howells down and announced, "I am a revolutionist—by birth, breeding, principle and everything else," then regretfully acknowledged that Gorki's role as persuader was obviously "impaired. I was about to say *destroyed*. . . . The man might just as well have appeared in public in his shirt-tail." He then announced he would not preside at the advertised dinner, adding "Gorki hits the public in the face with his hat and then holds it out for contributions. It is more than ludicrous, it is pitiful!"[31]

President Theodore Roosevelt promptly canceled the White House dinner he had ordered to honor the Russian novelist.

Characteristically, Gorki himself refused to take the general hostility passively. He lashed out at the furor as a "scandal staged by pious Americans." Anatole France telegraphed him to keep on fighting.

Gorki's mission then took a personal turn. The three visitors were ejected from one hotel after another. At one hotel their trunks were piled up on the sidewalk. Gorki planted himself on one trunk, folded his arms defiantly, determined to sit the storm out. He called on the mob of embattled sympathizers surrounding him to raise their red banners even higher.

Fortunately, the trio were offered temporary lodging at an apartment where five writers were living in a "commune" hosted by Leroy Scott's wife, a Russian Jew. It was a beehive of revolutionary activity. Gorki kept issuing bulletins on the ongoing Moscow insurrection, pleaded for relief funds for his revolutionist brothers, and bitterly assailed pot-bellied puritanical American imperialists.

By a stroke of fortune, the Fabian English-born socialist John Martin, now rich and influential, invited him to share his Staten Island home. H. G. Wells, then in America to do some journalism, visited him to offer comfort and support. "To me it was astonishing, it was terrifying," he said.

Years later Wells wrote in his *Experiment in Autobiography* that in 1919 he met Gorki again, now a rehabilitated expatriate in Soviet Russia. "He is ruddy and white-haired; if Bernard Shaw were to trim and brush his hair and beard they would be almost indistinguishable. He is eighty-five and he wants to live to a hundred-and-five just to see how the work he has in hand will turn out."[32]

Martin succeeded in persuading the authorities to release the Gorkis from Ellis Island, where they were awaiting deportation as undesirable aliens. He let them use his lodge in the Adirondacks. During that summer the author wrote in white heat a play, *Enemies*, and the famous novel *Mother*, a story of an old woman bewildered by her son's revolutionary activities.

He ridiculed the moral turpitude charge with a pamphlet in which he has an American multimillionaire pontificate ironically:

"It is impossible for an American to recognize Christ! . . . He was born out of wedlock! . . . A man born out of wedlock cannot even be an official in America to say nothing of a god. He is not received anywhere in decent society. Not a single girl will agree to marry him. Oh, we are very strict! And if we were to recognize Christ, we would also have to accept all the illegitimates born as respectable people . . . even if they were born of a Negro and a white woman. Think how horrible that would be!"[33]

Gorki had come to the United States gushing praise for the American sense of fairness and sympathy for the plight of the downtrodden rebellious Russian people. When he left, he called America "the garbage bin of Europe" and the people here "blind tools in the hands of the Yellow Devil-Gold." In his pockets he kept ten thousand dollars, some of the devil-gold contributed to his cause.

Unable to return to Russia, he headed straight for what he saw as a quieter, more hospitable refuge, Capri, not yet a tourist playground. There he stayed with Andreyeva for seven years. Capri became a second Yasnaya Polyana. Dozens of Russian artists and revolutionaries visited him, including Lenin, with his mistress.

Taking a leaf out of Lenin's testament, Gorki endorsed his view of women "as not only the source of physiological enjoyment, but as a faithful comrade and helpmate in the difficult business of life."

A TASK OF BRITISH PRUDERY

On his six-month South American lecture tour, Anatole France thoroughly enjoyed the attention and services of his latest mistress, middle-aged Jeanne Brindeau, a member of a touring theatrical group he had met aboard the *Amazon*. It was taken for granted wherever he lectured and was feasted that the beautiful lady constantly at his side was his wife. As a matter of fact she nodded charmingly on being introduced and addressed as Mrs. Anatole France. No complications ensued until he returned home to face Mme. Léontine Arman, his mistress for twenty-seven years, who had been informed confidentially ahead of time that *cher maître* was enjoying what he termed "a second youth abroad." Léontine was ready for him at the threshold, having nursed her wrath to keep it boiling hot.

It was another story when Anatole France visited England in 1913, where his sponsors included the cream of English authors—Shaw, Bennett, Harris, Kipling, and Galsworthy. He came accompanied by Mme. Arman's former maid, Emma Laprévotte, who was now living with him at the Villa Saïd as housekeeper-mistress after Mme. Arman had died. France always invited her to sit beside him among his distinguished guests; she listened attentively, smiled appreciatively at witticisms, but otherwise was placid and surprisingly silent. Obviously, she was no Mme. Arman. France called her affectionately Tico, his pet name abbreviation of *petite coco* (little cuckold).

The social conventions were still strictly observed in Georgian England, and the stodgy reception committee were at a loss to know how to receive her. How address her? Tico was out of the question. They presumed the two were husband and wife.

One or two committeemen, however, suspected that the lady hanging on to the visitor's arm was probably not his wife. There were rumors abroad, but then every celebrity attracts gossip. Then again, how could one be certain? Actually, they did not know what to make of her: she spoke no English. None ventured to speak French; an Englishman's French is notoriously atrocious. Emma smiled affably and accepted greetings graciously but responded with only, "Merci, bien." Clearly, Anatole France was in love with her. The Paris salons knew how he had once bragged to a friend: "Tico is a rare woman. She has an opinion on every subject but never gives it."

The committee chairman, J. Lewis May, veteran translator of many of France's books, tells us that the only strategy he could contrive was silence, noting that France "when he went to visit the 'great houses' could not for the life of him understand how it was that they always tried to persuade him to leave her at the hotel." In each instance France refused, in violent French no doubt, and brought her along wherever he went.

At the Fabian Society dinner, where France gave his address in French to thunderous applause, Bernard Shaw, who took the chair, for once yielded to instinct rather than convention. He met the couple warmly, cavalierly bent half a foot over to let the visitor kiss him on both cheeks and then exchanged kisses with Madame. Shaw's wife, Charlotte, who always saw through such things, acted as interpreter but what she thought of the visiting couple she never revealed. She too, like Tico, was that rare being who knew when to shut up. But St. John Ervine did report that in the exchange of cheek pecks Shaw "blushed like a shy schoolgirl."[34]

Edward Marsh was one of the dozen who came up to the rostrum to shake France's hand. France gave him the thrill of a lifetime, he says. "I can still see the heavy jowls which gave him the looks of a sagacious hound." He overlooked Emma altogether.[35]

No one yet knows how Lord Redesdale, who presided at another grand banquet in London, where every writer of some note showed up to do France honor, managed in his welcome speech to camouflage Emma's relationship to the grand old man of French letters. David Tylden-Wright is of the opinion that Emma was tactfully "dissembled somewhere in the body of the room."[36]

The most embarrassing confrontation the committee chairman had to cope with on France's visit to London was when he had to introduce Emma to Mrs. Asquith at the tea party at 10 Downing Street.

As Laurence Sterne would have observed, and Anatole France would have seconded, "They order such things better in France."

THE AMERICAN KAFKA

When Budd Schulberg was preparing a memoir of Nathanael West (Pep, to friends) he asked a well-known literary agent who knew the author of *Miss Lonelyhearts* when she was a shopgirl in Stanley Rose's bookstore during his early scriptwriting days in Hollywood what words come to her mind when she thinks of Pep. And she reflected: "Sad. Everything about him was sad. Even his mustache was sad. And melancholy. Strange. Remote. Detached. And at the same time he was terribly warm and friendly, but in a strange, detached way."[37]

But her remembrance says little of the inner man in the Brooks Brothers suit.

For the root of the deep gloom one must go to perceptive intimates, or better still, a poet's eye. W. H. Auden suggests the core of this disturbed novelist when he defined the malaise of society in the 1930s as "West's disease."

S. J. Perelman, who fought West's battle for literary recognition, saw his brother-in-law as the direct descendant of Franz Kafka. Both writers were indeed strange, but lonely, enigmatic, frustrated, perplexed. Schulberg writes that West shared with Kafka "a dark vision of a man in a frenzy of futility, like a beetle on its back. Man flails, man gropes, man scrambles for identity, man sweats to pull himself hand over hand toward the prize of dignity at the top of the pole. But in the dizzy climb man falters, loses his grip, slips and slides and tumbles in a grotesque acrobatic that becomes even more ridiculous. You look at man and you can't help laughing until you cry. That's how I read Franz Kafka and Nathanael West."[38]

West himself identified his condition in the credo he included in his first novel, *The Dream of Balso Snell:* "I must laugh at myself, and if the laughter is 'bitter' I find it necessary to burlesque the mystery of feeling its source."

The personal view of West was given by Stanley Rose, who ran a literary bookshop with a back-room gallery where one could come across William Faulkner, Erskine Caldwell, Scott Fitzgerald, Dashiel Hammett, Pep, and others hard up for Hollywood cash who jawed, joshed, talked politics and shop. Stanley Rose summed up his lumbering, slouching, gifted shy lounger: "Pep would rather hunt than write, hunt than eat, hunt than hump."[39]

Rose touched the human nerve there. For Pep, dogs made existence tolerable. He romped with them, lived in close quarters with them, nuzzled them paternistically, and cuddled up in bed with them.

And if his dogs were the bright spot in his life, sex was the "troubling" (Yeats's favorite word). A stiff dose of gonorrhea crippled his sexual urges. It congested his prostate beyond repair, infected his urethra, and hampered gratification of the sexual drive to the point where he associated having sex with excruciating pain and disease. The irony of it was that the more he suffered below the belt, the more he craved sexual fulfillment.

Convinced that fate had slated him for premature impotence, he went for relief and reassurance to whores. And the case of clap got worse. Like Kafka's amatorial experiences, Pep's were comedies of the absurd. "Clearly he was more at ease with prostitutes than with those girls he regarded as 'nice,' " says his definitive biographer Jay Martin, who adds that Pep "was personally divided between a desire to marry and fears over the consequences of marriage, including doubt about his ability to continue as a writer."[40]

A further ironic twist for the creator of Shrike. Here he was a man with a gift for analyzing love acutely, who could lead hundreds of hotel visitors out of their sexual frustrations as he did so successfully in *Miss Lonelyhearts* and yet could not manage his own parallel disorders. Like Kafka, he wanted desperately to marry, felt like the author of *Metamorphosis*, that he needed the stability only marriage could provide, and yet, was terribly afraid of the consequences.

But Pep went on trying. His first serious attachment his mother interdicted successfully. "What? Another *shiksa*! Aren't there enough Yiddishe girls around any more, Nadie?"

The next love prospect turned him down. He was madly in love. Perhaps out of fear, she wavered: he might infect her. Teasing, she called his professed virility just talk. To prove it wasn't, he volunteered to bring in the prostitute next door to show that he had more than the average gimmicks in bed. He was sure he would eventually win her, he carried around in his wallet a blank wedding license application for days. Then, characteristically, when hope of marriage brightened, he got cold feet and stuck to his dogs. The whole thing suddenly loomed up as ridiculous. He hadn't a cent in the bank. But he never forgot her. He dedicated his first novel to her.[41]

At thirty-seven, furiously writing film scripts for the Hollywood studios, he resolved he wouldn't die a bachelor. He admired his sister's ideal marriage to his Brown University classmate and now fast friend Perelman. The moment came when Lester Cohen introduced him at a party to Eileen McKenney, ten years younger than himself, the heroine of her sister Ruth's best seller *My Sister Eileen*. She was charming, witty, and a natural, "a delicious featherhead," someone called her. She had, says Schulberg "that unmistakable Irish-colleen beauty, and she was hearty, funny, warm, outgoing, constitutionally cheerful, and loving." Ruth says that even before Eileen met Pep she was "determined to marry him." It was love on pre-sight. She had admired the image that came through his books. Her life had already been wrecked by one marriage—"entrapment," she called it—and separated from her husband after a child was born. She was desperately lonely. Pep was even lonelier. He lost his shyness the moment he laid eyes on her. He was enchanted. This was the wife he had hungered for. And this time Mama was not around to cry havoc. Sidney Behrman and his wife, Laura, were wild about her. After two months of passionate courtship, the pair agreed they were to be married by a judge. His brother-in-law was to be best man.

Again Pep got the Kafkaesque chills. He thought seriously of fleeing to Mexico, then dismissed it as unfair to Eileen. His checkbook told him he couldn't afford supporting a wife. How could he then even consider taking on a "ready-made family"? The funny thing about the idea was that at least it was original. Pep was a born romantic; originality had always appealed to him. Then, half-seriously, he checked his enthusiasm: how could he break faith with his two comforting hunting dogs, Danny and Julie, his dependents, who had for years slept in bed beside him? It would hit them hard.[42]

Pep hit on a major compromise before he and Eileen came forward to the judge. Pep would agree to sleep with Eileen alone and find a way to appease the hounds provided she'd join him without cavil on his duck-hunting expeditions. Eileen, says Jay Martin, "ostensibly regarded his passion for hunting as a gentle madness and made it a sort of comedy."[43] Besides, you do meet so many famous writers as hunting partners. Faulkner often joined Pep on pheasant hunts. At any rate, in marrying, one has to give hostages to fortune.

Pep got the better deal. Eileen brought a measure of regularity into his introverted life. She gave him more time to write and added the serenity he sorely needed.

Days later, Eileen stuttered ecstatically in a telephone call to Ruth: "Oh, I'm happy. . . . It's a l-l-lovely day out here. Pep is s-s-s-sort of nervous, we're both so . . . h-h-happy."

Ella Winter and Donald Ogden Stewart sent Pep a telegram: "REQUEST AUTHORITY USE YOUR NAME MESSAGE TO PRESIDENT ROOSEVELT AND BISHOP MANNING QUOTE MARRIAGE IS A WONDERFUL INSTITUTION UNQUOTE AND A LONG KISS FOR EILEEN TOO."

A friend hit a prophetic note when he said of Pep: "Disaster fascinated him, not in the puerile sense, but from the standpoint of human tragedy."[44]

Terribly myopic and crazy at the wheel, he was warned to cut down driving at catastrophic speeds. The fabulously euphoric marriage was in its eighth month. As they were returning to California from a duck-hunting trip, which didn't net them a single bird, looking back at his dog puffing and enjoying the wind in the back seat, Pep passed a stop sign and smashed into another car.

The accident killed Pep and Eileen. The dogs survived without a scratch.

Death handed Pep a new deal. Kafka received a similar postmortem fortune. At the time of his death, Pep was already becoming a cult figure. His readership had surged to the point where his four novels sold a million copies. He was in his writing prime and one can only speculate as to what heights he might have reached had he lived just a few years longer. Ironically, he had earned more money in one year from his hotel night-clerkships, the inspiration and source of his *succès d'estime, Miss Lonelyhearts,* than he had in the fourteen years of writing novels. Perelman, friend Budd Schulberg, and critics Edmund Wilson and William Carlos Williams, who backed Pep through all the dismaying frustrations, lamented that he was not around to enjoy the universal recognition and cultist admiration that zoomed after he died.

ELINOR WYLIE: ALL FOR LOVE

Dreamy, visionary, beautiful, and even in adolescence a gifted versifier, Elinor Hoyt, daughter of a United States solicitor general in Washington, saw herself as the reincarnation of the hounded poet P. B. Shelley:

> Down to the Puritan marrow
>   of my bone
> There's something in this
>   richness that I hate[45]

The *revenante* went into action at twenty, raw and inexperienced, when she leaped into an unfortunate marriage with the preeminent and wealthy but dull and unstable Philip Hichborn. After the birth of her child, she realized that the union did not provide the romance or flight she had sought.

> Avoid the reeking herd,
> Shun the polluted flock.
> Live like that stoic bird,
> The eagle of the rock.

She startled the polluted Washington flock by falling in love with Horace Wylie, a distinguished lawyer, fifteen years older and conspicuously vulnerable to scandalous tongues: he was a married man with four children.

She had made a decision and was impatient to fly off. No persuasion could get her to wait until Mrs. Wylie could be brought around to agree to divorce. She took the only resort left, elopement. She left her husband, child, and horrified friends, and ran off with her lover to Canada; then mocking growing public scandal, she sailed for England to live the independent poetic life as Mrs. Waring.

> If you would keep your soul
> From spotted sight or sound,
> Live like the velvet mole;
> Go burrow underground.[46]

The couple were happy in their burrow, a country cottage where they eluded potential tattlers. She published her first book of poetry, *Incidental Numbers*, in England, anonymously.

The concealment worked until the Warings collided with a Washingtonian buzz-buzzer at one of her rare country house weekends.

Her close friend Mary Colum tells what happened: "But now, here in this house she had felt so happy to be invited to, she came against the potential enemy, the woman who thought it her duty to tell her hostess that a fellow guest was not what she seemed to be, that she bore an assumed name, that the man with her was not her husband but a lover.

"When, some time after dinner, her hostess approached Elinor and said she wanted to speak to her privately in her room, Elinor felt herself quaking, and something in her mind snapped; I think it never really came together again. . . . The hostess informed her of the tale she had just heard from the American guest and inquired if it were all true. Elinor acknowledged everything and suggested it might be well if she and Horace left early the next morning." She could not be persuaded otherwise.[47]

The disclosure was only a prelude to the disasters that ensued. Tragedy upon tragedy drove her out of her hitherto screened underground refuge. Hichborn committed suicide. Night after night, accusatory fingers and hideous gestures drove sleep off and brought her to the verge of a nervous breakdown. In a flash the clouds then lifted. She contained her consuming tension with the self-assurance that since Hichborn's suicide had taken place some years after the elopement, she could not be held responsible.

Time slowly brought in other revenges. One of her children by Horace died stillborn; another died months after birth. Interestingly, the hostess in whose home the Warings had had the catastrophic encounter helped her during the trying period.

The decisive blow to their security came from an unforeseen source, driving the expatriates out into the open. With the outbreak of World War I, a government edict ordered everyone, domestic and foreign, living under an assumed name to report forthwith to the police. The Warings were left only one course of action, immediate return home to face the music, which they knew could only be a dirge.

It took months of distasteful conferences in lawyers' offices before Horace would wrest a divorce from his wife that would free him and Elinor to rehabilitate themselves by legally marrying.

The promised freedom proved illusory. In Washington, Elinor found that her enfranchisement could not keep the Grundys from her door. Her native city never let her forget the earlier brouhaha. Moving to Westchester, where they built a beautiful house, did not help. In fact it stifled her spirit and leadened her pen even more, and after months of acute depression, she concluded that the marriage to Horace lacked the romantic glamour she had hoped for when she wrecked her life to be his "enchanting companion." They separated preliminary to divorce and for the first time in her life she felt free. The Shelleyan scenario of escape and love ended. Tragedy had made her mature and a sophisticate.

She took up residence on the fringe of Greenwich Village at a famous address, 1 University Place. Her circle of literary celebrities widened, thanks to Edmund Wilson, who lived on the floor above. He introduced her to the Algonquin coterie and opened the door for

her at *Vanity Fair,* where he had an influential voice on the editorial
board. Her poetic gift blossomed. *Nets to Catch the Wind,* her first
important work, received immediate acclaim. She was talked about
as America's most promising writer. After her divorce from Horace,
she published her novel *Jennifer Lorn,* which became an immediate
best seller.

Her beauty became legendary. Jean Gould described her as another St. Vincent Millay, only more fragile, though still secure, a
charmer with "a cameo-like aristocratic face framed by the marcelled
hair she wore in the Twenties; her tall, slim figure, always perfectly
groomed, in keeping with the imagery of her poems."

Romance showed its alluring head once more. She fell in love with
William Rose Benét, brother of the gifted Stephen, the popular critic
and poet. He became her third husband, the most dependable and
affectionate man she had ever known. The spirit of Shelley still moved
her to write her best known novel, *The Orphan Angel,* a fantasy in
which the English poet visits America. One critic noted, too, that
"Shelley's poems served as chief model for much of her poetry."

The Talmudist wrote: "Thy friend has a friend, and thy friend's
friend has a friend, so be discreet." But even at the risk of her health
Elinor had by now reached the age where she scoffed at discretion.
To her considerable alarm, however, she felt she was not yet free of
foul whisperings threatening and that she had to fight every inch of
the way to acceptance by the literary world. Influential critics kept
up their stinging crusade. George Oppenheimer called her "extraordinarily talented and good-looking. In her youth she had startled society by eloping with Horace Wylie while she was married to another
man. She had been, in fact, something of a seductress, and with her
looks and charm, there were scores of willing victims."[48]

One incident showed that she still had one friend—Edna St. Vincent Millay, whose loyalty gave no quarter to detractors. Invited to
be a guest of honor at a dinner of the League of American Pen-
women in Washington, Edna thanked them for the honor, but added
an indignant note that she would not attend any affair that had in a
previous scathing letter condemned "and insulted one of the most
distinguished writers of the day." She wrote "she would consider it
unbecoming for her to sit as guest of honor at a gathering of writers
which placed 'the circumspection of one's personal life above literary
accomplishment,' " Jean Gould reports in *The Poet and Her Book,* and
ended her denunciation by saying that she, too, was " 'eligible for

their disesteem,' and wished to be struck from their lists, to share with Elinor Wylie a 'brilliant exile' from their 'fusty province.' She enclosed a note to her 'darling' with the letter, sending it to Elinor with instructions to read it over, change the address if necessary 'on the typewriter,' and mail it at once."[49]

Other poets could not resist cattiness. At a luncheon of the Poetry Guild, where Elinor was to read from her *Nets to Catch the Wind*, Jean Starr Untermeyer recalls in her autobiography *Private Collection:*

I had barely entered the foyer leading to the private dining room of the Biltmore when a beautiful, slender young woman, a wrinkle of annoyance marring her brow, approached me. "You are Jean Starr Untermeyer, aren't you? I recognized you from your photograph." . . . "I am Elinor Wylie, and your husband," she continued accusingly, "has reviewed my book, and called me cold. Me, me—who have lost two children!" Her voice was not that of the turtle dove, and her reasoning seemed to me to lack cogency. Death brings grief, but does not necessarily bestow depth of soul or warmth of heart. Elinor took out her powder puff and her lipstick and surveyed herself in her pocket mirror. Then she gave a start, "Oh, I have forgotten to bring my book. I must find Bill." And forthwith she sent her newly affianced into the gale. My thoughts were ironic. . . .

Another time, in 1925, when I first visited the MacDowell Colony, I found myself seated next to Elinor at a long table. She began telling me about having lived in Westchester. To keep the conversation moving, I asked, idly: "Had you a nice house?"

She turned to me like an outraged goddess. "Jean! Can you imagine me living in any place that was not exquisite?"

Indeed, she assisted her legend by her social demeanor and by her finely wrought verses. . . . I admired her looks and her gift, but not her all-pervading narcissism.[50]

The thirst for vindication, tinged with a shade of vengeance, drew Elinor to London, where she was now recognized as a literary celebrity and the legal wife of a first-rate poet. She was welcomed with open arms to inner literary circles. Arnold Bennett noted in his journal that he and Dorothy had gone to a supper at Sybil Colefax's home where he met A.E.W. Mason, Geoffrey Scott, Katherine Cornell, now Mrs. McClintok, and Elinor Wylie, author of *The Venetian Glass Nephew.*

In another entry, in 1927, he reported meeting a glittering array

of writers at lunch, among them H. G. Wells (a tolerated womanizer), "and there was Otto Kahn, a vast amount of chatter. Otto was
in lovely form." Elinor was thrilled.[51]

The end came suddenly. She had been writing at a furious pace,
inviting at "the cost of desperate nervous strain," her admirer Edmund Wilson wrote. She had just finished preparing her last volume
of poems, *Angels and Earthly Creatures*, and had taken her pen up to
write when she called out frantically from the kitchen to her husband. She had fainted, and as he handed her a glass of water, she
murmured "Is that all it is?" and died of a stroke. She was forty-three.

Millay was getting ready to read her poems at the Brooklyn Acad-
emy of Music when one of the staff told her rather casually that Elinor Wylie had just died. Shaken and holding back her tears, Edna
walked onto the platform, says Jean Gould, and "instead of her own
poetry, began to recite the lines of Elinor Wylie that she had loved
and learned by heart. It was a beautiful gesture, and one made spon-
taneously, unconsciously. She hardly knew what she was doing."[52]

Edmund Wilson in his "The Death of Elinor Wylie" eulogized her
brilliant and all too brief career before her death in 1928.

"When I first knew her, only five years ago, Elinor Wylie was a
brilliant amateur, who had produced a few striking poems and started
a novel or two, but who had never worked with much application.
Yet by the time *Jennifer Lorn* was published, she had become one of
the most steadily industrious and most productive of my acquaintances."[53]

Edna dedicated *Fatal Interview* to Elinor. One of her sonnets bears
the classic first line:

"Oh, she was beautiful in every part!"

THE RABBI SAID NO

"It seems so dreadful to be a bachelor," Franz Kafka confided to his
diary in his late twenties, ". . . never being able to run upstairs beside one's wife; to lie ill and have only the solace of the view from
one's own window."[54]

But how does one take the leap into matrimony? "Only recently,"
he wrote about a prostitute after roaming about Prague's shadiest al-

leys, "one of them said something very intelligent: 'Ah, if I could only see you naked once, then you ought to be really pretty and kissable.' . . . I intentionally walk through the streets where there are whores. . . . One woman probably knows me by now. I met her this afternoon. . . . We looked at each other fleetingly. . . . Then I really ran away."[55]

Fortunately, he was introduced to Fräulein Felice Bauer in his friend Max Brod's apartment. At twenty-nine, Kafka was still clerking in the Workmen's Accident Insurance Association, bored by figures and writing furiously. Felice had come to Prague on a short visit. They took to each other from the first, and she met all his requirements: she was sprightly, attractively feminine, and intelligent. She hung on every word he uttered. This fräulein, he thought, would make a good wife and mother. He was restive at home, where he had to please a martinet father, and Felice, "stirred him to the very depth of his being."

But their courtship stretched out over five years, bubbling mostly in correspondence. Their few rare meetings usually came when Franz suffered a critical bout with frightening illness. Felice would have married him instantly, but she could not prod him into his ultimate proposal. The delays were terribly frustrating.

Never did an ardent young woman receive such torrents of lacerating, self-abusive letters as she had from Franz: *Weltschmerz*, agonizing complaints about his illnesses, interminable vexations. Given his bag of neuroses, it is no wonder that their engagement was broken off twice, the first time when he warned her that anyone who married him was doomed to a hectic and woeful existence.

Before sending Felice his first proposal of marriage, Kafka sweated through sleepless nights. Finally, an accountant to the bone, he drew up a double-column inventory of points pro and con. The self-analysis is *echt* Kafka:

"Inability to live alone . . . it is even unlikely that I understand how to live together with someone; but to bear the onslaught of my own life, the onset of time and old age, the vague pressure of the itch to write, my sleeplessness, the near approach of madness—I am unable to bear this alone. . . .

"I must be alone a great deal. All that I have accomplished is the result of being alone. . . .

"Fear of being tied to anyone, of overflowing into another personality. Then I shall never be alone any more. . . .

"Single, I might perhaps one day really give up my job. Married, it would be impossible."

Kafka shrank from the sight of the trial balance, crying, "Miserable me!"[56] But desperate for marriage and fatherhood, he sent the letter off anyway.

Nevertheless, he felt compelled to defend his decision in "A Letter to My Father": "To get married, to found a family, to accept all the children that arrive, to maintain them in this uncertain world, and to lead them a little on the way is, in my opinion, the utmost that a man can ever succeed in doing."[57]

When a jubilant Felice sent back an affirmative response, Kafka got cold feet. In a few months he broke off the engagement, as much out of anxiety over his own incompetence as fear of hurting Felice.

A few months later, emotionally replenished, he decided a second time to propose. Again he drew up a checklist:

To Remain Chaste	To Get Married
I preserve all my powers in coherence	You will remain without your coherence;
	you will become an idiot, will follow
	every wind, but will never get any forwarder . . .
Responsible only for myself	The more infatuated with yourself
No worries, concentration on work	As I grow in strength I shall stand now.
	But there is a certain kernel of truth in this.[58]

Chaste won—at first.

Then, after a wrenching night, *chaste* lost.

This time he felt he was in deep trouble: "The very idea of a honeymoon fills me with horror,"[59] he confided to Brod. Apparently, deep down Kafka feared he was sexually inadequate. Philip Toynbee thought, and Max Brod hinted, that when Felice came to stay with Kafka at a sanatorium in Marienbad, he slept with her for four or five nights. Kafka commented in his diary: "To be smiled at by her in a boat. That was the most beautiful thing of all. Always the longing to die, and yet keeping oneself alive, that alone is love."

Sexual inadequacy is hinted at in what he told Felice: "You are a girl and want a man, not a flabby worm on the earth." And again he warned her that as his wife she was doomed to lead "a monastic life."

Accountants constitutionally respect written contracts. So Kafka wrote down items in the compact they drew up: "Getting married shortly after the war is over; take two or three rooms in a Berlin suburb; leave each one only his own economic worries. F. will go on working as before, and I, well I, that I can't say yet."[60]

During this stabilizing period he wrote *The Trial* and *The Castle*.

Shortly before the planned wedding, he began to cough up blood. Kafka called it his "final defeat. . . . Tormented soul!" The doctor diagnosed it as TB—Kafka called the symptoms psychic and wrote Felice that he feared that because of the sudden turn of events, the marriage would have to be called off again, because it held a mortal threat to her life.

When she received the letter, Felice immediately traveled thirty miles to see him at the sanatorium. Kafka said that a permanent parting was the only way out. "She is an innocent woman condemned to be severely tortured," he wrote. "I have committed the fault for which she is being tortured, and even the rack."

She left for Berlin, leaving Kafka weeping. "It was the only time I saw him cry," Brod writes.

Fifteen months later, Brod heard that Felice had married a businessman who promised fewer marital migraines. They left for America where she died forty years later.

"I broke the news gently to Franz. He was moved, full of the most sincere good wishes for the new marriage, wishes that then to his great joy were daily fulfilled. 'It is a good thing that some things which are insoluble seemed to find a solution after all.' "[61]

Kafka turned to Zionism with feverish zeal, going off to Berlin to stay with friends. There he fell in love with a nineteen-year-old Hebrew scholar and Orthodox Jew, Dora Diamant. He met her in a Berlin Jewish people's home. She was scaling fish. "Such gentle hands," he told her, "and such bloody work." Dora felt humiliated, but his gentleness and burning dark eyes, the "Byzantine bird-face," captivated her. She chose another chore.

Dora, like Kafka, was a rebel, striking out against her Orthodox Polish Jewish family, but she retained a good deal of respect for her parents. She read Isaiah to Kafka in the original Hebrew; he took pains to teach her how to develop her latent dramatic talent.

Living together with Dora in Berlin gave Kafka more happiness than he had ever had, despite his fast deteriorating health. She became his sympathetic companion, nurse, mistress, daughter, mother figure, all that he had sought in a wife. At last he felt he was achieving his ideal of complete independence. As he said, "a home of his own, he was no longer a man living with his parents, but to a certain extent himself a pater familias."

Brod tells a pathetic story of how Franz made a last-ditch effort to make the relationship with Dora legal and holy. "He wanted to marry Dora, and had sent her pious father a letter in which he explained that, although he was not a practicing Jew in her father's sense, he was nevertheless a 'repentant one, seeking to return,' and therefore might hope to be accepted into the family of such a pious man. The father set off with the letter to consult the man he honored most, whose authority counted more than anything else for him, to the 'Gerer Rebbe.' The rabbi read the letter, put it to one side, and said nothing more than the single syllable, 'No.' Gave no further explanation. The miracle-working rabbi's 'No' was justified by Franz's death, which followed soon afterwards."[62]

Franz had taken the rebuff as one more bad omen in his life. Dora and Brod tried to comfort him. Franz smiled weakly. One night before the rejection came, an owl appeared at Franz's window—the bird of death. He realized he was a doomed man.

By Appointment Only

Only a precisionist and routine-freak like Samuel Butler could have written the utopian classic *Erewhon* (*Nowhere* spelled, approximately, backward), in which mankind is cut down to automatism.

In *The Way of All Flesh*, he has a character voice the author's complaint wearily, "Oh, why, why, why could not people be born into the world as grown-up persons?"

The course he took in bookkeeping was designed to give him expert management of detail accounting of his household affairs. Samuel Butler kept a double-entry record of his appointments as well as household expenditures.

All his adult life this self-termed "incarnate bachelor" adhered to an unbending schedule for rising and sleeping, eating, brushing his hair—a hundred strokes each morning—and laying out the same daily ration of cigarettes. He had a set time for sex as he had for writing. Even as he lay dying, he begged his valet to bring him his checkbook to see his cash balance.[63]

Three women shared his adult life: a lame spinster who did not requite his attention, an intellectual; another, a striking beauty but sexually frigid; and another, useful though passably dull, a prostitute. The intense attachments he reserved for men. When a close male companion went off and married, Butler instantly dropped him. To his most affectionate friend and crony, Henry Festing Jones, like himself possessing strong bisexual tendencies, nineteen years his senior, who later became his Boswellian biographer and literary and financial executor, he gave an annual allowance of two hundred pounds provided he gave up his law profession, drop his lover, remain Butler's constant companion, and be readily available to talk to and travel with. There shall be no other gods than Butler. Malcolm Muggeridge explains: "Butler was most comfortable with people when his relationship to them had a clear financial basis."

Butler picked up Lucie Dumas, a twenty-one-year-old French whore, at the Angel, a public house in Islington. For twenty years he and Jones shared her bed. In return she agreed to give up their predecessors and take on no new patrons. At least she said she would. In practice, she kept other lucrative clients discreetly closeted.

By prearrangement, Butler visited her in her Handel Street rooms regularly every Wednesday, punctually at 2:30 P.M., and he returned home on the dot of five. Jones went Tuesdays at 2:00 P.M. They each paid Lucie one pound, even when they were out of town and missed the appointed hour. They called her Madame. It was only after fifteen years of service that Butler gave her his name and address, when he made an exception and brought her up to his rooms for tea.

With the exception of Jones, no one else knew about the schedule, though one day, apropos of nothing, Butler blabbed the secret to his friend W. B. Yeats. "I have a little needle woman, a good little thing," he said. "I have given her a sewing-machine, a good little thing." Gissing, it may be recalled, also gave his steady whore a sewing machine. Keep them busy! "While making this confession," Yeats reported, "Butler retired backwards, bowing several times as in mockery of himself, an acknowledgement of a sad necessity from which even he was not exempt."

Alfred Cathie, Butler's valet and housekeeper, told Malcolm Muggeridge, who interviewed him in his old age, that his master used to say to him, "Oh bother, Alfred, it's Wednesday, and I've got to go to Handel Street."

"She was a fine woman," Alfred commented, "dark and large, not a regular street-walker, but receiving gentlemen in her room . . . I took her out once or twice myself."[64] Probably brag.

Lucie kept her side of the arrangement as far as her two clients knew. For Butler it had obvious advantages. Philip Henderson points out: "He was able to keep his rooms to himself and order his time as best suited his work."

During his hour in Handel Street, Jones occasionally forgot what he had come for, complaining about his carbuncles, rheumatism, and other ailments; Butler's conversation must have been on a loftier plane, for Lucie is reported to have once said of him: "He knows everything; he knows nothing; he is a poet." One is inclined to agree with Ronald Pearsall: "Never, one thinks, did a prostitute earn £2 so laboriously."[65] Nevertheless, for Lucie it was a bargain compact, and with a few others on the string she prospered.

Butler kept the relationship on a strictly commercial basis. Lucie understood. When she died in her early forties, he dutifully paid all the funeral expenses and, in a rare show of sentiment, possibly also to keep his memory green, he pinned the kettleholder she had knitted for him above the mantelpiece. It spelled *finis* for the major heterosexual relationship in his life.

• • •

Samuel Butler was brokenhearted when his young Swiss lover Hans Faesch, whom he shared with Henry Festing Jones for twenty-three years, left permanently for Singapore. They embraced and kissed the "dear little fellow" at the railway station.

Butler had offered Hans, "in the name of all the affection a dear father can bear to a very dear son," to "draw on me for your passage money and necessary expense." Hans readily accepted the offer.

For months Butler longed for a memento, and in a rush of emotion wrote to ask him for a lock of his hair, pretending it was wanted by a mutual lady admirer. Hans complied. Butler wore it for the rest of his life in a locket on his watch chain.

MAUGHAM LOOKS BACK

In his last years, Somerset Maugham kept whimpering privately to close friends and publicly to the press that everything about his marriage to Syrie Bernado Wellcome embittered his life: the unsettling overlong liaison; their utter incompatibility; the pervasive emotional drain; the doubtful parentage of his child; and the vast sums of money his wife squeezed out of him. The litany of complaints increased in number and ferocity as years went by. One would imagine that by forty-three, the successful novelist and playwright should have known better than to fall for the wiles of a woman he later called "a harlot, a vulgarian, a sponge and a fool."

Wrath over the liaison and marriage festered inside him for more than four decades until his misgivings blew up in an explosion that devastated everyone it touched, most of all himself. No one, not even Jonathan Swift, could have bid the world farewell with as much venom as Maugham poured into three articles he titled "Looking Back" which were published when he was eighty-eight in *The Sunday Express* and reprinted in the American magazine *Show*.

Maugham once indicated the source of his rage to his nephew Robin Maugham: "I was a quarter normal and three quarters queer, but I tried to persuade myself it was the other way round. It flattered me that she cared for me more than anyone else in the world. And she wanted to bear my child. I was so vain and stupid that I believed her. . . . But she ruined my life. She made my life utter hell."[66]

Since the publication of "Looking Back," various accounts of his marriage ceremony have appeared in print. His closest friend and longtime bridge partner, Garson Kanin, gave in *Remembering Mr. Maugham* what is considered the authentic version of the ceremony and what led up to that event. "Syrie was pregnant, came to New York, and asked WSM to marry her. He refused. Edward Sheldon [American dramatist, 1886–1945] sent for him and convinced him to do the the the right thing. Maugham agreed. A ceremony was held at the Hotel Brevoort. Maugham kissed the bride and went to the South Seas with Gerald Haxton."

Kanin says that Maugham filled him in on the climate in the courtroom: "My wedding lacked not only . . . sentiment, but what is more important . . . glamour. I remember that immediately before the judge in New Jersey married us he . . . fined a drunk; and immediately after, he fined another."

Kanin adds, "But hold. In WSM's account, he agrees to marry his pregnant girl friend, but cannot, since her divorce from Mr. Wellcome is not yet final. So he goes to Tahiti (yes, with Gerald Haxton as secretary-assistant) to research *The Moon and Sixpence*. Upon his return, he leaves Haxton in Chicago, returns to New York, and marries Syrie in New Jersey. Their child . . . is one or two years old."[67]

Maugham himself expatiates on circumstances leading to the vows. He writes in "Looking Back" that Syrie lied to him, tricked him, and used him. He asserts that he had been maneuvered into the marriage after an exclusive liaison with her for at least seven years. He had taken Syrie at her word that her husband, Sir Henry Wellcome, on separating from her, had given her *carte blanche* to live as promiscuously as she wanted. This she proceeded to do, concentrating on the open affair with the novelist. However, Maugham later learned to his utter bewilderment that Wellcome had set a pack of detectives on her trail. In due time, he sued for divorce, naming Maugham co-respondent.

Maugham goes on to give details about his premarital entrapment and how he was pushed into marrying Syrie. Sir George Lewis, the fashionable London solicitor who had handled James Barrie's divorce so successfully and discreetly, counseled Maugham: "She's up against it and you're sure to be the mug to save her. You're cruelly trapped and you'd be a fool to marry her."

"What else can I do?" stammered Maugham, convinced that as co-respondent he was expected to marry the woman with whom he had committed adultery.

"You can afford to give her twenty or thirty thousand pounds, couldn't you?" asked Sir George.

Maugham felt he was in a bind. Seeing his client's predicament, the solicitor asked him, "Do you want to marry her?"

Maugham paused, then replied emphatically, "No, but if I don't I shall regret it all my life."[68]

The divorce settled only some of Maugham's anxieties, but Syrie, he points out, got the better end of the stick: a bigger income. For him, the scandal produced a host of rumors, most of them distasteful and discreditable. He complained he had been given a bad press. The facts of his relationship with Syrie had not been heard. His inner rage kept boiling up to the point where he felt that for peace of mind he had to get the poison out of his system. And he took up his pen and wrote "Looking Back" in hot fury. He was then in his late eighties.

The confession was a shocker. He had met Syrie on a blind date, he wrote, and "after a decent delay we went to bed. It was all very delightful. I laughed when Syrie told me she was madly in love with me. . . . One day when we had driven to Richmond, she took me aback by suggesting that we should have a baby. I thought she was joking. I pointed out the difficulties it entailed." She had not yet been granted the divorce. Then, traveling on to Spain with Syrie, he writes, "At last I yielded. We returned to Biarritz and arranged to drive to Paris. It was there that for the first time we had sexual congress with the idea that Syrie should conceive. It gave me a peculiar feeling that I was engaging in a pleasant act, but, absurd as it may seem, a sacred one."

Syrie had a miscarriage, and when he visited her at the hospital she told him she wanted to break off their affair. Nevertheless, the two continued the relationship.

Several months later, Syrie told him she was pregnant again. "I was dismayed," Maugham wrote. "She burst into tears. She sobbed that it was only because she loved me that she wanted to have a baby. She made me feel an awful brute."

When Wellcome suddenly sued for divorce, Maugham went into shock and on recovery jeered that the reason he was picked out for the action as the star player among her lovers (Gordon Selfridge, the shopkeeper was another) was that he was rich and unmarried.[69]

Departing from his recital in his account of the sequence of events, Maugham raved, "She is grasping and will hesitate at no dishonesty to get what she wants. She is a climber but with the paltriness of her mind is satisfied with the second rate. She is vindictive, jealous and envious. She is a quarrelsome bully. She is vain, vulgar and ostentatious. There is real badness in her."[70]

Besides Maugham's stated motive for writing "Looking Back" was the sudden suit his daughter, Liza, filed to invalidate his much-publicized bequest of his vast estate to Alan Searle, his secretary-companion-lover. Liza's plea in court was that her father was *non compos mentis*. In a counter move, Maugham demanded that she return all his gifts, particularly the valuable pictures he had given her. He asserted in his brief that he had only lent them to her. Then he went even further: he disowned her and adopted Alan as his son. Liza brought suit to prevent this. In court, Maugham affirmed: "I have always considered her as my daughter, but legally she is the daughter of Henry Wellcome. She was born in 1915. Wellcome never denied paternity." Liza, he declared, was conceived before her mother's divorce from Sir Henry.[71]

While the briefs were being argued in court, public accusations and counter accusations were filling the front pages of the London newspapers. Liza's father-in-law tried to intercede. Appealing to Maugham's love of money, he suggested to him that he give his daughter the bulk of his estate *now* and thus avoid heavy death taxes. To this, Maugham apparently not yet totally in his dotage, responded with a grin, "I also have read *King Lear.*"

When Gerald Haxton died in 1944, Maugham was beside himself with grief: "For thirty years he had been my chief care, my pleasure, and my anxiety. Without him I am lost and lonely and hopeless. . . . I am too old to endure so much grief. I have lived too long."

But Maugham survived.

Maugham continued openly to begrudge Syrie the alimony awarded her by the court. He poked fun at her venality. He chafed at her success as an interior decorator. When Beverley Nichols told him that Syrie was complaining that the price of her favorite white camelias had gone up, Maugham retorted, "I made her an allowance of £3000 a year. If she cannot buy her c-c-camelias on £3000 a year, she should change her f-f-florist."

Years later Maugham was playing a game of solitaire in the Villa Mauresque when he was handed the message that Syrie had died. He laid down his cards and began to drum on the table.

"Tra-la-la," he sang. "No more alimony! Tra-la, tra-la."[72]

Maugham's jubilation was short-lived. The appearance of "Looking Back" opened a new can of worms. Many friends of both Maugham and Syrie leaped to her defense. Shortly after Maugham died, Beverley Nichols was the most vehement; he wrote *A Case of Human Bondage* and dedicated it "To the Memory of Syrie Somerset Maugham with love." In a foreword he wrote that before the publication of "Looking Back" he had for many years "enjoyed with him a friendship of some intimacy," but reading the master's "squalid paragraphs" he felt compelled to publish a response. "This book," he wrote, "is not an attack upon a dead man; rather it is a refutation of a libel upon a dead woman."[73] "As for her vindictiveness, where is the proof? Her only defense . . . was that she loved Willie and continued to live with him for the rest of her life. Of this I had the most poignant proof before her death. She was ill in bed, but she had tried to make herself pretty because she had a vain hope that he might come to see her."[74]

Nichols wrote that Syrie loved Maugham not for his money or his fame as a dramatist but for himself "with his stumpy little body, his trembling lips, and his shimmering contorted brain. She loved him warts and all. And she went on loving him until the end." [75]

Noel Coward joined the proliferating chorus of Syrie's defenders. He told Garson Kanin, "The man who wrote that awful slop has been my friend for so many years. Some evil spirit has entered his body." [76]

Coward was even more horrified later when Maugham refused to lend his name to a petition calling for the repeal of the law regarding homosexuality. What made Coward particularly furious was that Maugham's support might have turned the tide to favor victims of the law. Ironically, the shadow of Oscar Wilde's disgrace had by then long disappeared and it was no longer criminal to admit one's homosexuality.

MRS. PERKINS NEVER KNEW

It was undoubtedly the best kept secret at Scribner's.

For nearly a quarter of a century, sober Maxwell Perkins, editor for Fitzgerald, Wolfe, and Hemingway, the father of five devoted daughters, exchanged passionate love letters with Elizabeth Lemmon, a spinster he had met years back, in 1922, falling instantly and madly in love with her. She wrote him from her Virginia home and he her from the inviolate letter drop at his Scribner's cubicle. Max had too heavy a conscience to leave his wife, Louise, whom he to all appearances loved, and to expose his liaison to his children.

The relationship consisted of a few clandestine encounters, but they were admittedly entirely sex-free. But it was definitely not an exercise in epistolary literature.

After twenty-one years Perkins concluded that a complete break was the only way out of what threatened to be a catastrophic link. At the climactic showdown in the Ritz Bar in New York, he told her crisply: "Oh, Elizabeth, it's hopeless." And she answered, no less laconic, "I know." And that spelled *finis* for the dragged out affair. It was the only extramarital love Perkins had experienced.

When Louise got wind of her husband's dalliance—it was just like Max to spill it out—she turned to drink, converted to Catholicism, and every month purged their marital bed of sin by sprinkling a few drops of holy water on their pillows. [77]

A Divided Heart

When Alfred E. Housman's younger brother, playwright Laurence (*Victoria Regina*), on a rare visit to Trinity College, Cambridge, asked him who the person in the portrait on the wall was, he replied in a strangely moved voice, "That was my friend Jackson, the man who had more influence on my life than anybody else."

> Ask me no more, for fear I
>   should reply;
>   Others have held their tongues,
>   and so can I;
> Hundreds have died, and told no
>   tale before:
>   Ask me no more, for fear I
>   should reply—
> How one was true and one was clean of stain
>   And one was braver than the
>   heavens are high,
> And one was fond of me: and all are slain.
>   Ask me no more, for fear I
>   should reply.[78]

It is amazing how cannily Housman managed to closet his homosexuality so effectively when it was writ so large in his *A Shropshire Lad*. Where were the literary Baker Streeters? No definitive biography has yet been written—he's been dead for over half a century—nor could one ever come out: the will saw to that. Even his brother said he knew of no Moses Jackson in Alfred's life. The index to Laurence's Housman's fat autobiography *The Unexpected Years* does not include Jackson's name. The full *New York Times* obituary skips Moses altogether. And yet Moses Jackson was the heart of Alfred Housman.

The most striking wonder about his great slim volume, boldly published at his own expense—since no publisher would dare touch it—came out slap in the middle of the 1896 brouhaha over the Wilde trials and imprisonment. Housman was taking chances for personal disaster in flaunting his "secret vice." But he played it cool. While the panthers fled in droves across the Channel, terrified of detection, he cooped himself up for five years in monastic academic isolation, mulling over Propertius and Manilius, "seldom visiting, seldom visited," as he said.

The two men got to talking to each other casually on the queue to register at Oxford University. Housman was short, taciturn, difficult of approach, stiff-necked, sensitive, still smarting from the shattering disillusionment over his mother's death when he was twelve, and isolated from his inadequate, cold father, who had turned to drink. In Jackson, Housman saw everything he himself was not, an all-around athlete, tall, an extrovert, interested in the new sciences.

Before the year was up the two were already alter egos. By the fourth year they were sharing digs. It was then that Housman discovered his homosexual nature and was distressed that Moses, familiarly called Mo, never reciprocated his mute adoration or advances.

"Oxford had not much effect upon me," he said in later years, "except that there I met my greatest friend."

Housman left Oxford feeling disgraced at his failure to receive a First in Classics. It put a possible fellowship at the university out of his reach. He entered civil service at a dismal salary in the London Patent Office and shared a *ménage à trois* with Moses and his brother Adalbert. Ten years later he was appointed professor of Latin at the University of London.

Then came an unexpected crushing blow. Mo suddenly informed him that he was in love with a widow and was going off to settle in Karachi, India, as a schoolmaster. The two faced each other stiffly as Mo took his whirlwind departure. "Shake hands," he said, "we shall never be friends, all's over."

The news, says G. L. Watson, gave Housman "a laceration of feeling akin to surgical shock."

> To put the world between us
> We parted, stiff and dry;
> "Good-bye," said you, "forget me."
> "I will, no fear," said I.[79]

Once more, as when his mother had died, he felt abandoned. "It tore my heart asunder," he said. For a time he contemplated suicide; for solace he turned to bury his "curse" in Propertius, and to Adalbert, who looked like Mo, and for a season took his brother's place in his affection.

The relationship with Adalbert was never so close as it was with Mo, though he later referred to his comforter in

> . . . that straight look,
>   that heart of gold,
> That grace, that manhood gone[80]

"I did not write poetry in earnest until the really emotional part of my life was over," he said.

The sore throat that followed the shock from Jackson's desertion lingered until he found relief in writing lyrics.

> Be still, my soul, be still; it is
> but for a season,[81]

But it was for more than a season: it was a lifetime.

Housman published A Shropshire Lad seven years after Mo left. He resented any mention of it among his fellow Cambridge dons. The lyrics surprised his closest friends. One quipped, "Alfred has a heart!"

He took his daily stroll the next twenty-five years, looking neither to left nor right, dismaying even colleagues by his refusal to return salutes, "a forced march-style, a spartan slender man of sorrowful visage with pale eyes and drooping gray moustache." He wore clothes that went out with Victoria.

Max Beerbohm remarked, "He was like an absconding cashier; we certainly wished he would abscond."

Abscond he did. On a holiday in Venice he befriended a gondolier. The pickup was twenty-three, Housman was forty-one. There seems to be something about brawny gondoliers that induces sexual attraction, perhaps their bewitching grace as they swing along the canals. J. A. Symonds enjoyed the favors of any number of gondoliers. Housman's Venetian idol was no stunner, certainly nowhere near the Apollonian Jackson, for Housman told his stepmother that the man "had one eye kicked out by a horse."

The affair lasted eight years. A quarter of a century later, when Housman was sixty-seven, on receiving a letter from Venice, "where my poor gondolier says he is dying and wants to see me," he dropped everything and rushed to Venice to do all he could to provide him with needed comforts.

To the surprise of his fellow dons, Housman never set foot in Shropshire, but took his holidays in Paris, where he was known as Monsieur Oozman, among the Burgundy vineyards, and Venice. No one dared ask him why he avoided Shropshire.

Housman died in 1936, at seventy-seven. A. W. Pollard, the famous bibliographer and the poet's most intimate friend, broke the seals. The information revealed a strange man and his half-century of intense inner travail. Some odd contradictions came to light. While George Meredith, who suffered long silences for his boldness in analyzing love and marriage, refused to sign a petition in 1898 urging that Wilde's maximum two-year prison sentence be reduced, Housman, for all his fears of being discovered, was openly sympathetic and signed. He was ecstatic about the *Rubáiyát*, saying he held Fitzgerald, who worshiped a six-foot Norfolk fisherman as a god, greater than his friends Tennyson and Carlyle, and even Shakespeare. Oddly, he thought more of *Gentlemen Prefer Blondes* than all Yeats's poetry.

Robert Ross, Wilde's friend, learned some of the lyrics in *A Shropshire Lad* by heart and recited them to the poet on his visit to Reading Gaol. Housman sent Oscar a complimentary copy when he left Reading.

Jackson undoubtedly recognized himself in *A Shropshire Lad* as the lover who filled Housman's heart with rue. Housman sent the first and only presentation copy of *A Shropshire Lad* to him in Karachi. Jackson flipped the pages, hurriedly ran his eyes down the lyrics here and there, then pushed the book aside, saying, "Stupid stuff." The author would not have taken offense at that: he knew all along that Mo had no use for poetry. Jackson's son testified, "My father jokingly professed to have contempt for Housman's poems."[82]

When Jackson came to London on one of his holidays every five years, Housman hurried down to embrace him, still hoping for a few crumbs of affection, but was disappointed at finding him a sedate pedagogue, a bit heavier, but still an eye-filler with his athletic build, handlebar moustache, and graying side-whiskers. The meeting was warm but hardly a thirst-quencher.

A year after Housman published *Last Poems* in 1922, he learned about Jackson's death. It made him ill for three months. He broke out in boils and carbuncles, and for relief he turned to other emotional outlets—wine, gourmet food, and his cherished scatological Roman poets.

THE SELF-MADE SAINT

George Sand called him Saint Rousseau. Tolstoy in adolescence wore a medallion bearing Rousseau's image around his neck. The English philosopher David Hume, who gave him and his mistress refuge in England, later branded him a traitor. His latest biographer, J. H. Huizinga, called the great romantic whose books unsettled a whole continent a liar, thief, plagiarist, and, above all, a hypocrite.[83]

Responding to his detractors, who figured in the hundreds—there were the same number of idolators, too—Rousseau ejaculated: "Show me a better man than me; if I am a scoundrel, how vile is the whole human race."

Probably the only one who stuck to Jean-Jacques Rousseau as "my man," through thick and thin for some thirty-seven-odd years, was his semiliterate mistress and common-law wife, Thérèse Levasseur, a sewing maid, waitress, and laundress.

"The man who thinks should not ally himself with a wife who cannot share his thoughts," Rousseau pontificates in *Émile*. Characteristically, he did just the opposite. What if she couldn't talk philosophy? He left her back home when he went to visit brilliant minds. He adored her for her faults and her virtues. We seem to hear Heine talking about his Mathilde. Thérèse, Rousseau concluded, "could not enumerate the twelve months of the year in order, or distinguish one numeral from another, notwithstanding all the trouble I took endeavoring to teach her. She neither knows how to count money, or to reckon the price of anything." But she did satisfy "the first of my wants, the greatest, strongest, and most insatiable."[84]

Rousseau wrote that sex was far from his immediate object in forming the liaison. But then he could rationalize himself out of any contradiction. Fresh from writing that children should be reared affectionately at home, suckled by their mothers as nature intended, he proceeded to put each of their five children into a foundling home. To Thérèse's tearful objections he argued that since she was not married, it was the only way he could "save her honor."

A better wife never made a man happier. She stood his tantrums without complaining. She solaced him, nursed him, cooked for him, and even inserted catheters in his penis to relieve his lifelong bladder disorder.

When at first she balked at going to bed with him, he concluded she was probably reluctant because she feared giving him the pox. But the real cause came out under pressure; rather, she feared he would discover she was not a virgin. After hearing her blurt out her confession, he burst into a "shout of joy," he says, forgave her magnanimously, and assured her that it was the rare twenty-year-old Parisienne who remained virginal. "Ah, my Thérèse," he exclaimed, embracing her tenderly, "I am only delighted to possess you good and healthy and not find something I was not looking for." He promised her he would never abandon her, but, he was quick to add, "I shall never marry you."[85]

Rousseau did not keep the reservation. Suddenly, on impulse, after twenty-five years of what he called the "trial" marriage, he decided to make her an honest woman. As he explained to a friend, "If all marriages started with such an attachment for twenty-five years, don't you think they mostly would prove harmonious?"

Calling in a few friends as witnesses, he conducted a threefold service as registrar, priest, and best man. He ended the travesty with an address congratulating the witnesses on their good fortune in being present. "One day," he said, "people will erect statues to me. . . . It will then be no empty honor to have been a friend of Jean-Jacques."[86]

Rousseau once advised a friend to take three mistresses concurrently—in memory of the Holy Trinity. This was just what Rousseau proceeded to do after he had disposed of his five illegitimates.

In his forty-third year he ceased having sexual intercourse with Thérèse as being too painful. "Until then I had been good; from that moment I became virtuous, or at least infatuated with virtue." But the fact is what he told his physician in Geneva when he was forty-two: "I have been subject for a long time to the cruelest sufferings, owing to the incurable disorder of retention of the urine, caused by a congestion in the urethra, which blocks the canal." He relieved his repeated overpowering sexual tension by masturbation.[87]

The return of spring, however, "redoubled my amorous delirium." At the Hermitage cottage, where he, Thérèse, and her mother boarded, he met his landlady's sister-in-law, the Countess Sophie d'Houdetot. Rousseau was never the one to be captivated by feminine beauty. The lady was pock-marked, cross-eyed, muddy com-

plexioned, but charming; to him she appeared like a "divine image."
Sophie had two added inducements: she could roll off reels of philosophy and was a love poet. Her "Hymn to the Breasts," Diderot
wrote, "sparkled with warmth and fire and voluptuous images." The
time for another sexual relationship was ripe. Her lover-husband, who
hadn't slept with her for years, was off to war.

The prospect of a kiss from her, Rousseau wrote in his *Confessions*,
"so fired my blood that my head was dizzy, my eyes were dazzled and
blind, my trembling knees could no longer support me, I had to stop
and sit down." That bladder acting up again! But he was so drunk
with passion, "she for her lover; I for her; our sighs and tears mingled," that when he bent to kiss her tender hand, he turned "weak,
exhausted, worn out, scarcely able to hold myself up . . . intoxicat-
ing tears." When he came to the point of the heavenly consummation, inspired by the flooding June moon, all he could do was embrace
her knees vigorously. "Never was there a man so tender," the countess whispered, "never a lover who loved like you."[88]

Later in life Sophie confessed that she spoiled *le moment suprême*
herself by giggling, not from his excitement but from seeing a rustic
within hearing distance swearing at his horse.

"Amid the delicious intoxication," he recalled, "she never forgot
herself for a moment, and I solemnly protest that if ever, led away
by my senses, I have attempted to render her unfaithful, I was never
really desirous of succeeding. . . . The duty of self-denial had elevated my mind. . . . I might have committed the crime; it had been
a hundred times committed in my heart; but to dishonor my Sophie!
Ah, was ever this possible? No! I have told her a hundred times it
was not. . . . Such was the sole enjoyment of a man of the most
combustible constitution, but who was at the same time one of the
most timid mortal Nature ever produced."

Faced with the possibility of losing her forever—she had to go to
Switzerland to cure her tuberculosis—he confessed, "I sighed and was
silent. I embraced her. What an embrace! But that was all!"

That was not all. He did not recover for several years from the
three months of continuous futile stimulation. It gave him a constant
reminder that their fierce amative wrestling had brought on a hernia
"that I shall carry with me to the grave."

In a final apology to cover his unmanliness, he wrote her: "I may
die of my passion but I will not soil your purity. . . . I cannot cor-
rupt the woman I idolize."[89]

He summed up her contribution to his emotional life: "She refused me nothing that the tenderest friendship could give, she granted me nothing that would make her unfaithful."

But Sophie did contribute a favor to literature: she inspired the model of Julie, the pure heroine in his *La Nouvelle Héloise*, probably the greatest novel of the eighteenth century.

When Rousseau recounted his traumatic experience from the novel to his other mistress, Thérèse, and her mother, they wept sympathetically. The first words Thérèse uttered after he died were, the report has it, "If my husband is not a saint, who is?"[90]

THIS IS GRATITUDE

Rousseau never ceased saying how "tender and virtuous" his common-law wife Thérèse was, "the heart of an angel," "a beautiful soul," and even when he returned from a whoring session, she gave him only "touching and tender reproaches without a trace of anger. She serves me with the attachment of a daughter for her father, rather than a servant for her master." She was "my sister, my only friend, the sweetest consolation of my life."[91]

Rousseau was proud of her "impeccable fidelity." And he gives an instance to prove it.

They were riding in a carriage taking them to Geneva. A friend was their fellow traveler, "a gouty old man of over sixty, impotent and worn out by his pleasures and dissipation." While Rousseau was taking a nap, the "he-goat" propositioned Thérèse in "the most shameful way. . . . He offered her his purse and tried to excite her by reading her a filthy book and showing her obscene pictures." Thérèse indignantly threw the "beastly" book out of the window and left the carriage.

When she told her husband about his trusted fellow traveler, Rousseau says, "I sustained a shock to my confiding nature. . . . For the first time in my life, I found myself compelled to . . . withdraw confidence and respect for a man whom I loved and who, I believe, loved me." He bit his tongue and refrained from reproaching the would-be seducer so as not to betray his wife.

So he said, but at bottom Rousseau was not so charitable. The fact is that the would-be seducer was too well known in Geneva and could prove useful to him during his exile.

Rousseau hailed Thérèse as a rare woman. "When I possessed her she still was not mine: so cool are her passions that she has seldom felt the want of a man even when I ceased to be one with her."[92]

On his European grand tour, James Boswell had set out to pick the brains of the two great heretics of the eighteenth century, Rousseau and Voltaire.

Boswell, who idolized Rousseau, crossed the Swiss border to the thatched cottage at Neufchâtel to interview the refugee philosopher. Although the philosopher had put in a side door to elude curiosity seekers, who managed to get past Thérèse, his "housekeeper," it would nevertheless take more than a No Admittance sign or a guard in petticoats to daunt the plucky Scot.

Bozzy did his homework: he brought the right letter of introduction from Rousseau's political patron, the Lord Marshal, and he drew up a list of questions so framed as to set the author of *The Social Contract* talking. He describes how he costumed himself: ". . . in a coat and waistcoat, scarlet with gold lace, buskskin breeches, and boots. Above all, I wore a greatcoat of green camlet lined with foxskin fur." In contrast, Rousseau wore a simple Armenian costume which he could remove easily when he had to rush, every half hour, to the chamber pot, dragging along the attached urethal dilator.[93]

Boswell had vowed "neither to talk to an infidel, nor to enjoy a woman before seeing Rousseau." Of course, he never kept such vows.

The night before his descent on Rousseau's cottage, he stopped at an inn and pumped the innkeeper's daughter for inside information on the man whom Kant hailed as "the Newton of the universe."

"Monsieur Rousseau often comes here and stays here several days with his housekeeper, Mademoiselle Levasseur," she told him. "He is a very amicable man. He has a fine face. But he doesn't like to have people come and stare at him as if he were a man with two heads. . . . Many, many people come and often he will not receive them. He is ill, and doesn't wish to be disturbed."[94]

When Bozzy got to meet the fifty-two-year-old Rousseau, he seized his hand and thumped him on the shoulder ("I was without restraint"); to prevent a snub, he informed him he was no mere tourist but came from an ancient Scottish family ("Though I am only a young man, I have experienced a variety of experience that will amaze you"). He had a pressing marriage problem, he said; "only the philosopher could resolve it." He had to see his "Enlightened Mentor" *alone.*

"In view of my condition kindly make it short," said his Enlightened Mentor.

The stipulated fifteen minutes stretched to five sessions, one even lasting one and a half hours. The two talked about doctors, religion, Frederick the Great, and Voltaire (whose name threw Rousseau into a tizzy). Once, irritably, Rousseau dismissed his guest, explaining that he was irksome to him: "It's my nature, I cannot help it." At another time, Rousseau said he couldn't promise to see him any longer. "I am in pain. I need a chamber pot every minute."

During one visit, Boswell cannily steered the conversation to his favorite subject, morality and women.

Boswell: "Morality appears to me an uncertain thing. For instance, I would like to have thirty women. Could I not satisfy that desire?"

Rousseau: "No!"

Boswell: "Why not?"

Rousseau: "Ha! Ha! If Mademoiselle were not here, I would give you a most ample reason why."

Boswell: ". . . but consider, if I am rich, I can take a number of girls; I get them with child [Thérèse at this point gets up and leaves]; propagation is thus increased, I give them dowries, and I marry them off to good peasants who are very happy to have them. Thus they become wives at the same age as would not have been the case if they had remained virgins, and I, on my side, would have had the benefit of a great variety of women."

Rousseau: "Ah! You will be landed in jealousies, betrayals, and treachery."[95]

Boswell returned to his hotel in a transport of emotion and recorded the conversation verbatim.

"I should have observed," Boswell commented in his diary, "that when I pushed the conversation on women, Mademoiselle Thérèse went out, and M. Rousseau said, 'See now, you are driving Mademoiselle out of the room.'"

Boswell also recorded that his idol kissed him several times and held him in his arms "with elegant cordiality."[96]

Shortly thereafter, before Boswell set out on his visit to Voltaire and his return to England to meet Hume, Swift, and Pope, Rousseau asked him if he would meet Thérèse when she stopped in Paris and escort her to London, where she was to join him. Boswell was thrilled: the slender thread that linked two souls now held a third. The gift of a beautiful garnet necklace he sent to Thérèse cemented a closer friendship with her.

When she showed Boswell to the gate after one meeting with his

Enlightened Mentor, she said: "I have been twenty-two years with Monsieur Rousseau; I would not give my place to be Queen of France. I try to profit by the good advice he gives me. If he should die, I shall have to go into a convent."[96]

Bozzy smiled: he knew better than to trust a woman's fidelity.

Durant tells us that Boswell "shared the same bed with Thérèse at an inn on the second night out of Paris, and several nights thereafter. They reached Dover early on February 11. The diary [according to pages now destroyed] proceeds: 'Wednesday 11 February: Yesterday morning had gone to bed very early, and had done it once; thirteen in all. Was really affectionate to her. At Two [P.M.] set out on the sly."[97]

Huizinga noted: Thérèse "congratulated him on his 'vigour' but complained of his 'lack of art.' "

As for "thirteen times," Huizinga added, "presumably not consecutively."

How authentic all this is we shall never know. Boswell was, after all, an egregious braggart about his amorous exploits.

A NOBLEMAN FROM BROOKLYN

One of the inside stories Wilfrid Sheed shares with his readers in *Clare Booth Luce* must surely come as a surprise and give no little amusement. Norman Mailer played more than a bit part in a Luce marital playlet.

During what Sheed refers to as Luce's "somewhat restless, tossing-and-turning mid-life," the father of *Time* was seriously thinking of divorcing his second wife, Clare, and marrying socialite Lady Jean Campbell, Lord Beaverbrook's granddaughter, who was at least a generation younger. "Clare," says Sheed, "knew she had a few wifely claims on Harry, and has always been very understanding in sexual matters, but she was embarrassed to tears over Harry, who appeared to be making an ass of himself, and tangentially herself."[98]

Clare told Harry she would not block his divorce, but cannily did just that with a stiletto comment in public: "If Jean marries Harry and I marry Lord Beaverbrook, then I'll be Harry's grandmother."[99]

Lady Jean saw the humor in the situation, Sheed noted, and let herself "settle for a piece of Norman Mailer, who has hinted in his roguish way that he got a kick out of replacing a press lord."[100]

The "nice Jewish kid from Brooklyn," as Norman characterized himself, promptly divorced his second wife, Adele, the one he had stabbed, and proceeded to marry into nobility. His first wife, Bea Silverman, regarded this marriage, Hilary Mills noted, as Mailer's "next step up the gentile ladder which he had been ascending since Harvard. 'She was the ultimate *shiksa*,' Bea says."[101]

Madame Zola Had to Grin and Bear It

When Madame Zola first discovered it she was furious, but then she reconciled herself to her husband's skirt-chasing and shameless infidelities. To appease him she even took care of his illegitimate children. When she first caught Émile making advances to their chambermaid, she promptly dismissed the girl, but naïvely replaced her with a prettier one despite her friends' warnings that she was doing the wrong thing.

Madame had to bite her tongue, in public at least, when the maid, Jeanne Rozerot, bore Émile two children. His wife was often seen walking them down the Champs Élysées in smug defiance of the inevitable gossip. The liaison's complexities provided the quidnuncs with hilarious copy.

When there was tattle you could be sure to find a Goncourt's bent ear. Edmond gives this piece about the crisis that nearly broke up Zola's friendship with Céard, whom he got to act as his go-between postmaster. "Whenever Zola was at Médan, the mother of his two children was installed in the vicinity, and Céard acted as postman for the letters he wrote to the young woman, letters, in which for some reason or other, Zola with his Italian duplicity, poked cruel fun at his postman. And one day, Mme Zola, irritated at the part Céard was playing in the affair, ridiculed the trust he placed in Zola's friendship, quoting the jokes her husband had made about him in certain letters which, somehow or other, she had seen.

"Then," Goncourt noted, "there was a scene between the two friends which nearly turned them into enemies. One evening at Médan, after a violent quarrel between husband and wife, Mme Zola started packing her bags and Zola went into his room, just letting her go. Céard, who was at Médan at the time, abandoned his tactful reserve and with praiseworthy indignation told Zola that he was a cad and a swine, if he let the woman go who had shared the poverty of his bad years and whom he was heartlessly throwing out now that he had got to the top."

Mme. Zola was forever threatening: "If this goes on, I shall cry
. . . if this goes on, I shall leave." But she stayed, swallowing her
pride. She could no longer go out trifling on her own, being wrinkled, and as Madame Daudet was reported to have said "looking like
an old doll in the window of a bankrupt toy shop."[102]

HATS OFF TO BASTARDS

Shakespeare, in a famous soliloquy, has one of his characters, Edmund, make such a powerful defense of the virtues of bastardy, one
is fairly tempted to prefer it to legitimacy. Wilkie Collins would be
the first to say amen to Edmund's triumphal speech.

Collins was one of the highly respected and most popular novelists
in Victorian England. His *Man in White* and *The Moonstone* set the
tone for all future Gothic mysteries. He is still a best seller the world
over. His life may be said to be one long novel of homage to illegit-
imacy.

Collins was walking home from dinner one summer evening with
Millais, the painter who had taken Ruskin's wife Effie off impotent
Ruskin's hands, when he picked up Mrs. Caroline Greaves, the
"woman in white." He lived with her for nine years and even adopted
her daughter. Dickens thought none the less of him for it. Even the
Dictionary of National Biography, with characteristic coverup, referred
to this and similar liaisons as "intimacies formed as young men."

When Mrs. Greaves left him to marry another, he set up house
with Martha Rudd, who bore him three children. Suddenly Mrs.
Greaves reappeared in his life, and he welcomed her with open arms.
He set up his two women in a *ménage à trois*, which he maintained
until he died twenty years later. Martha appeared to be his favorite,
and she gave birth to another illegitimate child four years after she
returned to Collins.

Collins was not a cad: he acknowledged all four bastards in his will
and made provisions for them.

FORSTER'S TICKET

How, James Joyce asked, could Henry James even dare to write novels about love without ever having lived with a woman? E. M. Forster apparently succeeded in producing one impressive novel exploring
the subject without having understood, let alone experienced, copulation.

Although many of his Bloomsbury friends had come out of the closet, Forster was afraid to risk exposure. "However gross my desires," he wrote in his diary, "I find I shall never satisfy them for fear of announcing them."

Forster wavered several times on the brink of coming out, and each time recoiled. In later years, in a rare exchange of views, he told his intimate friend Leonard Woolf about a doctor who claimed he could "convert" homosexuals. "And would you like to be converted?" Woolf asked him. "No," Forster replied unhesitatingly. To Joe Ackerley, a reputable journalist and his homosexual companion, he confided: "I am rather prone to senile lechery . . . want to touch the right person in the right place, in order to shake off bodily loneliness. . . . Licentious scribblings help, and though they are probably fatuous I am never ashamed of them." [103]

After Forster, already a celebrated novelist, visited D. H. Lawrence for three days, the latter wrote Bertrand Russell about Forster: "I hope to see him pregnant with his own soul. . . . He sucks his dummy—you know, those child comforters—long after his age. . . . Why can't he take a woman and fight clear of his own primal being?" [104]

Forster couldn't do this while his widowed mother and his doting priggish aunt were around. His aunt had the money!

It began at prep school, when a classmate remarked, loud enough for "Maurie" to hear, "Have you seen Forster's cock? A beastly brown thing." The word was new to him. He kept praying to God "to help me get rid of the dirty trick." Once, when he dutifully reported to his mother his first masturbatory spasm, she told him to call the offending organ "dirty." Later, home for the holidays, P. M. Furbank tells us, he volunteered that he now knew what "committing adultery" was: "A man placed his stomach against a woman's and it was a crisis when he warmed her." Lily Forster, startled, ordered him to silence: "You understand now how dreadful it would be to mention it, especially if a gentleman was there." [105]

During his second term at Kent House, Forster experienced a sexual trauma when he met a man on the downs, urinating in full view, who asked the youth to play with his penis. Forster obeyed, more startled than alarmed by the sight of the man's inflamed organ. The man quickly lost interest, "asked Morgan where he lived, and offered him a shilling, and when Morgan refused it, he let him go without

much ado." Next day, Forster wrote obscurely to his mother about
the incident, and at her insistence, her son's schoolmaster escorted
him to report to the police. No further action was taken by them,
and on his diary page for that day, Forster wrote: "Nothing."[106]

If Lily Forster was aware of her son's sexual problem, she never let
on. Later, when the rector gave a sharp look at Roger Fry's portrait
of her son and said to her, "I hope your son isn't queer?" she took
the picture down as soon as he left.

Though Forster customarily read aloud his novels to the ladies at
home, he didn't dare tell them he was also writing about his sexual
preference in *Maurice*.

The sense of frustration continued unabated, privately. He hung
around Hyde Park corner and public lavatories for male pickups. He
approached guardsmen and window cleaners, consorted with gam-
blers and cat burglars, giving them money and clothes. He had picked
up a sailor in Toulouse. To his diary, he confided: "I want to love a
strong young man and be loved by him and ever and ever hurt by
him. That is my ticket."

Forster was handed that ticket when he visited Love of Comrades,
the Uranian shrine set up by the aging Edward Carpenter, the homosexual poet and yogi-Christian socialist. Carpenter was living with
George Merrill, who had a habit of caressing the behinds of male
visitors. The visit gave Forster the enlightenment he'd been seeking
for years and spurred him to write *Maurice*, which he showed to Lytton Strachey, Virginia Woolf, G. Lowes Dickinson, and others.

Long after he had put the novel aside, Forster wrote in his *Terminal Note*:

"It must have been on my first or second or third visit to the shrine
that the spark was kindled and he and his comrade George Merrill
combined to make a profound impression on me and to touch a creative spring. George Merrill also touched my backside - gently and
just above the buttocks. I believe he touched most people's. The sensation was unusual and I still remember it, as I remember the position of a long vanished tooth."

In the *Terminal Note*, written just before his death at ninety-one,
he told in *Maurice*, "I was determined that in fiction anyway two should
fall in love and remain in it for the ever and ever that fiction al-
lows."[107]

Forster never set up house with a male lover, as Lytton Strachey and others in Bloomsbury were doing. In other matters he had courage enough; he volunteered in 1960 to come forward in public defense of Lawrence's *Lady Chatterley's Lover* and his brief but eloquent testimony in court was highly effective; the consensus was that it disarmed censors of the novel. However, he could not get himself to come out of the closet. Across the first page of *Maurice*, completed in manuscript form as early as 1914, he had written: "Publishable—but is it worth it?"

Furbank writes: "One can't picture him doing it [taking a male lover publicly]. He could imagine two lovers living together in the 'greenwood' [his solution in *Maurice*] but hardly in a flat in Kensington or a house in Potter's bar."

The novel was published posthumously, when Forster knew he could not hurt his mother or his aunt or himself.

The Age of Wisdom

"I had been taught only two things in my childhood: the modern languages and good manners," said Edith Wharton late in life. No nice girl asked questions about whoremongering in the Bible or the meaning of the seventh commandment; only the lowborn would publicly covet a neighbor's wife.

Enlightenment came soon enough for the debutante of Washington Square. A few days before Edith Jones, a virginal twenty-three, was to marry Edward Wharton, an agreeable and wealthy Boston bachelor, she came to her mother.

"I'm afraid, Mamma—I want to know what will happen to me."

"I never heard such a ridiculous question!" said Lucretia Jones impatiently. Then Mamma, after a pause, said frigidly to Pussy: "You've seen enough pictures and statues in your life. Haven't you noticed that men are . . . made differently from women?"

"Yes," she faltered, still perplexed.

"Well, then—then for heaven's sake don't ask any more silly questions. You can't be as stupid as you pretend."

Edith retreated, more confused than ever. An avid reader who had already written some romances, she had gone to the New York parties and balls, one of the more attractive debutantes in town, with her mother's injunction foremost in mind, that the business in life for a young lady was to get married. And so she accepted Mr. Wharton, with Mamma's encouragement. There were whispers that Edith was really marrying to get away from Mamma.

The wedding night was such a trauma for Edith that the marriage was not consummated for three weeks. Teddy was as inept and fearful as his wife. After the first try, all sexual contact between them ceased, though the marriage endured, and they remained on good terms through the early years, polite and without recriminations.[108]

However, Teddy learned much. He formed a number of liaisons unknown to Edith. She too was maturing, becoming disenchanted not so much with marriage as with the stuffy pre-Gilded Age New York. She escaped to Paris, taking Teddy along (said a friend) "more as an equerry than an equal." To keep up appearances, she told people they were going abroad for Teddy's health.

In her book A Backward Glance, Wharton glosses over the sexual bleakness of her life with Teddy: "Since the first years of our marriage, his condition, in spite of intervals of apparent health, had become steadily graver. His sweetness of temper and boyish enjoyment of life struggled long against the darkness of neurasthenia."[109]

Teddy's boyish enjoyment of life, however, was still strong enough for him to shuttle to and from Boston, where he set up a love nest, embezzling fifty thousand dollars of his wife's money (he was a trustee of her estate). She had more than enough to spare; she had a legacy of half a million.

Paris quickened Edith into emotional maturity. When an old friend, Walter Van Renssalaer Berry, came over from America, she fell in love with him. He was three years older, a "man's man," as her biographer R.W.B. Lewis describes him; "strikingly tall, six foot three, and strikingly thin, with probing blue eyes set in an oval face . . . and an aristocratically prominent nose." Berry was knowledgeable, witty, and gregarious. He gave Edith self-confidence and stature. Through the years of her arid marriage, she and Berry were platonic lovers. Doubts persist about the extent of their intimacy. Wharton's close friend Henry James thought that she and Berry traveled together like lovers ("even like another George Sand and another Chopin"), but Lewis calls the statement "only a piece of James' magisterial fooling, for he rarely joked about an actual illicit affair." Lewis adds, however, that it was safe to assume "that there was a hovering and gratifying sexual element in the relationship, and that she embraced Walter Berry with special tenderness. She loved him very much." She expected him to marry her if and when she divorced Wharton. Berry did in fact propose, but backed out at the last moment.[110]

Then she met Morton Fullerton, a brilliant journalist for *The Times,* "a sexual wizard"—with both sexes. Now forty-five, Edith was for the first time "bowled over by the glory of physical passion." Freed by Fullerton from sexual inhibitions, she proceeded to make up for twenty-three years of frustration. She was now launched on a career of writing novels about what she thoroughly understood—illicit love and disillusionment.

Fullerton once said he could take love with one woman for only three years. Though he appreciated his late-blooming mistress (admitting Edith was as passionate as George Sand), he kept to his code in the end. As for Teddy, when he popped in from time to time crying adultery, he had his own blatant adulteries thrown in his face by his wife.

After three years of living with Fullerton, Wharton realized she had lost him. On their last night together in a Charing Cross hotel, they had it out. She retreated from the defeat with an impassioned poem, "Terminus." Fullerton hung on as a member of her widening circle of friends, and she made use of the love affair in her masterpiece, *The House of Mirth,* whose theme is again personal, that of a higher nature destroyed by a baser one.

It took her several years to make up her mind to sue Teddy for divorce. What would the social consequences be? But twenty-eight years after their marriage, she was freed from her husband.

Second only to Henry James, Walter Berry was the strongest influence in her life; she named him her literary executor and in her will asked that she be buried beside him.[111]

After her death at seventy-five, her secret erotic life became public. In a locked desk drawer in her château, Pavillon Colombe, were found her highly compromising journal and a pornographic fragment about father-daughter incest. These from the formidable lady who not long before her death condemned *Ulysses* as "a welter of pornography" and thought *The Well of Loneliness* "dull twaddle." Lewis suggests that she thought she could improve on Joyce's work "with a truly accurate portrayal of a woman's sexual response."[112]

A story is told which shows how far Wharton came from her early sexual inhibitions. In her sixties, an international celebrity, she was visiting Aldous Huxley at his villa in the south of France, not far from her own winter home. The thirty-four-year-old author, himself a celebrity after *Chrome Yellow* and *Brave New World,* treated her with "elegant formality." But as they were going down the steep step into the dining room, Huxley could not resist pressing her ample, tightly corseted derrière with his cupped hand, in full view of the other guests. Everyone froze. But instead of the expected reaction from the grand dame, reports Sybille Bedford, "Mrs. Wharton turned her head, not abruptly, identified, and gave him a sweet smile."[113]

Though Huxley's sight was going, his hand had not lost its cunning. And Edith Wharton was now enjoying her age of wisdom.

Scott Fitzgerald Meets the Unshockable Edith Wharton

F. Scott Fitzgerald had sent Edith Wharton a copy of *The Great Gatsby* "with a friendly dedication," and in her letter to him praising the novel, she invited him and Zelda to lunch or tea at her villa, Pavillon Colombe.

In anticipation he had gone on the wagon for a week, but on the way down he fell off it and stopped at several cafés to brace himself for the occasion with stiff drinks. Feeling that she couldn't face Wharton, Zelda stayed home in their walk-up apartment. One version has it that Scott took Theodore Chanler along for moral support; another, that Esther Arthur, Gerald Murphy's sister, drove Scott down.

When Fitzgerald swayed into the Wharton drawing room an hour late, his hostess offered him a warm hand of welcome.

"Mrs. Wharton," Scott began humbly, "you don't know what it means to come here."

Reportedly there were a dozen or more others in the room, Paul Claudel and "lots of bluestocking French duchesses." Mrs. Wharton seated Fitzgerald on her right as the guest of honor.

Later, during an awkward pause, Scott felt he had to break the ice and asked his hostess whether he might tell "a couple of—er, rather rough stories." He was bent on shocking the sedate novelist. Surprisingly, not only was she not shocked, but she smiled and nodded approval and said she loved such stories provided they had real humor and weren't raw.

According to one account of what happened next (Turnbull's), Scott told about an American couple who had spent three days in a Paris bordello, mistaking it for a hotel. He faltered to a halt. Mrs. Wharton said, "But, Mr. Fitzgerald, your story lacks data"—which flustered him.

A likelier account has Fitzgerald bragging about how he had just come from a bordello, at which point she reduced him to a purgatory of silence by asking, "But what, Mr. Fitzgerald, did you *do* there?"

As he stumbled out of the room, shaken by drink, and supported by Chanler—or, in one version, by Wharton's lover Walter Berry— she turned to one of her guests, Gaillard Lapsley, and said, "There must be something peculiar about that young man."

On his return to Paris, sober again, Scott collapsed in a tearful rage, says Roderick Coupe: "They beat me!"

In her diary that night, Mrs. Wharton noted: "To tea, Teddy Chanler and Scott Fitzgerald, the novelist (awful)"—and she added next to Fitzgerald's name, "Horrible"—which meant, of course, he would never be invited again.[114]

Woman, Liberated and Unliberated

By the time that Edith Wharton settled permanently in France, she had freed herself from insularity and prudishness. In defiance of the moral code practiced in the red brick mansion in Washington Square, she lived openly with her lover, Walter Berry, although she was still legally married to Teddy Wharton.

When the world-famous Wharton was touring French Morocco with Berry, she made her first port of call a visit to the sultan's seraglio in the summer palace in Fez. Her friend Henry James would have been shocked by her daring.

R.W.B. Lewis says that as she studied the passive faces of the concubines, "Edith felt all her feminism rising up in futile anger and helpless compassion. The Eastern world had again laid its magic upon her, but she had never been more conscious of the irreplaceable Western value of personal freedom."[115]

It was a far cry from the captive houris in the carpeted, scented cell of the Moroccan harem to Mrs. Edith Wharton in the fashionable Paris apartment, living with the man of her choice.

• • •

"When Elinor [Wylie] and Horace [Wylie] got to Paris," Edmund Wilson wrote, "Wylie's attention one day was attracted by a man who recognized him on the other side of the street. He told Elinor to stay where she was but went over to speak to the friend. When he came back, he warned Elinor to note and remember the other man and never have anything to do with him. 'He has syphilis. His name is Walter Berry.' "[116]

HAPPY CHANUKAH

Richard Ellmann, in his updated biography of James Joyce, exposed for the first time the Irishman's extramarital love affair with a young Swiss woman in Zurich—Marthe Fleischmann. Joyce put practically every woman who inspired him with emotional stirrings into *Ulysses*, and Marthe became the limping Gerty MacDowell and Bloom's Martha Clifford.

The first time Joyce laid eyes on Marthe was in Zurich in December 1918—he was then thirty-seven—when he was peeping down from his upstairs window into the next building and saw her pull the toilet chain. She reminded him of a woman sixteen years back tucking her skirts up to wade in the Irish Sea. He wrote Marthe a letter about his reminiscence, adding that he was then as old as Shakespeare when he fell in love with the Dark Lady of the Sonnets.[117]

When Joyce met Marthe, Ellmann says, one topic that came up was "the titillating subject of women's drawers," and another that he had a passionate desire for a Semitic woman, "who would envelop him in her arms."[118]

They agreed to meet in the studio of Joyce's friend Frank Budgen. In preparation for the appointment, Joyce borrowed a ceremonial candlestick used during the Jewish festival of Chanukah, as befitting Marthe's ancestry.

Budgen was not overjoyed at Joyce's arranging the rendezvous in his studio, but yielded when Joyce told him, "If I permitted myself any restraint in this matter it would be spiritual death to me."[119]

As part of the decor, Joyce made Budgen hang his painting of a nude so that her "ample bottoms" would reflect the light of the candlestick," something certain to lend color and inspiration to the meeting." Joyce later took Marthe home and saw her often.

Joyce confessed ecstatically to Budgen, "I have explored the coldest and hottest parts of a woman's body." He did not have sexual intercourse with Marthe, but "fingered only."

Richard Ellmann comments that Joyce was "more onlooker than lover." However, the three-month affair did give him material for his book—always a priority for Joyce. Although he insisted that Nora tell him even the trivia touching any of her affairs, he kept silent about this momentary passionate fling. Fortunately, Marthe's longtime but not openly discarded lover returned to Zurich from his convalescence in a sanatorium and put *finis* to the whole Joyce-Marthe affair.[120]

THIS THING CALLED LOVE

Madame Casanova! Peggy Guggenheim would have given her legacy for that reputation.

Artists and writers were the meat she fed on; she couldn't paint or sing or write, but she more than made up for it by her eagerness to give her money to support them, lots of money to throw in as entrance fees to membership in the literary and artistic world. She met more than all the requirements: good looks, irrepressible high spirits, an Olympian bank account, and an overcharged sex battery. What more could any writer stepping out in Paris in the 1920s ask for in a mistress?

When Peggy suddenly inherited tons of money, she headed straight off to the City of Light to shoot the works. But her virginity bothered her. "I found it burdensome," she wrote. "All my boy-friends were disposed to marry me, but they were so respectable they would not rape me. I had a collection of photographs of frescoes I had seen at Pompeii. They depicted people making love in various positions, and of course I was very curious and wanted to try them all out myself. It soon occurred to me that I could make use of Florenz. . . . He now told me he was about to take a little apartment, and I asked if I could pay half the rent and share it, hoping by this maneuver to get somewhere. He said yes, but soon changed his mind. The next time I saw him he told me he had taken a hotel room in the Rue de Verneuil on the Left Bank, in the Latin Quarter. He came to see me at the Plaza-Athénée Hotel where I was living and started to make love to me. When he pulled me toward him I acquiesced so quickly that he was surprised by my lack of resistance. However, I told him that we could not do anything there as my mother [who came with Peggy to Paris as her chaperone] might return at any moment. He said we would go to his hotel room sometime. I immediately rushed to put on my hat, and he took me to his hotel in the Rue de Verneuil. I am sure he had not meant to. That was how I lost my virginity. It was as simple as that. I think Florenz had a pretty tough time because I demanded everything I had seen depicted in the Pompeian frescoes. I went home and dined with my mother and a friend gloating over my secret and wondering what they would think of it if they knew."[121]

There followed a long line of high-pressured seductions, husbands, liaisons, and divorces before Samuel Beckett got a toe hold in her apartment. Her first husband was the poet Laurence Vail, and his successor another poet John Holms. She took on half a dozen artists as diversions. Years later, *hors de combat* but no less eager for sexual tilts, she reminisced to a *New York Times* reporter: "I have always found husbands much more satisfying after marriage than during." Artists, she said, do not make good lovers. "They're often so wrapped up in themselves. Tanguy was warm and lovely, though. Ernst was interesting but definitely not nice."

Samuel Beckett turned out somewhat of a disappointment. He was far too phlegmatic to suit her; he was too reticent and enigmatic. But then Peggy was still learning the initial steps in the art of sexual arousal.

Peggy has a lot to say about her Beckett experience in the original edition of *Out of This Century*, where she screens his real name by *Oblomov*, the character in Goncharov's novel, describing him as "the strange inactive hero who finally did not have the will power to get out of bed." "Oblomov," she recalled many decades later, "was such a strange creature. He needed a lot of drink in him before he'd even talk."

She met the lanky Irishman with the green eyes and sharp stare and tight-fitting French clothes at several parties in Paris. She was then living with John Holms. Beckett's *Murphy* was already in the hands of a publisher and he was often invited out. At one party she kept staring at him with quiet fascination from a distance, measuring him for an eventual plucking. He surprised her by asking whether he could walk her home. On entering her flat, she wrote, he "did not make his intentions clear but in an awkward way as he asked me to lie down on the sofa next to him. We soon found ourselves in bed where we remained until the next evening at dinner time." In bed they had long talks about literature, art, and his own *More Pricks Than Kicks* and *Murphy*. During a lull, when she told him she liked champagne he leaped out of bed, hurried out, and brought back several bottles.[122]

Years later, in Venice, she was still thinking of their idyll. "Looking back on it now, I don't think he was in love with me for more than ten minutes. He couldn't make up his mind about anything. He wanted me around but he didn't want to have to do anything about it."[123]

Peggy was bemused by Beckett's flinty, sometimes puzzling, sense of humor, but she found him stimulating because his ideas on art and literature struck her as so original. "The thing I liked best about our life together was that I never knew what hour of the night or day he might return to me. His comings and goings were completely unpredictable, and I found that exciting. He was drunk all the time, and seemed to wander around in a dream. I had a lot of work to do because of my gallery and often I had to get up in the afternoon to see Cocteau, who was to have the opening show. Oblomov objected to this, he wanted me to remain in bed with him."[124]

Beckett's attitude toward women, his recent biographer, Bair, writes, "ranged from careless indifference to basic distrust and irritated dislike. He gave the impression that women were necessary inconveniences and in an attitude that his French friends found 'very Irish' professed to find true happiness only in the company of good male companionship late at night in a pub."[125]

Beckett once gave soberly to a group of friends in a pub his view of romance and lovemaking. "This thing called love, there's none of it, you know, it's only fucking. That's all there is—just fucking."[126]

CHRISTOPHER AND HIS KIND

At St. Edmond's School in Hindhead, Christopher Isherwood had many romantic crushes. However, they didn't go beyond linking arms, giggling over off-color stories, shouting sex-slang, comparing penises, and making clumsy attempts at buggery. Isherwood's first serious homosexual experience occurred when he was in his early teens, at the all-boys' Repton College. An aggressive older classmate dragged "Beesh" into bed with him. When the mother-dominated, puritanical Christopher shrieked objections, the bully locked the door and forcibly engaged him in genital play.

Surprisingly, the initiation left him with a good taste. Fifty years afterward, he wrote, in *Christopher and His Kind*, "I am still grateful to him. I hope he is alive and may happen to read these lines."[127]

Other homosexual experiences that followed were enjoyable but somehow lacking flavor. After much self-analysis, Isherwood realized that there was an inhibitory element; he could not relax with a member of his own class or nation; his partner had to be working-class or foreign. In this respect he was not different from many other upper-class homosexuals, among them E. M. Forster.

A more favorable sexual climate presented itself several years later, in 1929, when his close friend and St. Edmond's bedmate, W. H. Auden, two and a half years younger, invited him to join him in Berlin on a study holiday. Isherwood hailed the visit as "one of the decisive events" in his life. He had planned to stay only a week, but "Berlin meant boys," he exulted, and remained for years, with brief interludes in England.

In the decadent German capital, he came to realize the "delicious nausea of initiation terror." He had the pick of any number of complaisant lower-class *Pupenjungen* (boy dolls), for Auden was on hand to give the decisive push to a heavy leather door-curtain of a boy-bar called Cosy Corner and to lead the way inside.

In the smoke-filled, noisy back room, Christopher was fascinated by a glamorous former boxer, Bubi (Germanized "Baby"), because "he had a pretty face, appealing blue eyes, golden blond hair, and a body which was smooth-skinned and almost hairless, although hard and muscular." Bubi was his first hero; he "could hold in his arm the whole mystery-magic of foreignness, Germanness." More: Christopher was thrilled by the realization that at last he had found "the masculine *yang*, mating the Christopher *yin*."[128]

Bubi gave Isherwood a symbolic engagement present, a gold-plated chain bracelet; in exchange for sexual favors, Isherwood gave Bubi money, clothes, and sundry treats, though he had to admit (apparently without dismay) that Bubi "had a weakness for whores and would pursue them desperately, giving them all the money he had."

There followed endless rounds of bars, balls for men, male prostitute pickups. Christopher donned frilly female clothes and used makeup. At one bar he glowed when he was introduced to the great film star Conrad Veidt, in evening tails, who "watched the dancing benevolently through his monocle as he sipped champagne and smoked a cigar in a long holder."

In the West End of Berlin there were also dens of pseudo-vice that catered to heterosexual tourists: "Here screaming boys in drag and monocled, Eton-cropped girls in dinner jackets playacted the high jinx of Sodom and Gomorrah, horrifying the onlookers and assuring them that Berlin was still the most decadent city in Europe."[129]

The flavor is in his Berlin stories, the first of which inspired John Van Druten's play *I Am a Camera* and the later musical and film *Cabaret*. His literary inspiration came from "the boys' world, their slang, their quarrels, their jokes, their outrageous demands, their girls, their thefts, their encounters with the police."

Exploring the infamous Dr. Hirschfeld Institute for Sexual Sciences with its whips and torture instruments, Isherwood saw André Gide, in cape and high-heeled shoes, making a tour of inspection, and knew that this was where he himself belonged.

Without relaxing his hold on Bubi, Christopher took up with a sixteen-year-old male prostitute (the Otto Novak in "Goodbye to Berlin"), who once cried out in Isherwood's arms, "This is how I'd like to die—doing this."

When Bubi took him to see a film about a psychopathic killer, he turned to Isherwood and beamed, "Thank God, Christopher, we're both normal." [130]

Isherwood fled from Berlin when Hitler came. With an attractive homosexual, Heinz, as his companion, he wandered around Europe for several years. Eventually he settled in California as an American citizen, wrote film scripts, became a disciple of the Hindu mystic Ramakushna, and converted to Vedanta.

Taking a clue from Merle Miller and others, Isherwood came out of the closet. He has described his one experience with heterosexual sex. His first—and last—completely voluntary heterosexual experiment took place at a seaside village near Amsterdam, where he was tutoring a youngster. Finding that there was nothing to do after dark but play cards, drink, or loaf, he took on a woman who was five years older than he and no longer married. They were both drunk.

He describes the episode in the third person, "he" being Christopher:

"She liked sex but wasn't in the least desperate to get it. He started kissing her without bothering about what it might lead to. When she responded, he was surprised and amused to find how easily he could relate his usual holds and movements to this unusual partner. He felt the curiosity and the fun of playing a new game. He also felt a loss which was largely narcissistic; she had told him how attractive he was, and now he was excited by himself making love to her. But plenty of heterosexuals would admit to feeling that way some time. What mattered was that he was genuinely aroused. After their orgasm, he urged her to come to his room, where they could take off all their clothes and continue indefinitely. She wouldn't do this because she was sobering up and getting worried that they might be caught together. Next day, she said, 'I could see that you've had a lot of women through your hands.' " [131]

In relief, Christopher returned to homosexual experiences. After fifty years of following the truth of his own nature, he is very proud of his sexual preference: "Damn Nearly Everybody. . . . If boys didn't exist, I should have to invent them."

AVOIDING THE "HICCUP"

Charles Baudelaire believed that only prostitutes or stupid women make suitable companions for serious writers. (He ignored the fact that he got a dose of clap in a Paris brothel in his early days.)

In his *Advice to Writers*, Baudelaire urged writers to avoid the sadness that follows coition. Orgasm is evil, he said, the trap of the devil. He classified the women who are dangerous to writers:

"The 'virtuous wife,' the blue-stocking, and the actress: the virtuous wife because she necessarily belongs to two men and thus provides poor pasture for the despotic soul of a poet; the blue-stocking, because she is simply an unsuccessful imitation of man; the actress, because she is all decked out in literature, and speaks the language of the street—in short, she is not a woman in the true sense of the word, her public being more precious to her than any lover."

"Generally speaking," Baudelaire added, "the mistresses of poets are ugly sluts of whom the least bad of the lot are those who know how to cook up a decent soup and turn over their money to another lover."[132]

As a young law student, Baudelaire made a grisette his mistress. Known as Squinting Sarah, she was red-haired and apparently Jewish. One of his earliest poems, "To a red-headed beggar girl," is addressed to her. She rewarded him with his first case of gonorrhea (then called *le mal de siècle*). Later he contracted syphilis. About this time he expressed a favorite sexual notion:

"A precocious taste for the world of women, *mundi muliebris*, for all its undulating appurtenances, its glimmer and its perfume, gives birth to the superior geniuses."[133]

Sexual fulfillment, he insisted, was death to literary creativity. The mental excitation from contemplating a woman was the truer sexuality, and inspirational. Alex De Jonge says, "He was not undersexed, nor truly a virgin poet; he simply felt there were greater pleasures to be derived from sex than the hiccup of orgasm."[134]

This view accounts for Baudelaire's singular way of gratifying his sexual desires. Visiting Jeanne Duval, his mistress of twenty years, he sat for hours and gazed at her in silent adoration. Jeanne turned to other men to satisfy her physically. Knowing this, Baudelaire tolerated it as the price he must pay for his passive brand of lovemaking; there were only a few outbursts of jealousy.

Enid Starkie, Baudelaire's painstaking biographer, writes:

"When Jeanne Duval came to the Hotel Lauzin, Baudelaire used to make her sit in an armchair opposite the window so that the light streamed in on her. He would then gaze at her in admiration, kneel before her in worship and kiss her feet. Sometimes he would read his poem to her . . . or else poems in a language which she did not understand but listened to with rapt attention. She used to remark, placidly reclining in her armchair, with scarcely a movement on her imperturbable face, dreaming perhaps of the distant land where she was born, but, every now and then, she yawned and stretched herself like a Persian cat, and her body rippled like the surface of the sea ruffled by a light breeze."[135]

Capricious, cruel, and tantalizing, Jeanne humiliated him pitifully before his friends, brought dogs into the apartment although she knew the very sight of them made him sick, and was openly unfaithful to him with tradespeople and mutual friends. But he always returned to her arms, with expensive gifts that nearly bankrupted him; just being with her or nestling in the hollow of her breasts was all he desired.

Baudelaire was fascinated all his life by female fragrances ("the soft atmosphere of women, in the odor of their hands, their breasts, their limbs, their hair, their supple, flowing garments"), which he believed were more gratifying than coition. In his prose poem *Les Vocations*, he tells how he succumbed early in life to this intoxication. His parents took him on a trip and when they stopped for the night at an inn there weren't enough beds and he had to sleep with the maid. He couldn't get to sleep, and while she slept he ran his hand along her arm and neck and breasts:

"She's built bigger than any other woman in the world, and her skin is so soft, so very, very soft, that you'd think it was fancy letter-paper, or that paper made out of silk. . . . Then I nestled my head in her hair which hangs all the way down her back, as thick as a lion's mane, and it smelled so good—honest!—as the flowers right here in the garden."[136]

CONTINGENT LOVES

The contractual "contingent loves" entered into by Jean-Paul Sartre and Simone de Beauvoir called for companionate living without marriage, each partner being faithful to the other and yet in fact separate—loving and caring for each other and yet playing the field so long as each came back home and told the other everything.

In a *Harpers* article in 1965, the American novelist Nelson Algren, who became involved with Simone de Beauvoir in the "contingent love" setup, gave his views in a moment of disillusionment on such arrangements:

"Anybody who can experience love contingently has a mind that has recently snapped. How can love be *contingent*? Contingent upon *what*? The woman is speaking as if the capacity to sustain man's basic relationship—the physical love of woman and man—were a mutilation; while freedom consists of 'maintaining through all deviations a certain fidelity'! What she means, of course, when stripped of its philosophical jargon, is that she and Sartre erected a facade of *petit-bourgeois* respectability behind which she could continue to search for her own femininity. What Sartre had in mind when *he* left town I'm sure I don't know . . ."[137]

Sartre spoke frankly about his ties to de Beauvoir in an interview with Catherine Chaine in *Playboy*:

Chaine: "That pact that you made with each other—not to dissemble, not to lie, not to have secrets—did you hold to it?"
Sartre: "Yes, all the way. . . ."

The pact, Sartre went on to say, was necessary: "She realized that it was best for her to have relationships with several men, and she didn't want her relationship with me to prevent her from having them. And, thus, her idea of relationships with others was in the plural—or, rather, pluralistic. She did not think that a sex life ought to be defined solely by a relationship with just one man. . . . I would tell the woman whom I was starting to date: There's this woman named Simone de Beauvoir who's the end-all of my life. They just had to put up with it."

Sartre said that his "secondary relationship" with a woman called M caused a misunderstanding with Beauvoir: "The woman whom she refers to as M had come to spend several months in France. During that time Simone de Beauvoir had gone to America, to Chicago, where she met Nelson Algren. Upon her return, the two of us met in Copenhagen. . . . This double changing of partners—with her going with Nelson Algren and me with M—produced a strain in our relationship. But it was just a misunderstanding."

Chaine: The fact remains that de Beauvoir was afraid, but you were not.

Sartre: I wasn't afraid, because I recognized as valid everything that she had told me. But she did misunderstand what I had told her. One evening, she asked me, "What does M mean to you? Is she very important?" And, as a matter of fact, she *was* very important to me at that time. I replied, "She means a great deal, but isn't it a fact that I am with you?" This response—which I must admit wasn't very nice—was, nevertheless, intended as affectionate. It was intended to mean: What is true, what is deep, is the relationship between us two. . . .

Chaine: And when de Beauvoir was seeing Algren, were you ever jealous?

Sartre: Never. On the contrary, my heart was with her. . . . Oh, on occasion, I've experienced a bit of jealousy. Not, however, on account of Simone de Beauvoir. Rather, it would manifest itself as a secondary feeling, which I could allow myself with other women. But with Simone de Beauvoir, I believed our relationship to be such that even an amorous adventure with a man like Nelson Algren did not concern me. It didn't deprive me of anything—which must sound very conceited. . . .

Chaine: What attracts you at first in a woman?

Sartre: Her appearance and her charm. I see a woman in a restaurant or a café and I like her because of her face and her body, because of what she says, the prospects that open up. . . .

Chaine: But all the women with whom you've been associated have been quite pretty.

Sartre: Well, I admit it. I think that for sexual relations to have a real meaning, in the majority of cases, the woman must have something that attracts the man physically. Call it pretty, if you like; it can be something else. . . .

Chaine: Your circle of friends is almost exclusively made up of women. Why do you prefer their company?

Sartre: Because I always love what a woman says, what she does. Even if she is very unpleasant and says stupid things. I don't care.

Chaine: Why?

Sartre: I love their sensitivity. . . . Not only am I comfortable with women but women are comfortable with me. I have to say it, since they say it. They like to spend time with me.[138]

Simone de Beauvoir, in her polemical *The Second Sex*, said: "Marriage kills love. Scorned too much, rejected too much, too much an everyday matter, the wife ceases to have attraction. . . . Hence, adultery can disappear only with marriage itself."[139]

She told an interviewer: "I think marriage is a very alienating institution, for men as well as women; it's a very dangerous situation— dangerous for men, who find themselves trapped, saddled with wife and children to support; dangerous for women, who aren't financially independent of men who can throw them out when they're forty; and very dangerous for children, because their parents vent all their frustrations and mutual hatred on them. The very words 'conjugal rights' are dreadful. Any institution which solders one person to another, obliging people to sleep together who no longer want to, is a bad one."[140]

COCTEAU STOPPED FOR NONE OF THE RED LIGHTS

It was boys, boys all the way for Jean Cocteau, with a few actresses thrown in for variety and diversion.

"I wonder how people can write the lives of poets," he once said. "There are too many mysteries, too many true lives, too much of a tangle."

Cocteau should have known. It is hard to trust any of his confessions, for he was a fabricator, a dazzling showman, a narcissist, an artful embellisher of fact. From his blue-rinse hair dye and powdered cheeks to his infinite variety of masks, he was a self-dramatizer and an exhibitionist.

One thing the "Prince of Poets" refused to do was hide his homosexuality. Actually, J. C., as his friends called him, was bisexual but with a strong preference for men. Coco Chanel, who like Colette and other celebrated salonières was fond of Cocteau, called him "a snobblish little pederast who did nothing in all his life but steal from people."

Cocteau traced his sexual awakening to the time in his pubescence when he was aroused by seeing a farmboy riding a horse. "As far back as I can remember," he remarked years afterward, "even at the age when the mind does not yet influence the senses, I find traces of my love for boys." At school, fascinated by the extraordinary muscles of the class bully, he latched on to him, and he never ceased worshiping muscular males, especially boxers. He had the artist's eye for form. In black pugilist Al Brown he saw a combination that dazzled him: an artist, a heavyweight champion, a conductor at the Caprice Viennoise in Montmartre ("galvanizing it, dominating it with a fist of bronze . . . practically a lyric creation").

When Cocteau was seventeen, a friend took him to a brothel run by a lesbian where he had his first experience of opium and homosexuality. He went in for heavy makeup and transvestism and haunted stage doors for the thrill of gazing at handsome male actors.

It wasn't easy for his mother to bring up this fatherless, precocious poet. At one time she had to haul him out of a Marseilles casbah into which he had disappeared for months, working in a house run by an old Annamite woman as a shelter for harried prostitutes, drug addicts, and thieves. "Marseilles," rhapsodized Cocteau, "was my real school. . . . It set me free."

When Maman's *enfant terrible* formed a torrid liaison with a singer in Mistinguette's company, Madeleine Carlier, who passed as twenty but was actually thirty, Cocteau out of traditional courtesy presented her at the family dinner table as his fiancée, announcing that he was in love and wanted the marriage blessing. Observing their sullen faces, he offered his ace card: he was an expectant father. Madeleine, who knew otherwise, blushed.

After Cocteau stayed away from home for several days, Maman convened a family council and sent several husky relatives to drag the truant out of the Café de l'Eldo. Jean was stood up as a target while the family laid down the law. He fought back with a tantrum but softened when Maman took him in her arms, wailing, "Poor Jean! Poor Jean—with an old woman!"

Poor Jean yielded, and went out for younger lovers—but boys.

At twenty-eight, Cocteau entered on the famous liaison with Raymond Radiguet. One summer day his valet announced, "There's a little boy with a cane here to see you, Monsieur Jean." The visitor wore a shabby winter coat. Cocteau had seen the boy before, at a café where he paid little attention to him in an admiring group. Someone described him as having "the profile of a Hindu, full lips, narrow-shaped eyes and strongly marked eyebrows." All of sixteen, and Cocteau's junior by more than ten years, Raymond Radiguet was a poet of extraordinary promise.

In *La Difficulté d'Être*, Cocteau describes the first meeting of the lovers:

"At my very first meeting with Raymond Radiguet I may say that I guessed his star quality. How? You may well ask. He was small, pale, short-sighted, his badly cut hair hanging round his collar and giving him side-whiskers. He puckered up his face as if in the sun. He skipped as he walked. It was as if for him the pavements were made of rubber. He pulled little pages of copy-books out of his pockets which he screwed into a ball. He smoothed them out with the palm of his hand, and hampered by one of the cigarettes he rolled himself, tried to read a very short poem. He glued it to his eye."[141]

For five years, Cocteau was bent on nurturing Radiguet's genius. He called himself "adoptive father" and called Raymond "Bébé" or "Monsieur Bébi." He went wild over his metallic voice, pampered him, took him to fairs, cafés, the Folies Bergères, to meetings with friends—and urged him, "Be a good boy, and wear large glasses. And write, write, write." When he found Bébé drinking a bottle of whiskey and a quart of gin every day, he lashed out like an angry parent and gave up his own public drinking as an example. To keep Radiguet working, Cocteau locked him in his room, succeeding so well that *tout Paris* took up the prodigy as their own.

Then the blow came, surprising no one but Cocteau: Bébé told J. C. that he intended to marry. He had given signs to everyone but Cocteau that he was passionately attracted to women and he had announced to café habitués that when he reached forty, he did not wish to be known as "Mrs. Jean Cocteau." Stormy quarrels followed; he avoided Cocteau whenever he could; and went downhill all the way. He died suddenly of typhoid. He was twenty.

" 'Listen,' he said to me on the 9th December, 'listen to something terrible. In three days I'm going to be shot by God's soldiers.'

"As, choked with tears, I remonstrated, Radiguet continued: 'Your information is not as good as mine. The order has been given. I heard the order.' "[142]

Radiguet's family kept accusing Cocteau of having encouraged the youth in his debauchery and of having led him to premature death. All that great promise squandered! "I am trying for Maman's sake not to die," Cocteau told his friend Abbé Mugnier. ". . . Death would be better than this half-death. . . . I suffer day and night. I shall not write any more."[143]

The death of Radiguet was the watershed of Cocteau's career. He plunged into well-publicized debauchery, fantastic capers, visits to homosexual parlors, boy pickups, and the crowning addiction, opium. On the rebound, he took up with twenty-year-old Jean Desbordes, supported him in grand style and, with him, frequented all the opium dens on the Left Bank, picking up sailors and bringing them to their hotel for opium and sex. Cocteau also had female crushes; he was familiar with every celebrated actress, female author, and horizontale in Paris, although none were as intimate as his dear boys. In his erotic *Le Livre de Blanc*, Cocteau tells how he met a young sailor just out of prison whose chest was tattooed with the words *Pas de chance* (no luck). Cocteau had no luck either; Desbordes went on to marry.

Though Cocteau was a unique and dominant intellectual figure in French life in the years between WWI and WWII—author of many novels, plays, ballets, and poems as well as a painter—he is known best today for his films, which are a must for college film societies. Jean Desbordes had appeared in his *Le Sang d'un Poète* in 1930–1932; and Cocteau's young Yugoslav chauffeur and gardener, Edouard Dermit (Doudou), with whom he lived in his last years and whom he made his adopted son and heir, appears in his *Le Testament d'Orphée* (1959). But much more closely associated with Cocteau now in the minds of American youth who know nothing of Radiguet, Desbordes, or Dermit is the gifted, handsome Jean Marais. The French cinema's Don Juan during the 1940s and 1950s, Marais collaborated closely with Cocteau, starring in his *La Belle et la Bête*, *L'Aigle à Deux Têtes*, *Les Parents Terribles*, and *Orphée*.

When Cocteau was nominated for membership in the Académie Française, one member who obviously was no friend of the nominee reported that he had obtained access to Cocteau's police dossier and the cover read: "Cocteau, Jean. Opium addict. Pederast. (Says he is a poet.)"

Hours after the death of his friend Edith Piaf, Cocteau was taken to the hospital. Coming out of a coma in the ambulance that was hurrying past red lights, he said to the attendant, "I have stopped at a red light, and I am wondering if it will ever turn green. . . . It's my birthday. Instead of blowing out candles I am blowing out red lights." When Igor Stravinsky, who had little liking for the celebrated Cocteau, was called to the phone and asked to comment for the Paris press on the now hospitalized Cocteau, he refused, and as he returned to his desk, he muttered, "Cocteau cannot even die without advertising." Cocteau died in the hospital.

8

STRICTLY PRIVATE

Poetry is made by the genitals.

—Remy de Gourmont

ONE-UPMANSHIP

In his early Paris days, when his wife, Zelda, was on the verge of her first breakdown, Scott Fitzgerald invited Hemingway to lunch at Michaud's, saying he had something pressing on his mind that he wanted to discuss with him, strictly confidential.

After lunch, Scott suddenly broke in: "You know, I never slept with anyone except Zelda." This was news to Hemingway. He looked sorry for him. Then Scott went on to say that this was not the thing he had in mind. He was desperately anxious to check up on something Zelda had told him. At least that is what Hemingway says in his memoir A *Moveable Feast*, which may be only an embellished yarn touching Scott's sexual relationship with Zelda.[1]

Hemingway writes that Scott told him, "Zelda said that the way I was built I could never make any woman happy and that was what upset me originally. She said it was a matter of measurements. I have never felt the same since she said that and I have to know truly."

Hemingway invited Scott to join him in the john. There they compared privates.

"You're perfectly fine," Hemingway assured him. "You're O.K. There's nothing wrong with you. You look at yourself from above and you look foreshortened. Go over to the Louvre and look at the people in the statues and then go home and look at yourself in the mirror in profile."

Scott appeared unconvinced: he still could not see why Zelda would have said what she did.

"To put you out of business," Hemingway told him. "That's the oldest way in the world of putting people out of business."

Scott thought Hemingway was putting him on and kept pursuing for a more convincing analysis.

So Hemingway took him to the Louvre to have a close look at the male nudes. Scott gazed long, but he was still unconvinced.

"It is not basically a question of the size in repose," Hemingway explained. "It is the size that it becomes. It is also a question of angle."

Then Scott blurted out that he was thinking about a certain girl who was then trying to make him, but after what Zelda had said he was hesitating.

"Forget what Zelda said," Hemingway grinned. "Zelda is crazy. There's nothing wrong with you. Just have confidence and do what the girl wants. Zelda just wants to destroy you."[2]

Hemingway turned more confidential. The very first time he saw Zelda, she confided that Scott was not good in bed. It was obvious to Hem that Zelda was jealous of Scott's writing. She took him to drinking parties; she kept pleading boredom. Hem countered: why was she continually telling him stories about men chasing her, if not to tease? Couldn't Scott see that all Zelda was doing was encouraging him to drink. He was wasting his talent and letting himself be put down by his envious erratic wife, and couldn't he see that her tantrums were only part of an escape syndrome, that the drunken capers were all part of an escape mechanism.

Sheilah Graham, Scott's mistress, testified long after he died: "As a lover, in terms of giving physical pleasure, he was very satisfactory. . . . Zelda had tried to emasculate Scott by telling him that he was too small in the vital area to give a woman satisfaction. I never thought of the size as there was no doubt about the satisfaction, either during intercourse or afterward."[3]

Hemingway was forever giving advice on the art of sexual intercourse, considering himself the authority on the subject.

Scott Donaldson wrote that Hemingway had some weird notions about copulation, one of which was that "if you had enough sexual intercourse you could eat all the strawberries you want without contracting hives."[4]

Zelda's friend and biographer Sara Mayfield, commenting on the lapsing sexual attraction of the Fitzgeralds, said that Zelda told her psychiatrist that she had no erotic feelings toward Scott "and refused to have sexual relations with her husband."[5] On this point, Andrew Turnbull writes that Scott "was normally but not oversexed. Perhaps one could say that with him a strong sex drive had been geared to beauty and creation, while the destructive side of his nature found an outlet in drink."[6]

There were numerous quarrels between Scott and Sheilah, especially over his drinking. About one particularly fierce quarrel, Graham writes she slapped him and struggled for his gun and cried, "Shoot yourself, you son of a bitch. I didn't raise myself from the gutter to waste my life on a drunk like you."[7]

Opinions differ about Hemingway's incessant bragging of his own sexual drive. Howard Jenkins, an ambulance driver who rode with him in Italy during World War I, recalls that when Hemingway was propositioned by a prostitute at the officers' brothel, Ernest blushed and turned away. Hemingway claimed that he had intercourse with Mata Hari, but Donaldson cuts in: "Chronology tripped him up here: the famous spy died a year prior to the supposed date of the affair."[8]

Scott Fitzgerald had his own theories about Hemingway's virility, as they were revealed in his series of marriages and divorces, and particularly his marriage to Pauline: "I have a theory," he said. "Ernest needs a woman for each book. There was one for the stories and *The Sun Also Rises*. Now there's Pauline—*A Farewell to Arms* is a big book. If there's another big book I think you'll find Ernest has another wife."[9]

Anita Loos once observed: "To me Scott was more virile and more of a man than Hemingway."

Yet one cannot lightly dismiss Zelda's recurrent jealous suspicions. They grew in intensity with the approach of each of her breakdowns; she was not so sure that her husband didn't have a homosexual relationship with Hemingway, whom she called "as phoney as a rubber check." She discounted Hem's "tough guy" boast that, "he had bedded every women he had ever wanted and some that he hadn't."[10] Hem bragged to Donaldson that "he maintained a black harem while on a safari with Pauline in 1933 . . . and that he made love to Delba, another native African girl, while on a safari with Miss Mary in 1933 . . ."[11]

Gregory Hemingway, a physician, put his father's dwindling sexuality in surprisingly blunt perspective: "His liver had been in poor shape for years. Even in the male, the adrenal glands produce estrogen, or female hormones, which are normally broken down in the liver. But if the liver is badly damaged, there can be a high concentration of estrogen in the bloodstream which will reduce the male libido."[12]

*   *   *

Sheilah Graham says she wrote her memoir on her affair with Fitzgerald to set the record straight, and she ends the first chapter: "I
will always remember Scott as the only person before or since to give
me such a compelling relationship. He remade me in many areas so
that I can still be more honest with myself and don't rationalize my
misdeeds. And however badly he may have treated me when he was
drunk, the pluses of our years together—his love of me, the education, and the marvelous happy times we had between the binges—
were much more than the anguish of the drinking quarrels. As long
as I live I will be grateful for my time with him."[13]

The last word has not yet been said. Recently a news item appeared that in 1949 Ernest Hemingway had an affair with eighteen-
year-old Adriana Ivancich. For the next six years he wrote her two
thousand letters. Gossip about this affair had grown to such propor-
tions that the Countess von Max, fifty years old in 1980, felt impelled to tell all in her yet untranslated confession *La Torre Bianca*
(The White Tower).

Their relations were chaste, she writes, and the consummation came
only in fiction. "I love you more than the moon and the sky," he
had written her. One year after he met Adriana, Hemingway put her
into his *Across the River* and *The Old Man and the Sea*. Adriana, says
Claudia Wallis in *Time*, "recognizes herself as the elusive fish, chased
and hooked by the masterful old fisherman."[14]

DIRTY THINGS

One would imagine that Anaïs Nin, eroticist par excellence and Henry
Miller's intimate friend, whom Girodias advised to turn out sex novels for a living, would have got to know the physiology of the male
instrument.

Not so, says Edmund Wilson, who knew her better than most, dis-
illusions his readers in his diary in *The Twenties*: "She had thought
that men's cocks were stiff all the time because whenever they got
close enough to her for her to notice, they always were—when men
danced with her and when she was a little girl and when they'd hold
her on their legs—(with sudden bitterness) 'The dirty things!' "[15]

THE TOYS OF MEN

When W. H. Auden, in his last decade, settled in rooms in Cambridge, friends noted that his conversation was liberally sprinkled with the words *fuck* and *phallus*.

He expounded a favorite theory to Anne Fremantle, that all weapons of war are "phallic toys . . . cannons and aeroplanes and all those things, and men need phallic toys and women do not. Now these toys are become too dangerous. Men's phallic toys are likely to bring the world to an end." [16]

THE PHALLUS

D. H. Lawrence said that the penis is the source of all real beauty and all real gentleness. "I put a phallus in each one of my pictures somewhere."

("Lawrence could not buy a bicycle," noted Beverley Nichols, "without investing it with a dark, mysterious, sexual significance.") [17]

Moreover, said Lawrence, "The tragedy is when you've got sex in the head instead of down where it belongs." There is a divinity that inspires the phallus. The flesh is wiser than the intellect, he professed.

"We can go wrong in our minds," Lawrence wrote. "But what our blood feels and believes and says is always true."

Lawrence's misfortune in becoming impotent before his climacteric often drove him to a mad fury. Knud Merrild, who was with him when Lawrence's little dog, Pips, was happily coupling on the lawn with a neighbor's mongrel, reports that Lawrence "kicked and mauled the defenseless pet within an inch of his life." Merrild had to step between the "tortured dog and the absolutely insane author"; he said that he felt as if he were looking "into the deepest whitest boiling inferno—a pair of burning, piercing eyes of such strength that I saw nothing else, only sensed the bloodless, pale-pink eyes in a wilderness of beard." [18]

PHALLIC POWER

I. B. Singer recently unfolded this defense of phallic power in a *New York Times Magazine* interview:

"The sexual organs are the most sensitive organs of the human being. The eye or the ear seldom sabotages you. An eye will not stop seeing if it doesn't like what it sees, but the penis will stop functioning if he doesn't like what he sees. I would say that the sexual organs express the human soul more than any other limb of the body. They are not diplomats. They tell the truth ruthlessly. It's nice to deal with them and their caprices, but they are even more *meshuga* than the brain."[19]

If Only Maupassant Knew English

Guy de Maupassant, who was given to gross exaggeration, told it to Oscar Wilde, who put it in an anecdote and told it to more trust-worthy Vincent O'Sullivan. It finally found a place in Montgomery Hyde's *Oscar Wilde* and in Leon Edel's *Henry James: The Middle Years*.

Although Henry James made sex his basic theme, he could be frig-idly puritannical. He admired Maupassant's literary gift but was slightly affronted by the Frenchman's attitude to women.

The final story goes that when Maupassant visited him in London in 1886, James took him to his favorite restaurant. After they were seated, says Montgomery Hyde, Maupassant "looked around the room and said to his host, "There's a woman sitting over there whom I would like to have. Go over and get her for me.'

"Henry looked rather shocked. 'My dear friend, I cannot possibly do that, she may be perfectly respectable. In England you have to be careful.'

"A few minutes later Maupassant spotted another woman. 'Surely you know her at least? I could do quite well with her, if you would get her for me.' Then after a sigh, he added, 'If only I knew En-glish!' "

When Henry had refused for about the fifth time, Maupassant observed sulkily, 'Really you don't seem to know anybody in London!'"[20]

The Recognition Factor

Interviewing himself in a chapter of his recent *Music for Chameleons*, Truman Capote is asked: "How do you handle the 'recognition fac-tor?' " and answers:

It doesn't bother me a bit, and it's very useful when you want to cash a check in some strange locale. Also, it can occasionally have amusing consequences. For instance, one night I was sitting with friends at a table in a crowded Key West bar. At a nearby table, there was a mildly drunk woman with a very drunk husband. Presently, the woman approached us and asked me to sign a paper napkin. All this seemed to anger her husband; he staggered over to the table, and after unzipping his trousers and hauling out his equipment, said: "Since you're autographing things, why don't you autograph this?" The tables surrounding us had grown silent, so a great many people heard my reply, which was: "I don't know if I can autograph it, but perhaps I can *initial* it."[21]

Apparently, Truman suffered a memory lapse barely four years later when he revised the earlier account in his memoir "Remembering Tennessee" for the January 1984 issue of *Playboy*. His later account is expanded, given a touch of art and imagination, and in a generous impulse, the hero badge is shifted from himself onto Williams, who was no longer around to enjoy the questionable kudos. The new account is more than a self-parody. Every writer, one is safe to suppose, has the right to embellish an experience of his own, and it appears that most memoirists take that liberty, but Capote's refurbished account leaves one asking how far one can believe some anecdotes and particularly this "funniest memory" as well as a good many others he recalls.

Here is Capote's amended version:

My funniest memory, though, is of four or five years ago, when I was staying with Tennessee in Key West. We were in a terrifically crowded bar—there were probably 300 people in it, both gays and straights. A husband and wife were sitting at a little table in the corner, and they were both quite drunk. She had on a pair of slacks and a halter top, and she approached our table and held out an eyebrow pencil. She wanted me to autograph her belly button.

I just laughed and said, "Oh, no. Leave me alone."

"How can you be so cruel?" Tennessee said to me, and, as everybody in the place watched, he took the eyebrow pencil and wrote *my* name around her navel. When she got back to her table, her husband was furious. Before we knew it, he had grabbed the eyebrow pencil out of her hand and walked over to where we were sitting, whereupon he unzipped his pants and pulled out his cock and said—to me—"Since you're auto-graphing everything today, would you mind autographing *mine?*"

I had never heard a place with 300 people in it get that quiet. I didn't know what to say—I just looked at him.

Then Tennessee reached up and took the eyebrow pencil out of the stranger's hand. "I don't know that there's room for Truman to autograph it," he said, giving me a wink, "but I'll initial it."

It brought down the house.[22]

PEGGY STRIKES BACK

For years Peggy Guggenheim, permanently settled in Venice as resi-dent and museum curator, was victimized by the paparazzi in a dozen ways out of distaste for her reputedly outrageous immorality and that of her visitors. The main police office was directly across the canal and faced her Palazzo Venier dei Leoni. Finding the feud unbearable, she took revenge by setting up a Marino Marin bronze of a nude youth astride a little horse, flaunting a well-polished erection several feet long pointed directly at the station house.

Eventually, Peggy won her point. The police found it in their in-terest to leave the American hussy alone.

9

TURNED OFF

Heav'n has no rage like love to hatred turn'd,
Nor hell a fury like a woman scorn'd.

—William Congreve

Flannel Forbid

When a friend, Jack Nettleship, an Oxford professor, asked Oscar Wilde why he didn't live with his wife Constance, the poet evaded what was common knowledge, his homosexuality, and quipped: "Who would go to bed with a woman who slept in a flannel nightgown?"

John Quinn gives what he believes was the real reason for the separation, averring that Oscar knew he had syphilis and abstained out of fear he would infect his wife.[1]

The Versatile Tease

Prosper Mérimée often went whoring with Stendahl. They had little trouble bedding opera dancers and chorus girls. Everybody in the less fashionable Paris salons and around the cafés in Montparnesse came to envy Mérimée's sexual expertise and chuckled over the juicy stories he loved to tell about his prolific womanizing. He had once boasted, in truth, that he had even paid court to Shelley's widow Mary.

As George Sand's reputation spread, Mérimée set his sights on getting her into bed not necessarily for a prolonged liaison—that could be sticky—but a night or two of dalliance, adding another notch to the record he kept in his book of conquests.

At first Sand proved difficult. The novelist with the see-through male shirts, fancy trousers, and belted dagger was not shy about boasting how she had seduced Chopin, de Musset, and a passel of other celebrities. But after a phenomenal career of debauchery, she was heard to complain, heaving a sigh, "If I had to start my life over again, I should choose to remain chaste." However, when Mérimée started making advances, she made it clear to him privately that she

283

was not yet ready for him. She usually started out playing hard to get, but her repeated snubs only made him redouble his efforts.

Eventually, she yielded. "I am disposed," she told him. "Let it be as you wish, since it gives you such pleasure. But for my part I must tell you that I am sure it will give me none whatsoever."[2]

Typical brag, he thought.

He has a surprise coming, she thought.

After an assignation supper in her Quai Malaquais apartment, Sand calmly led him to her bedroom. Biographer Curtis Cate vividly describes what followed. It is the most authentic report we have.

"Unaccustomed to this total lack of coquetry, Mérimée was further amazed, as the decisive moment approached, to see George Sand calmly prepare the bed with her maid and then proceed to disrobe while he sat in an armchair, as though they were an old couple who had lived together for forty years. Whatever erotic appetite might have been aroused by the champagne consumed at supper had completely evaporated by the time he had undressed in his turn and climbed in under the sheets. Mérimée, though a skilled seducer, was also, it seems, a somewhat fastidious lover, having already once been thrown off his erotic stride by the sight of two wrinkled stockings being unrolled down the veiny shanks of a lady with the celestial name of Madame Azur. Contact under the sheets with Madame Sand's strangely immobile limbs proved equally chilling—with the result that the would-be Don Juan suffered what Stendahl in *De l'Amour* had described as the 'fiasco of imagination.' It was so complete that the impassive Madame Sand refused to lend a 'helping hand.' According to another account, which sounds like an apocryphal embellishment, she hit Monsieur Mérimée in the shoulder in a desperate effort to arouse him."[3]

Sand suffered a pang of remorse and the next day dropped him a note asking him to have *le courage* to come to her bed again. "If this bores you, don't do so. I am more resigned than you think. I have made a great deal of progress since yesterday. No, I'm not mad, believe me. I wouldn't blush at being so, but I feel that I'm not even very exalted."[4]

The first experience had been a shock to his dignity and he knew that the whole Left Bank would soon be gossiping. He saw his reputation slipping. So he wrote her a mocking note: "You have the tone of a young girl without her advantages, and the pride of a marquise with none of her graces."[5]

Sand took no time telling her friend, Marie Dorval, an actress and reputedly her lesbian lover, who rushed to tell Alfred de Vigny, who told others; the line of communication went on and on.

Mérimée himself is alleged to have added a denigrating embellishment to his own account, saying how even during their bed session the reputed hot lover Sand lay back, quill in her free hand, writing. Nothing but nothing must interfere with her professional routine. She was as cold as ice. From midnight to dawn her quill kept scratching away, as *horrible dictu,* she kept puffing on a smelly cigar. Was she teasing him? She knew that Mérimée was allergic to tobacco fumes! Hot lover, this Sand? She wasn't even tenth-rate! *Sacre nom,* how could one screw a woman while she's lying, knees up, composing?

One of the Goncourts wrote in his diary that everyone knew de Musset and the whole lot of her amourists, and they were amazed that one of the group, Mérimée, shouldn't have known that the alleged indefatigable sexist was a tease and far from expert in bed at all, "with a basic coldness which allowed her to write about her lovers when practically in bed with them," Goncourt wrote. "When Mérimée got out of her bed one day and picked up a sheet of paper lying on the table, she snatched it out of his hand: it was a pen portrait she had of him."[6]

Alexandre Dumas volunteered his own bit of mockery. "What do you expect?" he asked. "Mérimée is five feet, five inches tall . . ."

EYELESS IN GARSINGTON

It is not certain who was seducing whom. Cute, uninhibited Dora Carrington? Or Aldous Huxley? Both Lady Ottoline Morrell's "darlings" were collectibles in her free-wheeling playground in Garsington. Ott (D. H. Lawrence's familiar name for her) approved. Everyone at the manor was playing around and Huxley saw a golden opportunity to try a *carpe noctem* for himself.

Seduction was as new to Dora as it was to Aldous. His fianceé, Maria Nys, was a thousand miles away with her mother in Florence. Lytton Strachey, Dora's steady, was leagues off at his Titmarsh enclave, sleeping blissfully in the arms of her future husband, Ralph Partridge.

Dora always told Lytton everything, and she couldn't get to a pen fast enough when she reached home. Lytton always asked for lubricious particulars.

"Such a nightmare last night with Aldous in bed, everything went wrong. I could not lock the door: all the bolts were crooked. At last I chained it with a watch chain on the nails. Then I had a new pair of thick pajamas on and he got cross because I wouldn't take them off and they were all scratchy. Everything got in a mess, and he got so angry, and kept on trying to find me in the bed by peering with his eye-glass, and I thought all the time how I could account to my mother for the mess on my pajamas."[7]

Maria never knew, but even if he had told her she would have smiled. She even encouraged him in his extramarital sexual involvements. She knew him and all his fumblings well and loved him for all his faults. "You can't leave it to Aldous," she said. "He'd make a muddle."[8]

Aldous Huxley was twenty-eight, now happily married to Maria Nys and the father of a son, when he became infatuated with Nancy Cunard. Nancy did not take much notice of him. "She liked him," writes Anne Chisholm, "and kept him dangling; he would wait miserably for her telephone calls or hang around her at parties or in nightclubs, which he detested. At one point she had a brief and, for her, unimportant affair with him, which left him more in love than ever; but his adoration bored her, and his jealousy irritated her. He once spent a whole night pacing the street below her window."[9]

Maria Huxley began to take notice and issued an ultimatum. She was leaving for Italy and ordered him to join her or she would go alone. He went sheepishly. In Italy he wrote his second novel, *Antic Hay*.

Apparently, the affair with Cunard did not end there. Decades later Nancy wrote that when Huxley asked her to live with him, she refused since he was married and had a baby son. "I did nothing to excite or tempt him. We saw much of each other for two or three days, without sex, then drifted apart. I never saw him again."

Nancy, whose list of lovers could fill a folio, once told a friend that she found Huxley physically repellent; being in bed with him was like "being crawled over by slugs."[10]

A Bitch Sans Reproche

Had Gertrude Stein accepted Ernest Hemingway's marriage proposal they would have made the oddest couple in literary history. How the macho youth ever came to make the proposal to the lesbian lady is still a mystery, and so is the exact reason why Stein rejected him— though Man Ray believed she did not do so out of hand. It was probably Alice B. Toklas who persuaded Stein to allow her to slam the door in Hem's face when he called.

Stein must have resented an obvious threat to her sovereignty; Hemingway was becoming better known than she was in the Stein circle and in the Paris colony of expatriate Americans. In her eyes *lese majesté* was a cardinal sin. No one can be better than Gertrude Stein, she insisted, not even Shakespeare.

Back home, Hemingway took off his shelf a presentation copy of Gertrude Stein's *Autobiography* crossed out Stein's "A Rose Is a Rose," and scrawled "A Bitch is a Bitch is a Bitch." Thereafter, that was his word for all lesbians.

Ernest Hemingway always had a woman in reserve ready to marry him before he divorced the previous wife. Other men might leave their wives for permanent mistresses in unsanctified liaisons, but Hemingway wed four times.

He told Matthew Josephson in 1937, "with an air that was only half-jesting, that as he was readying to leave his wife #2 he already had in hand wife #3 ready to marry him. 'The trouble is I'm a fool for women; I always have to marry 'em.' "

The author of *The Sun Also Rises* could be brutally frank. When he was asked by Bill Bird why he and his first wife, Hadley, were divorcing, he replied, "Because I am a son of a bitch." Nothing was going to stop his bitchiness, he told Scott Fitzgerald. He had made up his mind to being "the son of a bitch *sans peur et sans reproche.*" And he lived up to his word.[11]

10

THE POSTMAN COMETH

The letter killeth.

—2 Corinthians 3:6

The Wrong Address Killeth

Charles Dickens ordered a well-known London shop to send an expensive gift package to the home of his mistress, Ellen Ternan, whom he was keeping in a love nest, all expenses paid. The clerk got the address wrong; it may have been that Dickens gave it wrong and the messenger brought it to the Dickens home.

Mrs. Dickens accepted it and put two and two together when she read the torrid note in the box. Their marriage started to crumble.

Dickens knew his Bible. *The letter killeth.* He proceeded to burn all the letters he had received for the past twenty years in a field behind Gad's Hill. His family completed most of the coverup: after he died, they burned piles of letters he had written to them.[1]

• • •

A post-office mixup occurred to Walter Lippmann, who was having a clandestine affair for weeks with Helen, the wife of his best friend, Hamilton Fish Armstrong. Lippmann wrote a letter to Helen in Europe and it accidentally was delivered to her husband. Armstrong arranged divorce proceedings at once.

It did not turn out well for either lover. When Lippmann became old and infirm, Helen, instead of arranging private nurse care, put him in a Park Avenue nursing home. Lippmann died at eighty-five, six years after Helen.

The Intercepted Letter

When John Marquand, author of *The Late George Apley*, divorced his wife and married Adelaide Ferry Hooker, one of his cousins snick-

288

ered, "Poor Adelaide never realized that she was being used as an instrument of revenge." She was so right.

What Marquand had in mind at his second altar performance we shall never know, but in short time he went forth and formed a torrid liaison with Carol Brandt, his literary agent's wife. Carol's husband acceped the division of his love, but Carol rejected Marquand's importunities to run off to Hollywood with him. Marquand never told his wife of the liaison but, like Mrs. Charles Dickens and some others in a like situation, she found out about it through an intercepted letter.

Adelaide was furious and proceeded to make Marquand's life at home a living hell, brawling in public, and continually engaging in other notorious actions socially with the object of tarnishing his reputation.[2]

"Too Much Is Too Much"

Reflecting on his approaching eightieth year, André Gide averred that if he had to live it over again, he would have given in to even more temptations. He parked his *angst* at home with his wife and anchor, Madeleine. He offered her no apologies for leaving her to go foraging abroad for boys in public squares and cafés. To stave off domestic squalls, she suppressed her feelings during the long stretches and was silent. "I think of her all the time,"[1] he said, affectionately apologetic.

The long armistice burst into a temporary war when Gide ran off to England with fifteen-year-old Marc Allégret, son of his wife's friend. The elopement hit Madeleine hard. "Too much is too much," she cried, and in the sudden rush of rebellion at the desertion, she burned all the letters he had ever sent her, even as far back as early adolescence.

On his return, Enid Starkie writes: "He asked to see the letters to refresh his memory, and then she told him what she had done to him. He was heartbroken . . . he felt that she had killed their child—his and hers—and that these letters had been the best things that he had ever written."[3]

After giving up on trying to convert Gide to Catholicism, Paul Claudel exclaimed at a lunch while watching a crêpe suzette flame up in brandy, "That is how Gide's soul will burn in hell!"

When his irreconcilable friend died, Mauriac wrote, "I don't know whether Gide is in heaven or hell. But wherever he is, it must be very interesting."

The week following Gide's death, a telegram was tacked up on a bulletin board in a Sorbonne hall. It read: "L'enfer n'existe pas. Préviens Claudel!" (Hell does not exist. Better warn Claudel!) It was signed "Gide."[4]

11

ENCOUNTERS

It is better to connect in print than in person.
—John Updike, *Picked Up Pieces*

MEDICINE AND MORALITY

Literary quidnuncs are still telling about how, on an Atlantic crossing, Hemingway met a homosexual actor and reported jubilantly, "Whenever he walked into the dining room, I raised my glass and smashed it on the table as every gentleman does in the presence of homosexuals."[1]

Tennessee Williams, therefore, told Kenneth Tynan (the noted British drama critic) that Hemingway's bias against gays made him the last person in the world he'd want to meet. But gradually the fear of confrontation wore off, and when Tynan told him he had an appointment with Hemingway at the novelist's favorite eating place in Havana, Tennessee thought he'd like to come along. "I will be there," Tynan told him, "to lend you what support I can."

"But, Ken baby, won't he kick me?" asked Tennessee, in a cold sweat. "They tell me Hemingway kicks people like me in the crotch."

"Nonsense," said Tynan, and to reassure the playwright, he picked up the phone. Hemingway said he'd be delighted to have Tennessee join him at the Floridita.

The meeting couldn't have begun more inauspiciously. Tynan and Hemingway were on time; Tennessee, who had been fortifying himself with stiff drinks since ten in the morning, was late. In disgust, Hemingway went to the john and had to be coaxed to come out.

At lunch, the booze in Tennessee spoke: "What I've always admired about your works, Mr. Hemingway, is that you care about honor among men. And there is no quest more desperate than that."

The remark made Hemingway see red.

"What kind of man, Mr. Williams, did you have in mind?"

Tennessee had plunged into the trap he'd set for himself. Seeing the novelist sprawling across the table, he shrugged his shoulders uneasily and replied, "People who have honor never talk about it."

More drinks. Slipping further in the noose, Tennessee became offensively personal:

"I used to know your second wife, Mr. Hemingway. I believe her name was Pauline. I knew her in Key West when I was young. She was very kind to me when I was poor—a lovely lady, a most hospitable lady. I often wondered what happened to her. They tell me she died. Did she die in great pain?"

Tynan reports: "Hemingway, who was profoundly attached to his second wife, replied with a stoical sentence that deliberately verged on self-parody: he often used this technique to avoid direct emotional commitment. 'She died like everybody else,' he said leaning portentously across the bar, 'and after that she was dead.' "

A blow-up might have been in the making, but the conversation veered to the relative importance of kidneys and liver and the sailing was smooth. At one point they exchanged names and addresses of their doctors. Finally they rose, swaying, and shook hands; as Tynan says, "linked at last by medicine and mortality."[2]

In his *Memoirs*, Williams notes:

"I had expected a very manly, super-macho sort of guy, very bullying and coarse spoken. On the contrary, Hemingway struck me as a gentleman who seemed to have a very touchingly shy quality about him. . . . I was not an *aficionado* of bullfighting, but one who had enjoyed the spectacle of it and I had become, the previous summer, a good friend of Antonio Ordóñez, who was, you might almost say, an idol of Ernest Hemingway's. I mentioned to Hemingway that I knew Antonio Ordóñez. Hemingway was pleased, I thought, and he was also pleased that I shared his interest in bullfighting."[3]

As for insights into literature, the meeting drew a blank. There was occasionally a flash of original opinion on a subject unrelated to either man's work. Fortunately for Tennessee, the two avoided sex. The luncheon did not make literary history.

ANDRÉ GIDE MEETS OSCAR WILDE

At the height of his fame—he had already published *The Picture of Dorian Gray*, and *Salome* was in the works—Oscar Wilde felt the need for diversion and went to Paris, leaving his wife, Constance, and their two small sons at home in Tite Street, London.

Pierre Loüys introduced Wilde to André Gide, then twenty-one. Gide later recalled their first meeting:

"In Paris, no sooner did Wilde arrive, than his name was on everybody's lips. . . . I had heard him spoken of at Mallarmé's; he was a brilliant talker and I wished to know him."

A friend arranged it; Wilde was invited to dinner at a restaurant. There were four guests, but Wilde was the only one who talked. Gide wrote: "Wilde did not converse; he narrated throughout almost the whole meal; he did not stop narrating. He narrated, gently, slowly; his very voice was wonderful. . . ."[4]

A short time later, seeing Wilde's photograph on Marcel Schwob's mantelpiece, one of Wilde's acquaintances, Jules Renard, said, "Gide is in love with Oscar Wilde."

After their first encounter, the two met practically every day until Wilde left Paris. It is reported that once, in a crowded drawing room at the home of Heredia, Wilde took Gide aside and said, "Do you know why Christ did not love his mother? . . . It's because she was a virgin!"—and burst into laughter. They became closer than ever.[5]

Before Wilde was convicted and sent to prison, in January 1895, the two writers met by accident in an Algiers hotel, when Gide saw Wilde's name on a blackboard guest list. (Wanting solitude, Gide rubbed out his own name, but feeling he had been cowardly he had a change of heart and put his name back again.)[6] It was during those last Algiers meetings that Wilde said he had written *The Picture of Dorian Gray* in a few days "because one of my friends claimed that I could not write a novel. It bores me—so much writing." It was at this time that Wilde made his classic remark—"Would you like to know the great dream of my life? It's that I've put my genius into my life; I've put only my talent into my works."

ANDRÉ GIDE MEETS CHRISTOPHER ISHERWOOD

In the 1920s and early '30s all roads led to Magnus Hirschfeld's Institute for Sexual Sciences. It was a shrine that observant homosexuals found it mandatory to visit.

André Gide journeyed all the way to view specialties in sexual kicks. It was a vacation from his boy hunting in Northern Africa.

Hirschfeld, internationally recognized as an expert on homosexual goodies, ran a highly specialized sex factory and it was only natural that Christopher Isherwood should occasionally look in on the museum, since he lived next door. He often brought W. H. Auden along.

Isherwood recalled that the first time he visited the emporium he giggled nervously from embarrassment when the good doctor's assistant took him on tour. "Here," he wrote, "were whips and chains and torture instruments designed for the practitioners of pleasure-pain; high-heeled, intricately decorated boots for the fetichists; lacy female undies which had been worn by ferociously masculine Prussian officers beneath their uniforms. Here were the lower half of trouser legs with elastic bands to hold them in position between knees and ankle. . . . Here were fantasy pictures, drawn and painted by Hirschfeld's patients. Scenes from the court of a priapic king who sprawled on a throne with his own phallus for a scepter and watched the grotesque matings of his courtiers. Strange sad bedrooms in which the faces of the copulators expressed only dismay and agony. 'And here was a gallery of photographs, ranging in subject matter from the sexual organs of quasi-hermaphrodites to famous homosexual couples—Wilde with Alfred Douglas, Whitman with Peter Doyle, Ludwig of Bavaria with Kainz, Edward Carpenter with Knud Merrild."

Isherwood thought it a fortunate coincidence that he met Gide there. He treated the Frenchman like visiting royalty. Gide had come in full regalia, wearing his hallmark Superman cape.

Both visitors looked hard, says Isherwood, at "a young man who opened his shirt with a modest smile to display two perfectly formed female breasts." Gide looked on, "making a minimum of polite comment, judiciously fingering his chin."

Meeting Gide at the institute made Isherwood, he says, now "love Hirschfeld," at whom he had been sneering a moment before—"the silly solemn old professor with his doggy mustache, thick peering spectacles. . . . Nevertheless, they were all three of them on the same side, whether Christopher liked it or not. And later he would learn to honor them back as the heroic leaders of his tribe."[7]

No doubt, Gide added a few more sexual kicks to his knowledge, but judging by his sober reaction, he probably personally preferred what he saw in the exotic dens in Algiers and Morocco.

James Whistler Meets Oscar Wilde

James Whistler said that when he first met Oscar Wilde, then newly arrived from Oxford to startle and entertain London, had he been aware of his pederasty, it "would certainly have prevented me from offering him a spontaneous invitation to my next Sunday breakfast."

Years later, after Whistler had shed half a dozen mistresses and settled down to traditional domestic routine, he took a different view of homosexuals and modified his original puritanical bias. The new view came after Oscar's fall from grace.

In his novel *I, James McNeill Whistler*, based on authentic facts, Lawrence Williams cites the turn Whistler took of homosexuals:

"The first fact about Oscar that I didn't know was that he was a pederast, but of course that would have had nothing to do with inviting him to my breakfast table, as dukes, curators or even Pre-Raphaelite painters are as welcome as long as they are entertaining. The whole notion of getting stuffy about how another man finds his sexual satisfaction has always seemed to me totally inexplicable. . . . Am I to shun a man because he prefers his stout to my champagne? . . . I will confess that the preference for the backside of a Wapping stable boy to the ineffable glories of a beautiful woman's body strikes me as a calamitous error in judgement, a self-deprivation of joy quite staggering to mention to someone like me. . . . Whoever introduced us failed to mention that he was a pederast, but that was only a show of manners, I suppose."[8]

Whistler called Oscar Wilde half-facetiously a thief for appropriating his epigrams. For a man like Whistler whose "Ha! Ha!" could be heard tens of yards away, *plagiarist* was rather a mild term.

Around 1883, privately the two wits were friends, and he had Oscar as his select breakfast guest and Wilde invited him to his wedding. Whistler, unpunctual as usual, telegraphed him at the church: "Fear I may not be able to reach you in time for the ceremony. Don't wait."

Whistler had heard of Marcel Proust, of course, and it was common knowledge that the French writer was homosexual. However, that did not deter him from readily accepting Malarmé's invitation to meet the then celebrated journalist. The translator of Whistler's *Ten O'Clock Lecture* felt he had to add that he was not so sure Proust would show. He rarely went out. This time Proust came.

At Malarmé's, Whistler found Proust charming, though just slightly less larcenous than Wilde.

Back home he wrote this memo:

"At one point I turned to speak to someone else sitting nearby, and as I did so I put my gloves, grey they were, tinted a little blue on the table. In a moment, only out of the edge of one eye, talking the while, I saw M. Proust pick up a single glove and surreptitiously only slip it into the pocket of his coat. Only one, mind you—not a thoughtful thrill, you see, but a hunter of souvenirs."[9]

GENDER GAP

Early in their careers in Berlin, Stephen Spender and Christopher Isherwood were lovers. Later in London, at a party, Spender got the impression that Isherwood was showing signs of irritation with him and suggested the next day to Christopher that when they returned to Berlin, for their mutual good, and to cut down on their increasing jealousies, they should see little or nothing of each other. As they parted, Spender put out his hand and said, "If we're going to part, at least let's part like men." To which Christopher replied, smiling, "But, Stephen, we aren't men."[10]

TWO GIANTS, HEAD-ON

In one of those confrontations in literary history that come once in a century, two titans met by prearrangement in the Albermarle Street drawing room of their publisher, John Murray, for an hour or two.

Sir Walter Scott was the conservative numero uno. George Gordon, Lord Byron, his junior by sixteen years, was the latest meteor in the literary sky—proud and notorious rake and flâneur. The two had already exchanged complimentary gifts; now they had come to exchange ideas.

They agreed on everything except politics, religion, and morality.

Byron snapped, "You are one of those who prophesy that I shall turn Methodist."

"No," replied Scott, "I don't expect your conversion to be such an ordinary kind. I rather look to see you retreat upon the Catholic faith and distinguish yourself by the austerity of your penance."

They broke lances on morals. Byron said he thought "a spot of adultery would do Scott no harm." The older poet rejoined that "a dash of chastity would do Byron some good."[11]

A witness to the meeting reported that it was an inspiring thing to see the two giants of the age stomping side by side down the stairs, Byron limping with a club foot and Scott unsteady on his lame leg.

ENOUGH IS ENOUGH

As Professor of Poetry in Residence in Oxford, W. H. Auden was expected to give three lectures a year and to hold himself accessible to callers presenting their respects or wanting him to read their work. Often they would join him as he sat sipping coffee at the Cadena Café in the Cornmarket, or if they had some prestige, he invited them to his digs in Brewer Street. He always showed an interest in what they were writing. It was worth his $7.50 monthly rental.

One morning two American Beat poets, Allen Ginsberg and Gregory Corso, were brought to his room by an Oxford student to shake his hand and read their poems. Though Auden did not have a high opinion of their poetry, he considerately kept his opinion to himself.

Time dragged on painfully for Auden. At length, finding that his two American guests would not budge, he volunteered to show them around the Christ Church Cathedral as a way of shaking them off. It was a device he adopted time and again. As he extended his hand in farewell after the tour, both guests dropped to their knees and attempted to kiss the bottom of his trousers. Auden was horrified.[12]

12

TAKE MY WIFE

The great trick with a woman is to get rid of her while she thinks she's rid of you.

—Sören Kirkegaard

THE TRAP THAT FAILED

"Don't please compare me to Casanova," Frank Harris roared early in his career to a flatterer. "Casanova, my dear man, is not worthy to tie my bootstrings—though I like the fellow."

Middleton Murry, one of any number of writers eager to exploit the bounder's literary influence, swooned before Harris: "Ave, imperator amoris!"

Harris fully admired his own image. He is alleged to have said "I always pray to God that He may let me live up to my vain opinion of myself."

It has always been a mystery to writers who knew Harris how women ever yielded to his persuasive whispers. His looks and general appearance were against him. He looked more like a tout or a horse auctioneer than the influential editor: undersized; mongrel muscular arms; dyed, pomaded moustache done up at night in curlers; flashy checked waistcoat with an enormous watch across his big chest; brown buckskin shoes; white spats; a roaring base voice. He reminded Malcolm Muggeridge of Mussolini.

No longer able to flaunt his superhuman sexual gymnastics to friends, who now couldn't afford to scorn the boss at *The Fornightly Review* and call his bluff openly, he took to publishing his reminiscenses in a four-volume *My Life and Loves*. Someone called the memoirs *My Life and Lies*. It was so erotic that he had to get friends like Hesketh Pearson to smuggle it into England to be sold under the counter. Muggeridge wrote: "I cannot imagine any single circumstance more calculated to enrage his ghost than the knowledge that his wife Nellie's heirs were benefiting financially from *My Life and Loves* on an infinitely greater scale than ever he did. 'Twenty-five thousand pounds for the paperback rights alone!' I hear him roaring in anguish out of Hades."[1]

Sweating profusely, Harris never ceased regretting having squandered his allotted ration of sperm all too soon despite his efforts years back "to bind himself up nightly to prevent spillage."

Now past his prime, he compensated for his losses in lewd fantasizing. A witty woman said, "Frank Harris seemed capable of sex in any language." Harris's daughter told Muggeridge that "there was nothing on earth which scared the daylights out of poor old Frankie as a truly passionate woman."[2]

Poor Nellie had all the evidence a wife needs to know that her husband was irrevocably impotent, for all his brag.

Agustus John was notorious for having a goat's conscience, but as he testifies in *Chiaroscuro*, when he visited Harris in his rented flat outside Nice, "I was shown to my room, which as Frank was careful to point out, adjoined Nellie's, his own being at a certain distance round the corner." The inuendo couldn't have been more obvious that he was giving his guest the green light. John went in and stayed the course.

The next day it dawned on him that he had been set up as "pliable if Frank needed money." Harris was still an undischarged bankrupt. Fearing blackmail, John crept out of the villa in the morning without saying good-bye, his wallet intact.[3]

A MORATORIUM ON MONOGAMY

Bertrand Russell, as usual pulling no punches, began his autobiography with his philosophy of life:

"Three passions, simple but overwhelmingly strong, have governed my life: the longing for love, the search for knowledge, and unbearable pity for the sufferings of mankind.

"I have sought love, first, because it brings ecstasy—ecstasy so great I would often have sacrificed all the rest of life for a few hours of this joy. I have sought it, next, because it relieves loneliness—that terrible loneliness in which one shivering consciousness looks over the rim of the world into the cold, unfathomable, lifelong abyss. I have sought it, finally, because in the union of love I have seen, in a mystic miniature, the prefiguring vision of the heaven that saints and poets have imagined. This is what I sought, and though it might seem too good for human life, this is what—at last—I have found."[4]

Will Durant admired Russell's search for knowledge, sympathized, in the abstract at least, with his longing for love. He was not so enthusiastic about the direction the longing for love fulfilled itself.

Will Durant claimed he was "an essential monogamist" but that he saw nothing wrong in an occasional deviation into infidelity by his wife, Ariel, so long as she came back to hubby.

In the Durants' joint memoir, A *Dual Autobiography*, Ariel tells what happened when their friend, a Communist cartoonist, stayed overnight at the Durants' bungalow in Staten Island's New Dorp section in 1914:

"When Robert Minor visited us in our New Dorp bungalow in 1914 I admired him for his art, his kindness, and his powerful figure that more than once I reached up and flung my arms around his neck. We put him up in a bed just a step away from the one in which I lay with Will. Slowly a desire came over me for physical union with Robert—not (if I may trust my memory) for any erotic intimacy (for I have never been very sexual) but just to feel the warmth and strength of the virile body that housed so big a heart. Like a good wife I asked my husband's permission: Might I get into bed with Bob for a little while? Will, who has never been bothered by the itch to possess, gave me his indulgent consent, as if understanding that it was the child, and not merely the woman, that was speaking. Suddenly Bob found me beside him. He smiled, offered me a paternal kiss, and sent me back to my proper bed. So far as I know, he was too much of a gentleman to tell this story to anyone, even when he sadly condemned us for expressing our disappointment with Soviet Russia in 1932. Will and I liked him to the end."[5]

Ariel was more discriminating when Bertrand Russell came to visit them in New York. It was common knowledge that an attractive woman in the same room with the English philosopher had to keep miles out of his reach. She had heard how his advances to Mrs. Alfred Whitehead nearly broke up their marriage and split the collaboration of two most eminent British philosophers. Will relished the after-dinner talk, which turned out to be strictly philosophical, but he became uneasy when Ariel readily accepted Russell's invitation to ride him home. For security she asked her brother Michael to take the wheel. Asking him to drive leisurely through Central Park, Russell began to fondle his hostess in the back seat.

Durant comments in A *Dual Autobiography*: "When I consider that Russell was soon to publish his view that a man compelled by his business to be absent from his wife for more than three weeks should be allowed a temporary moratorium on monogamy, I tremble to think what might have happened in Central Park."[6]

Fortunately, Russell was staying only a short distance from the Durant apartment, and Michael, keeping his eye on the rear-view mirror, headed straight for the philosopher's hotel will all due dispatch.

A Friend in Need

Among the many speculations in T. S. Matthews's biography of T. S. Eliot is whether Bertrand Russell seduced Vivienne Eliot, the poet's first wife. The matter is shrouded in fog and a welter of contradictory evidence. The remark by Matthews that Russell "had a first-rate mind, humane aspiration, and the sexual morals of an alley cat" would not have been rebutted by Bertrand Russell himself. Whether myth or fact, the alleged seduction is discussed in practically every biography of Eliot. Russell himself has much to say on the subject. And he should know.

Russell invited the newly married Eliots to his small two-bedroom flat in London. He noted that Vivienne was cruel to Eliot: "I am every day getting things more right between them," Russell said, "but I can't let them alone at present, and of course, I, myself, get very much interested. She is a person who lives on a knife-edge and will end as a criminal or a saint. I don't know which yet. She has a perfect capacity for both."[7]

A few months later, Russell invited Vivienne, who was suffering from depression, to spend a holiday with him in Torquay. Eliot consented, and remained in London. "Did Russell seduce Vivienne," Matthews asks, and goes on to say "and was Eliot, at least for a time, unaware of the fact? The probable answer to both questions, in the light of the circumstantial evidence and of the characters concerned, is yes. How could Vivienne, married only a few months and supposedly much in love with her husband, have taken part in so cruel an adultery? One possible answer is that she was a flirt, and flirts sometimes go too far, sometimes get themselves into situations they can't get out of; sometimes, a determined seducer is one too many for them."[8]

Apparently, Eliot later expressed his gratitude: "Dear Bertie," he wrote. "This is wonderfully kind of you; really the last straw, so to speak, of generosity. I am very sorry you have to come back, and Vivienne says you have been an angel to her . . . I am sure you have done *everything* possible, and handled her in the very best way; better than I. I often wonder how things would have turned out but for you. I believe we shall owe her life to you, even."[9]

We have only Russell's vague word to go on. There is some doubt among biographers whether the "angel" referred to in Eliot's note was in fact, an adulterer—and we can't put it beyond Russell—or just a friend in need.

Sainte-Beuve: A Double Agent

In an attempt to resolve the major crisis in his marriage, Victor Hugo gave his wife license to continue her affair with their mutual friend Sainte-Beuve, provided his friend's love sessions with Adèle take place in the afternoon, when Hugo was engaged at his own love nest a few miles away.

Joanna Richardson tells us that in public, Victor Hugo and Sainte-Beuve acted correctly, but in private it was another matter, as Sainte-Beuve recorded in the notebooks later published as *Mes Poisons*. In it he gave an account of his love affair, which he privately printed as *Le Livre d'Amour*. In 1885, when Sainte-Beuve and Hugo and Adèle were dead, Léon Daudet and the poet's grandson, Georges, went to Guernesy; there, in Hugo's library, they found an envelope sealed with three black seals and inscribed, in Hugo's hand, PUDENDA. It contained letters from Adèle to Sainte-Beuve. "We know," said Daudet, "that these significant letters had been sent to Hugo by Sainte-Beuve himself. He wanted—apart from *Le Livre d'Amour*—to make him understand the extent of his Adèle's betrayal!"[10]

13

GOOD TO THE LAST DROP

There is no man so decrepit whilst he has Methuselah before him who does not think he has still twenty years of life in his body.

—Montaigne

Old lovers are soundest.

—John Webster

FUNERAL DIVERSION

Edmund Gosse, panjandrum of English letters and a repressed homosexual, whom Aldous Huxley called "the bloodiest little man I have ever seen," enjoyed the bundles of photos of male nudes his gay friend J. A. Symonds sent him from abroad. Symonds had tried in vain to get Gosse to admit, in the way he himself had done, that he was homosexual.

At Robert Browning's funeral in Westminster Abbey, while the organ was pealing the requiem, the *arbiter elegantarium* couldn't restrain himself from stealing glances at a pack of photographs of young attractive males Symonds had sent him from Italy.[1]

AN UNQUENCHABLE TORCH

John Ruskin, doddering past seventy and verging on senility, got his greatest thrill dancing ring-around-the-rosy with little girls at the school he had set up and financed. He was then still carrying the torch for a thirteen-year-old Rosie and writing her letters in baby talk, several of them telling her he would marry her when she grew to mature age.

RESEARCH DIVIDEND

On the pretext that he had to go off to London to research at the British Museum, septuagenarian and more lustful than ever, Thomas

Hardy spent many afternoons atop a bus goggling at the pretty ankles and hefty bottoms of young ladies sashaying down Regent Street, the venue of prostitutes.[2]

ETERNALLY OLYMPIO

On the evening that Victor Hugo, still virginal, married his wife, Adèle, his brother, who was an unflagging rival for her hand, put a bullet through his head. Victor went right ahead with the ceremony and for years boasted that he had made up for lost time that night and possessed his bride nine times. Tolstoy was an amateur by comparison.

Hugo collected mistresses by the dozens. To the very year he died he boasted that no labor, whether of love or anything else, could drain his Olympian strength. He could crack walnuts with his natural complement of teeth, walk miles without tiring, take on three mistresses in an afternoon.

After hearing Hugo, well past seventy, make a very long speech, a friend told him, "You must be exhausted!"

"Yes," he said, for the first time confessing a trace of fatigue, "it is a great effort for me to talk: to make a speech is more exhausting for me than making love three times." Then pausing not for breath but recollection, he added: "Or even four!"[3]

Hugo's friends were amazed at the old man's unabated vitality. *Mon Dieu,* it must be a gift of the Gods! Even his old rival, his wife's lover Sainte-Beuve, had to admit: "He's got an amazing constitution, that man. His barber told me that his beard was three times as stiff as anybody else's and that it nicked all his razors. . . . And his eyes! When he was writing his *Feuilles d'automne* we went up to the top of the towers of Notre Dame nearly every evening to see the sunsets— which, incidentally, didn't amuse me very much. Well, from up there, he could tell the colour of the dress Mademoiselle Nodier was wearing on the balcony of the Arsenal."[4]

When he got his first toothache, well into his seventies, he asked "What is all this?" His apartment was on the third and fourth floors and he climbed them without getting out of breath. Every evening he would entertain from ten to fourteen guests, talking, reading his poetry, discussing literary feuds, and end up being the only one without glazed eyes.

Two of Hugo's biographers add this bit about his funeral: "Another detail about the *fucking* funeral rites for the great man—a detail which comes from the police. For the last week all the Fantines of the big brothels have carried on their trade with their natural parts draped in a scarf of black crêpe—*their cunts in mourning.*"[5]

Making Up for Lost Time

"Ah, if I were but fifty years old!" said Anatole France with a heavy sigh to his secretary Jean-Jacques Brousson. He was then enjoying sleeping with his duenna in Argentina. But his candid mirror depressed him. To his eternal regret it was obvious he could no longer cosmetize his three score years.

"Why, what would you do if you were but fifty?" Brousson asked. "Would you change your path?"

"Ah, yes, indeed. I would send literature to the dickens! I was born among books and I have made books—but books are not the only things in the world. If I were only fifty, my friend, I should not go back to France."

Another sigh, much sadder reflection: if he had the choice, he would never be "sleeping two days running in the same bed with the same woman. There are so many women! And so many beds!"[6]

But back to Paris he came, continually grumbling even more over *les temps perdus.*

Years came, years went, and the older Anatole France got, the more insistent the itch became.

It is incredible that this true-born Parisian had reached seventy without ever having been to a single girlie show or a striptease joint. Even goggle-eyed tourists from the American Midwest couldn't wait to taste the Place Pigalle on their first stop.

With Mme. de Caillavet securely buried, France stepped out for the first time in his life into the metropolis he had never really known. On the town with his friend Calmette he qualified his opposition to World War I, remarking that "the only practical results the long agony of the war seemed to have achieved were Summer Time and short skirts."

"Bonheur appréciable!" he commented on the welcome new fashion of abbreviated skirts, "but just my luck, they have come at a time when I could no longer see clearly."[7]

His friend Wasserman took him one night to the Casino de Paris, but it proved an exasperating experience. Even with the thousand dazzling lights exposing hundreds of soubrettes on stage wiggling their powdered bottoms, France couldn't enjoy the sight of a single rump. Nature had played him dirty!

For years, even when he was under the sleuthing eyes of Mme. de Caillavet, France had stashed a collection of Frenchie postcards in his desk drawer. Once she was out of sight and shopping, having alerted Josephine not to let her *malheureux* slip out, he nevertheless managed to get out. In his rue Hoche study, wearing his cardinal red cap and lounging robe, he would push the pile of books off his cluttered desk, take out his stereoptican machine, and feast his eyes on the slides. There was always the hidden telescope buried among the books on the floor. He got another set of thrills squinting through it at a disrobing female neighbor across the way.

Recovering from a slight stroke at eighty, France, in the Hugo tradition, proudly attributed it to "a moment of passion with a beautiful visitor."

PRIVATE LUST

A. E. Housman ordered that "my executor shall destroy without exception all my unpublished Mss." Despite this precautionary measure, his secret homosexual affairs with Moses Jackson and the Venetian gondolier leaked out after he died. Somehow gondoliers on the wharf had proved persuasive homosexual bait to homosexuals like Housman.

After Housman died, the executors found a collection of pornographic clippings and materials in his locked desk drawer. He had intended to use them for a book he was writing, but no English publisher would dare take it. Eventually it was published in *Hermes*, a German periodical, with the title *Praefando* (Dirty Words).

W. H. Auden, who sympathized with Housman's suppressed urges,[8] wrote:

> Deliberately he chose the dry-as-dust,
> Kept tears in dirty postcards
> in a drawer. . . .[9]

A.E.H. was a stickler about personal record-keeping. Among the private papers the executors found in the locked drawer was a list of names of male prostitutes who had serviced him during his two-week jaunts to Paris, their avocations, and the price he paid them for servicing him.

MORE THAN ART AT I TATTI

Long after age sixty, Bernard Berenson, the greatest art critic of his century and a reputed memoirist, was tickled pink when attractive ladies dropped in on him at I Tatti. He was an incurable flirt who took advantage of his age to fondle lady visitors and ask questions about their intimate lives. He relished an occasional affectionate pat on the rump. Even at eighty-five he was still writing love letters.

The Marchesa Lulu Torrigiani, whose estate was next to Berenson's, was eighty-five, a few years older than B.B., and she dropped in on him again and again. He got a kick out of kissing her and holding her hands. Her naughty stories titillated him no end.

"One of her mildest," Harold Acton says in his *Memoirs of an Aesthete 1939–1969*, "concerned two policemen on the prowl for indecent behaviour in a public park. Hiding behind a bush they heard a feminine voice implore: 'Oh, do let me take a last look before you put it in!' Leaping forth to catch a couple in 'flagrant delight' they found two old women burying a cat."[10]

Acton tells us that once when B.B. told Lulu how much he enjoyed her visits, she replied seductively, "But you don't know how amusing I could be in bed." Whether B.B. took her up on that has not been told.

Mary and Ernest Hemingway were invited to tea at Berenson's villa. B.B. was then eighty-three.

At the introduction, the art connoisseur asked Mary, "What number are you?"

"Sir?" she replied. "Do you number your guests?"

"Wife," he said.

"Number four."

Then B.B. asked her how Hemingway had managed to "get through so many wives."

"I have no simple answer for that, sir," she said. "Of course, Ernest is a man of tremendous energy and exuberance."

B.B. was still not satisfied, and he asked, "Does he demonstrate those characteristics in bed?" Silence.

The colloquy stopped when they sat down to tea.[11]

As they were leaving, he said in a jocular pursuit, "You may not leave until you have given me a kiss."

"Then he said," Mary recalled in *How It Was*, "awaiting my salutation, his eighty-three-year-old lips still full and sensuous, I gave him a generous kiss and muttered: 'You and H. G. Wells.' "[12]

14

TOUCHING BOTTOM

If your posterior's cute, let it be seen from behind.
—Ovid, *The Art of Love*

A BUM RAP

"Madame Sand has a great soul and a perfectly enormous bottom," the French critic Sainte-Beuve said.

In Sand's day women prided themselves on having enormous rear ends; bustles were high style, petticoats were multitudinous. Internationally famous as the greatest female novelist, Sand was envied even more in the cafés along the Left Bank for her extraordinary rear end.

Tout Paris chuckled for years over the report that when she quarreled with her son-in-law, Clésinger, the sculptor and painter, she screamed, "I'll publish an account of your behaviour." And he screamed back, "Then I'll do a carving of your backside, and everybody'll recognize it!"[1]

Caricatures flaunting her bum, and they were numerous, never really upset her. It was after she died that her bottom became a problem. The funeral had to be delayed for hours because at the last moment the undertaker discovered that the lead coffin sent to Paris from Nohant was too small to accommodate her prodigious rear. A larger coffin arrived scarcely an hour before the scheduled service.

FAME AT BOTTOM

Outwardly a conformist to British sexual hyprocrisy, Sir Arthur Wing Pinero, the darling of the Dress Circle ladies, could drop a bombshell on occasion. In his lively melodrama *The Second Mrs. Tanqueray*, the leading character is a prostitute, and there is the memorable line about another character: "I believe she kept a thermometer in her stays and always registered ten degrees below zero."

Like other London gentlemen at the turn of the century, Pinero escaped to Paris when he was surfeited with respectability. On the

Left Bank was fresher air and an infinite variety of sex. He once induced playwright Alfred Sutro to join him for a round of the Paris hot spots. At one of the naughty revues, they were sure they would not be recognized. An English dancer onstage, however, recognized Pinero in the front row. Approaching the footlights and stopping the show, she called out, "Hullo, there's Sir Arthur Pinero! I must salute him."

Whereupon, in his honor, she turned three somersaults, revealing a considerable part of her bare bottom.

Sir Arthur could not restrain his delight.

"This," said Sutro, turning to Pinero, "this is fame!"[2]

REAR VIEW

The expatriates went wild in Montmartre and Montparnasse in Paris during the twenties. Morley Callaghan tells about one midnight frolic in which he, McAlmon, and the French model Kiki, communal lover of Hemingway, Apollinaire, and a dozen others, all restless and hungry for thrills, decided to raise hell at a midnight party at the Whidneys', close but more serious friends.

"Down the street we went, laughing and giggling, and on the stairs to the Whidneys' apartment house we began to make a lot of noise. Going up the stairs ahead of me was Kiki, and being the lovely clown she was, she began to go up the stairs on all fours. Whereupon I reached down, and threw her skirt up over her head. Undisturbed, she continued to go on up on all fours while I played a drumbeat with both hands on her plump behind."[3]

The Whidneys in dressing gowns—Mrs. Whidney's hair still up in curlers—invited them in for drinks and a night of noisy revels.

TAPS

In old age, Goethe, in bed before his shut-eye, or awakening in the middle of the night, used to hammer out some of his lyrics on the back of Christiane, his child-wife, before publishing them. She inspired him, he said, to poetic activity. After living with her for nineteen years, he married her.

Robert J. Clements paraphrased in *Merchants of Light* the quatrain that Goethe once composed on Christiane's behind while in Rome:

If sleep overcomes her, I lie
back in her arms
While my fingers the measure of
hexameter
Have mounted on her back

TOUCH AND RUN

One winter afternoon, window-shopping along Fifth Avenue, Frank Sullivan spied Kathleen Norris looking intently into one of the store windows. Alexander Woollcott reports that Sullivan thought "it might be fun to steal up behind her and pinch her playfully. If ever in his life he was to acquire the memory of thus roguishly accosting a famous writer of wholesome fiction, here was his chance. He knew her slightly, admired her profoundly, and it was all, mind you, in the spirit of clean fun. . . ."

He had hardly touched her fanny, says Woollcott, when she turned to him and, in a ringing voice that could be heard above all the hubbub of the avenue, cried out:

" 'Not a penny. Not one penny more. No,' she continued, with a rush that bore down any feeble attempt at interruption which occurred to his startled mind, 'you and your family have had all the money you'll ever get out of me. The back of my hand to you, Frank Sullivan.'

"Frank fled through the jostling crowd and hailed the first taxi that he could stop, all the while Norris kept hurling at him a deluge of histrionic abuse: 'It's useless for you to call me stingy. Only last week I gave you a hundred dollars to buy medicine for your poor sick wife. Did she get a penny of it? Not she! No, you spent it on the drink, my lad. You guzzled it, Frank Sullivan, and they found you in the gutter.' "[4]

THE COFFEE WAS WONDERFUL

When Vachel Lindsay, the troubador hobo, came to Urbana, Illinois, to give a recital-lecture, the Stuart P. Shermans invited him to be their weekend guest. They accorded him regal hospitality. He slept in the best upstairs room, propped up in bed, swilling half-pints of hard liquor or punch. Mrs. Sherman sent his meals up. He made endless long distance calls.

After a sumptuous five-course dinner, Lindsay rose, as the report has it, "reached around and patted her gently on the backside. Mrs. Sherman reeled with a horrified gasp. Then Lindsay said, 'The coffee was wonderful!' "

Before he left, he stuffed a dozen of Sherman's silk stockings into his knapsack.[5]

Reach Out and Touch Someone

At a bar in New Orleans, says Rex Reed, a "waiter with a rather large behind passes the [Tennessee Williams's] table. Tennessee reaches out and pinches it. The waiter hurls around, his fists doubled. 'What the . . . oh, it's you, Mr. Williams. . . . What are you doing in town?'

"Tennessee looks innocent-guilty like a choirboy who has just been caught sneaking a bullfrog into the collection plate. 'We all heah fo' Holy Week,' he says, exploding with laughter. The waiter leaves, laughing too, and rubbing his derrière."[6]

George Moore Had an Eye for Bottoms

For George, the female bustled backside was an irresistible invitation for the soft touch, a delicate pat. He would have been flattered to be characterized, however vulgar the term might sound, as an *arse-man*. He was an incurable pincher, given to pawing ladies' bottoms with his tapering long fingers.

Once a pretty lady came to see him, presumably to ask his help in getting a part in a play. She took a reclining position on his sofa, whispering languorously, "Shall I? Shall I?" Nancy Cunard noted in her diary: "Apparently they did! I could hardly believe this. George Moore was *gross* at moments, but most lovable."

One person who knew Moore well said that the novelist's descriptions of his amatory ventures were imaginary and that the self-advertised philanderer was "a man with whom any pretty girl might walk safely through the deserts of Sahara."[7]

There was one occasion when an affair threatened to become serious and the lady overplayed her advances. Moore lost his cool and, as he reported, "lifted my foot and I kicked her while we were walking in the park. . . . I kicked her in the behind—in the bustle if you prefer."[8] Nancy Cunard has suggested that the offender was Pearl Craigie, who wrote under the name of John Oliver Hobbes.

Though Moore dared satirize contemporary sexual reticence in his early novels, in private he would drivel on hearing a bawdy joke and give his characteristic hysterical *khk! khk! khk!* in enjoying it.

"At times salacious," Nancy Cunard recalled, "he saw no harm in coming out with a gross word or two when applicable: 'Why object to old English—surely 'belly,' a word in Shakespeare and the Bible, cannot be asked to make way for 'tummy?' "[9]

On his first visit to the Holy Land to do research for a novel, when his fellow passenger travel agent Thomas Cook volunteered to show him the Holy Sepulchre, Moore threw up his hands and pleaded "Oh, for goodness sake, nothing so hackneyed, Cook! . . . Bring me where the woman was taken in adultery."

With Nancy and her mother, Lady Emerald, he was an uninhibited rogue. Nancy recalls his jubilation when they went hunting through dozens of antique shops for an old-fashioned French porcelain bidet, made about 1850, that he had longed for years to install in his home: "A bidet on a wooden case with a lid on it . . . the inside prettily painted with flowers. At the bottom there *must* be painted a human eye gazing upward."

Some of his anecdotes, to be sure told in private, had a punch line touching his favorite obsession:

" 'She was losing her husband's affections, you see. So she went to Paris and took lessons from some of the ladies in the Chabanel. A French cocotte has a good deal to teach you may be sure! When she returned she began to put these lessons into practice in bed with her husband. Oh, it must have been a dreadful moment when she heard him say: *"Dora, ladies never move!* khk! khk! khk!" ' "[10]

Dublin gossips never ceased conjecturing that he was Lady Emerald Cunard's lover and the father of inflammatory Nancy. He neither confirmed nor denied it. There must have been some good reason for his being Lady Emerald's most constant visitor at the Cunard estate, Nevil Holt. The Bache Cunards had long been separated. Moore admitted he had loved Nancy's mother for over forty years. Why didn't he marry her? "If we were married," he answered, guffawing, "we should be very happy—for six months."

He "must be my father," Nancy wrote in her diary. "But what of my long limbs? Shall we ever know? It seemed to me that if it were true I should become a different personality and a more contented one." She herself often wondered how she ever came to be sired by the likes of the dull Sir Bache Cunard. When Moore was asked about her paternity, as he often was, he evaded it delicately, saying, "Oh my Lord! Oh my Lord! Never ask your mother that . . . I wish I could think so, Nancy. . . . But I fear not. I fear not."[11]

He never faulted Nancy for her promiscuity and notorious sex orgies, and when everybody condemned her for marrying the still-married General Marsh's black chauffeur Henry Crowder, Moore was unreservedly her defender. The novelist was Nancy's father figure.

Moore, who knew all about Nancy's lesbian proclivities, often teased her about them. " 'Oh well, lesbians,' " she quoted him as remarking, " 'one says "dearest" and the other replies "darling" and then they gaze into each other's eyes, and then they tick-el each other a little. But what can they do? khk, khk, khk.' "[12]

Nancy later described an episode of a visit to him in Paris. G.M., as she called him familiarly, was then an old man and he would twaddle on nostalgically for hours about his past affairs. His blue eyes would light up mischievously, then he would abruptly change the subject and ask, in his velvety voice, "Tell me about *your* lovers." Nancy smiled, pressed his hand lingering on his lap, and say, "George Moore, you have the soul of fire."

After one fine dinner at Foyote's, his favorite Parisian restaurant, out of the clear blue he taunted her, "I wish you would let me see you na-aked . . . I am an old man. I am sure you have a lovely body, now won't you let me see it? Oh, at least let me see your naked back." Unshocked, she writes, "I told him there was a long scar on one side of me, he would hate the sight of that."

In her biography, Anne Chisholm cites Nancy's uninhibited response:

"Now equally suddenly, something within me said 'Do this!' and without more ado, facing away from him, I took off all my clothes, standing motionless a few feet from where he sat. How lightly, how easily it came about. My clothes left me, lying in a graceful summer pool on the floor, as if they had slipped away of themselves. The night was warm and the mood serene. Without hesitation, my long, naked back and legs were at last in front of him and the silence was complete. It would be full-on he was looking at them and I did not turn my back. Of what could he be thinking? At length came a slow, murmuring sigh. 'Oh, what a beautiful back you have, Nancy, it is as long as a weasel's. What a beautiful back!' " [13]

Ilka Chase tells how Horace Liveright, the publisher and a notorious rake, took her to call on George Moore in Ebury Street:

"We [Horace Liveright and Ilka] went to Ebury Street one evening after dinner, and there were just the three of us. I felt that history was in the making, but the occasion somehow lacked stature. Moore was a spindly-legged, potbellied, bejowled little man, and he unexpectedly pinched my behind. I felt rather honored that my behind should have drawn the attention of the great master of English prose, but it was embarrassing too, as I didn't know whether to respond or whether it wouldn't be kinder to let the whole thing drop. I listened respectfully, however, while he and Horace discussed literature, and at last ventured to ask him what he thought of Conrad. There was a slight pause. 'I don't know, my child,' he said testily, 'I can't read Polish.' " [14]

THE UNDOING OF GEORGE MOORE

W. B. Yeats kept prodding Dr. Oliver St. John Gogarty on the subject. "I've just been reading George Moore's *Memoirs of My Dead Life*," he said to Gogarty. "And a question keeps rising in my mind which you can answer. Do you think George Moore was impotent?"

"I don't know," replied Gogarty. "It is rare for a man to be impotent. He may be unable to propagate, but organic impotence must be rare."

For years George Moore kept bragging in conversation and in several memoirs about his extraordinary seductions, his ardent lovemaking, and a whole string of women who were pressing their attentions on him.

Moore took much kidding over his professed amours. Susan Mitchell, A. E. Russell's secretary, who knew Moore better than was comfortable for him, is alleged to have said (some attribute the quote to Sarah Pusser, says Mary Cardozo in *The Life of Maud Gonne*) that he was fearful, and in fact incapable, of going through the ultimate act: "Gentlemen kiss but never tell. Cads kiss and tell. George Moore doesn't kiss but he tells." But no one had proof one way or another. Susan refused to go further than the quote. [15]

Moore somehow always managed to step out of set traps. Until Oliver St. John Gogarty spilled the beans. The trap came ready-made. Gogarty, Dublin's legendary wit and prankster, prototype for Buck Mulligan in Joyce's *Ulysses*, was physician-surgeon to many Irish writers, including Moore. Living directly across the street from Moore, he had an exceptional opportunity to witness all who came and went through Moore's vivid green door. One of Gogarty's rooms looked out on Moore's garden.

One afternoon Moore came running across the street, Gogarty recalls. Moore often came cadging for free medical aid. He was obviously disturbed. He pointed to a rash of red spots on his face and asked for a diagnosis. Were the vesicles on his forehead eczema or irritation? Gogarty saw his chance at last to show his blabber-mouth patient up.

"What are those loathsome things?" Moore asked.

"Why, it's hard to tell," he told him. "It might be serious and it might not be serious. A few days will tell. Such things take time to develop." He told him to stay indoors out of the sun.

Three days later Moore came running into Gogarty's office again. The red spots had multiplied and deepened in hue. Gogarty examined him intently, then shook his head and said, "You were with a woman, Moore. The evidence is clear. Venereal disease. Quite a serious thing, Moore."

Horrified, Moore asked, "How can we be sure?"

"Oh, a doctor can tell easily."

"But how is it possible? I haven't had a woman these last ten years."

Moore himself said it. Susan Mitchell was confirmed.[16]

15

REMEMBERING MAMA

Children begin by loving their parents; as they grow older they judge them; sometimes they forgive them.

—Oscar Wilde

A man who has been the indispensable favorite of his mother keeps for life the feeling of a conqueror.

—Sigmund Freud

Look Who's Coming to Chelsea!

The prospect did not appear so pleasant to Whistler.

At long last, his career as an artist was beginning to look up when he received a letter from Mama informing him that she had run the Union blockade after the catastrophe at Gettysburg and was en route to London. The news threw "your own darling son, Jamie" into a panic. What to do about Jo, his current mistress, who was living with him? Even more alarming: his mother was coming with intentions to live with him in his Chelsea flat. Permanently!

Mrs. Anna Matilda Whistler was an uncompromising puritan with "cadence from the Bible singing in her ears." She was now fifty-six and frail. He was not going to abandon her in that condition. She had a very close relationship with her firstborn. A devoted son, he never forgot her birthday, corresponding with her, giving her mostly good news to cheer her up, but he had kept her in discreet ignorance of his free life abroad. When she blamed his current lagging career on his having violated the Sabbath she made him vow, and he kept this promise, never to paint on the Holy Day. Even parted across three thousand miles he was still in subconscious fear of her disapproval. There was no question where his prime loyalty stood.

How could he ever manage to prevent a confrontation between Jo and his mother? Like Ruskin's evangelical mom, Anna made it a point to live with her boy whenever it was possible. Whistler's family, then living in London, made matters for him even worse. His brother-in-law, Seymour Haden, now a surgeon and an aspiring painter, refused to provide Jo with lodging, even temporarily. Ironically, though he

317

was a lecher himself, he put his foot down against Jimmy's bringing Jo as a guest in his home. And, as DuMaurier notes, he wouldn't let his wife, Whistler's half-sister, even go "to see her mother in a house which had once been polluted by Jo's presence."

After Whistler had been sweating it out for a week, a flat fell vacant a few doors down the street, and with difficulty, he managed to appease Jo by setting her up there, though hardly in the fashion she was enjoying in her lover's rooms.

Mama never knew, or if she did, pretended she didn't, though few things could escape her suspicious eye. One thing Whistler insisted upon, however: his mother could not enter the studio part of his house.

Biographer Stanley Weintraub reports: "Once she made the mistake of going to the studio uninvited and discovered the model standing to Whistler in the nude. It was a shock, although she might have consoled herself with the fact that the maid was standing; and afterwards she visited only on invitation, usually to take trays of lunch and tea when a prospective purchaser or a model was present, or when her son worked alone. . . . Although Whistler regretted the inconvenience to Jo, after ten years' absence he found that he truly loved his mother in his own fashion and settled comfortably into the new domestic arrangements, while expecting Jo to remain to him what she had always been."[1]

Whistler was at bottom a sentimentalist. In his eyes, Anna Matilda was saintly. And if he had to shuffle a mistress out of his home so as not to upset his mother, that was the way it had to be. Actually, he had idealized the mild and charming old southern lady in his famous portrait. In truth, she was a tough, no-nonsense, dominating parent—"bittersweet," Ted Berkman called her. Whenever Anna Matilda laid down the law to Jamie, which was often, he invariably gave deferential compliance. He could never bring himself to argue with Mama.

Whistler visited her regularly, during her last days at Hastings, cracked jokes to ease her pain, patted her hand fondly, and told her how well his paintings were selling. When she died, he expressed deep regret that he had not arrived in time for the funeral. One afternoon later he broke down: "It would have been better had I been a parson as she wanted!" But he solaced himself with reflecting that at least she had come to Chelsea in time to be proud of his success—"succès d'exécration," as he called it.

MAMA'S BOY

Jack Kerouac was not really the hard-boiled tough his public thought him to be. He had greater regard for what his mother thought of his work than he did of his fellow Beats. In deference to her, he cut the coarser obscenities and toned some of the sex exploits he had put into his published writing lest they offend her.

For all his wild careening across the American continent to San Francisco and Mexico City, Jack never really left his Lowell, Massachusetts, home.

Kerouac once picked up a picture of his mother as a young mill girl, gazed at it with visible tenderness, and vowed: "That's the picture of the girl I want to marry someday."

He never did. Repeatedly, in periods of crisis he fled to the old homestead. He left his first two wives to stay with mémère, as he invariably referred to her. Even when he married Stella, he insisted on living in Lowell in a *ménage à trois*.

Mémère constantly reminded her boy, whom she called Jean, that it was her job in the shoe factory that had put him into classy Horace Mann prep school in Riverdale and into Columbia College. It was she who slaved to give him time to write. Never forget, Jean. She never let him forget where his prime duty lay. The fight had gone out of that once pudgy-faced athletic muscled boy. He offered no protest to her watchdog injunctions. Mémère knew best. He promised her no more getting stoned on Benzedrine; no alcohol; and above all, none of the foul smelling evil-spreading cronies, Burroughs, Cassady, Greeley, Kesey, and Ginsberg, who came to visit him there to lure him back to the San Francisco jazz joints.

Ginsberg's *Howl* was inspired by Kerouac. Kerouac's mother barred the door especially to Allen, as Kerouac explains: "He wasn't allowed to come and see me by my mother. I can't say I blame her, though. He scared the hell out of her, with his beard and bald head."

Ann Charters describes the last agony in mother and son devotion: "He paid a friend to drive him, mémère and Stella [Kerouac's wife] from Lowell to St. Petersburg, where he hoped the sun and warmth would help mémère's convalescence. . . . Death was on his mind, his mother paralyzed in a back room, whispering his name to come sit beside her so she could ask him why God had punished her mercilessly. Stella moved low and steady. . . . In important matters he tried to be responsible, worrying about the money coming in, settling his will and with his lawyers, putting the deed to his home in his mother's name so he'd know he'd kept his promise to his father to take care of mémère even after his death."[2]

Kerouac had finally realized his wish of dying in his mother's arms.

MOTHER CONFESSOR

Every day, while Alfred de Musset, the great French romantic poet, was honeymooning with George Sand in Venice, he sent maman a detailed report on how he was making out. There were constant squabbles, acrimonious threats to go home, public shouting matches— all were set down for his mother to read.

The day following their honeymoon night, Sand complained to her friend Boucoiran about her Byronic lover: "Oh, my God, my God, what a spectacle! He came near to strangling me while kissing me. The two men [doctors] could not get him to let go of the collar of my dress."[3]

The irony of all this was that his mistress was paying for the heavy postage, as she had paid for all the expenses of the trip.

MAMA BLEW THE WHISTLE

Tennessee Williams recalls Mama's scream ringing in his ears when he was a child. Who can tell how much of his deviant sexual urge is attributable to what he experienced?

"Mother could not bear the idea of anything sexual," he told a reporter. "Every time she had sexual intercourse with my father she would scream. Rose [Tennessee's sister] and I would hear her and we would run out of the house, screaming, off to a neighbor's. My mother had three children, so I imagine she was raped rather frequently."[4]

After publishing his *Memoirs*—he desperately needed the $50,000 it brought him—Tennessee Williams told Madeleine Blais of the *Miami Herald*:

"It shocks me when women are coarse. Women should preserve grace and femininity. These are the things that attract me to women. Of course, a woman has to let down during moments of desire in private; she can't always be the reserved lady. I proposed marriage twice in my life, once to a childhood sweetheart and once to a nym-

phomaniac. I am so glad I didn't get married. I would have no freedom, saddled with a family. Now I have nothing to tie me down except
my sister Rose." [5]

How about coarseness in men? Even in our frank four-letter age,
Williams's *Memoirs* establish something of a record. For Williams *fuck*
has always said it best. At a rehearsal once, he shouted at a group of
female stagehands, "What the fuck are you crepehangers barging in
for? Take your drinks and get on, we've got a play in trouble and
we've got to discuss it strictly among ourselves."

In his *Memoirs*, he also tells of trying to break out of a hospital
despite doctor's orders.

"I started down the corridor of the hospital. On the way down the
corridor, I encountered the nurse. 'Mr. Williams,' she said, 'what are
you thinking of?'

" 'Nothing,' I said, 'but getting the fuck out of here.'

" 'But, Mr. Williams, a hospital isn't a hotel that you can check
out of before we dismiss you.'

" 'Fuck that, I'm dismissing myself and I only want you to get me
a cab at the door.' " [6]

16

POTPOURRI

Love is the whole history of a woman's life, it is but an episode in man's.

—de Staël

One exists with one's husband—one lives with one's lover.

—Balzac

SHAW, A TRANSVESTITE?

Bernard Shaw's maid came in haste into the kitchen and fairly gasped to the housekeeper, who was also Mrs. Shaw's nurse, "What do you think? Mr. Shaw is in the passage upstairs trying on one of your frocks!"

Mrs. Laden could hardly believe it. She scrambled upstairs and, sure enough, found the old man wearing one of her dresses and posing in front of the full-length mirror. She had to admit he looked a stunner.

"What do you think you are doing?" she howled.

"This Chinese robe Sir Robert Ho Tung gave me is most attractive," he said calmly. "I thought I'd try it on."

"That's my dress," she retorted. "Sir Robert gave you a blue robe—this one is black."

"I knew he was fond of nice clothes," she later told R. J. Minney. "But why my frock? I couldn't believe it."

She tried to put a good face on the discovery, chalking it up to his vanity, but changed to reserving judgment. As she explained to Minney: "I knew he was a little colour blind. He couldn't distinguish blue from green as a rule, though he did get the colour of his wife's eyes right: they certainly were green. But black and blue!

"The confusion arose because my clothes cupboard stood in the passage between his section of the house and ours and he had an overflow cupboard there for the clothes he no longer wore. I brought out the Chinese robe for him and he was later photographed in it."[1]

Shaw gave the postcard-size print to Sybil Thorndike, who used it as a book marker in, of all books, her Bible.

Virginia Woolf in Person

Virginia Stephen (later Woolf) was prudish to such an extent that when she went out shopping at Harrod's, she slipped furtively past the department featuring women's undergarments, too frightened to be seen even taking a fleeting look.

Home was something different. Her father, Sir Leslie Stephen, was one of the directors of the London Library and consistently voted banning women from its shelves. At home, however, he had a library liberally stocked with some of the smuttiest Restoration novels and plays, and he gave his own daughters full run of the library.

Gawky, adolescent Virginia was forever losing her underpants in public and on social visits. One such contretemps occurred while she was walking in Kensington Gardens, when, neither for the first time nor the last, she felt her drawers slipping. Finding that no amount of juggling would keep them up, she retired behind a bush and burst out singing "The Last Rose of Summer" while she pinned up her knickers.[2]

Quentin Bell tells of an occasion when she was at a party: ". . . her drawers fell down while she was in the very act of saying goodbye to her hostess: she gathered everything up in a bundle and shuffled away as best she could; but on returning to Hyde Park Gate [her home] and finding [her brother] George at home she came into the drawing-room and flourished the errant garments in his face. George was speechless with indignation."[3]

All her married life Virginia openly envied her elder sister Vanessa's fertility. She desperately wanted to have children but remained barren. Once she was certain she was pregnant. Whether this was so no one knows for sure, but Virginia believed it. Apparently her cousin and lesbian companion thought so and gave her a cradle as a delayed wedding present. "My baby will sleep in it," she said, thrilled. She knitted toddler clothes and pressed them to her bosom.[4] The cradle remained conspicuous in a corner of her bedroom for years.

A Clear-cut Option

The historian Luigi Barzini records that Julius Caesar's "gallantries were notorious. In his youth he was sleeping with the wives of some of the most important gentlemen in Rome and the famous beauties of his time. Rumor whispered that he often slept with their husbands as well. As with many ambitious men beds were stepping stones in his career."[5]

Lytton Strachey relished this tidbit of history.

At a literary party the guests were exchanging banter and off-color jokes when someone popped the question, "Which historical figure would each of you have liked to go to bed with?"

One man said Cleopatra. Another chose the contemporary beauty Kitty Fish. When Lytton Strachey's turn came, everyone was sure he would pick his current historical obsession, the widow Queen Victoria. But Strachey stroked his beard, his eyes lit up, and he piped, "Julius Caesar!"[6]

THE RED LIGHT TURNS GREEN

When a writer's will prohibits unsealing his diaries until twenty years after his death, we can be sure he must have a secret he wants to hide. Invariably, the injunction is futile.

Pieces of one secret came out with the publication of Thomas Mann's suspiciously vague diary entries, recently published. In his early forties, Mann recorded, he suffered "sexual failure" with his wife Katia. He had married her at twenty-nine and lived with her in an otherwise affectionate bond for fifty years before he died in 1955. He fathered six children.[7]

Mann had acted out his homosexuality in his masterpiece *The Magic Mountain*. Obviously, from several diary notes we now know that he had turned by then to a relationship with a young male painter. Where were the probing psychoanalysts? So surely did he conceal his homoeroticism that it is still not certain whether he had consummated his sexual desires.

Any year now some literary sleuth will expose the shredded facts.

FOUR-LETTER SHOCK

Painter Robert Haydon's all-male dinner parties sometimes took a shocking turn. Charles Lamb, hilariously drunk, made the evening he was present immortal by bursting out with one of his nonsensical improvisations of a traditional nursery rhyme. At another dinner John Keats, bored stiff by the pedantic interchanges, decided to shake the party up by steering it into a discussion of the word *cunt*. Keats relished the new turn immensely. So did most guests. But prudish Haydon was obviously uncomfortable and set the word down as C––t in his journal.[8]

PRIVATE FILE

Norman Mailer penned his own obituary notice for *Boston Magazine:*
"Norman Mailer passed away yesterday after celebrating his 15th divorce and 16th wedding. When asked on one occasion why he married so often, the Pulitzer Prize winner replied, 'To get divorced. You don't know anything about a woman until you meet her in court.' "[9]

WORDS, WORDS, WORDS

Dylan Thomas had the reputation of being a notorious womanizer. Not necessarily, said Anthony Burgess, who knew Dylan intimately. The fact is that later on, the poet was almost impotent. In a *Playboy* interview, Burgess said: "My first wife, who was Welsh, slept with him frequently—was by way of being his mistress. I discovered—and she told me all he really wanted was to get into bed with a woman and be comforted by her, to feel her warmth and hold her tight. His sexual activities normally took place in the bathroom; he was a great masturbater. I was amazed when I first came to America and I met a woman, a drunken faculty wife at a party, who said, 'Can you *screw* as good as Dylan?' Obviously, she had no experience of Dylan's screwing."[10]

• • •

Dylan Thomas's wife observed that the only adjective her husband unfailingly used in his conversation was *fuckin'*.

Donald Hall tells in *Remembering Poets* that Archibald MacLeish asked Dylan Thomas after he had given a reading at Harvard, "We all know what you've done in the first thirty-five years of your life. What will you do in the next thirty-five years of your life?" And Thomas replied, not entirely sober: "I will write poems, fuck women, and annoy my friends."[11]

ALL IN LOVE WITH MISIA

In a rapturous *Time* review of the Arthur Gold-Robert Fizdale biography of Misia Sert, Margaret Duffy could not restrain her jubilation:

"What a life Misia Sert lived! Faure gave her piano lessons. Ravel presented her with a score of *Le Sacre du Printemps* . . . Cocteau modeled the heroine of his novel *Thomas L'Imposteur* on her . . . Proust also used her as one of the inspirations for Mme. Verdurin . . . For 40-odd years she was the godmother of European artists. If she was a climber, the mountain was Parnassus."

How can anyone recall the opalescent ambience of literary life in nineteenth-century France and omit a profile of Misia Sert? The *Epoque* would hardly be *Belle* without her. The twentieth century had its Peggy Guggenheim; the nineteenth glitters through Misia, the Renoir princess, Russian-born Pole, born Godeska, married and divorced three times.

"It was the thing to be in love with Misia," say Arthur Gold and Robert Fizdale. "She had tremendous allure in the French meaning of the word—a sense of how to carry herself with style . . . she listened attentively and responded with enthusiasm, candor, and an independence of judgment startling in one so young. Her speech was salted with irony and peppered with four-letter words, which on her lips escaped vulgarity. She was a rough-and-ready princess."[12]

A salty little thin woman in a sailor hat who made the literary carousel spin round in Paris for years, Misia is too precious to be forgotten after thirty years.

Such a woman comes only once in a century.

WHAT PRICE FORNICATION?

Graham Greene says in his autobiographical *Ways of Escape* that he once saw his vitriolic friend Evelyn Waugh in characteristic action. They were having dinner in Carol Reed's home with guests Alexander Korda and his fiancée when for no apparent reason Waugh suddenly delivered a shocking tonguelashing on Korda. The director kept his cool. Greene, who was fond of Korda, was visibly embarrassed.

Riding in a taxi with Waugh the next day, Greene asked, "What on earth induced you to behave like that?"

"Korda," responded Waugh, "had no business to bring his mistress to Carol and Pempe's house."

"But I was there with my mistress," said Greene.

"That's quite different; she's married."

Greene, an orthodox Catholic, wondered: "Fornication more serious than adultery?"

The two drove on in silence.[13]

IBSEN NO WOMEN'S LIBBER

When Ibsen's most famous play, A Doll's House, was produced to international acclaim he was hailed as a pioneer proponent of greater
freedom for women. The Social Democrats in England, Shaw among
them, claimed him as a socialist, and his name became synonymous
with radical feminism.

Ibsen countered that his view on the subject had been distorted.
Contrary to popular supposition, he insisted, he was only advocating
that the Noras of the world, victims of male chauvinists, should leave
even their children and wedded mates to enter the battlefield to fight
for equality in marriage. He never intended that all women should
act like Nora.

To a request for permission to use his name as honorary member
of the Society for Extended Female Education, Ibsen wrote back a
snappy refusal and repeated that A Doll's House was not one about
women's rights but about the rights of human beings generally.[14]

When he proposed that the Scandinavian Club in Rome admit
women to their meeting, they rejected it out of hand. Ibsen de-
nounced them.[15]

Michael Meyer, Ibsen's definitive biographer, expressed Ibsen's view
thus: "A Doll's House is no more about women's rights than Shakespeare's Richard II is about the divine rights of kings. . . . Its theme
is the need of every individual to find out the kind of person he or
she really is and to strive to become that person."[16]

We still do not know what Henrik Ibsen's last words were—an ex-
plosive "No!" or a defiant "Tvertined" (On the contrary). However,
his daughter-in-law, Berghot, declares that Ibsen's wife told her that
his last words were, "Suzannah, my sweet, sweet wife, how kind and
good you've been to me!"

Ibsen's relations with his wife have been the subject of much spec-
ulation and theorizing. He did not treat his plump, adoring hausfrau
with even half the consideration Helmer accorded Nora in A Doll's
House.

It has been said that after the birth of their only child, Sigurd, the

Ibsens never slept together again. In later years, when rumors reached Suzannah from abroad that Ibsen planned to put her aside for one of his young women disciples, she wrote him asking whether it was true. His fondness for little girls she could tolerate. But mistresses? Ibsen replied that she had nothing to worry about; he did not have divorce in mind.

Suzannah must have known that her aging husband couldn't have gone beyond some lustful petting. He was impotent.[17]

HOLY EROTICA

Replying to readers who wondered about the eroticism in his books, Nobelist I. B. Singer explained to a *New York Times* reviewer: "Eroticism is a very interesting part of life, and eroticism and religion are not contradictions. There's a lot of eroticism in the Bible, although it's wrong if one writes it just to excite the reader."

"Besides," Singer went on, "I'm not much of an eroticist in comparison with the way they write today. I never write four-letter words. But since I'm a Yiddish Writer, readers used to complain that they were afraid their daughters might get spoiled from what I write. Now they don't worry so much because people know that sooner or later their daughters will know all about it."

A critic asked him why he wrote so much about Jewish thieves and Jewish prostitutes. He answered, "Shall I write about Spanish thieves and Spanish prostitutes? I write about the thieves and prostitutes I know."[18]

BUT FOR A NOSE

Dozens of free-thinking, free-loving loungers around publisher John Chapman's parlor tried to choose a wife for the philosopher Herbert Spencer. He vetoed several and called the most promising candidate too "morbidly intellectual. Though she was sufficiently good-looking, young, extremely open, a poetess and heiress, I do not think that the spirit will move me."

At first Mary Ann Evans (later George Eliot) looked promising. It has been said that Chapman tried to seduce her and she resisted his plea to elope with him.

Gossips have had a field day. One story went that Spencer was joshed about his love affair with Miss Evans when he admitted he had once been in love with her but had never had the courage to propose.

Henry James passed on a different piece of gossip. H. Montgomery-Hyde, in *Henry James at Home*, writes that William Rossetti, the brother of D. G. and an art critic and editor, told him that he saw Spencer propose to Eliot on the leads of Somerset House Terrace: "I have as a matter of fact," James said, "frequently meditated on the motives which induced the lady's refusal of one so distinguished; and after mature consideration, although Mr. Spencer with correctness went down upon one knee and grasped the lady's hand, he completely omitted the ceremony of removing his high hat, a proceeding which her sense of the occasion may have demanded."[19]

But it was not the high hat that posed the obstacle, but Eliot's long nose, which Spencer found made kissing impossible.

Eliot wrote her friends, the Brays: "We have agreed that we are not in love with each other and there is no reason why we should not have as much of each other's society as we like. He is a good, delightful creature and I always feel better for being with him."[20]

Sour grapes? Perhaps. Spencer himself explained: "After all it does not much matter, if as somebody said (Socrates was it not?)—marrying is a thing which you do it or not you will repent, it is pretty clear that you may as well decide by a toss up. It's a choice of two evils, and the two sides are pretty nearly balanced."

Spencer ended up a celibate workaholic.

Of the numerous stories told about Eliot's ugliness one is so delicious that it has endured. It appears that a German professor and Eliot buff had heard that the great novelist was still a spinster. He had not yet been told about Eliot's indomitable paramour G. H. Lewes. When he saw one of her rare photographs—she justifiably hated to be photographed—he was ecstatic. He wrote her a proposal saying he wanted a wife who could translate German, but she had to be ugly. Regarding the offer as a *jeu d'esprit*, she wrote back an acceptance and enclosed her most ill-favored snapshot. In reply he regretted he had to retract his offer saying no, she was not ugly enough.

Henry James wrote a letter to his father about his meeting with George Eliot: "To begin with she is magnificently ugly—deliciously hideous. She has a low forehead, a dull grey eye, a vast pendulous nose, a huge mouth, full of uneven teeth, and a chin and jaw-bone *qui n'en finissent pas*. . . . Now in this vast ugliness resides a most powerful beauty which, in a very few minutes steals forth and charms the mind, so that you end as I ended, in falling in love with her. Yes, behold me literally in love with this great horse-faced blue-stocking."[21]

HOMAGE TO VIRGINITY

Barbara Cartland has reached her eighties and is still gung-ho for premarital virginity.

In her extraordinary career she has poured out more than three hundred novels (like *Kiss the Moonlight, Love Under Fire*, etc.), all paeans to contented virgins, which have sold millions of copies. Her campaign is not over; it seems as if every fortnight a new Cartland romance hits the bookstands.

"About twenty years ago," she has said, "publishers told me I should modernize. They wanted more sleeping about. I refused." And who came out right? she asks proudly. "We had a survey in America a while ago. It was found that when the bride was a virgin, the marriage lasted longer. I think young people are coming around to that way of thinking again."

Asked recently what she thought of women's lib, she responded, "I'm the opposite. I want to feel loved, and protected. . . . Women are having a miserable time now."[22]

During a TV interview at the time of the Prince Charles-Lady Diana wedding, she strongly defended her favorite thesis of premarital virginity. "*Everybody* wants to believe that Cinderella's going to marry the prince. Of course they do. They *all* want it. It's ridiculous to say not."

She sat back in an elegant chair before the cameras like one of her own heroines and beamed. "I didn't have any idea how babies were born until I was 19, and yet, see, I came out unscathed with a perfect marriage. That tells you something, doesn't it?" She had six marriage proposals. "You don't need vulgar words if a man makes love."[23]

WITH THIS RING . . .

Lord Byron was waiting impatiently at Newstead for Annabella Milbanke's letter of response to his final marriage proposal. She had already turned him down several times. The match was critical: only her dowry could save him from bankruptcy.

At the moment that Byron was handed the Milbanke letter, the gardener came in with milord's mother's heavy gold wedding ring, lost for years, that he had just dug up.

Characteristically, Byron saw an omen in the coincidence. Tearing the letter open, he exclaimed, "If it contains a consent, I will be married with this ring."

Miss Milbanke accepted, but he lived to regret it. Later Byron told his friend Thomas Medwin: "I thought the ring was sent on purpose for the wedding; but my mother's marriage had not been a fortunate one, and this ring was doomed to be the seal of an unhappier union still."[24]

* * *

Honoré Balzac wore a ring on every finger, each a gift from a favorite mistress.

* * *

At their wedding, his third and her fourth, Eugene O'Neill and Carlotta Monterey exchanged gold wedding bands with engraved quotations inside from his play *Lazarus Laughed:* "I am your laughter," his ring was inscribed; hers, "and You are mine!"

* * *

Tired of battling social disapproval of their living in sin together, D. H. Lawrence induced Frieda Weekley, not without a quarrel, after her divorce became absolute, to taxi down with him to the registry office behind Harrod's and legalize their relationship. Their neighbors Katherine Mansfield and her lover John Middleton Murry came along as witnesses. On the way, Lawrence dashed into a goldsmith's and bought a wedding ring.

Although Frieda thought the ritual was farcical, she went along anyway. Lawrence believed in the solemnity of the ceremony, although he later reported that he had gone through it "with his heart in his boots and neuralgia in his left eye."[25]

Frieda gave her own account: "It was quite a simple and not undignified ceremony. I didn't care whether I was married or not, it didn't seem to make any difference, but I think Lawrence was glad that we were respectable married people."[26]

When Lawrence kissed his bride, Katherine was deeply moved, and blushed. On an impulse, Frieda took the old Weekley wedding band off her finger and handed it to her. Katherine proudly wore the ring, says Murry, "nor would she change it when we married. She was buried with it on her finger at Fontainebleau."[27]

• • •

At twenty-two, while madly in love with another, Alan Paton (*Cry the Beloved Country*) married a widow six years his senior. On their wedding night he was shocked to see her still wearing her late husband's wedding ring. No, she would not take the ring off, and taunted him with the explanation that she could never love him as she had loved her first husband. After all, *he* was still smitten with his literary friend. Only when she was sure Paton had given up his earlier love did she remove the offending ring.[28]

FOREHEAD PREFERRED

Whenever Robert Browning returned to London with his wife, and on every visit there after her death, he commemorated the anniversary of his marriage by kissing the paving stones in front of Marylebone Church, where their union had been solemnized.

After observing an extremely long period of mourning for his wife, Browning turned full circle. He took up permanent residence in London and became a socialite: he was sought by Park Lane widows for their dinner parties and musicales. He did not have to be coaxed to recite his favorite poems. Columnists speculated about Elizabeth Barrett Browning's successor.

"Most of the ladies who came to the house were taller than the master," said his valet, "and whenever I let a taller lady in, and Mr. Browning greeted her, she would bend down a little, and he kissed her on the forehead, always on the forehead."

The valet told William Connolly that one day he had heard the poet's sister Sarianna, who kept house for him, suggest that Browning should marry: "Miss Browning said—she could not pronounce her *l*'s and *r*'s—'Wobbit, why don't you mawwy one of those nice young wadies you take out in the evening?'

"The master looked up, and rested his eye on a painting of his wife on the wall opposite his chair. He spoke one word: 'Never!' It was only then that I knew why he always kissed the ladies just on the forehead."[29]

HEROINE WORSHIP

Every time that Thomas Carlyle passed the spot at Hyde Park Corner where his wife, Jane, suffered her fatal heart attack when trying to rescue her dog from the wheels of a passing vehicle, he paused, removed his hat, and stood for a minute in silence.

SALVAGING SANDBURG

Carl Sandburg's marriage to Lillian Steichen was one of the most idyllic in American literary life. Before their marriage, Carl and his socialist Phi Beta Kappa love slept in a double bed during the two nights before the wedding in a hotel room, to save money.

"They called the room their 'home,' " Sandburg's daughter Helga writes, "and while they were in love, my mother said they didn't have intercourse. When I asked her why, she said they wanted to wait until their wedding. . . . They lay in each other's arms and it seemed enough she said."[30]

Carl Thompson, a minister and colleague at the Social-Democratic Party headquarters, married them. Sandburg did not tell his parents anything of the wedding plans. Lillian never wore a wedding ring, as she later told her daughter. "I gave up wearing rings about 10 years ago because they seemed to me to be relics of barbarism on a level with earrings and nose-rings!" Lillian got the license. The certificate listed her as "teacher" and Charles A. Sandburg as "party organizer." There was no honeymoon since Carl had to run off to report to party headquarters in Milwaukee.

"Never to my knowledge," says Helga, "did my father bring my mother flowers, candy, diamonds, or rings. From the beginning he placed his earnings in her care, and if in later life he kept a separate bank account, she spoke of it to me with some interest, but not to him. 'He ought to have what he wants,' she said.

Their whole life together was "a great and glorious romance." "Do you see that woman down there tying my laces?" he told Herbert Mitgang in Lillian's presence, "If it wasn't for her, I'd still be a bum today."[31]

FOR KING AND COUNTRY

During the War of the Roses, the Black Prince ransomed adolescent warrior Geoffrey Chaucer for the then princely sum of sixteen pounds, just slightly less than the price of a good horse. Thereafter, the court poet was indebted to King Edward III's household for life.

Apparently, fealty included obedience to the king in matters relating to love affairs at court.

Recently John Gardner has produced evidence that the author of *The Canterbury Tales* was "a ludicrously unsuccessful lover, a man pious by default—that is, a man devoted to God because the ladies won't have him."

Gardner conjectures that when Chaucer was called upon to marry a lady of the court who had been made pregnant by King Edward's son John of Gaunt, the poet complied because one good turn deserves another. Gardner's evidence also shows that Gaunt sired Chaucer's second son several years later.[32]

GEORGE MOORE'S PRICE TAG

Instead of marrying, George Moore restricted his amorous activities to pinching bottoms, kissing cheeks, and squeezing hands. And he wrote letters, hundreds of letters, to women. He said, "We woo at intervals, but in art we are always wooers." Moore, whom the French would have called "an exquisite," confessed: "My thoughts run upon women. And why not? On what would you have them run? On copper mines?"

But one marriage almost came about because his thoughts did run on copper mines. He proposed to Miss Mary de Ross, who (he told his mother breathlessly) had a guaranteed income of £2000 a year. "I will marry for 700,000 francs, and not a penny less," he said.

Moore's Irish cousins, who knew the heiress but knew their kinsman better, said that he proposed and was refused. Moore insisted that he backed off when he learned Miss Mary's income was only £800.

"I do not think that this is enough," he told his uncle; "there are plenty with more."[33]

Apparently Moore never found them; he remained a bachelor.

THE BEST MAN WORE GREEN

When poet Countee Cullen married Yolande DuBois, daughter of venerable black writer Dr. W.E.B. DuBois, in the Harlem church where his father was pastor, it was heralded as the social and literary event of the season. The bridesmaids came in a special car all the way from Baltimore, where Miss DuBois had been teaching. The wedding was held at dusk. Multitudes were turned away, even though it was one of the largest churches in Harlem.

The best man was Countee Cullen's closest friend, poet Langston Hughes. Hughes himself never married. At one time he had a mistress in the USSR and had many affairs here, but he never took a bride. In his autobiography, *The Big Sea,* Hughes tells what happened at Countee Cullen's wedding:

"We held a rehearsal of the wedding on Good Friday and it was my job to escort the bride's mother to her seat. Unfortunately, I didn't own a pair of tails, so I had to rent a set. In the rental shop the suit looked black, but once outside, it looked rusty green. It was one of those cheap, dull blacks that had been faded with time, and the trousers were stove-pipe. I felt very self-conscious in a green, rented pawnshop dress suit, so I said to myself: 'I will never go into society again if I have to rent my clothes.' "[34]

17

CAUSERIE

> Good sense about trivialities is better than nonsense about things that matter.
>
> —Max Beerbohm

> Even listing trivia can be important.
>
> —Nikolai Gogol

> Il n'y a d'originalité et de vérité que dans les détails.
> (There is no originality or truth except in details.)
>
> —Stendahl

When the prominent painter John Everett Millais wed Effie after the court had annulled her marriage to John Ruskin, the *Leader*, a popular London newspaper, inadvertently slipped the news item in among its death notices.[1]

• • •

James Joyce, whose novels, particularly *Ulysses*, shocked the literary world by its prolific use of "dirty" words, was in private life a notorious prude. He would never utter an obscenity in public or tell an off-color joke in the presence of women, and if he heard a joke in mixed company he'd walk away in a huff. He railed against Henry James for daring to write "love novels." How, he asked, could James talk about love, never having lived with a woman?

• • •

When Henry Miller was interviewed in 1970 for his obituary, he complained: "The majority of readers of *Tropic of Cancer* have never read another book of mine, and they only looked for those pages where is the sex they wanted. That disgusts me!"

• • •

When David Frost asked Tennessee Williams point-blank in a TV interview whether he was homosexual—this before Tennessee disclosed his answer in *Memoirs*—he replied, grinning as usual, "I cover the waterfront."[2]

• • •

George Bernard Shaw refused to file a joint income tax return, arguing that it was humiliating to a wife with her own income to be treated as an appendage of her husband.[3]

• • •

Charles Osborne tells how W. H. Auden rejected out of hand André Gide's claim in *Si le grain ne meurt* that he had spent a whole night having sex with an Arab youth and followed it up at sunrise with sex on the dunes. "He's a conceited liar," Auden said. "How could he have an orgasm after a night of fucking. I'll bet he can't even produce an erection!"[4]

• • •

Auden, who had written a considerable number of erotic poems, privately enjoyed pornography, which he defined as "any material that gives a male an erection." He joined the ranks of celebrities, Shaw among them, who were revolted by D. H. Lawrence's *Lady Chatterley's Lover*. E. M. Forster, on the other hand, joined the defenders of the novel and even went so far as testifying in court in Lawrence's behalf.

• • •

Dylan Thomas once observed that but for one misplaced letter, T. S. Eliot's name spelled *toilets* backward.

• • •

T. S. Eliot was an outspoken prude. He found the very sound of the word *whorehouse*, or any of its euphemisms, offensive. He never shaved in the presence of either of his two wives, and though hard to prove, rumor has it he never saw them in the nude.

• • •

John Evelyn, the learned seventeenth-century diarist and a noted cleric, secretly bought up many bawdy pamphlets and books for his private library.

• • •

Samuel Pepys, diarist par excellence, kept the pornographic poems of the wicked earl of Rochester in a secret drawer. Neither his servants nor his wife were allowed entry into his library, still regarded as one of the most extensive in Great Britain.

• • •

J. M. Barrie, who built a reputation on sentiment about children, had none of his own and thought that children were "heartless creatures."

• • •

Bertrand Russell, past master of satyriasis, showed embarrassment when an American gynecologist showed him a frontispiece picture of a uterus in his textbook, yet Bertie thought nothing of sleeping with the man's daughter the second night they met, while her sisters stood guard outside the door to warn them of their parent's approach.

*   *   *

Eugene O'Neill made no bones about sleeping with John Reed's wife while both men were buddies, yet when he saw his own wife, Agnes Boulton, sit cozily near another man, he slapped her across the face until blood ran.

*   *   *

D'Annunzio kept a couch at home exclusively for sexual intercourse. Harold Acton reports that on his visit to the playwright's home he saw above a couch the Salimbeni motto *Per non dormire* (not for sleeping).[5]

Rumor had it that D'Annunzio slept on a pillow he had stuffed with the locks of a hundred mistresses. Before he went to sleep, he put on lace underwear. (He had forty-eight pairs of undies). Then he took out his case of assorted perfumes and doused himself with a special brand of toilet water that he himself had blended, which he called Aqua Nunzio, supposedly derived from a recipe used by nuns.[6]

*   *   *

It has been said that when Brendan Behan happened to come across the phrase "Dublin, city of gentle dastards" in John Mitchell's *Jail Journal,* he asked his father whether the author had not meant "bastards."

"No, son," replied his father. "You see, you're born a bastard, you can't help that. But you've got to work at being a dastard."

Brendan's father was once asked why he hadn't produced a book himself: he was witty and could tell a story better than most Irish authors. "Produce books?" he replied. "Why should I? I produced Behan."[7]

*   *   *

Gertrude Stein, says Virgil Thomson, addressed her live-in companion as Pussy: Alice privately called Gert Lovie.

Charlotte Shaw addressed her husband as Gee Bee. Ironically, he called her Mother, a considerate idealization of her pathetic refusal to have children. As an old man, after she died, he bewailed the fact that they had no children.

* * *

John Updike has another distinction besides being one of America's greatest novelists, a nonliterary record: he obtained the first no-fault divorce in Massachusetts history.

* * *

Rainer Maria Rilke, the Austrian lyric poet, was so intent on courting his muse that he begrudged the two hours he allotted to love-making on his honeymoon and spent the rest of the "blissful" period versifying. The obsession to write was so overpowering in the following years that he refused to take a job to support his wife and baby. He could not spare the time even to go to his daughter's wedding.

* * *

When William Godwin, author of the intellectually revolutionary *Political Justice*, learned that his daughter Mary had eloped with Percy Bysshe Shelley, who was still married and the father of two small children, he sent the poet a blistering letter.

"Why the fuss?" Shelley wrote back. "You yourself have preached the doctrine of free love and I was converted."

"Fool!" Godwin replied. "That was meant as an abstract theory. It doesn't apply to my family!"

* * *

When Jessie Conrad informed her husband that she was having labor pains, he rushed up to his own room, visibly annoyed, locked the door, and stayed there for hours fuming over the inconvenience to his writing schedule. Jessie couldn't get him to stir out of his study. "I really don't care who suffers," he shouted through the locked door; "I have enough of my own trouble." He remained barricaded for days.

In point of fact he was going through his own labor pains: he was writing *The Recruit*.

Mrs. Conrad understood her Joseph well and later defended his action at the time their first son, Borys, was born:

"One had to remember that a genius is not a common mortal to live with, and such license must be allowed. His meal must be served to the moment. Five minutes grace either was seldom allowed, even to a distinguished guest. And incongruous as it may appear, if for instance lunch was delayed, tea must be ready precisely at the right time, even if that meal should follow so closely on the heels of the one preceding it as to leave guests no time to leave the table."[8]

• • •

When Len Deighton and his wife Shirley decided to go to the law to split up finally after living apart for five years, she petitioned the London Divorce Court for a "quickie" *in absentia* unhitching in order to spare the horror of having to face him in court. She feared that seeing him in person would lead her to change her mind.

The court yielded. The proceedings in chambers took just ten seconds.[9]

• • •

Long after they had been written, the Browning love letters covering little over a year sold recently for $35,000, a sum considerably more than Elizabeth Browning had ever received for any of her poems and vastly more than her husband had ever had from his.

• • •

At Hamilton College, one of Alexander Woollcott's classmates jeered: "I wonder whether he has to sit down to pee." None of the frats wanted to pledge him. So he founded his own fraternity. In all of the plays put on by the college's first dramatic club, The Charlatans—which Aleck founded—he played the feminine leads. In an *esprit de jeu* his calling card read: "Alexandra Woollcott."

Even Aleck didn't know to what category he belonged until he dug into Kraft-Ebbing's *Psychopathia Sexualis.* Eventually, he came to terms with himself. Acquaintances gossiped. One Hamiltonian said: "Aleck Woollcott was a fag but nobody ever caught him at it." One of his biographers, Samuel Hopkins Adams, said that Aleck was a closet homosexual. Another, Edwin P. Hoyt, suggested that a bout with mumps put him *hors de combat* sexually. His latest biographer, Howard Teichmann, concludes that Woollcott was "not a practicing homosexual—even though he did have urges in that direction."[10]

Dr. Shepard Aronson, an endocrinologist, said that Woollcott was born with a chromosome abnormality that gave him a hormonal imbalance at puberty. It left him with thwarted "clusters of desire." In Dr. David Abrahamsen's opinion: "He is an outstanding example of what to do with an abnormal inclination. I hardly know anyone who has succeeded in sublimating his thwarted sexual feeling in such a way as Woollcott did. He had to fight daily to overcome it and in order to sustain the loss of never feeling completely potent."

Dr. Mortimer Shapiro, psychiatrist, is quoted by Teichmann as explaining Aleck's inadequate testicular system:

"Woollcott had the fat, stuffy, amuscular appearance which one usually associates with testosterone deficiency. Testosterone is a hormone secreted by a part of the testicle that provides the secondary male characteristics such as beard and distribution of fat. The absence of it tends to give a softness to the skin and a plumpness around the hip area generally associated with female appearance."[11]

SOURCES

CHAPTER 1

1. Mina Curtiss, *Other People's Letters* (Boston: Houghton Mifflin, 1978).
2. *Time*, 12 June 1978.
3. Joanna Richardson, *Victor Hugo* (New York: St. Martin's, 1976), p. 270.
4. Georges Victor Hugo, *Mon Grand-Père* (Paris: Calmann-Levy, 1902), p. 58.
5. Robert Baldick, ed. and trans., *Pages from the Goncourt Journal* (New York: Oxford University Press, 1962), p. 307. Reprinted by permission of Oxford University Press.
6. Henri Guillemin, *Victor Hugo par lui-même* (Paris: Editions du Seuil, Collection, 1951), p. 58.
7. Robert Baldick, *op. cit.*, p. 307. Reprinted by permission of Oxford University Press.
8. Jean-Jacques Brousson, *Anatole France Himself*, trans. John Pollock (Philadelphia: Lippincott, 1925), pp. 109–10.
9. Obituary, *The New York Times*, 15 May 1977.
10. Alan Levy, *The New York Times Magazine*, 31 Oct. 1971, p. 30.
11. Cass Canfield, *Up & Down & Around* (New York: Harper & Row, 1971), p. 144.
12. Irving Mansfield, *Jackie* (New York: Bantam, 1983), p. 83.
13. Charles Osborne, *W. H. Auden* (New York: Harcourt Brace Jovanovich, 1979), p. 242.
14. Max Herzberg, *Insults* (New York: Dell, 1941), p. 204.
15. Leonard Lyons, "The Lyons Den," *New York Post*, 12 Apr. 1966.
16. *Newsweek*, 29 Nov. 1976, pp. 76–77.
17. Hesketh Pearson, *Horizon*, Nov. 1958, quoted by Janet Dunbar in *Mrs. G.B.S. A Portrait* (New York: Harper & Row, 1963), pp. 199–200. Reprinted by permission of *The Society of Authors*, London.
18. Janet Dunbar, *Mrs. G.B.S. A Portrait* (New York: Harper & Row, 1963), pp. 200–201. Reprinted by permission of the Executor and Trustees of Charlotte Shaw's estate, the Bank of Ireland, Trustee Department, Dublin, Ireland.
19. Janet Dunbar says her opinion is based on the draft of Mrs. Shaw's letter now in the Hanley Collection, University of Texas.
20. *Playboy*, Sept. 1975. Reprinted by permission of *Playboy* magazine.
21. Quoted by Gordon S. Haight in *George Eliot* (New York: Oxford University Press, 1968), pp. 452; 535–36.
22. *Ibid.* pp. 550–51.

23. Hilary Mills, *Mailer* (New York: Empire Books/Harper & Row, 1982).
24. Patricia Bosworth, "Fifth Estate at the Four Seasons," *Saturday Review,* Mar. 1973.

CHAPTER 2

1. Scott Donaldson, *By Force of Will* (New York: Viking, 1977), p. 177.
2. *Ibid.* pp. 176–77.
3. *Ibid.* p. 177.
4. Ariel & Will Durant, *Interpretation of Life* (New York: Simon and Schuster, 1970), p. 46.
5. Robert Baldick, ed. and trans., *Pages from the Goncourt Journal* (New York: Oxford University Press, 1962), pp. 215–16. Reprinted by permission of the publisher.
6. Peggy Guggenheim, *Out of This Century* (New York: Dial, 1946), p. 208. Reprinted by permission of Universe Books Inc.
7. *Paris Review,* Summer 1971, p. 190. Reprinted by permission of Viking Penguin, Inc.
8. Anthony Burgess, *Playboy,* Sept. 1974, p. 74. Reprinted by permission of *Playboy* magazine.
9. *Ibid.* p. 78.
10. *International Herald Tribune,* quoted in *Encounter,* June 1978, p. 97.
11. Fenton Bresler, *The Mystery of Georges Simenon* (London: Heinemann, 1983).
12. *The Times Literary Supplement* (London), 1 April 1983.
13. *Playboy,* Sept. 1975. Reprinted by permission of *Playboy* magazine.
14. André Gide, *Journal,* Vol. I, 1918, ed. and trans. Justin O'Brien (New York: Viking, 1947), p. 293.
15. *Miami Herald,* 27 Jan. 1977.
16. *Ibid.*
17. *Ibid.*
18. Jack Lindsay, *William Blake* (New York: Braziller, 1979), p. 256.
19. *Ibid.,* quoting A. Gilchrist, *Life of William Blake* (1863), edited by Todd, 1942, p. 72.
20. *Ibid.* p. 72.
21. Robert Baldick, *op. cit.,* p. 95. Reprinted by permission of the publisher.
22. Henri Troyat, *Tolstoy* (Garden City, N.Y.: Doubleday, 1967), pp. 570–71. Copyright © 1967 by Doubleday & Company, Inc. Reprinted by permission of the publisher.
23. John Stewart Collis, *Marriage and Genius* (London: Cassell, 1963), p. 228.
24. *Ibid.* p. 224.

25. Cyril Pearl, *The Girl with the Swansdown Seat* (Indianapolis: Bobbs-Merrill, 1955), p. 204.
26. Susan Chitty, *The Beast and the Monk* (New York: Mason-Charter, 1974), p. 82.
27. Edmund Wilson, *The Twenties* (New York: Farrar, Straus & Giroux, 1975), p. 215. Copyright © 1975 by Elena Wilson, Executrix of the Estate of Edmund Wilson. Reprinted by permission of Farrar, Straus & Giroux, Inc., publisher.
27. W. C. Rogers, *Irish Literary Portraits* (B.B.C. Broadcast, April 1952), pp. 81–82.
28. Norman and Jeanne Mackenzie, *The Time Traveller* (London: Weidenfeld & Nicolson, 1973), pp. 251–52.

CHAPTER 3

1. Jim Bishop, *A Bishop's Confession* (Boston: Little, Brown, 1981), p. 3. Reprinted by permission of Little, Brown and Company, Inc.
2. *Ibid.* p. 17.
3. *Ibid.* p. 24.
4. S. N. Behrman, *The Suspended Drawing Room* (New York: Stein and Day, 1939), p. 203.
5. *Book Digest,* Aug. 1980, p. 23.
6. Karl Fleming and Anne Taylor Fleming, *The First Time* (New York: Berkley Medallion/Simon and Schuster, 1975), p. 61. Copyright © 1975 by Karl Fleming and Anne Taylor Fleming. Reprinted by permission of Simon and Schuster, Inc.
7. Avrahm Yarmolinsky, *Turgenev* (New York: Crowell-Collier, 1961), p. 36. Copyright © 1959 by Avrahm Yarmolinsky. Reprinted by permission of Macmillan Publishing Company, Inc.
8. There have been at least three translations of Goncourt's account of Turgenev's first sexual experience: Yarmolinsky's, Robert Baldick's, and Pritchett's, each markedly different from the others. The most authoritative translation, in the author's view, is Yarmolinsky's. V. S. Pritchett, *Turgenev: The Gentle Barbarian* (New York: Random House, 1977), p. 17.
9. Michael Meyer, *Ibsen* (Garden City, N.Y.: Doubleday, 1967), p. 689.
10. Bertrand Russell, *The Autobiography of Bertrand Russell* (Boston: Little, Brown, 1967), pp. 183–84. Reprinted by permission of Little, Brown and Co. Inc. and copyright © 1967 George Allen & Unwin, Publishers Ltd.
11. *Ibid.* p. 114.
12. WPBT, Channel 2, Florida, 6 May 1978.

13. *M.D.*, October 1979, p. 94; Giacomo Casanova, *History of My Life*, trans. Willard R. Trask (New York: Harcourt Brace World).
14. *Ibid.* p. 94.
15. *M.D.*, October 1979, p. 98.
16. *Ibid.* p. 98.
17. Klaus Völker, *Brecht*, trans. John Nowell (New York: Seabury Press, 1978), p. 16.
18. *Ibid.* p. 35.
19. *Ibid.*
20. Tennessee Williams, *Memoirs* (Garden City, N.Y.: Doubleday, 1975), p. 43. Copyright © 1972, 1975 by Tennessee Williams. Reprinted by permission of Doubleday & Company, Inc.
21. *Ibid.* p. 43.
22. *Ibid.* p. 43.
23. *The New York Times*, 21 Feb. 1976.
24. Cole Lesley, *Remembered Laughter* (New York: Knopf, 1976), p. 19.
25. R. J. Minney, *Recollections of George Bernard Shaw* (Englewood Cliffs, N.J.: Prentice-Hall, 1969), p. 16. Copyright © 1969 by R. J. Minney. Reprinted by permission of Prentice-Hall, Inc.
26. *Ibid.* pp. 17–18.
27. *Ibid.* p. 19.
28. G. B. Shaw, "To Frank Harris on Sex in Biography," *Sixteen Self-Sketches*, (New York: Dodd, Mead and Company, 1949), p. 178. Reprinted by permission of the Public Trustees and The Society of Authors and the Bank of Ireland, Trustee of Charlotte Shaw's Estate, Dublin, Ireland.
29. G. B. Shaw, *op. cit.* pp. 175–78.
30. St. John Ervine, *Bernard Shaw* (New York: William Morrow and Company, 1956). Reprinted by permission of the publisher.
31. James Atlas, *The New York Times*, 16 June 1980, quoting Keith Sagar, *The Life of D. H. Lawrence* (New York: Pantheon, 1980).
32. G. H. Ford, *The New York Times Book Review*, 9 Mar. 1969, reviewing *Letters to Louie Burrows*, ed. James T. Boulton (Southern Illinois University Press, 1969).
33. Henri Troyat, *Tolstoy* (Garden City, N.Y.: Doubleday, 1967), p. 69. Copyright © 1967 by Doubleday & Company, Inc. Reprinted by permission of the publisher.
34. *Ibid.* pp. 62–63.
35. *Ibid.* p. 63.
36. *Ibid.* p. 63.
37. A. Alvarez, reviewing *First Love* in *The Observer* (London), 15 Nov. 1973.
38. Deirdre Bair, *Samuel Beckett* (New York: Harcourt Brace Jovanovich, 1978), pp. 83–84. Copyright © 1978 by Deirdre Bair, Copyright © 1978

by Harcourt Brace Jovanovich. Reprinted by permission of Harcourt Brace Jovanovich, Inc.

39. *Ibid.* p. 100.

40. Richard Ellmann, *James Joyce* (New York: Oxford University Press, 1959), p. 662.

41. Deirdre Bair, *op. cit.* p. 84.

42. *Ibid.* p. 101.

43. Samuel Beckett, *Krapp's Last Tape* (New York: Grove Press, 1960), copyright © 1958 by Grove Press, Inc. Reprinted by permission of Grove Press, Inc. and Faber & Faber, Ltd.

44. Rupert Hart-Davis, ed., *The Letters of Oscar Wilde* (New York: Harcourt Brace & World, 1962), p. 76.

45. Frank Harris, *Oscar Wilde: His Life and Confessions* (New York: Frank Harris, 1916), Vol. I, pp. 1–21.

46. H. Montgomery Hyde, *The Three Trials of Oscar Wilde* (New York: University Books, 1948), p. 369.

47. H. Montgomery Hyde, *The Love That Dared Not Speak Its Name* (Boston: Little, Brown, 1970), p. 142.

48. William Rothenstein, *Men and Memories* (London: Tudor, 1872), Vol. I, p. 187.

49. Quoted by Cecil Roberts, "Oscar Wilde," *Books and Bookmen*, April 1973, p. 55.

50. Philippe Jullian, *Oscar Wilde* (New York: Viking, 1968), p. 363.

51. H. Montgomery Hyde, *Oscar Wilde* (New York: Farrar Straus & Giroux, 1975), p. 144.

52. Philippe Jullian, *op. cit.* p. 277.

53. H. Montgomery Hyde, *The Three Trials*, p. 144.

54. Bernard Shaw, "Memories of Oscar Wilde," in Frank Harris, *Oscar Wilde: His Life and Confessions*, Vol. II, p. 15.

55. Cecil Beaton, *Self-Portrait with Friends*, ed. Richard Buckle (New York: Times Books, 1979), p. 168.

56. *Ibid.*

57. Hesketh Pearson, *Oscar Wilde* (New York: Grosset and Dunlap, 1946), p. 316.

58. Horace Traubel, *With Walt Whitman in Camden* (New York: Small, Maynard, 1906).

59. Justin Kaplan, *Walt Whitman* (New York: Simon and Schuster, 1980), pp. 141–42. Copyright © 1980 by Justin Kaplan. Reprinted by permission of The Sterling Lord Agency, Inc.

60. *Ibid.* p. 47. Walt Whitman, *Leaves of Grass*, eds. Horace V. Blodgett and Sculley Bradley, in *The Collected Writings of Walt Whitman*, Comprehensive Readers Edition (New York: New York University Press, 1965), pp. 109–10.

61. Justin Kaplan, *op. cit.* pp. 311–12.
62. *Ibid.* p. 314.
63. Paul Lauter, in *Psychological Studies of Famous Americans: The Civil War Era,* ed. Norman Kiell (New York: Twayne, 1964), pp. 287–89.
64. Justin Kaplan, *op. cit.* p. 43.
65. *Ibid.* p. 43.
66. Chard Powers Smith, *Annals of the Poets* (New York: Charles Scribner's Sons, 1935), p. 454.
67. W. R. Brett, *The Infirmities of Genius* (London: Christopher Johnson, 1952), pp. 54–55.

Chapter 4

1. W. A. Swanberg, *Dreiser* (New York: Charles Scribner's Sons, 1965), p. 133. Reprinted by permission of W. A. Swanberg.
2. *Ibid.* p. 375.
3. Bennett Cerf, *At Random* (New York: Random House, 1977), p. 38.
4. W. A. Swanberg, *op. cit.* p. 20.
5. *Ibid.* pp. 134–35.
6. *Ibid.* pp. 279–80; *The New York Times,* 23 Dec. 1923.
7. *Ibid.* pp. 484–85.
8. *Ibid.* pp. 56–57.
9. *Ibid.* p. 520.
10. *Ibid.* p. 505.
11. *Ibid.* p. 375.
12. *Ibid.* p. 526.
13. *Newsweek,* 1 Nov. 1982.
14. *The Paris Review,* 1958, Vol. II, pp. 112–13. Copyright © 1963 by *The Paris Review.* Reprinted by permission of Viking Penguin, Inc.
15. Joseph Hone, *The Life of George Moore* (Gollancz, 1936), p. 144.
16. Erasmus, *Defence of the Colloquies* (1526), quoted in *The Times Literary Supplement* (London), 3 June 1965.
17. Ulick O'Connor, *Oliver St. John Gogarty* (New York: Ivan Obolensky, 1964). Copyright © 1963 Ulick O'Connor. Reprinted by permission of Davin-Adair, Inc.
18. Anaïs Nin, *The Diary of Anaïs Nin,* ed. Gunther Stuhlmann (New York: Harcourt Brace Jovanovich, 1966), Vol. I, pp. 58–60. Reprinted by permission of the publisher.
19. Stanley Weintraub, *Shaw: An Autobiography: 1898–1950* (New York: Weybright and Talley, 1971).
20. Malcolm Cowley, *A Second Flowering* (New York: Viking Penguin, 1973), p. 92. Copyright © 1956, 1967, 1968, 1970, 1972, 1973 by Malcolm Cowley. Reprinted by permission of Viking Penguin Inc.

21. *Time*, 6 Feb. 1956.
22. Somerset Maugham, "Looking Back," *Show*, June 1962, p. 66. Reprinted by permission of A. P. Watt, Ltd. and the Executors of the Estate of W. Somerset Maugham.
23. Ted Morgan, *Maugham* (New York: Simon & Schuster, 1980), p. 278. Reprinted by permission of Ted Morgan.
24. *Ibid.* pp. 338–40.
25. *Ibid.* p. 297.
26. *Ibid.* p. 525.
27. Evelyn Waugh, *Diary*, ed. Michael Davie (Boston: Little, Brown, 1976), p. 240. Copyright © The Diary of Evelyn Waugh 1976.
28. *Ibid.* pp. 339–40.
29. Emir Rodriguez Monegal, *Jorge Luis Borges* (New York: E. P. Dutton, 1978). Quoted by John Leonard, *New York Times*, 12 Dec. 1978.
30. *The New York Times*, 8 Aug. 1971, p. 34.
31. Noel Coward, interview with David Frost, WPBT 2, Florida, 16 Dec. 1969.
32. Bennett Cerf, *At Random* (New York: Random House, 1977), p. 87.
33. Tennessee Williams, *Memoirs* (Garden City, N.Y.: Doubleday and Company, 1972), pp. 97–98. Copyright © 1972, 1975 by Tennessee Williams. Reprinted by permission of Doubleday and Company, Inc.
34. Robert Baldick, ed. and trans., *Pages from the Goncourt Journal* (New York: Oxford University Press, 1962), p. 106.
35. Robert Baldick, *Dinner at Magny's* (New York: Coward, McCann & Geoghegan, 1971), pp. 104–5.
36. *Ibid.* p. 105.
37. H. G. Wells, *Experiment in Autobiography* (New York: Macmillan, 1934), p. 246.
38. *Ibid.* p. 145.
39. Max Brod, *Franz Kafka* (New York: Schocken, 1963), p. 151. Copyright 1937 by Heinr. Mercy Sohn, Prague. Copyright 1947, 1960 by Schocken Books, Inc. Reprinted by permission of Schocken Books, Inc.
40. Franz Kafka, *The Diaries of Franz Kafka 1914–1923*, ed. Max Brod (New York: Schocken Books, 1965), p. 159. Copyright 1949 by Schocken Books. Reprinted by permission of Schocken Books, Inc.
41. *Ibid.* pp. 278–79.
42. Céleste Albaret, *Monsieur Proust*, ed. Charles Belmont and trans. Barbara Bray (New York: McGraw-Hill, 1977), pp. 196–97.
43. William Sanson, *Proust and His World* (New York: Charles Scribner's Sons, 1974).
44. Patrick O'Higgins, *Madame: An Intimate Biography of Helena Rubinstein* (New York: Viking, 1971), pp. 92–93. Reprinted by permission of Viking Penguin, Inc.

45. Enid Starkie, *Baudelaire* (New York: New Directions, 1958), pp. 88–89. Copyright © 1958 by New Directions.

46. Alex de Jonge, *Baudelaire: Prince of Clouds* (New York: Paddington Press, 1976), p. 110. Copyright © 1976 by Paddington Press, Ltd.

47. *Ibid.* p. 110.

48. H. C. Andersen, *Diaries*, Vol. III, ed. Tue Gad and Kirsten Weber (Copenhagen: G E C Gad, 1850); review in *The Times Literary Supplement* (London), 17 Sept. 1971.

49. H. C. Andersen, *Diaries*, Vol. XI.

CHAPTER 5

1. Louis Kronenberger, *No Whippings, No Golden Watches* (Boston: Little, Brown and Company, 1965), pp 116–17.

2. Larry Adler, *Sunday Times* (London), 23 Dec. 1973. Howard Teichmann in *George S. Kaufman* (Angus and Robertson, 1973) says that Astor's "twenty—count them, diary" is probably "referring to the number of clubs she and Kaufman visited one night."

3. Larry Adler, *op. cit.*

4. *Time*, 21 Feb. 1969.

5. Richard Freedman, *Book World*, 28 Feb. 1971.

6. Margaret Morris, *My Galsworthy Story* (London: Peter Owen, 1967), p. 54. Reprinted by permission of Peter Owen, Ltd.

7. *Ibid.* p. 69.

8. Catherine Dupré, *John Galsworthy* (New York: Coward McCann & Geoghegan, 1976), p. 213.

9. Frank Swinnerton, *Background with Chorus* (London: Hutchinson, 1956), p. 190.

10. John Updike, *The New Yorker*, 21 Mar. 1977, reviewing *The Letters of Wallace Stevens*, ed. Holly Stevens (New York: Knopf, 1966).

11. Emund Wilson, *The Twenties*, ed. Leon Edel (New York: Farrar, Straus & Giroux, 1975), pp. 255–56. Copyright by Elena Wilson, Executrix of the Estate of Edmund Wilson. Reprinted by permission of Farrar, Straus & Giroux, Inc.

12. *Ibid.* pp. 315–16.

13. *Ibid.* pp. 407–8; 410; 411–13; 417; 432; 445–46.

14. Edmund Wilson, *The Forties: from Notebooks and Diaries of the Period* ed. Leon Edel (New York: Farrar, Straus & Giroux, 1983). Reprinted by permission of the publisher.

CHAPTER 6

1. Walter Allen, *As I Walked Down New Grub Street* (London: Heinemann, 1981), pp. 55–56.

2. Humphrey Carpenter, *W. H. Auden* (Boston: Houghton Mifflin, 1981), pp. 175–76. Many fantastic legends have sprung up about the Auden-Mann wedding, but according to Charles H. Miller, in *Auden, An American Friendship* (New York: Charles Scribner's Sons, 1983), pp. 52–53, the only true version is the one Isherwood gave in *Christopher and His Kind.*

3. Walter Allen, *op. cit.* pp. 57–58.

4. *Ibid.* p. 58.

5. James Harding, *Sacha Guitry* (New York: Charles Scribner's Sons, 1968), p. 206. Copyright © 1968 James Harding. Reprinted by permission of Charles Scribner's Sons, Inc.

6. *Ibid.* pp. 66–70.

7. *Ibid.* p. 119.

8. *Ibid.* p. 161.

9. *Ibid.* p. 172.

10. *Ibid.* p. 176.

11. *Ibid.* p. 170.

12. *Ibid.* p. 200.

13. *Ibid.* p. 227.

14. Cecily Mackworth, *Guillaume Apollinaire* (London, John Murray, 1961), p. 37.

15. Margaret Davies, *Apollinaire* (New York: St. Martin's, 1964), p. 85.

16. W. B. Yeats, *Memoirs*, ed. Denis Donaghue (New York: Macmillan, 1973), pp. 132–33.

17. Richard Ellmann, "At the Yeats' " *New York Review*, 17 May 1979. Reprinted by permission of A. Whitney Ellsworth, Publisher, *New York Review.*

18. *Ibid.* p. 22.

19. B. L. Reid, *The Man from New York* (New York: Oxford University Press, 1968), p. 308.

20. Richard Ellmann, *The Man and the Masks* (New York: E. P. Dutton, 1948), p. 208 fn.

21. Richard Ellmann, "At the Yeats.' "

22. W. B. Yeats, *The Collected Poems of W. B. Yeats* (New York: Macmillan, 1956), p. 177. Copyright 1924 by Macmillan Publishing Co., Inc.; renewed copyright 1952 by Bertha Georgie Yeats.

23. Richard Ellmann, "At the Yeats.' "

24. *Ibid.*

25. Lillian Hellman, *An Unfinished Woman* (Boston: Little, Brown and Company, 1969), p. 217. Reprinted by permission of Little, Brown and Company, Inc.

26. Alden Whitman, obituary, *The New York Times*, 8 June 1967.

27. John Keats, *You Might As Well Live* (New York: Simon and Schuster,

1970), p. 58. Copyright © 1970 by John Keats. Reprinted by permission of The Sterling Lord Agency, Inc.

28. Dorothy Parker, "Enough Rope," *The Portable Dorothy Parker* (New York: Boni & Liveright, 1926), p. 51. Copyright 1946 Viking/Penguin. Reprinted by permission of Viking Penguin, Inc.

29. *Ibid.* p. 157.

30. Lillian Hellman, *op. cit.* p. 214.

31. John Keats, *op. cit.* p. 214.

32. Wyatt Cooper, *Esquire,* July 1968, p. 112.

33. *Ibid.* p. 112.

34. *Ibid.*

35. John Keats, *op. cit.* p. 250.

36. *Ibid.* p. 251.

37. *Ibid.*

38. Lillian Hellman, *op. cit.* p. 228.

39. Maisie Ward, *Gilbert Keith Chesterton* (New York: Sheed and Ward, 1943), p. 110. Copyright by Sheed and Ward, Inc. Reprinted by permission of Andrews and McMeel, Inc.

40. G. K. Chesterton, *The Autobiography of G. K. Chesterton* (New York: Sheed and Ward, 1936), pp. 154–55. Copyright by Frances Chesterton. Reprinted by permission of Andrews and McMeel, Inc.

41. Maisie Ward, *op. cit.* p. 92.

42. *Ibid.* pp. 94–96.

43. Chesterton, *op. cit.* p. 30.

44. *Ibid.* pp. 29–30.

45. Dudley Barker, *G. K. Chesterton* (London: Constable, 1973), p. 110.

46. *Ibid.* pp. 111–12.

47. *Ibid.* pp. 112–13.

48. Maisie Ward, *op. cit.* pp. 651–52.

49. Maisie Ward, *Return to Chesterton* (London: Sheed and Ward, 1952), pp. 77–78. Copyright 1952 by Sheed and Ward. Reprinted by permission of Andrews and McMeel, Inc.

50. *Ibid.* p. 88.

51. Elizabeth Cobb, *Cosmopolitan,* August 1945.

52. Kitty Muggeridge and Ruth Adam, *Beatrice Webb: A Life* (London: Secker & Warburg, 1967), pp. 89–93.

53. *Ibid.* p. 119.

54. Norman MacKenzie, ed., *The Letters of Sidney and Beatrice Webb* (London: Cambridge University Press-London School of Economics, 1978). Copyright © 1978 by the London School of Economics and Political Science, London. Reprinted by permission of Subsidiary Rights Department, Cambridge University Press.

55. Norman and Jeanne MacKenzie, *The Fabians* (New York: Simon and Schuster, 1977), p. 153.
56. Malcolm Muggeridge, *Chronicles of Wasted Time*, Vol. I (London: Collins, 1972), pp. 146–47.
57. Margaret Cole, reviewing *The Letters of Sidney and Beatrice Webb*, in *Books and Bookmen*, Nov. 1979, p. 32.
58. Kitty Muggeridge and Ruth Adam, *Beatrice Webb: A Life*, p. 140
59. A. L. Rowse [reviewing Jeanne Mackenzie, *A Victorian Courtship* (London: Weidenfeld & Nicolson, 1979)] in *Books and Bookmen*, Nov. 1979, p. 19.
60. Malcolm Muggeridge, *Chronicles of Wasted Time*, p. 149.
61. A. L. Rowse, *op. cit.* p. 20.
62. R. J. Minney, *Recollections of George Bernard Shaw* (Englewood Cliffs, N.J.: Prentice-Hall, 1969), p. 44. Copyright © 1969 by R. J. Minney. Reprinted by permission of Prentice-Hall, Inc.
63. Malcolm Muggeridge, *The Green Stick* (London: Collins, 1970).
64. Hesketh Pearson, *George Bernard Shaw* (New York: Atheneum, 1963), p. 200.
65. *Ibid.* p. 203.
66. St. John Ervine, *Bernard Shaw* (New York: Morrow, 1956), p. 31.
67. Hesketh Pearson, *op. cit.* pp. 204–5.
68. *Ibid.* p. 206.
69. Unsigned notice in *The Star*, quoted by Janet Dunbar, *Mrs. G.B.S.* (New York: Harper and Row, 1963), p. 151.
70. R. J. Minney, *op. cit.* p. 49.
71. *Ibid.* pp. 54–55.
72. *Ibid.* p. 55.
73. Hesketh Pearson, *op. cit.* pp. 315–16.
74. George Bernard Shaw, *Sixteen Self-Sketches* (New York: Dodd-Mead, 1949), p. 178–79. Reprinted by permission of the Public Trustees and the Society of Authors and Trustees for Mrs. Charlotte Shaw Estate.
75. R. J. Minney, *op. cit.* p. 54.
76. W. C. Rogers, *Irish Literary Portraits* (London: B.B.C., 1972), pp. 131–32.
77. Justin Kaplan, *Mr. Clemens and Mark Twain* (New York: Simon and Schuster, 1966), pp. 91–92. Copyright © 1980 by Justin Kaplan. Reprinted by permission of The Sterling Lord Agency, Inc.
78. Clara Clemens, *My Father Mark Twain* (New York: Harper and Brothers, 1931), p. 63.
79. *Ibid.* p. 371.
80. S. L. Clemens, *Letters, The New York Times*, 9 Aug. 1972.

81. Charles Angoff, *H. L. Mencken* (New York: Thomas Yoseloff, 1956), p. 70.
82. *Ibid.* p. 175.
83. *Ibid.*
84. Sara Mayfield, *The Constant Circle* (New York: Delacorte, 1968), p. 163. Copyright © 1968 by Sara Mayfield. Reprinted by permission of the publisher.
85. Guy J. Forgue, ed., *The Letters of H. L. Mencken,* (New York: Knopf, 1961), p. 319.
86. Sara Mayfield, *op. cit.* p. 165.
87. Guy J. Forgue, *op. cit.* p. 320.
88. Charles Angoff, *op. cit.* p. 170.
89. Guy J. Forgue, *op. cit.* p. 318.
90. *Ibid.* p. 320.
91. Sara Mayfield, *op. cit.* pp. 167–68.
92. Guy J. Forgue, *op. cit.* p. 319.
93. Charles Angoff, *op. cit.* pp. 175–76.
94. Sara Mayfield, *op. cit.* pp. 183–85.
95. Charles Angoff, *op. cit.* p. 176.
96. *Ibid.* pp. 177–78.
97. Guy J. Forgue, *op. cit.* XI-XII.
98. Mark Shorer, *Sinclair Lewis* (New York: McGraw-Hill, 1961), p. 334. Copyright © 1961 by Mark Shorer. Reprinted by permission of Brandt & Brandt, Inc.
99. Vincent Sheean, *Dorothy and Red* (Boston: Houghton Mifflin, 1963), pp. 87–94.
100. *Ibid.* p. 123.
101. Mark Shorer, *op. cit.* p. 505.
102. *Ibid.* p. 503.
103. Vincent Sheean, *op. cit.* pp. 123–25.
104. Mark Shorer, *op. cit.* p. 638.
105. *Ibid.* p. 675.
106. *Ibid.* p. 676.
107. *Ibid.* p. 677.
108. *Ibid.*
109. Arthur H. Calder-Marshall, *The Times Literary Supplement* (London), 10 Feb. 1978, p. 156.
110. Andrew Birkin, *J. M. Barrie and the Lost Boys* (New York: Potter/Crown, 1979), pp. 26–29.
111. Janet Dunbar, *J. M. Barrie* (Boston: Houghton Mifflin, 1970), p. 231. Copyright © 1970 by Janet Dunbar. Reprinted by permission of Houghton Mifflin Company, Inc.
112. Janet Dunbar, *op. cit.* pp. 222–23.

113. Denis Macail, *The Story of J.M.B.* (London: Norwood Editions, 1941), p. 414.

114. Diana Farr, *Gilbert Cannan* (London: Chatto & Windus, 1978); quoted by Arthur H. Calder-Marshall in *The Times Literary Supplement* (London), 10 Feb. 1978, p. 156.

115. *Ibid.*

116. Diana Farr, *Gilbert Cannan* (London: Chatto & Windus, 1978), pp. 249–50.

117. Cynthia Asquith, *Portrait of Barrie* (London: James Barrie, 1954), pp. 157–58.

118. André Gide, *Si le grain ne meurt*, Vol. II (Paris: Gallimard, 1951), p. 369.

119. Jean Delay, *The Youth of André Gide* (Chicago: University of Chicago, 1963), p. 419.

120. *Ibid.* p. 421; letter of 17 Sept. 1895.

121. André Gide, *L'Immoraliste* (New York: Knopf, 1948), p. 12. Reprinted by permission of A. A. Knopf, Inc.

122. Jean Delay, *op. cit.* p. 451.

123. Albert J. Guerard, *André Gide* (Cambridge, Mass.: Harvard University Press, 1969), p. 10. Quoted from *André Gide, Si le grain ne meurt*, p. 369.

124. André Gide, *Et nunc manet in te* (New York: Knopf, 1952), p. 49. Trans. Justin O'Brien. Reprinted by permission of A. A. Knopf, Inc.

125. André Gide, *The Journals of André Gide: 1889–1913*, trans. Justin O'Brien (New York: Knopf, 1947), p. 49; 30 Dec. 1895 entry. Reprinted by permission of A.A. Knopf, Inc.

126. André Gide, *Et nunc manet in te*, p. 30.

127. *Ibid.* pp. 17–18.

128. Frank MacShane, *The Life of Raymond Chandler* (New York: Dutton, 1976), p. 188. Copyright © 1976 by Frank MacShane. Reprinted by permission of E. P. Dutton, Inc.

129. *Ibid.* p. 188.

130. *Ibid.* p. 32.

131. *Ibid.* p. 33.

132. *Ibid.*

133. *Ibid.* pp. 37–38.

134. *Ibid.* p. 225.

135. *Ibid.* p. 224.

136. *Ibid.* p. 227.

137. *Ibid.* p. 211.

138. *Ibid.* p. 232.

139. *Ibid.* pp. 238; 203.

140. *Ibid.* p. 203.

141. T. S. Matthews, *Great Tom* (New York: Harper & Row, 1973), p. XII.

142. Robert Sencourt, *T. S. Eliot* (London: Garnstone Press, 1971), pp. 119–21; 152.

143. T. S. Mathews, *op. cit.* pp. 111; 138.

144. *Ibid.* pp. 43–44.

145. William Plomer, "Urban Invader," *London Magazine,* 3 Feb. 1972. p. 176.

146. Laurance Thompson, *Robert Frost,* Vol. I (New York: Holt, Rinehart, Winston, 1966), p. 211.

147. *Ibid.* p. 212.

148. Eileen O'Casey, *Sean* (New York: Coward, McCann & Geoghegan, 1972), pp. 45–46.

149. Sean O'Casey, *Rose and Crown* (New York: Macmillan, 1952), p. 65. Copyright © by Sean O'Casey; renewed 1980 by Eileen O'Casey.

150. *Ibid.* p. 76.

151. *Ibid.* p. 67.

152. Eileen O'Casey, *op. cit.* p. 47.

153. *Ibid.* pp. 110–11.

154. Andrew Turnbull, *Scott Fitzgerald* (New York: Charles Scribner's Sons, 1962), p. 104. Copyright © 1962 by Andrew Turnbull. Reprinted by permission of Charles Scribner's Sons, Inc.

155. Nancy Milford, *Zelda* (New York: Harper & Row, 1970), p. 41. Reprinted by permission of Charles Scribner's Sons, Inc.

156. Andrew Turnbull, *op. cit.* p. 110.

157. *Ibid.* p. 108.

158. Michael Arlen, *Exiles* (New York: Farrar, Straus & Giroux, 1970), p. 77.

159. Nancy Milford, *op. cit.* p. 60.

160. Emily Hahn, *Lorenzo* (Philadelphia: Lippincott, 1975), pp. 103–5. Reprinted by permission of Andrew Wylier Agency.

161. Emily Hahn, *op. cit.* p. 107.

162. Richard Aldington, *D. H. Lawrence: Portrait of a Genius, But . . .* (New York: Collier Books, 1961), p. 66.

163. Frieda Lawrence, *Not I But the Wind* (New York: Viking, 1934), pp. 4–6. Reprinted by permission of Laurence Pollinger, Ltd., and the Estate of Mrs. Frieda Lawrence Ravagli.

164. *Ibid.*

165. David Garnett, *Great Friends* (New York: Atheneum, 1980), p. 78.

166. *Ibid.*

167. Frieda Lawrence, *op. cit.* p. 40.

168. *Ibid.* p. 35.

169. H. T. Moore, ed., *Collected Letters of D. H. Lawrence* (New York: Viking, 1962), pp. 133–34. Copyright © 1962 by Angelo Ravagli and C. Montague Weekley, Executors of the Estate of Frieda Lawrence Ravagli. Copyright 1932 by the Estate of D. H. Lawrence and 1934 by Frieda Lawrence. Copyright 1933, 1948, © 1953–54 and each year 1956–1962 by Angelo Ravagli and C. Montague Weekley, Executors of the Estate of Frieda Lawrence Ravagli. Reprinted by permission of Viking Penguin, Inc.

170. Frieda Lawrence, *op. cit.* p. 34.

171. Douglas Goldring, *Life Interests* (London: MacDonald, 1948), p. 86.

172. Sylvia Beach, *Shakespeare and Company* (New York: Harcourt Brace and Company, 1959), p. 42.

173. Oliver St. John Gogarty, *It Isn't This Time of Year* (Garden City, New York: Doubleday & Company, 1954), p. 99.

174. Bryher, *The Heart to Artemis* (New York: Harcourt Brace & World, 1962), p. 201.

175. Malcolm Cowley, *A Second Flowering* (New York: Viking, 1973), p. 61. Copyright © by Malcolm Cowley, 1956, 1967, 1968, 1970, 1972, 1973. Reprinted by permission of Viking Penguin, Inc.

176. Morley Callaghan, *That Summer in Paris* (New York: Dell, 1964), pp. 76–77. Copyright © 1963 by Morley Callaghan. Reprinted by permission of Don Congdon Associates, Inc.

177. S. N. Behrman, *Portrait of Max* (New York: Random House, 1960), pp. 14–15. Copyright © 1960 by S. N. Behrman. Reprinted by permission of Brandt & Brandt, Inc.

178. *Ibid.* p. 15.

179. David Cecil, *Max* (Boston: Houghton Mifflin, 1965), p. 495.

180. Henri Troyat, *Tolstoy* (Garden City, N.Y.: Doubleday, 1967), pp. 250–60. Copyright © 1967 by Doubleday and Company, Inc. Reprinted by permission of the publisher.

181. *Ibid.* pp. 443; 479.

182. Ernest J. Simmons, *Leo Tolstoy* (New York: Vintage, 1945), p. 334.

183. Ilya Tolstoy, *Tolstoy, My Father* (Chicago: Cowles, 1971), pp. 178; 267.

184. Henri Troyat, *op. cit.* p. 479.

185. Sergei Tolstoy, *Tolstoy Remembered* (New York: Atheneum, 1962), p. 172.

186. J. M. Whistler, quoted in "Scalaway of Genius" by Cecil Roberts in *Books and Bookmen*, Apr. 1973.

187. Robinson Jeffers, "Let Them Alone," *The Selected Poetry of Robinson Jeffers* (New York: Random House, 1963). Copyright © 1963 by Stephen Glass; copyright © 1963 by Garth Jeffers and Donnan Jeffers. Reprinted by permission of Random House, Inc.

188. Quentin Bell, *Virginia Woolf: A Biography*, Vol. I (New York: Har-

court Brace Jovanovich, 1972), p. 141. Copyright © 1972 by Quentin Bell. Reprinted by permission of Harcourt Brace Jovanovich, Inc.

189. Leonard Woolf, *Beginning Again* (New York: Harcourt Brace World, 1963), p. 53. Copyright © 1963, 1964 by Leonard Woolf. Reprinted by permission of Harcourt Brace Jovanovich, Inc.

190. Quentin Bell, *op. cit.* II, p. 2.

191. Leonard Woolf, *Sowing* (New York: Harcourt Brace, 1960), pp. 46–47. Reprinted by permission of Harcourt Brace Jovanovich, Inc.

192. Quentin Bell, *op. cit.* II, p. 3.

193. *Ibid.*

194. *Ibid.* p. 4.

195. Leonard Woolf, *Beginning Again* (New York: Harcourt Brace World, 1963), pp. 69–70. Copyright © 1963, 1964 by Leonard Woolf. Reprinted by permission of Harcourt Brace Jovanovich Inc.

196. Phyllis Grosskurth, *The Times Literary Supplement* (London) 31 Oct. 1980.

197. Quentin Bell, *op. cit.* II, pp. 155; 209.

198. Quentin Bell, *op. cit.* II, p. 5.

199. *Ibid.* p. 6.

200. Leonard Woolf, *Beginning Again*, pp. 76–82.

201. Jessica Mitford, *A Fine Old Conflict* (New York: Knopf, 1977), pp. 139–40. Copyright © 1977 by Jessica Mitford. Reprinted by permission of Alfred A. Knopf, Inc., and Random House, Inc.

202. *Ibid.* p. 140.

203. *Ibid.*

204. *Ibid.* pp. 140–42.

205. *Ibid.* p. 143.

206. *Ibid.* p. 145.

207. *Ibid.*

208. *Ibid.* pp. 150–51.

209. *Ibid.* p. 156.

210. *Ibid.* p. 157.

211. Richard Stonesifer, *W. H. Davies: A Critical Biography* (Middletown, Conn: Wesleyan University Press, 1978).

212. Arthur H. Calder-Marshall, *The Times Literary Supplement* (London), 1953.

213. *Books and Bookmen*, July 1978, p. 26.

214. W. H. Davies, *The Complete Poems of W. H. Davies* (Middletown, Conn.: Wesleyan University Press, 1963), p. 87. Reprinted by permission of Wesleyan University Press.

215. Royal A. Gettmann. Introduction to *George Gissing and H. G. Wells* (Champaign, Ill.: University of Illinois Press, 1961), pp. 14–15.

216. R. W. Stallman, *Stephen Crane* (New York: Braziller, 1968), p. 239.

217. *Ibid.* p. 254.
218. Nicholas Delbanco, *Group Portrait* (New York: Morrow, 1982), p. 46.
219. *Ibid.* pp. 54–55.
220. *Ibid.* p. 47.
221. Stallman, *op. cit.* p. 457.
222. *Ibid.* p. 468.
223. Stallman, *op. cit.* p. 468.
224. Delbanco, *op. cit.* p. 49.
225. *Ibid.*, p. 66.
226. Stallman, *op. cit.* p. 510.
227. *Ibid.* p. 529.

CHAPTER 7

1. Lewis Browne, *That Man Heine* (New York: Literary Guild, 1927), p. 270. Copyright 1927 Macmillan. Reprinted by permission of Pauline Mosley, Executrix of the Lewis Browne Estate
2. *Ibid.* pp. 374–75.
3. *Ibid.* p. 269.
4. *Ibid.* p. 322.
5. *Ibid.* pp. 317–18.
6. *Ibid.* p. 363.
7. *Ibid.* p. 389.
8. *Ibid.* pp. 379; 396.
9. *Ibid.* p. 381.
10. *Ibid.* pp. 318–19.
11. George and Jean Beardmore, *Arnold Bennett in Love* (London: David Bruce & Watson, 1972), p. 28.
12. *Sunday Times* (London), 21 Jan. 1973.
13. George and Jean Beardmore, *op. cit.* p. 28.
14. *Ibid.* p. 74.
15. *Ibid.* p. 69.
16. *Ibid.* p. 85.
17. *Ibid.* p. 86.
18. *Ibid.* p. 84.
19. *Ibid.* pp. 71–72.
20. *Sunday Times* (London), 21 Jan. 1973.
21. George and Jean Beardmore, *op. cit.* p. 87.
22. Frank Swinnerton, *A Last Word* (London: Hamish Hamilton, 1978), pp. 86–88. Copyright © 1978 by Frank Swinnerton.
23. *Ibid.* p. 86.
24. *Ibid.*

25. Sherwood Anderson, *Memoirs*, ed. R. L. White (Chapel Hill, N.C.: North Carolina University of North Carolina Press, 1969), p. 458.
26. W. A. Swanberg, *Dreiser* (New York: Charles Scribner's Sons, 1965), p. 386. Copyright © W. A. Swanberg. Reprinted by permission of W. A. Swanberg.
27. John Dos Passos, *The Best of Times* (New York: New American Library, 1966), pp. 207–8. Copyright © 1966 by John Dos Passos.
28. W. A. Swanberg, *op. cit.* p. 387.
29. *Ibid.*
30. Nina Gourfinkel, *Gorky* (New York: Evergreen, 1960), p. 48. Copyright © 1960 Evergreen/Grove, Inc. Reprinted by permission of Georges Borchardt, Inc.
31. Justin Kaplan, *Mr. Clemens and Mark Twain* (New York: Simon and Schuster, 1966), pp. 367–68. Copyright © 1966 by Justin Kaplan.
32. H. G. Wells, *Experiment in Autobiography* (New York: Macmillan, 1934), p. 697.
33. Nina Gourfinkel, *op. cit.* p. 163.
34. St. John Ervine, *Bernard Shaw* (New York: William Morrow and Company, 1956), p. 307. Copyright © 1956 St. John Ervine.
35. Christopher Hassall, *Edward Marsh* (New York: Harcourt Brace and Company, 1949), p. 254.
36. David-Tylden Wright, *Anatole France* (London: Collins, 1967), p. 285.
37. Budd Schulberg, *The Four Seasons of Success* (Garden City, N.Y.: Doubleday & Company, 1972), p. 151.
38. *Ibid.* p. 156.
39. *Ibid.* p. 150.
40. Jay Martin, *Nathanael West: The Art of His Life* (New York: Farrar, Straus & Giroux, 1970), pp. 134; 372. Reprinted by permission of Farrar, Straus & Giroux, Inc.
41. *Ibid.* pp. 135–38.
42. *Ibid.* pp. 376–77.
43. Jay Martin, *op. cit.* p. 376.
44. *Ibid.* p. 385.
45. Elinor Wylie, "Wild Peaches" (New York: Harcourt Brace, 1921). Copyright © 1921 by Alfred A. Knopf, Inc.; copyright renewed 1949 by William Rose Benét. Reprinted from *Collected Poems* of Elinor Wylie, by permission of Alfred A. Knopf, Inc.
46. Elinor Wylie, "The Eagle and the Mole," *Nets to Catch the Wind* (New York: Harcourt Brace, 1921) from *Collected Poems*, copyright 1921 by Alfred A. Knopf, Inc.; copyright renewed 1949 by William Rose Benét. Reprinted by permission of Alfred A. Knopf, Inc.
47. Mary Colum, *The Life and the Dream* (Garden City, N.Y.: Doubleday & Company, 1947), p. 337.

48. George Oppenheimer, *The View from the Sixties* (New York: David McKay, 1966), pp. 87–88.
49. Jean Gould, *The Poet and Her Book* (New York: Dodd, Mead, 1969), pp. 180–81. Reprinted by permission of Dodd, Mead & Company, Inc.
50. Jean Starr Untermeyer, *Private Collection* (New York: A. A. Knopf, 1965), p. 142. Reprinted by permission of A. A. Knopf, Inc.
51. Arnold Bennett, *The Journal of Arnold Bennett* (Garden City, New York: Doubleday, 1932), 7/16/26, p. 884; 6/8/27, p. 958.
52. Jean Gould, *op. cit.* p. 194.
53. Edmund Wilson, *The Shores of Light* (New York: Vintage, 1952), p. 394.
54. Franz Kafka, *Diaries 1910–13* (Vol. I, Schocken Books, 1965), p. 150. Copyright 1948 by Schocken Books, Inc., copyright renewed 1975 by Schocken Books, Inc. Reprinted by permission of the publisher.
55. *Ibid.*, Vol. I, p. 19.
56. Max Brod, *Kafka* (New York: Schocken Books, 1963), pp. 141–42. Copyright 1937 by Heinr. Mercy Sohn, Prague. Copyright 1947 by Schocken Books, Inc.; copyright © 1960 by Schocken Books, Inc. Copyright renewed © 1975 by Schocken Books, Inc. Reprinted by permission of the publisher.
57. *Ibid.* pp. 141–42.
58. *Ibid.* p. 151.
59. *Ibid.* p. 144.
60. *Ibid.* p. 152.
61. *Ibid.* pp. 166–67.
62. *Ibid.* p. 208.
63. Phyllis Greenacre, *The Quest for the Father* (New York: International Universities Press, 1963), pp. 72–73.
64. Cyril Pearl, *The Girl with the Swansdown Seat* (Indianapolis: Bobbs-Merrill, 1955), p. 86; Philip Henderson, *Samuel Butler* (London: Cohen & West, 1967), pp. 93–94.
65. Ronald Pearsall, *The Worm in the Bud* (New York: Macmillan, 1969), pp. 269–70; 428–29.
66. Robin Maugham, *Somerset and All the Maughams* (New York: New American Library, 1966), pp. 201–2.
67. Garson Kanin, *Remembering Mr. Maugham* (New York: Atheneum, 1965), pp. 92–93. Copyright © 1966 by T.F.T. Corporation. Reprinted by permission of Atheneum, Inc.
68. Somerset Maugham, "Looking Back," *Show*, July 1962, p. 44. Reprinted by permission of the Society of Authors and the Maugham Estate.
69. *Ibid.* pp. 42–44.
70. Beverley Nichols, *Books and Bookmen*, May 1980, p. 13.

71. Ted Morgan, *Maugham* (New York: Simon and Schuster, 1980), pp. 607–8. Reprinted by permission of Ted Morgan.
72. *Ibid.* p. 523.
73. Beverley Nichols, *A Case of Human Bondage* (London: Secker & Warburg, 1966), p. 7.
74. Beverley Nichols, *Books and Bookmen*, May 1980, p. 13.
75. *Ibid.*
76. Garson Kanin, *op. cit.* pp. 225–26.
77. A. Scott Berg, *Max Perkins* (New York: E. P. Dutton, 1978).
78. A. E. Housman, "Additional Poems," *The Collected Poems of A. E. Housman* (New York: Holt, Rinehart & Winston, 1922). Copyright © 1965 by Holt, Rinehart & Winston. Copyright © 1967, 1968 by Robert E. Symons. Reprinted by permission of Holt, Rinehart and Winston.
79. *Ibid.* p. 190.
80. Reprinted from A. E. Housman, *The Collected Poems of A. E. Housman* in George L. Watson, *A. E. Housman* (London: Rupert Hart-Davis, 1967), p. 123. Reprinted by permission of Holt, Rinehart and Winston, Inc.
81. From "A Shropshire Lad"—Authorized Edition from *The Collected Poems of A. E. Housman.* Copyright 1939, 1940, © 1965 by Holt, Rinehart and Winston. Copyright © 1967, 1968 by Robert E. Symons. Reprinted by permission of Holt, Rinehart and Winston.
82. George Watson, *op. cit.* p. 157
83. J. H. Huizinga, *Rousseau: The Self-Made Saint* (New York: Grossman/Viking, 1976). Copyright © 1976 J. H. Huizinga.
84. Will and Ariel Durant, *Rousseau and Revolution* (New York: Simon and Schuster, 1967), pp. 17–18.
85. *Ibid.*; (Quoted from Rousseau, *Confessions*, trans. J. M. Cohen, Vol. I (Pennsylvania State University Press, 1954), p. 309.
86. Huizinga, *op. cit.* p. 171.
87. Durant, *op. cit.* p. 152.
88. Huizinga, *op. cit.* pp. 95–96.
89. Jean-Jacques Rousseau, *Confessions*, trans. J. M. Cohen (Baltimore: Penguin, 1953); quoted by J. H. Huizinga, *op. cit.* pp. 95–96.
90. Huizinga, *op. cit.* p. 172.
91. *Ibid.* p. 173.
92. *Ibid.* p. 173.
93. Durant, *op. cit.* p. 202.
94. James Boswell, *Boswell on the Grand Tour: Germany and Switzerland, 1794* (New York: McGraw, 1953), p. 150

95. Frederick A. Pottle, *James Boswell: The Early Years* (New York: McGraw-Hill, 1966), pp. 162–81; Durant, *op. cit.* pp. 202–3.
96. Durant, *op. cit.* p. 202.
97. *Ibid.* p. 210.
98. Wilfrid Sheed, *Clare Boothe Luce* (New York: Dutton, 1982), pp. 125–26.
99. *Ibid.* p. 126.
100. *Ibid.*
101. Hilary Mills, *Mailer* (New York: Empire Books, 1982), p. 238.
102. Robert Baldick, ed. and trans., *Pages from the Goncourt Journal* (New York: Oxford University Press, 1962), p. 385.
103. P. N. Furbank, *E. M. Forster: A Life*, Vol. II (New York: Harcourt Brace Jovanovich, 1978), p. 317. Reprinted by permission of Harcourt Brace Jovanovich, Inc.
104. *Ibid.*, II, pp. 10–11.
105. *Ibid.*, I, pp. 36–37.
106. *Ibid.* pp. 37–38.
107. E. M. Forster, *Maurice* (New York: W. W. Norton, 1971), p. 249.
108. R.W.B. Lewis, *Edith Wharton* (New York: Harper & Row, 1975), p. 53. Reprinted by permission of Charles Scribner's Sons, Inc.
109. Edith Wharton, *A Backword Glance* (New York: Charles Scribner's Sons, 1964). Copyright 1933, 1934 William R. Tyler; copyrights © renewed 1961, 1962. Reprinted by permission of Charles Scribner's Sons, Inc.
110. R.W.B. Lewis, *op. cit.* pp. 48–49; 343–44.
111. *Ibid.* p. 460.
112. *Ibid.* p. 525.
113. *Ibid.* pp. 444; 497–98.
114. Andrew Turnbull, *Scott Fitzgerald* (New York: Charles Scribner's Sons, 1962), pp. 153–54. Copyright © 1962 Andrew Turnbull. Printed by permission of Charles Scribner's Sons, Inc.; Roderick Coupe, "Letters to Cyril Connolly," *The Times Literary Supplement* (London), 7 Sept. 1966.
115. R.W.B. Lewis, *op. cit.* p. 405.
116. Edmund Wilson, *The Twenties*, ed. Leon Edel (New York: Farrar, Straus & Giroux, 1975), p. 76.
117. Richard Ellmann, *James Joyce* (New York: Oxford University Press, 1982), p. 449.
118. *Ibid.* pp. 450–51.
119. *Ibid.* p. 451.
120. *Ibid.*

121. Peggy Guggenheim, *Out of This Century* (New York: Dial, 1946), p. 31. Reprinted by permission of Universe Books, Inc.

122. *Ibid.* p. 194.

123. Deirdre Bair, *Samuel Beckett* (New York: Harcourt Brace Jovanovich, 1978), p. 276. Copyright © 1978 by Deirdre Bair. Copyright © 1978 by Harcourt Brace Jovanovich, Inc. Reprinted by permission of the publisher.

124. *Ibid.* p. 277.

125. *Ibid.* p. 481.

126. *Ibid.*; John Montague, Jean Martin, and Roger Blin quoted.

127. Christopher Isherwood, *Christopher and His Kind* (New York: Farrar, Straus & Giroux, 1976), p. 3. Copyright © 1976 by Farrar, Straus & Giroux, Inc. Reprinted by permission of the publisher.

128. *Ibid.* pp. 2–4.

129. *Ibid.* pp. 15–19; 29–34.

130. *Ibid.* p. 43.

131. *Ibid.* p. 11.

132. Charles Baudelaire, "Advice to Writers" in Pascal Pia, *Baudelaire* (New York: Evergreen/Grove, 1961), p. 41. Copyright © 1961 by Evergreen/Grove. Reprinted by permission of Georges Borchardt, Inc.

133. *Ibid.* p. 39.

134. Alex De Jonge, *Baudelaire, Prince of Clouds* (London: Paddington Press, 1976), p. 55. Copyright © 1976 by the publisher.

135. Enid Starke, *Baudelaire* (New York: New Directions, 1958), pp. 88–89.

136. Pascal Pia, *op. cit.* pp. 35–36.

137. Nelson Algren, *Harper's*, May 1965.

138. *Playboy*, Jan. 1978. Copyright © 1978 *Le Nouvel Observateur*, Paris, France. Reprinted by permission of *Le Nouvel Observateur* and *Playboy* magazine.

139. Simone de Beauvoir, *The Second Sex* (New York: Knopf, 1957), p. 182.

140. *The New York Times Magazine*, 2 June 1974.

141. Elizabeth Sprigge and Jean-Jacques Kihm, *Jean Cocteau: The Man and the Mirror* (New York: Coward-McCann, 1968), p. 69. Copyright © Elizabeth Sprigge & Jean-Jacques Kihm.

142. *Ibid.* p. 92.

143. *Ibid.* p. 93.

CHAPTER 8

1. Ernest Hemingway, *A Moveable Feast* (New York: Bantam, 1964), pp. 188–89. Copyright © 1964 Ernest Hemingway Ltd. Reprinted by permission of Charles Scribner's Sons.
2. *Ibid.* Malcolm Cowley, in his interview on the Dick Cavett Show (Channel 2, WPBT, 29 Jan. 1979), said that Hemingway didn't always tell the truth about this episode. As Cowley recalled it, the measurement occurred in Paris at a party when Edmund Wilson, F. Scott Fitzgerald, and Hemingway were present, and it was Cowley who said to Hemingway: "Did you ever hold a mirror up to the organ, because the mirror gives an elongated image of it."
3. Sheilah Graham, *The Real Scott Fitzgerald: Thirty-Five Years Later* (New York: Grosset and Dunlap, 1976), p. 120.
4. Scott Donaldson, *By Force of Will* (New York: Viking, 1977), p. 150. Copyright © 1977 by Scott Donaldson. Reprinted by permission of Scott Donaldson.
5. Sara Mayfield, *The Constant Circle* (New York: Delacorte, 1968), p. 132. Reprinted by permission of the publisher.
6. Andrew Turnbull, *Scott Fitzgerald* (New York: Charles Scribner's Sons, 1962), p. 262. Copyright © 1962 Andrew Turnbull. Reprinted by permission of the publisher.
7. Sheilah Graham, *op. cit.* p. 19.
8. Scott Donaldson, *op. cit.* p. 178.
9. Morley Callaghan, *That Summer in Paris* (New York: Dell, 1963), p. 158. Copyright © 1963 by Morley Callaghan. Reprinted by permission of Don Congdon Associates, Inc.
10. *Look,* 29 Apr. 1969.
11. Scott Donaldson, *op. cit.* p. 178.
12. Gregory Hemingway, *Papa* (Boston: Houghton Mifflin, 1976), p. 15. Copyright © 1976 by Gregory H. Hemingway. Reprinted by permission of Houghton Mifflin Company.
13. Sheilah Graham, *op. cit.* p. 17.
14. *Time,* 1 Dec. 1980.
15. Edmund Wilson, *The Twenties,* ed. Leon Edel (New York: Farrar, Straus & Giroux, 1975), p. 223. Copyright © 1975 by Elena Wilson, Executrix of the Estate of Edmund Wilson. Reprinted by permission of the publisher.
16. Anne Fremantle, "W. H. Auden" in *A Tribute,* ed. Stephen Spender (London: Weidenfeld & Nicolson, 1975), p. 92.
17. Beverley Nichols, *The Sweet and Twenties* (London: Weidenfeld & Nicolson, 1958), p. 58.

18. Richard Aldington, *Portrait of a Genius, But . . .* (New York: Collier Books, 1961), pp. 254–55.
19. I. B. Singer, *The New York Times Magazine*, 26 Nov. 1978.
20. Vincent O'Sullivan, *Aspects of Wilde* (New York: Henry Holt, 1936), p. 206.
21. Truman Capote, *Music for Chameleons* (New York: Random House, 1980), p. 251. Reprinted by permission of Random House, Inc.
22. Truman Capote, "Remembering Tennessee Williams," *Playboy*, January 1984, p. 234. Reprinted by permission of *Playboy* magazine.
23. As told to the author by Peggy Guggenheim.

CHAPTER 9

1. B. L. Reid, *The Man from New York* (New York: Oxford University Press, 1968), p. 108.
2. Curtis Cate, *George Sand* (Boston: Houghton Mifflin, 1975), p. 246. Copyright © 1975 by Curtis Cate. Reprinted by permission of Houghton Mifflin Company, Inc.
3. *Ibid.* p. 246.
4. *Ibid.* p. 247.
5. *Ibid.*
6. Robert Baldick, ed. and trans., *Pages from the Goncourt Journal* (New York: Oxford University Press, 1962), p. 87. Reprinted by permission of the publisher.
7. *The Times Literary Supplement* (London), 4 Sept. 1971, p. 421.
8. Michael Holroyd, *Lytton Strachey*, Vol. II (London: Heinemann, 1967), p. 187.
9. Anne Chisholm, *Nancy Cunard* (New York: Knopf, 1973), pp. 74–75. Reprinted by permission of A. A. Knopf, Inc.
10. *Ibid.* p. 75.
11. Matthew Josephson, *Life Among the Surrealists* (New York: Holt, Rinehart and Winston, 1962), p. 319.

CHAPTER 10

1. Norman and Jeanne MacKenzie, *Dickens* (New York: Oxford University Press, 1979), p. 327.
2. Stephen Birmingham, *The Late John Marquand* (Philadelphia: Lippincott, 1972).
3. H. J. Nersoyan, *André Gide* (Syracuse University Press, 1969), pp. 109–10.

4. Claude Mauriac, *Conversations with Gide*, trans. Michel Lebec (New York: Braziller, 1965), p. ix.

CHAPTER 11

1. Kenneth Tynan, "Papa and the Playwright," *Playboy*, May 1964. Reprinted by permission of Kathleen Tynan.
2. *Ibid.*
3. Tennessee Williams, *Memoirs* (Garden City, N.Y.: Doubleday, 1975), pp. 67–68. Reprinted by permission of Doubleday and Company. Kenneth Tynan, *op. cit.*
4. H. Montgomery Hyde, *Oscar Wilde* (New York: Farrar Straus & Giroux, 1975), pp. 128–29.
5. André Gide, *Oscar Wilde* (New York: Philosophical Library, 1940), p. 9.
6. Albert J. Guerard, *André Gide* (Cambridge, Mass.: Harvard University Press, 1969), p. 9.
7. Christopher Isherwood, *Christopher and His Kind* (New York: Farrar Straus & Giroux, 1976), p. 17. Reprinted by permission of the publisher.
8. Lawrence Williams, *I James McNeill Whistler* (New York: Simon and Schuster, 1972), pp. 223–24. Copyright © 1972 by Lawrence Williams.
9. Cecil Roberts, *Books and Bookmen*, Apr. 1973, p. 60.
10. Christopher Isherwood, *op. cit.* pp. 106–7.
11. Carola Oman, *The Wizard of the North: The Life of Sir Walter Scott* (London: Hodder and Stoughton, 1973), pp. 194–95. Copyright © 1973 by Carola Oman.
12. Charles Osborne, *W. H. Auden* (New York: Harcourt Brace Jovanovich, 1979), pp. 245–46.

CHAPTER 12

1. Malcolm Muggeridge, *The Most of Muggeridge* (New York: Simon and Schuster, 1966), p. 183.
2. *Ibid.* p. 187.
3. Augustus John, *Chiaroscuro* (London: Readers Union, Jonathan Cape, 1954), pp. 94–95.
4. Bertrand Russell, *The Autobiography of Bertrand Russell 1872–1914*, Vol. I (Boston: Little, Brown, 1967), p. 3. Copyright © 1967 by George Allen & Unwin, Publishers, Ltd.
5. Ariel and Will Durant, *A Dual Biography* (New York: Simon and

Schuster, 1977), p. 84. Copyright © 1977 by Will (iam J.), Ariel and Ethel Durant. Reprinted by permission of Simon and Schuster, Inc.

6. *Ibid.* p. 119.

7. Bertrand Russell to Ottoline Morrell, quoted in T. S. Matthews, *Great Tom* (New York: Harper & Row, 1973), p. 47.

8. *Ibid.* p. 47.

9. *Ibid.* p. 47.

10. Joanna Richardson, *Victor Hugo* (New York: St. Martin's Press, 1976), p. 53.

CHAPTER 13

1. Rupert Croft-Cooke, *Feasting with Panthers* (London: W. H. Allen, 1967), p. 14.

2. Robert Gittings, *Thomas Hardy's Later Years* (Boston: Little, Brown, 1978).

3. George J. Becker and Edith Phillips, *Paris and the Arts 1851–1896, From the Goncourt Journal* (Cornell University Press, 1971), p. 125.

4. Robert Baldick, ed. and trans., *Pages from the Goncourt Journal* (New York: Oxford University Press, 1962), pp. 81–82.

5. *Ibid.*

6. Jean-Jacques Brousson, *Anatole France Himself* (Philadelphia: Lippincott, 1925), p. 249. David Tylden-Wright, *Anatole France* (London: Collins, 1967), p. 320.

7. *Ibid.* p. 321.

8. George A. Watson, *A. E. Housman* (London: Rupert Hart-Davis, 1917), p. 219.

9. W. H. Auden, *A. E. Housman, Collected Shorter Poems, 1927–1957* (New York: Random House; London: Faber & Faber, 1966). Copyright © 1966 by W. H. Auden. The poem was first published in W. H. Auden, *New Writing* (1939) and *Another Time* (1940).

10. Harold Acton, *Memoirs of an Aesthete 1939–1969* (New York: Viking, 1971), p. 202. Reprinted by permission of Viking Penguin, Inc.

11. *Ibid.* p. 201.

12. Mary Hemingway, *How It Was* (New York: Knopf, 1976), p. 230.

CHAPTER 14

1. Robert Baldick, ed. and trans., *Pages from The Goncourt Journal* (New York: Oxford University Press, 1962), p. 7. Reprinted by permission of the publisher.

2. Alfred Sutro, *Celebrities and Simple Souls* (London: Duckworth, 1933), p. 175.
3. Morley Callaghan, *That Summer in Paris* (New York: Dell, 1964), pp. 194–95. Reprinted by permission of Don Congdon Associates, Inc.
4. Alexander Woollcott, *While Rome Burns* in *The Portable Woollcott* (New York: Viking Penguin, 1946), pp. 149–50. Reprinted by permission of Viking Press, Inc.
5. Vachel Lindsay, "Lost Weekend in Urbana," *Horizon*, Winter 1967.
6. Rex Reed, *Esquire*, September 1971, p. 222.
7. Joseph Hone, *The Life of George Moore* (London: Gollancz, 1936), p. 269.
8. Nancy Cunard, *G.M.: Memories of George Moore* (London: Rupert Hart-Davis, 1956), pp. 114–15.
9. *Ibid.* p. 171.
10. *Ibid.* pp. 38–39.
11. Anne Chisholm, *Nancy Cunard* (New York: Knopf, 1979), p. 303. Reprinted by permission of A. A. Knopf Inc.; Nancy Cunard, *op. cit.* p. 48
12. *Ibid.* p. 187.
13. Anne Chisholm, *op. cit.* p. 92.
14. Ilka Chase, *Past Imperfect* (Garden City, N.Y.: Doubleday, 1942), p. 37. Copyright Ilka Chase Brown. Reprinted by permission of Doubleday and Company, Inc.
15. Mary Cardozo, *Lucky Eyes and a Little Heart: The Life of Maude Gonne* (Indianapolis: Bobbs-Merrill, 1978), p. 163.
16. Burton Rascoe, *We Were Interrupted* (Garden City, N.Y.: Doubleday and Company, 1947), p. 205.

CHAPTER 15

1. Stanley Weintraub, *Whistler* (New York: Weybright and Talley, 1974), pp. 90–91.
2. Ann Charters, *Kerouac* (San Francisco: Straight Arrow Books, 1973), pp. 364–67. Copyright © 1973 Ann Charters.
3. Curtis Cate, *George Sand* (Boston: Houghton Mifflin, 1975), p. 291. Copyright © 1975 Curtis Cate. Reprinted by permission of Houghton Mifflin Company.
4. Madeleine Blais, *Miami Herald*, 1 Apr. 1979. Reprinted by permission of Madeleine Blais.
5. *Ibid.*
6. Tennessee Williams, *Memoirs* (Garden City, N.Y.: Doubleday, 1972),

p. 182. Copyright © 1972, 1975 Tennessee Williams. Reprinted by permission of Doubleday and Company, Inc.

CHAPTER 16

1. R. J. Minney, *Recollections of George Bernard Shaw* (Englewood Cliffs, N.J.: Prentice-Hall, 1969), p. 172. Copyright © 1969 R. J. Minney. Reprinted by permission of the publisher.
2. Quentin Bell, *Virginia Woolf*, Vol. I (New York: Harcourt Brace Jovanovich, 1972), p. 24. Copyright © 1972 by Quentin Bell. Reprinted by permission of Harcourt Brace Jovanovich, Inc.
3. *Ibid.* p. 79.
4. *Ibid.* Vol. II, pp. 6–7.
5. *Life*, 9 March 1966, p. 70.
6. Michael Holroyd, *Lytton Strachey*, Vol. II (London: Heinemann, 1968), p. 19.
7. Thomas Mann, *Diaries 1915–39*, trans. Richard and Clare Winston (New York: Harry N. Abrams, 1975).
8. Robert Haydon, *Diary*; entry reported in *The Times Literary Supplement* (London), 2 Apr. 1971.
9. *Boston Magazine*, Nov. 1979; reprinted in *Encounter*, Dec. 1979, p. 93.
10. *Playboy*, Sept. 1974. Copyright © 1974 by *Playboy*. Reprinted by permission of *Playboy* magazine.
11. Donald Hall, *Remembering Poets* (New York: Harper & Row, 1979), p. 10.
12. Arthur Gold and Robert Fizdale, *The Life of Misia Sert* (New York: Knopf, 1980).
13. Graham Greene, *Ways of Escape* (New York: Simon and Schuster, 1980), pp. 269–71.
14. Michael Mayer, *Ibsen* (Garden City, N.Y.: Doubleday, 1971), p. 662.
15. *Ibid.* p. 260.
16. *Ibid.* p. 457.
17. *Ibid.* pp. 807–8.
18. *The New York Times*, 13 Feb. 1977.
19. H. Montgomery Hyde, *Henry James at Home* (London: Methuen, 1969), p. 76.
20. Gordon S. Haight, *George Eliot* (New York: Oxford University Press, 1968), p. 121.
21. *Op. cit.* p. 47.
22. *The Dick Cavett Show*, 20 Mar. 1979.
23. *60 Minutes*, WPBT, 2 Aug. 1981.

24. Ernest J. Lovelace, Jr., ed., *Medwin's Conversations of Lord Byron* (Princeton, N.J.: Princeton University Press, 1966), pp. 35–36.
25. Richard Aldington, *D. H. Lawrence: Portrait of a Genius, But . . .* (New York: Collier, 1961), p. 147.
26. Frieda Lawrence, *Not I but the Wind* (New York: Viking, 1934), p. 77. Reprinted by permission of Lawrence Pollinger, Ltd. and the Estate of Mrs. Frieda Lawrence Ravagli.
27. John Middleton Murry, *Between Two Worlds* (London: Jonathan Cape, 1935), p. 286.
28. *Saturday Review*, 8 Nov. 1969, pp. 51–52.
29. Willard Connely, *Adventures in Biography* (New York: Horizon Press, 1960), p. 30.
30. Helga Sandburg, *A Great and Glorious Romance* (New York: Harcourt Brace Jovanovich, 1978).
31. Herbert Mitgang, "An Unfinished Life," *The New York Times Book Review*, 25 Sept. 1983.
32. John Gardner, *The Life and Times of Chaucer* (New York: Knopf, 1977), pp. 125 ff; 153 ff; 167.
33. Joseph Hone, *The Life of George Moore* (London: Gollancz, 1936), pp. 55–59.
34. Langston Hughes, *The Big Sea* (New York: Hill and Wang, 1940), pp. 274–75.

CHAPTER 17

1. *The Leader* (London), 8 July 1955.
2. *Sunday Times* (London), 17 Mar. 1974.
3. Michiko Kakutani, *The New York Times*, 27 Sept. 1981, p. 14.
4. Charles Osborne, *W. H. Auden* (New York: Harcourt Brace Jovanovich, 1979), p. 215.
5. Harold Acton, *Memories of an Aesthete* (London: Methuen, 1948), p. 46.
6. Bertha Harding, *Age Cannot Wither* (Philadelphia: Lippincott, 1947), pp. 139–40.
7. Ulick O'Connor, *Brendan* (Englewood Cliffs, N.J.: Prentice-Hall, 1970), p. 23.
8. Jessie Conrad, *Joseph Conrad As I Knew Him* (London: Heinemann, 1926).
9. *Miami Herald*, 26 Nov. 1976.
10. Howard Teichmann, *Smart Aleck* (New York: William Morrow and Company, 1976), p. 38.
11. *Ibid.* p. 38.

INDEX